PHOTOSHOP
IN A NUTSHELL

A Desktop Quick Reference

PHOTOSHOP
IN A NUTSHELL

A Desktop Quick Reference

Donnie O'Quinn & Matt LeClair

WITHDRAW

O'REILLY™

Cambridge · *Köln* · *Paris* · *Sebastopol* · *Tokyo*

Photoshop in a Nutshell: A Desktop Quick Reference

by Donnie O'Quinn and Matt LeClair

Copyright © 1997 O'Reilly & Associates, Inc. All rights reserved.
Printed in the United States of America.

Published by O'Reilly & Associates, Inc., 101 Morris Street, Sebastopol, CA 95472.

Editor: Tim O'Reilly

Production Editor: Nancy Wolfe Kotary

Printing History:

    October 1997:   First Edition.

This book is printed on acid-free paper with 85% recycled content, 15% post-consumer waste. O'Reilly & Associates is committed to using paper with the highest recycled content available consistent with high quality.

ISBN: 1-56592-313-8

[10/97]

Table of Contents

Part II: Menus

Chapter 12—The Select Menu 246

Part III: Palettes

Part IV: Appendixes

Preface

Traditionally, computer books target novice, intermediate, or advanced users. As we collectively gain more and more experience with computers, those distinctions don't always make sense. The *In a Nutshell* series of books targets a new class of user, which we call the "sophisticated user." A sophisticated user may be a novice at using a particular program, but he or she has experience with other programs, and is a quick study. Or the sophisticated user may be very experienced with a program, but still need to look up details.

Because they target sophisticated users, the *In a Nutshell* books are oriented towards reference use, although they may include elements of a fast-paced tutorial or overview to get a new user quickly up to the point where the reference material makes sense.

Topics like UNIX or Java lend themselves readily to the *In a Nutshell* reference format, because they include a lot of hard to remember syntax. GUI-based programs like Photoshop may at first seem less appropriate for this format. We've all seen application books that walk through the GUI, repeating only the facts that are already obvious from the GUI itself.

In *Photoshop in a Nutshell*, we've avoided this problem by going deep. When we talk about a menu or a dialog box, we tell you the things that are not obvious, providing the deep knowledge that typically comes only with years of experience.

Overview

Adobe Photoshop is one of the most intensive applications in the graphics arts industry.

On one hand, it's one of the few universally indispensable tools. Enthusiasts in all graphics industries—print, the Web, multimedia, and video—turn to Photoshop again and again to refine the images that define our world.

On the other hand, it's nearly impossible to master. Photoshop is sprawling. It is immense. It caters to an incredible variety of needs. In a deadline-driven world, it's hard enough to fully explore the tools that apply to one line of work. Now, with more crossover than ever between industries, all users face a daunting challenge. To generate the flexible, high-quality images that your work demands, you will soon push your understanding of Photoshop and all of its issues to the limit.

That's where this book comes in. Even after you've learned the basics, it's difficult to remember the function of every tool, every palette, every item of every dialogue of every command.

Most Photoshop books spend a great deal of time and energy trying to teach you Photoshop from the beginning, leaving neither time nor space for the small details that even the most experienced Photoshop user can't always remember. *Photoshop in a Nutshell* focuses specifically on the details that a user is going to need to look up again and again.

Each tool and command in Photoshop receives the following treatment:

Specific Function

A summary of each item's purpose and function, as well as its context in a production environment.

Common Uses

A list of the most frequent applications of each item. Every use is fully described, and over 170 appear as step-by-step techniques in the back of the book.

Common Errors

A list of complex but avoidable misuses of the software. Since many aspects of Photoshop are nonintuitive, this section explains the common mistakes—and offers real-world solutions.

Special Notes

A list of tips, warnings, notes, and shortcuts. No single part of Photoshop works in a vacuum, and this section fleshes out the relationship one item has with any other.

The Dialog

Definitions and recommended settings for each option in every dialog. Because the real power of Photoshop rests in its on-screen controls, a user must understand the cause-and-effect relationship of every setting.

Like many professionals, we use Photoshop for a living. When the clock is ticking, we know you don't have the time to pore through unnecessary text for the information you seek. We've presented the facts—and only the facts—so you can get in, get out, and get back to work.

Cross References

The contents of this book follow the exact structure of Photoshop's tools, menu commands, and palettes.

We've taken great pains to include as many cross-references as possible—each item contains a "See Also" section, which lists the tools, commands, and palettes most commonly encountered when using a specific part of Photoshop.

We mention tools and palettes by their full names, which dovetail with the appropriate chapter title. A menu command might be buried two or three levels deep, so we include its location in the program as part of its title.

For example, when we discuss converting an RGB image to CMYK mode, we mention the importance of the Separation Setup dialog. This command is found under the File Menu, under the Color Settings submenu. We refer to it as "the File: Color Settings: **Separation Setup** dialog." If you desire more info, turn to the Table of Contents and follow the hierarchy—find the File Menu chapter (Chapter 8), find the "Color Settings" section, and get the page number for Separation Setup. Or, simply use the headers listed at the top of each page as a guide.

Macintosh and Windows Commands

Whenever we mention a keyboard technique, we've included key commands for Mac and Windows users. Mac keys appear in parentheses, and Windows keys appear in brackets.

For example:

- Hold down the (Command) [Control] key and click an image layer to make a selection.

- Choose (Option-Command-Shift) [Alt-Control-Shift]-V to paste into an active selection.

The Techniques Appendix

We've constructed a comprehensive list of over 170 step-by-step Photoshop techniques. These range from simple selections to layer- and channel-based editing, to methods of color correcting.

All techniques are listed in the "Common Uses" sections of the main text. Easy to find and easy to follow, they appear in the same order as the chapters. This list further illustrates the most demanding and production-enhancing uses of Photoshop.

Contents

This book is divided into three sections: Tools, Menu Commands, and Palettes. In turn, each section is split into chapters that pertain to one specific category of items. Some chapters are more information-intensive than others—some are 60 pages long, while others are three or four.

Part I, Tools

The first section covers the contents of Photoshop's Toolbar.

Chapter 1, Selection Tools
Covers the Marquee, Crop, Move, Lasso, and Magic Wand Tools.

Chapter 2, The Paint Tools
Covers the Airbrush, Paintbrush, Eraser, Pencil, Rubber Stamp, Smudge, Focus, and Toning Tools.

Chapter 3, Special Tools
Covers the Pen, Type, Line, Gradient, Paint Bucket, and Eyedropper Tools.

Chapter 4, The View Tools
Covers the Hand and Zoom Tools.

Chapter 5, The Color Controls
Covers the Foreground Color, Background Color, Default Colors, and the Color Picker.

Chapter 6, Quick Mask Tools
Covers the Make Mask and Make Selection Tools.

Chapter 7, The View Controls
Covers Window View, Full View with Window, and Full View.

Part II, Menus

The second section covers Photoshop's menus, from left to right.

Chapter 8, The File Menu
Covers all items under the File Menu, in descending order.

Chapter 9, The Edit Menu
Covers all items under the Edit Menu, in descending order.

Chapter 10, The Image Menu
Covers all items under the Image Menu, in descending order.

Chapter 11, The Layer Menu
Covers all items under the Layer Menu, in descending order.

Chapter 12, The Select Menu
Covers all items under the Select Menu, in descending order.

Chapter 13, The Filter Menu
Covers all items under the Filter Menu, in descending order.

Chapter 14, The View Menu
Covers all items under the View Menu, in descending order.

Part III, Palettes

The third section covers Photoshop's palettes, in the order they appear under the Window Menu.

Chapter 15, The Navigator Palette
Covers the use of the Navigator Palette and its submenu commands.

Chapter 16, The Info Palette
Covers the use of the Info Palette and its submenu commands.

Chapter 17, The Color Palette
Covers the use of the Color Palette and its submenu commands.

Chapter 18, The Swatches Palette
Covers the use of the Swatches Palette and its submenu commands.

Chapter 19, The Brushes Palette
Covers the use of the Brushes Palette and its submenu commands.

Chapter 20, The Layers Palette
Covers the use of the Layers Palette and its submenu commands.

Chapter 21, The Channels Palette
Covers the use of the Channels Palette and its submenu commands.

Chapter 22, The Paths Palette
Covers the use of the Paths Palette and its submenu commands.

Chapter 23, The Actions Palette
Covers the use of the Actions Palette and its submenu commands.

Part IV, Appendixes

This book contains four appendixes, which further expand the information covered in the main text.

Appendix A, Common Techniques
Includes over 170 step-by-step techniques referenced by the Common Uses sections of the main text.

Appendix B, Photoshop Shortcuts
Includes almost 300 Photoshop keyboard shortcuts.

Appendix C, Resolution Types
Defines the six resolution types referred to in the book.

Appendix D, Image Credits
Attributes the images used from the John Foxx Images CD-ROM collection.

How to Contact Us

We have tested and verified all the information in this book to the best of our ability, but you may find that features have changed (or even that we have made mistakes!). Please let us know about any errors you find, as well as your suggestions for future editions, by writing to:

O'Reilly & Associates, Inc.
101 Morris Street
Sebastopol, CA 95472
1-800-998-9938 (in the U.S. or Canada)
1-707-829-0515 (international/local)
1-707-829-0104 (FAX)

You can also send messages electronically. To be put on our mailing list or to request a catalog, send email to:

nuts@oreilly.com

To ask technical questions or comment on the book, send email to:

bookquestions@oreilly.com

You can also contact the authors by sending email to:

Donnie O'Quinn at *donnie@maine.rr.com*
Matt LeClair at *matty@maine.rr.com*

Acknowledgments

We offer thanks to the multitude of people who helped us complete this book:

David Rogelberg and Brian Gill, the boogie-woogie bugle boys of StudioB. Tim O'Reilly, editor of the *In a Nutshell* series, who gave us the initial thumbs-up. Troy Mott, who scrutinized our chapters with his eagle eye. Edie Freedman, whose tech-editing and real-world advice helped shape the book. John Foxx Images of Amsterdam, for the use of their most excellent stock images. Adam Cassel, for his steadfast support and expert advice. Robert Romano, for handling all the graphics. Richard Koman, Steve Clark, Susan Bailey, Larry Watson, Kristen Throop, and Bob Schmitt, for their contributions.

Also, thanks to the production staff of O'Reilly & Associates. Nancy Wolfe Kotary was the project manager and production editor. Mike Sierra provided technical support and worked with the tools to create the book. Deborah Lillie copy-edited the book. Seth Maislin wrote the index. Ellie Fountain Maden and Sheryl Avruch performed quality control checks.

On a personal note, Donnie thanks Colleen Caron (who has inspired, tantalized, and tormented me, often all at once) and Harvey Kail (who, as it turns out, taught me more about writing in a single class at the University of Maine than I ever dreamed possible).

Matt thanks Rachel Dyer, without whose love and support he wouldn't have finished this book. He'd also like to thank his mom, Ethel LeClair, and his sister, Caritha Curti, for keeping him from starving to death.

PART I

Tools

This section covers the contents of Photoshop's Toolbar. The order of the chapters follow the appearance of the tools from top to bottom. The Toolbar is actually a palette, much like the Layers Palette or Info Palette, and appears as an option under the Window Menu.

Access the Adobe Web Site

The button at the top of the Toolbar is a shortcut to the Photoshop portion of Adobe's corporate website.

Click it once to reveal the About Adobe Photoshop splash-screen. If you click the box in the upper left corner, Photoshop launches your Web browser and loads the basic web page information that ships with the software.

As soon as you click one of the links, your browser attempts to connect to Adobe's site. If you do not wish to connect, choose (Command) [Control]-period to cancel.

Context-Sensitive Menus

The Mac version of Photoshop features a series of context-sensitive menus. These are designed to mimic the menu that appears when you hold down the second mouse button on a Windows-based computer.

To access these menus, hold down the Control key, then press the mouse button anywhere on the active image. The items that appear on these menus depend on the following:

- The currently chosen tool.
- Whether or not an active selection exists.
- Whether or not the image contains multiple layers.

No unique commands appear. These menus only provide shortcuts to standard menu commands.

The Options Palette

Many tools are actually comprised of a series of tools and options, all of which are controlled by the Options Palette. Each tool has its own set of options. If this palette is not already visible, select either View Tool and press the Return key (unlike other tools, double-clicking on their icons does not reveal the Options Palette).

The Options Palette submenu contains only two items, regardless of the selected tool:

Reset Tool
> Choose this item to restore the default setting for only the selected tool. If the active tool does not have any options, this item is unavailable.

Reset All Tools
> Choose this item to restore the default settings for every tool in the Toolbar. You cannot save these settings like you can with other palettes, so be certain you are not deleting importing information.

CHAPTER 1

Selection Tools

The vast majority of image editing techniques involve an active selection. Selections are simply boundaries, or a sort of mask that allows you to work on one part of an image without affecting the color content of the rest. Without them, you could only apply commands to an entire image or layer.

Selecting information in Photoshop is much different from selecting elements in a page layout or illustration program. These applications are *object-oriented*, meaning every visible element can be individually selected, edited, layered, and moved. You select one of those objects by clicking it with an arrow-shaped tool. The edges highlight with a series of dots, indicating that future actions will affect only that particular page element.

These separate objects do not exist in a pixel-based image. In a scan, for example, Photoshop doesn't know the difference between a piece of fruit and the table it sits on, or a man's eyeglasses and the bridge of his nose, or a piece of furniture and the surrounding walls of the room. There's no way to click and automatically select what you only perceive to be an object in the image.

The only elements recognized by Photoshop are the individual pixels that comprise every image. Each pixel contains one color. When the pixels are small enough, they resolve into what you see as the image, much like an Impressionist painting. To make a selection, you must create an outline that surrounds your targeted area.

Common Reasons to Select

On its own, a selection does nothing. It must be used in conjunction with other commands to produce a visible result. The most common uses of a selection include the following:

- **Editing specific image areas.** Make a selection to edit the color or tone of a specific part of your image. For example, you can safely raise or lower the value of one color without compromising the remaining pixels. You can also protect sensitive areas from erroneous mouse-clicks when painting or retouching.

- **Creating multiple layers.** Active selections allow you to create new layers based on the contents of an open image. After making a selection, this is done by copying and pasting, choosing one of the Layer: **New** options, or holding down the Command key and dragging the selection to another open image.

- **Creating masks.** Aside from reloading a saved selection, mask channels can be used for additional spot color plates in a page layout, the transparent pixels of a Web graphic, advanced image composition, and techniques like specialized drop shadows. See the Channels Palette (Chapter 21) for more information.

- **Creating geometric shapes.** Nearly every other graphic arts program has a series of box and circle tools for drawing and coloring geometric shapes. To do this in Photoshop, draw a selection with the appropriate tool and use the Edit: **Fill** and **Stroke** dialogs.

- **Cropping.** Any rectangular selection can be used as a basis for reducing the overall canvas size. Also, the **Cropping Tool** is found among Photoshop's selections tools.

Editing Selections

When creating a selection, your first attempt does not need to be perfect. Each selection tool can be used to further alter the shape of an active selection outline:

- **Add to a selection.** Hold down the Shift key and use a selection tool to add to the existing outline. The cursor displays a small plus sign.

- **Subtract from a selection.** Hold down the (Option) [Alt] key and use a selection tool to remove pixels from the existing outline. The cursor displays a small minus sign.

- **Intersect two selections.** Hold down the (Option-Shift) [Alt-Shift] keys and use a selection tool to deselect all but the overlapping portions of the two outlines. The cursor displays a small "x".

Partial Selections

When you initially draw a selection, its contents are 100% selected. This means that the selected pixels are completely affected by any commands you apply. For example, if you fill one of these selections with black, all the pixels are uniformly recolored, obliterating any pre-existing detail.

It's possible to partially select the pixels, thereby reducing the effect of your edits. The effect is similar to lowering the opacity of a layer, but the semi-opacity is built into the selection itself. If you fill a 40% selection with black, the result is a 60% opaque black.

Although they remain active, pixels less than 50% selected are not surrounded by an outline.

Partial selections are encountered in four different places:

- **Soft selection edges.** The edges of any selection can be softened, or made to gradually increase in transparency. When you apply a command, soft edges result in a smoother transition between the selected and unselected pixels. The most common occurrence is *anti-aliasing*, which surrounds a selection with a one-pixel transition that conceals the jagged edges commonly associated with pixel-based edits. Increase the width of the transition by applying a *feather* value. (See Select: **Feather** for more information.)

- **Mask channels.** When Photoshop loads a saved selection, it reads the information in the Grayscale mask channel: 0% black areas are completely selected and 100% black areas are ignored. Gray pixels result in partial selections. The same values apply when you make a selection by (Command) [Control]-clicking on a color channel. (See Select: **Save Selection** and the **Channels Palette** for more information.)

- **Quick Mask selections.** Using a soft brush or applying a blur filter to a selection in Quick Mask mode results in feathered edges. Lowering the opacity of a brush results in a partial selection. (See **Quick Mask Tools** for more information.)

- **Select: Color Range selections.** When you tell the Color Range dialog to make a selection based on a predefined range, only full color intensities are 100% selected. The remaining values result in partial selections. (See Select: **Color Range** for more information.)

Floating Selections

A floating selection is a temporary layer created by the following actions:

- Repositioning a selection with the **Move Tool.**
- Duplicating a selection by holding down the (Option) [Alt] key while dragging it with the **Move Tool.**

As long as a floating selection remains active, it exists as a separate item in the **Layers Palette.** After creating one, you can handle it in one of two ways:

- **Add the selection to a new layer.** Double-click the Floating Selection item in the **Layers Palette** and enter a name in the Make Layer dialog, or simply reposition the item in the Layers Palette.

- **Add the selection to the current layer.** Choose Select: **None** after positioning the floating layer as desired.

Editing a Floating Selection

You can safely perform the following actions on a floating selection:

- **Moving the selection.** Drag with the Move Tool to reposition the floating selection.

- **Scrolling the window.** Drag with the Hand Tool to reposition the image in the window.

- **Filling the selection.** Use Edit: **Fill** to color a floating selection. All the Fill shortcuts can be used except pressing the Delete key, which removes the item altogether. You can also use the **Paint Bucket Tool.**

- **Resetting the opacity.** Move the Opacity slider in the **Layers Palette** to make the contents of a floating selection semi-transparent. If the underlying layer contains transparent pixels, the Preserve Transparency box underneath the slider applies only to that layer. Check the box to prevent pixels from the floating selection from appearing over the transparent areas.

- **Subtracting pixels from the selection.** Hold down the (Option) [Alt] key while using a selection tool to remove pixels from the floating selection. Hold down the (Option) [Alt] and Shift keys to produce the opposite effect—any part of the floating selection included in the new outline remains active, while the rest is discarded.

- **Applying a transformation.** Use any of the Layer: **Transform** commands. When you finish editing the transform box and apply the new values, it reverts back to a floating selection.

- **Choosing a Blend Mode.** Choose any of the Blend Mode options from the **Layers Palette** pop-up.

- **Saving the selection.** At any time, create a mask channel by choosing Select: Save Selection.

Defloating a Floating Selection

The following actions defloat a floating selection:

- **Choosing Layer: Defloat.** Whenever a floating selection exists, this item appears in the Layer Menu instead of Layer: **Merge Layers**. The effect of the command is the same—the contents of the selection merge with the underlying layer.

- **Deactivating the selection.** This includes making a new selection, clicking on-screen with a selection tool, or choosing Select: **None**.

- **Choosing the Quick Mask command.** You get an editable mask, but the selection itself defloats.

- **Applying a paint stroke, adjustment, or filter.** To use any of these commands, turn the floating selection into a new layer.

- **Applying any of the Select Menu commands.** With the exception of Select: **Save Selection**, they all defloat the selection.

- **Adding to the selection outline.** You cannot increase the area of a floating selection by holding down the Shift key while using a selection tool.

Marquee Tool
(type "M")

Use this tool to draw geometrically shaped selections. When you click and drag to create a selection, a preview outline extends outward from your starting point. When you release the mouse button, the preview converts to an active selection. From there, continue editing the selection or apply a command to the selected pixels.

Common Uses

See Appendix A for full descriptions of the following:

- Selecting a constrained circle or square
- Radiating a marquee from a center point
- Radiating a constrained marquee
- Adding a constrained marquee to an existing selection
- Subtracting a constrained marquee from an existing selection
- Adding a radiating marquee to an existing selection
- Adding a constrained, radiating marquee to an existing selection
- Subtracting a radiating marquee from an existing selection
- Subtracting a constrained, radiating marquee from an existing selection
- Creating geometric shapes

Common Errors

- **Making the right selection, but choosing the wrong layer.** You can choose any item in the **Layers Palette** while a selection is active. When you apply a command, it affects the current layer within the boundary of the selection.

- **Forgetting that the selection edges are hidden.** After choosing View: **Hide Edges**, you must still choose Select: **None** when finished with the selection. Otherwise, future edits will be confined to the selected area.

Special Notes

- If you need to reposition the entire preview marquee, hold down the space bar and continue dragging. You don't have to release any keys you may be holding down. Release the space bar to continue shaping the selection.

- You can only select to the edge of the image window. Any pixels that exist beyond that point cannot be included in any selection. These hidden pixels can be edited only after clicking on the appropriate layer in the **Layers Palette**, without making a selection.

- The Single Row and Single Column options create selections that are only one pixel thick. The ultimate thickness depends on the current resolution. This makes them best suited for editing low-resolution images such as screen-captures or web graphics. Their effects may not be visible in a 300 ppi print image.

- The aspect ratio of your monitor is 1.3 to 1, the same as your television set. Duplicate this by entering 1.3 under Width and 1 under Height. Other noteworthy aspect ratios include most modern movies (1.8 to 1), and wide-angle Panavision (2.4 to 1).

Marquee Options Palette

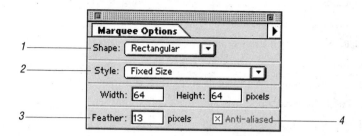

Make any changes to this palette *before* creating your selection. Otherwise, the following options have no effect.

1. Shape

Choose the basic shape of your marquee selection from this pop-up. These options reflect the different tools under the Marquee pop-up in the Toolbar (with the exception of the **Cropping Tool**). When you choose a shape, the appropriate tool appears in the Marquee position of the Toolbar.

Rectangular

Choose this option to create rectangular or square selections. Anti-aliasing has no effect on rectangular selections, since they never result in jagged edges; the outlines are always fully horizontal or vertical, aligning perfectly with the pixel grid.

Elliptical

Choose this option to create elliptical or round selections. Since these selections do not align with the pixel grid, the Ellipsis Tool uses anti-aliasing by default.

Single Row

Choose this option to select a single row of pixels. When you click and drag, a horizontal line appears, which can only be positioned up or down.

Single Column

Choose this option to select a single column of pixels. When you click and drag, a vertical line appears, which can only be positioned left or right.

2. Style

The options under the Style pop-up control the process of drag-selecting with the rectangular or elliptical Marquee Tools.

Normal

The most common option, this allows you to manually shape the selection by watching the preview outline while you click and drag.

Constrained Aspect Ratio

This option fixes the ratio between a selection's width and height, regardless of how big or small you draw the outline. The ratio is based on the values in the Width and Height fields. These values are based on proportion units instead of actual measurements. For example, if you enter 2 under Width and 1 under Height, the width of your selection is always twice the height. This option is only available for the rectangular and elliptical Marquee Tools.

Fixed Size

Here, you can enter values for a single-sized selection. The values can only be in pixels, the units recognized by a selection outline. Instead of dragging to create a selection, a simple click places a pre-measured selection onto the image. Or, you can hold down the mouse button and drag after clicking to position the outline.

3. Feather

This value applies a feathered edge to the next selection. See Select: **Feather** for more information.

4. Anti-aliased

Check this box to anti-alias the edge of the next selection, or apply a one-pixel transition into the surrounding image information. Unless you have a reason for turning it off, leave this box checked.

See Also

Appendix A (Selection Tools: **Marquee Tool**)
Cropping Tool
Select: **None**
Select: **Feather**
View: **Hide/Show Edges**
The Layers Palette

Cropping Tool
(type "C")

When cropping an image, you mimic the conventional technique of cropping a photograph. There, you'd mark the photo to specify the rectangular portion you wish to use. In Photoshop, you accomplish the same thing by drawing a crop marquee and discarding the pixels falling outside its boundaries.

To create a crop marquee, select the Cropping Tool and drag. This marquee is easily edited, so you needn't drag a perfect box the first time. Use the following techniques:

- **Move.** Place the cursor inside the marquee and drag to reposition it.

- **Resize.** Drag any of the points on the corners and sides of the marquee to resize it. Hold down the Shift key while dragging to scale the marquee proportionately.

- **Rotate.** Drag anywhere outside the marquee to rotate it. Now when you crop the image, the contents of the marquee rotate to become a vertically rectangular image.

- **Cancel.** Press the Escape key at any time to remove the crop marquee from the image.

- **Crop.** Double-click inside the crop marquee to apply the crop command.

Common Uses

Refer to Appendix A for full descriptions of the following:

- Simultaneously cropping and rotating crooked scans
- Editing image dimensions using Fixed Size variations

Common Errors

Confusing the Cropping Tool with the remaining Marquee Tools. In the Toolbar, the Cropping Tool appears with the rest of the Marquee Tools. The Cropping Tool uses a marquee as the basis for its commands, but that is the only similarity between the toolsets. The crop marquee cannot be used as a selection, and only perfectly rectangular selections can be used to crop an image (see Image: **Crop**).

Special Notes

- If you click on the Cropping Tool after drawing a crop marquee, an alert appears, allowing you to apply the crop or discard the marquee.
- Page layout programs have their own tools to crop imported images. Unlike cropping in Photoshop, they only hide portions of the image from view. This can cause problems during printing, since an output device must still process the hidden pixels. At the very least, the image takes longer to output. In extreme cases, the file may not output at all. Whenever possible, crop your images in Photoshop.

Cropping Tool Options Palette

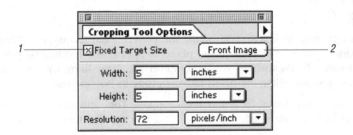

Make any changes to this palette *before* creating your crop marquee. Otherwise, the following options have no effect.

1. **Fixed Target Size**

   Check this box to set the final width, height, and resolution of the cropped image. This command combines the Cropping Tool with the effects of the Image: **Image Size** dialog. This is useful when you want to crop a series of images to the same dimensions. When the box is checked, the following options are available:

Width and Height

Enter the desired width and height of the cropped image in these fields. Choose your preferred unit of measurement from the pop-up menus. Now, as you draw the crop marquee, the ratio between the width and height is constrained. When you crop, the image is resized to match your settings.

Resolution

Enter the desired resolution of the cropped image in this field. When you crop, the image resolution is increased or decreased, depending on your setting.

2. **Front Image**

Use this button to automatically enter the dimensions of a pre-existing image. Open the image in Photoshop, bring it to the front of any other images, and click this button.

See Also

Appendix A (Selection Tools: **Cropping Tool**)
The Marquee Tool
Image: **Image Size**
Image: **Crop**

Move Tool
(type "V")

The sole function of this tool is to reposition the contents of an image layer, a channel, or a selection.

Click and drag with the Move Tool to reposition an item, similar to doing so in a page layout or illustration program. If no selections exist, the Move Tool affects the entire contents of the active layer or channel.

Common Uses

Refer to Appendix A for full descriptions of the following:

- Constraining the motion of a repositioned object
- Nudging in 1-pixel increments
- Nudging in 10-pixel increments
- Cloning a selection, channel, or layer

Common Errors

- **Moving the selection outline instead of the selection contents.** If you click and drag a selection while a selection tool is still chosen, only the outline is repositioned. In earlier versions of Photoshop, this would affect the selected pixels. Now, the outline moves independently. To move the selected pixels, you must use the Move Tool.

- **Accidentally moving a layer instead of a selection.** Click and drag *within* the selection outline to move its contents and create a floating selection. If you initially click and drag *outside* the outline, you move the contents of the entire layer—the selection moves with the layer, maintaining its relative position, so no floating selection is created.

Special Notes

- Holding down the (Command) [Control] key to access the Move Tool works for every tool except the Pen Tool (it accesses the Path Select Tool) and the Hand Tool (it accesses the Zoom Tool).
- When repositioning an element, refer to the upper-right panel of the Info Palette for precise measurements.
- If the selection is in an image layer, transparent pixels are left behind. If the background layer is active, the underlying pixels are filled with the current background color.
- If the background layer is active and you drag outside the selection outline, it automatically converts to an image layer.

Move Tool Options Palette

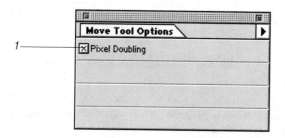

1. **Pixel Doubling**

   When this box is checked, Photoshop cuts the on-screen resolution of an image element in half as you drag it with the Move Tool. This allows the image to refresh more quickly, allowing you to reposition it in real time. The speed increase is most noticeable on high-resolution images and less-powerful workstations.

See Also

Appendix A (Selection Tools: **Move Tool**)
Selection Tools: Selections Overview (**Floating Selections**)
Layer: Layers Overview (**Background Layer**)

Lasso Tool
(type "L")

The Lasso Tool allows you to create a selection outline by hand. As you click and drag, you draw a thin line. Make a selection by drawing a free-form outline around the desired portion of the image. When you release the mouse button, the ends of the line automatically connect, completing the selection. From there, continue editing the selection or apply a command to the selected pixels.

Common Uses

Refer to Appendix A for full descriptions of the following:

* Adding straight segments to a freehand selection

* Including edge pixels in a freehand selection

Common Errors

Failing to "close the loop." For best results, always end on the same point you started from. Otherwise, the straight line that connects the start and end of the outline may cut off part of the image you want to select.

Lasso Tool Options Palette

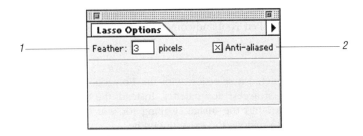

1. **Feather**

   This value applies a feathered edge to the next selection. See Select: **Feather** for more information.

2. **Anti-aliased**

   Check this box to anti-alias the edge of the next selection, or apply a one-pixel transition into the surrounding image information. Unless you have a reason for doing so, leave this box checked.

See Also

Appendix A (Selection Tools: **Lasso Tool**)
Select: **Feather**
The **Polygon Lasso Tool**

Polygon Lasso Tool
(type "L")

Use this tool to create a selection by clicking a series of straight lines.

Rather than drag to draw a selection, you click a series of points. Each mouse-click adds a straight segment to the outline. To complete the outline and convert it to a selection, you must end on the same point you first clicked. Before you click to complete a selection, the cursor displays a small circle which indicates a closed outline. If desired, you could double-click anywhere on the image to complete the selection, but this method gives you less control over the position of the final segment.

Common Uses

Refer to Appendix A for full descriptions of the following:

• Adding freehand segments to a polygon selection

• Including edge pixels in a polygon selection

Common Errors

Using the Polygon Lasso Tool for curved selection edges. If you're uncomfortable with the **Lasso Tool**, it's tempting to use the Polygon Lasso Tool to click a multitude of tiny straight lines. Unfortunately, it's easy to spot these edges. If you need to draw curved selections but cannot effectively use the Lasso Tool, consider drawing a path with the **Pen Tool** and converting it to a selection.

Special Notes

If you have not completed a selection with the Polygon Lasso Tool, you cannot select any other tools or access any palettes. Instead, the current straight segment follows your cursor around the image, waiting for you to click the next point. Press the Escape key to remove the existing outline.

Polygon Lasso Tool Options Palette

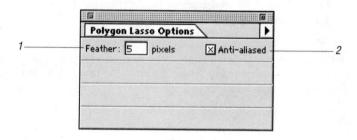

1. **Feather**

   This value applies a feathered edge to the next selection. See Select: **Feather** for more information.

2. **Anti-aliased**

   Check this box to anti-alias the edge of the next selection, or apply a one-pixel transition into the surrounding image information. Unless you have a reason for doing so, leave this box checked.

See Also

Appendix A (Selection Tools: **Polygon Lasso Tool**)
The Lasso Tool
The Pen Tool
Select: **Feather**

Magic Wand Tool
(type "W")

This tool allows you to create a selection by clicking on an image. A specific range of pixels is included in the outline, controlled by the Tolerance setting in the Magic Wand Tool Options Palette.

Starting from where you click, the Magic Wand Tool only selects adjacent pixels that fall within the established tolerance. For example, if an image contains two separate red circles on a black background, clicking on a circle only includes that one shape in the selection. To select the other, you must do one of the following: hold down the Shift key and click the second circle with the Magic Wand Tool, or choose Select: **Similar** to add all similar image colors to the current selection.

Common Uses

- Selecting areas of strongly defined color, such as logos or imported Illustrator or FreeHand artwork
- Selecting the white area surrounding a flattened silhouette

Common Errors

- **Attempting to select objects in continuous-tone images.** Because of the method it uses to recognize pixels, the Magic Wand Tool is a poor choice for making selections in continuous tone images. (See "Tolerance" in the following list.)
- **Attempting to make selections in a bitmap image.** Although the solid colors seem perfect for the Magic Wand Tool, this is the only selection tool that doesn't work when an image is in Bitmap mode. Convert the image to Grayscale to use the tool. If necessary, convert the image back to Bitmap when editing is complete.
- **Selecting the transparent pixels of an image layer.** This results in an inaccurate selection, because the edge pixels of the layer's contents can be mistakenly

included in the selection. For the best results, (Command) [Control]-click the appropriate item in the **Layers Palette**, then choose Select: **Inverse**.

Special Notes

- Try examining the individual color channels when using the Magic Wand Tool. If the object you wish to select appears solidly colored and highly contrasting, the tool may work more efficiently. Make the selection in the color channel, then switch back to the composite channel to continue editing. If you cannot make a clean selection, you'll have to resort to other selection tools.

- The Magic Wand Tool generates different results in RGB, CMYK, and Lab Color images, even if you click on the same color with the same Tolerance value. This is due to the different information in the color channels.

- There are three ways to increase the Tolerance of an active selection:

    - **Shift-click to add pixels to a selection.** This method is inaccurate. You increase the number of selected pixels, but the exact range is determined by the value of the second pixel you click.

    - **Increase the Tolerance and try again.** This method is also inaccurate. Unless you click on precisely the same pixel, the selected range will differ from the first selection.

    - **Choose Select: Grow.** This method automatically increases the Tolerance of the existing selection, using the value currently entered in the Tolerance field. If desired, enter a new value before choosing the command.

Magic Wand Tool Options Palette

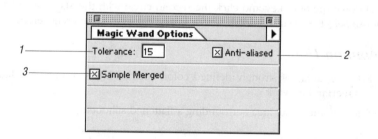

1. Tolerance

This value determines the range of pixels included in your selection. Choose a number between 0 and 255. A value of 0 includes only the exact color of the targeted pixel in the selection. Higher numbers gradually increase the range.

Contrary to popular belief, the Magic Wand Tool does not base a selection on color values. It measures the brightness values of the targeted pixel. The value you enter in the Tolerance field actually corresponds to the 256 possible tones in an 8-bit color channel. If the image is in RGB, CMYK, or Lab Color mode, it reads the values of each color channel.

Photoshop defines the range by adding and subtracting the Tolerance from the brightness value of the initial pixel. Assuming the Tolerance is set to its default of 32, clicking a pixel with a brightness value of 100 expands the range to include adjacent pixels between 68 and 132 in the selection. If you select an RGB pixel with values of R: 160, G: 50, and B: 35, the range includes all adjacent pixels with values between R: 128 and R: 192, G: 18 and G: 82, and B: 3 and B: 67.

The range cannot extend beyond values of 0 or 255. For example, if you click on a pixel valued at 10 and the Tolerance is set to 32, Photoshop selects all adjacent pixels between 0 and 42. Because of this, you select the greatest range when you click on a pixel in the midtones. Clicking lighter or darker pixels results in smaller selections.

2. **Anti-aliased**

   Check this box to anti-alias the edge of the next selection, or apply a one-pixel transition into the surrounding image information. Unless you have a reason for doing so, leave this box checked.

3. **Sample Merged**

   Check this button to allow Photoshop to use all visible pixels when defining the range of a selection. Otherwise, it uses only the pixels of the active layer. Even if you use the Magic Wand Tool with the Sample Merged box checked, the selection only affects the currently active layer.

See Also

Select: **Similar**
Select: **Grow**

Additional Selection Tools

The following tools are not officially selection tools, but they are often used to either create or edit selection outlines.

Layers and Channels

Create a selection based on the contents of a layer or channel by holding down the (Command) [Control] key and clicking the item in the appropriate palette:

- If you click a layer, you create a selection based on the exact outline of the layer's contents. Semi-transparent pixels result in partial selections.

- If you click a channel, you get a selection of varying opacity, based on the channel's gray values.

Pen Tool

You can convert any path created with the Pen Tool into an active selection. When a path is saved, it can be converted into a selection, quickly edited if necessary, and converted again. This provides a very precise and flexible method of saving a selection outline. (See the **Pen Tool**, in Chapter 3, for more information.)

Paths from Illustrator

When you copy information from an Adobe Illustrator graphic, you have the option of pasting it into Photoshop as a path. Then, like any path created with the Pen Tool, you can convert it into a selection. (See Edit: **Paste** for more information.)

Quick Mask

The Quick Mask feature allows you to graphically edit the shape of an active selection. (See **Quick Mask Tools** for more information.)

Type Outlines Tool

When you use the **Type Outlines Tool**, you don't actually create colored type. Rather, you create a selection in the exact shape of the type defined in the Type dialog. (See the **Type Outlines Tool** for more information.)

CHAPTER 2

The Paint Tools

The Paint Tools provide three functions:

- **Painting**. The **Airbrush**, **Paintbrush**, and **Pencil Tools** apply new colors to an image.

- **Retouching**. The **Eraser**, **Rubber Stamp**, and **Smudge Tools** primarily use existing pixel values as the basis for editing.

- **Tone editing**. The **Focus** and **Toning Tools** affect the sharpness and saturation of the existing image information.

These tools are placed in the same category because they all use a brush shape to apply or affect image colors, similar to traditional paintbrushes. (See Chapter 19, *The Brushes Palette*, for more information.)

Pressure-sensitive drawing tablets allow you to further emulate traditional brush techniques. The appropriate Options Palette item is available only when a tablet is properly connected to your workstation.

Stylus Pressure

As you apply pressure to the stylus of a drawing tablet, you dynamically change the function of the current brush. The following options control this effect:

1. **Size**

    Different levels of pressure affect the thickness of the brushstroke. Full pressure applies the current brush at its full width; less pressure results in a thinner stroke.

2. **Color**

    Full pressure applies the current foreground color; very slight pressure applies the current background color. As you apply levels of pressure in between, the result is a blend between the two colors, creating a sort of flexible gradient.

3. Opacity

Full pressure applies the foreground color at full opacity, assuming the opacity slider in the Options Palette is set to 100%. Less pressure results in increasingly transparent brushstrokes.

Fade

The Airbrush, Paintbrush, Eraser, and Pencil Tools allow you to apply tapered brushstrokes. You must enter a number of steps for this effect to work.

The steps value refers to the Spacing setting of the current brush. A brushstroke is actually a repeating series of brush shapes—when you taper a brushstroke, the distance of the fade is based on a specific number of these shapes. Therefore, brushes with higher Spacing values take longer to fade.

A brushstroke can fade to one of two values:

Transparent
Choose this option to fade the current foreground color into completely transparent pixels.

Background
Choose this option to fade the current foreground color into the current background color.

Brush Modes

The Options Palette for every Paint Tool contains a pop-up menu of different brush modes. These options affect how the color of a brush stroke combines with the colors of the existing image pixels.

When you apply any Paint Tool, the basic effect is the same: the color of every pixel involved is recalculated, or changed to a new value. Therefore, painting involves three values:

Base Color
The base color is the value of a pixel before you apply a brushstroke.

Blend Color
The blend color is the value you wish to apply. It can be a single value, such as applying the foreground color, or a series of colors, such as cloning with the Rubber Stamp Tool.

Result Color
The result color is the value ultimately determined by a brush mode, or the color that results from combining the blend color and base color.

Special Notes

Do not confuse brush modes with the *blend modes* found in the **Layers Palette**. Although the options of both lists are largely the same, the techniques required to apply them are different. Blend modes affect the contents of an entire layer; using the Paint Tools, brush modes can affect a smaller portion of a layer.

Normal

This mode applies the full value of the current blend color. If a tool does not apply color—such as the Blur or Sharpen Tools—it simply edits the existing colors based on the remaining settings in their Options Palette.

Threshold

Images in Bitmap or Indexed Color mode contain this option instead of Normal. Since both modes contain a limited number of colors, painting in this mode applies the available value closest to the current blend color.

Dissolve

This option affects soft-edged or semi-opaque brushes. Any application of a blend color less than 100% opaque is converted to randomly scattered, 100% opaque pixels. The result is a rough-textured brushstroke with no anti-aliasing.

The quantity of scattered pixels is determined by the transparency value of the brush. If its opacity slider is set to 60%, then 60% of the pixels within the painted area are changed to the foreground color. Forty percent of the pixels retain the original base color.

Behind

This mode is available only when an image layer is active. Here, only pixels less than 100% opaque are affected by the blend color. Fully transparent pixels are painted with 100% of the foreground color. Semi-transparent pixels are colored at opacity levels equal to the inverse of their transparency levels. For example, a 40% transparent pixel is colored with 60% of the blend color.

Clear

Only the **Line** and **Paint Bucket Tools** can use Clear, and only when an image layer is selected. Instead of applying color, this option changes pixel transparency. A fully opaque blend color results in completely transparent pixels. A semi-opaque blend color sets the transparency of the base pixels to the inverse value of the Options Palette's opacity slider. For example, an opacity setting of 80% results in 20% opaque pixels.

Special Notes

This option also appears in the Edit: **Fill** and **Stroke** dialogs.

Multiply

This mode multiplies the brightness values of the base color and blend color to create a darker tone.

To multiply color values, Photoshop regards the 256 brightness values as a range that extends from 0 to 1. Zero is black, or a brightness value of 0. One is white, or a brightness value of 255. The remaining values are treated as fractions.

For example, a brightness value of 100 is regarded as 100/255. A value of 200 is regarded as 200/255. If you apply one value to the other using Multiply, the resulting color value is the product of the two fractions, or 78 (78/255). Treating the values as fractions guarantees that all subsequent values fall between 0 and 255. Since multiplying two fractions always results in a smaller fraction (or lower brightness value), the result color is always darker.

When the blend color is white, the base color is not affected. When the base color is white, the blend color is unaffected. When either color is black, the result color is black as well.

Special Notes

When the blend color is a shade of gray, Multiply darkens the base color without changing its hue. This makes it an effective choice for applying shadows to a color image.

Screen

This mode produces the opposite effect of Multiply, resulting in lighter colors.

To create a Screen value, Photoshop multiplies the inverted values of the base color and blend color. It then inverts the new brightness value, creating the lighter tone. (A tone is inverted by subtracting its brightness value from 255. Therefore, inverting a value of 50 results in 205. See Image: Adjust: **Invert** for more information.)

For example, if you apply a value of 100 to a value of 200 (similar to the example described under Multiply), Photoshop inverts the values and multiplies 155/255 and 55/255. The product is 33, which is inverted to create the resulting tone of 222.

When the blend color is black, the base color is not affected. When the blend color is white, the result color is always white.

Special Notes

Shades of gray lighten pixels without changing their hue, making it an effective choice for applying highlights to a color image.

Overlay

The effect of this mode is the same as either Multiply or Screen, depending on the values of the base color. The hues of the base color shift toward the blend color, and the general contrast is increased.

Brightness values lower than 128 are multiplied by the blend color. Brightness values higher than 128 are screened by the blend color. Generally, light pixels become a lighter shade of the blend color, while dark pixels become a darker shade of the blend color.

When either the blend color or the base color is middle gray, this mode has no effect.

Soft Light

The effect of this mode is similar to Overlay, only less intense.

Hard Light

The effect of this mode is similar to Overlay, only more intense.

Color Dodge

This mode lightens the base color, using the values of the blend color as a basis. Lighter blend colors cause more intense changes, while darker colors cause a more subtle effect. The result of Color Dodge is similar to using the **Dodge Tool**, only the resulting hues are shifted toward the blend color.

When the blend color is black, this mode has no effect.

Color Burn

This mode darkens the base color, using the values of the blend color as a basis. Darker blend colors cause more intense changes, while lighter colors cause a more subtle effect. The result of Color Burn is similar to using the **Burn Tool**, only the resulting hues are shifted toward the blend color.

When the blend color is white, this mode has no effect.

Darken

This mode compares the brightness values of each color channel. The result color is formed by the darkest channel values of the blend color and base color.

For example, if you apply R: 160, G: 70, B: 220 to a base color of R: 80, G: 120, B: 155, the result color is R: 80, G: 70, B: 155.

Lighten

This mode compares the brightness values of each color channel. The result color is formed by the lightest channel values of the blend color and base color.

For example, if you apply R: 160, G: 70, B: 220 to a base color of R: 80, G: 120, B: 155, the result color is R: 160, G: 120, B: 220.

Difference

This mode compares the brightness values of each color channel. The result color is formed by subtracting the smaller values from the larger values.

For example, if you apply R: 160, G: 70, B: 220 to a base color of R: 80, G: 120, B: 155, the result color is R: 80, G: 50, B: 65.

When the blend color is white, the base color inverts. When the blend color is black, this mode has no effect.

Exclusion

The effect of this mode is similar to Difference, but the result color is more likely to contain neutral grays.

When the blend color is white, the base color inverts. When the blend color is black, this mode has no effect. When the blend color is middle gray, it replaces the base color completely.

Hue

This mode replaces the hue value of the base color with the value of the blend color. The saturation and lightness levels of the base color are not affected. (See "The HSB Model" in the Image: Mode **Overview** for more information.)

Saturation

This mode replaces the saturation value of the base color with the value of the blend color. The hue and lightness levels of the base color are not affected. (See "The HSB Model" in the Image: Mode **Overview** for more information.)

Color

This mode replaces the hue and saturation values of the base color with the values of the blend color. The lightness level of the base color are not affected. (See "The HSB Model" in the Image: Mode **Overview** for more information.)

Special Notes

Use this mode to recolor part of an image while keeping the image details intact.

Luminosity

This mode replaces the lightness value of the base color with the value of the blend color. The hue and saturation levels of the base color are not affected. (See "The HSB Model" in the Image: Mode **Overview** for more information.)

Airbrush Tool
(type "A")

This tool applies a continuous feed of color, similar to an actual airbrush. While painting, holding the cursor in one position results in a wider application of color. Use the Airbrush Tool to create soft, gradual brushstrokes.

Airbrush Tool Options Palette

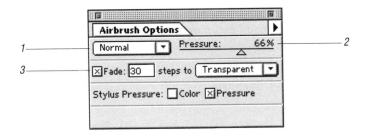

Make any changes to this palette *before* applying the Airbrush Tool:

1. **Brush Modes**

   These options determine how the Airbrush Tool affects existing image colors. (See "Brush Modes" earlier in this chapter for more information.)

2. **Pressure**

   This value controls how quickly color is applied to the image, simulating the flow of paint from an airbrush. It defaults to 50%, which applies a diffuse, semi-translucent line.

3. **Fade**

   Check this box to create a tapered brushstroke. (See "Fade" earlier in this chapter for more information.)

Paintbrush Tool
(type "B")

This tool applies a brushstroke of uniform width. Its brushes have either soft or anti-aliased edges.

Paintbrush Tool Options Palette

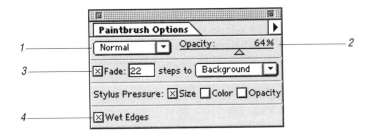

Make any changes to this palette *before* applying the Paintbrush Tool:

1. **Brush Modes**

   These options determine how the Paintbrush Tool affects existing image colors. (See "Brush Modes" earlier in this chapter for more information.)

2. **Opacity**

   This slider controls the opacity of a brushstroke. The value is applied in addition to the opacity of the current layer.

3. **Fade**

   Check this box to create a tapered brushstroke. (See "Fade" earlier in this chapter for more information.)

4. **Wet Edges**

   When this box is checked, the resulting brushstrokes resemble a watercolor. The color in the center of the brush is washed out and semi-transparent, while the edges appear slightly darker.

   This effect appears to be a blend mode, but it's not. Rather, Photoshop manipulates the opacity of the brush: the center of the brush is set to roughly half of the current opacity setting. The edges are set to roughly three-quarters of the current opacity.

Eraser Tool
(type "E")

Although the Eraser Tool appears to delete pixels, it actually does no such thing. Instead, it changes existing color values to one of two values:

- **Background color.** When the Eraser Tool is used on the background layer, it applies the current background color. This effect is the same as making a selection and pressing the Delete key.

- **Transparent.** When this tool is used on any other image layer, it applies no color at all. Rather, it converts colored pixels to fully transparent. This effect most closely resembles "erasing" pixels.

Special Notes

- By lowering the opacity setting for the Paintbrush or Pencil option, you can use the Eraser Tool to add transparency to specific parts of an image layer. For example, applying a 40% erasure to a 100% opaque layer results in 60% opaque pixels.

- If a layer's Preserve Transparency box is checked, the Eraser Tool applies the background color.

- Hold down the (Option) [Alt] key while using any brush type to access the Erase to Saved option.

Eraser Tool Options Palette

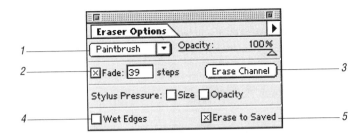

Make any changes to this palette *before* applying the Eraser Tool:

1. Brush Type

The Eraser Tool can mimic the characteristics of the Airbrush, Paintbrush, or Pencil Tool. The fourth option is Block, the same non anti-aliased square brush shape used by earlier versions of the program.

When you choose a Paint Tool from the pop-up, the Options Palette displays the appropriate slider and Stylus Pressure controls.

2. Fade

Check this box to erase with a tapered brushstroke. (See "Fade" earlier in this chapter for more information.)

3. Erase Image/Erase Layer

When an image contains only the background layer, click this button to fill it completely with the background color. When an image layer is active, click this button to remove all colored pixels.

4. Wet Edges

This option is available only when Paintbrush is chosen from the Brush Type pop-up. Here, the brushstroke resembles a watercolor, similar to using Wet Edges with the Paintbrush Tool. The effects are reversed, however, to create the appearance of erasing.

This effect appears to be a blend mode, but it's not. Rather, Photoshop manipulates the opacity of the brush: the center of the brush is set to roughly half of the current opacity setting. Its edges are set to roughly one-quarter of the current opacity.

5. Erase to Saved

When this box is checked, the Eraser Tool *selectively reverts*, or applies information from the last-saved version of the image. Although this option is always available, it doesn't work if you've changed the width, height, resolution, or color mode since the last save.

Pencil Tool
(type "Y")

This tool applies a brushstroke of uniform width. Like an actual pencil, its brushes have hard edges. Closely related to the very first digital paint tools, the Pencil Tool cannot use soft or anti-aliased brushes.

Pencil Tool Options Palette

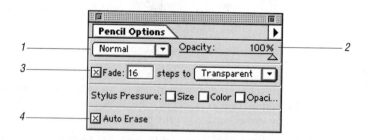

Make any changes to this palette *before* applying the Pencil Tool:

1. **Brush Modes**

   These options determine how the Pencil Tool affects existing image colors. See "Brush Modes" in the **Paint Tools Overview** for full descriptions.

2. **Opacity**

   This slider controls the opacity of a Pencil Tool brushstroke. The value is applied in addition to the opacity of the current layer.

3. **Fade**

   Check this box to create a tapered brushstroke. See "Fading Brushstrokes" in the **Paint Tools Overview** for a full description.

4. **Auto Erase**

   This option allows you to apply the background color over areas colored with the current foreground color.

   Although it's available in all color modes, the effect of Auto Erase is most apparent on a Bitmap image. Assuming the colors are set to default black and white, painting on white pixels applies black, similar to drawing on paper. If you start painting by clicking on a black pixel, the Pencil Tool applies white, similar to erasing black from a white page.

Rubber Stamp Tool
(type "S")

This is essentially a cloning tool, used to copy and paste brush-sized segments of pre-existing image pixels. Since Photoshop can invisibly store different variations of an image, the Rubber Stamp Tool allows you to clone the following information:

- Visible image pixels.
- Pixels from the last saved version.
- Pixels from a snapshot created with Edit: **Take Snapshot** or **Merged Snapshot**.
- Pixels from a pattern created with Edit: **Define Pattern**.

Although every Rubber Stamp option involves cloning, most of the options simply require clicking and dragging like any other Paint Tool.

As a production tool, however, the Rubber Stamp is most often used to retouch an image. For example, scratches or dust on a 35 mm slide may become visible when the image is scanned. To retouch the flaw, the Rubber Stamp Tool requires that you do two things:

- **Sample.** Typically, you'll copy pixels from an area with similar color, tone, and texture to the pixels surrounding the flaw. When you sample, you specify the exact pixels you want to clone. Do this by holding down the (Option) [Alt] key and clicking the appropriate area. This results in no visible changes.

- **Clone.** To apply the sampled pixels, move the cursor over the flaw and click. This act copies pixels from the defined sample area and pastes them wherever you clicked. By using the surrounding pixels, you keep visible artifacting to a minimum.

The exact behavior of the sample and clone commands depend on which Clone item is chosen from the Options pop-up in the Options Palette. No other option requires this technique.

Special Notes

- The Rubber Stamp Tool can read information from a separate image. Open the image and (Option) [Alt]-click to define a sample area. Open another image and click to clone the sampled information.

- When you retouch an image using Clone (aligned), avoid cloning by dragging the cursor. This often results in visible artifacting and the inclusion of unwanted details. For the best results, start with a small, soft-edged brush and clone one click at a time.

- When using the From Saved option on a large image, Photoshop may need to pause for a moment as it loads the saved information into active RAM. To avoid a lag between your brushstroke and the on-screen effect, click once on the image before applying additional strokes. After the pause, continue editing.

Rubber Stamp Tool Options Palette

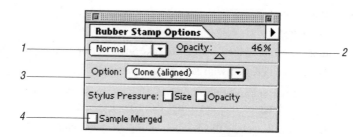

Make any changes to this palette *before* applying the Rubber Stamp Tool:

1. **Brush Modes**

   These options determine how the cloned pixels interact with the existing image colors. See "Brush Modes" in the **Paint Tools Overview** for full descriptions.

2. **Opacity**

   This slider controls the opacity of the cloned information. The value is applied in addition to the opacity of the current layer.

3. **Option**

   These options determine two things: where pixels are cloned from, and the relative position of the cloned information to the visible information. Choose one of the following:

   Clone (aligned)

   This option samples and clones visible pixels, as described above. Its title refers to the relationship between the sample area and the clone area— here, their relative positions remain constant. For example, assume your sample area is two inches to the right of the clone area. If you continue clicking various spots throughout the image, you continue sampling information from a point two inches to the right of every click.

   Clone (non-aligned)

   This option also uses visible pixels. Here, the sample area remains constant, regardless of where and how many times you click to define a clone area.

   Pattern (aligned)

   This option uses the pixels contained in a pattern, and is only available after you've created one using Edit: **Define Pattern**. As you paint, the pattern is always aligned, regardless of the number of times you click or drag. The illusion is that the pattern has already been applied to the image, and the Rubber Stamp Tool is simply revealing it.

   Pattern (non-aligned)

   This option also clones pixels from a defined pattern. Here, the pattern is re-aligned every time you click with the Rubber Stamp Tool. Rather than align to an invisible grid, the center of the pattern aligns to the center of every brushstroke.

From Snapshot

As you paint, this option continually refers to a snapshot, or a temporarily stored version of the image. This allows you to refer back to the status of an image before you applied any series of edits. Although this option is always available, it doesn't work if you've changed the width, height, resolution, or color mode since the last save.

From Saved

As you paint, this option refers to the last saved version of the image. Like From Snapshot, this option doesn't work if you've changed the width, height, resolution, or color mode since the last save.

Impressionist

Like From Saved, this option refers to the last saved version of the image. As you paint, it applies a smudged, "Impressionistic" rendition of the original image contents. Unfortunately, you have no control over the length, placement, or colors of the smudges.

4. **Sample Merged**

Ordinarily, the Clone options can only sample pixels from the active image layer. By checking this box, you can sample any visible color values, regardless of the layer in which they exist. As you clone, the new colors appear in the currently active layer.

Smudge Tool
(type "U")

This tool smears existing color values as you apply a brushstroke, similar to running your finger through wet paint.

Special Notes

Hold down the (Option) [Alt] key as you paint with the Smudge Tool to temporarily access the Finger Painting option.

Smudge Tool Options Palette

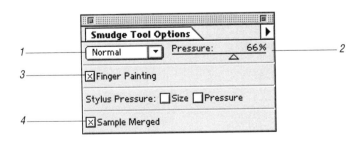

Make any changes to this palette *before* applying the Smudge Tool:

1. **Brush Modes**

   Since it doesn't apply new color values, this tool ignores most of the brush modes. The remaining modes affect the redistribution of the existing colors. See "Brush Modes" in the **Paint Tools Overview** for full descriptions.

2. **Pressure**

   This controls the intensity of the smudge, similar to the pressure of your finger as you smear wet paint. Lower values result in very slight smudging, while higher values exaggerate the effect. When the value is 100%, the Smudge Tool lifts the portion of the image you initially click, and repeats the edge pixels of the brush as you drag.

3. **Finger Painting**

   When this box is checked, the Smudge Tool initially applies the current foreground color, similar to dipping your finger in pigment before smearing wet paint. The length of this effect is determined by the Pressure setting. Lower values result in short applications of the foreground color, while higher values extend the distance. When the value is 100%, the Smudge Tool applies only the foreground color, just like the **Paintbrush Tool**.

4. **Sample Merged**

   Ordinarily, the Smudge Tool only affects pixels in the active image layer. By checking this box, you include any visible color values, regardless of the layer in which they exist. As you smudge, the new colors appear in the currently active layer.

Focus Tools
(type "R")

Use these tools to manually increase or decrease an image's clarity. The basic effect is similar to the Blur and Sharpen filters, only the Focus Tools are used to "paint" the intended effect. This method lacks the numerical precision of Filter: Blur: **Gaussian Blur** or Filter: Sharpen: **Unsharp Mask**, but it does allow you to specifically target part of an image.

Special Notes

You cannot use one Focus Tool to reverse the effect of the other. If you are unhappy with the effect of a brushstroke, choose Edit: **Undo** and try again.

Focus Tools Options Palette

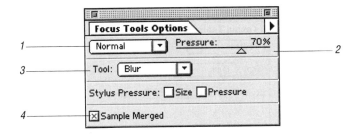

Make any changes to this palette *before* applying the Focus Tools:

1. **Brush Modes**

    Since they don't apply new color values, this tool ignores most of the brush modes. The remaining modes affect the redistribution of the existing colors. See "Brush Modes" in the **Paint Tools Overview** for full descriptions.

2. **Pressure**

    This slider controls the intensity of the Focus Tools. Lower values result in very slight blurring or sharpening, while higher values exaggerate the effect.

3. **Tool**

    Choose your desired Focus Tool from either the Toolbar or this pop-up menu:

    Sharpen
    Painting with this tool sharpens the image, further increasing the amount of contrast between colored areas. It achieves this effect by increasing the saturation values of the edge pixels of neighboring colors.

    Blur
    Painting with this tool blurs the image, further reducing the amount of contrast between colored areas. It achieves this effect by averaging the color values of the edge pixels of neighboring colors.

4. **Sample Merged**

    Ordinarily, the Focus Tools only affect pixels in the active image layer. By checking this box, you include any visible color values, regardless of the layer in which they exist. As you apply a tool, the new colors appear in the currently active layer.

Toning Tools
(type "O")

Use these tools to manually affect the tone and saturation of the existing image colors. All three of the Toning Tools mimic conventional photographic techniques.

Toning Tools Options Palette

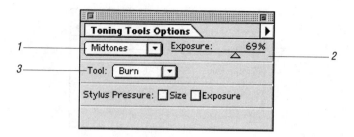

Make any changes to this palette *before* applying the Toning Tools:

1. **Brush Modes**

   These tools cannot apply color or redistribute pixels, so the standard brush modes do not apply.

   For the Dodge and Burn Tools, choose a tonal range from this pop-up menu:

   Shadows
   Here, the tool targets the darkest image tones, although the remaining tones are edited as well.

   Midtones
   Here, all tones except the very lightest and darkest are targeted.

   Highlights
   Here, the tool targets the lightest image tones, although the remaining tones are edited as well.

   For the Sponge Tool, choose one of the following:

   Desaturate
   This option reduces the saturation value of the painted colors, bringing them closer to neutral gray. (See "The HSB Model" in the Image: **Mode Overview** for more information.)

   Saturate
   This option increases the saturation value of the painted colors, or increases their intensity. (See "The HSB Model" in the Image: **Mode Overview** for more information.)

2. **Exposure/Pressure**

   The Exposure value mimics the intensity of light a photographer uses to expose a negative. The pressure value controls the intensity of the Sponge Tool. For both, lower values result in slight edits, while increasing the value exaggerates the effects.

3. **Tool**

Choose your desired Toning Tool from either the Toolbar or this pop-up menu:

Dodge

As you paint with this tool, you lighten the tones of the image colors. In photography, this affect is achieved by diffusing the light used to expose a negative.

Burn

As you paint with this tool, you darken the tones of the image colors. In photography, this affect is achieved by focusing the light used to expose a negative.

Sponge

As you paint with this tool, you only affect the saturation value of the colors. On a Grayscale image, however, this tool affects overall contrast. The Desaturate mode lowers the contrast, bringing all tones closer to middle gray. The Saturate mode increases the contrast, or brings all tones closer to black or white.

Paint Tools

CHAPTER 3

Special Tools

Pen Tool
(type "P")

The Pen Tool is used only for manually creating object-oriented paths. These are based on *Bézier curves*, the same technology employed by vector-based programs like Adobe Illustrator or Macromedia FreeHand.

Paths offer an impressive array of editing capabilities. However, the techniques required to create and modify a path are completely different from any other facet of Photoshop. Before you begin using the Pen Tool, you must understand the fundamental concepts of paths (see Figure 3-1).

Common Uses

Refer to Appendix A for full descriptions of the following:

- Drawing a basic path
- Continuing an existing path
- Creating multiple open paths
- Joining two open paths
- Transforming a path
- Deleting an entire path

Common Errors

Attempting to output Photoshop paths. These shapes—although they are object-oriented, just like Illustrator's or FreeHand's—can only be used to further affect a Photoshop image. If you want to print a Photoshop path, you must choose File: Export: **Paths to Illustrator**, open the new file in a vector-based editing program, apply color, and print from there.

Special Notes

- Any path you create automatically appears in the **Paths Palette**, which contains all the commands you need to make the path interact with your image. Once a path appears there, however, the terminology changes: there, a path is any specific grouping of object-oriented shapes. One specific shape, whether open or closed, is called a *subpath*.

- The Pen Tool is only used to create the initial path. Unless you create a path perfectly the first time—which rarely happens—you must use the remaining path tools to modify its shape.

- Each curve handle affects a segment on one side of a point. Therefore, a segment can be controlled by two curve handles—one on each end.

- After creating a path, you must use the Convert Point Tool to change a point from one type to another.

Path Components

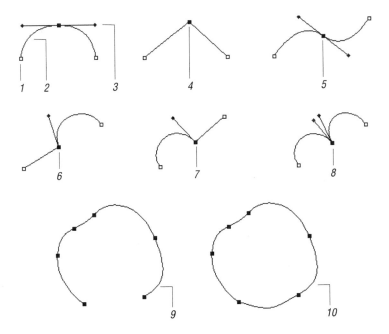

Figure 3-1: Path components

1. **Point**

   Click with the Pen Tool to place a single point. Paths are created one point at a time—they're the hot-spots, acting like the dots in a connect-the-dots puzzle.

2. Segment

As you click, a line connects the new point with the previous point. These segments ultimately form the shape of a path.

3. Curve Handles

Each point contains two curve handles. When you simply click to place a point, both handles are hidden. If you drag the cursor before you release the mouse button, you extend the handles. Manipulate them with the Arrow Tool to curve the segments connected to the point. It's not necessary to reveal the handles, but without them, you can only create straight lines.

4. Corner Point

This point displays no handles, resulting in straight segments. Place a corner point by simply clicking with the Pen Tool.

5. Smooth Point

This point displays two locked and symmetrical handles, allowing two segments to meet in a smooth, continuous curve. Place a smooth point by click-dragging with the Pen Tool to place a smooth point.

6. Single-curve Point (straight segment into curved)

This point displays one handle, resulting in a straight segment meeting a curved segment. After clicking to place a corner point (which forms the straight segment), click and drag from the same point to reveal one handle. This adds curve to the following segment, which appears when you place the next point.

7. Single-curve Point (curved segment into straight)

This point displays one handle, resulting in a curved segment meeting a straight segment. After placing a smooth point (which forms the curved segment), hold down the (Option) [Alt] key and click the same point to hide the forward handle. This results in no curve being added to the following segment, which appears when you place the next point.

8. Double-curve Point

This point displays two unlocked handles, allowing you to separately adjust the two segments on either side of the point. To create a double-curve point with the Pen Tool, start by placing a smooth point. Hold down the (Option) [Alt] key and drag from the same point to redirect the forward handle. This adds an independent curve to the following segment, which appears when you place the next point.

9. Open Path

A path with a distinct beginning and end is considered *open*. A path consisting of two points and a connecting segment is the simplest example. Using the Stroke Path command in the Paths Palette, this type of path is commonly used as the basis for creating curved lines in an image.

10.Closed Path

A path with no distinct beginning and end is considered *closed*. As you create a path, close it by targeting your last mouse-click on the very first point of the path. A circular path—a shape with no beginning or end—is the simplest example. Depending on the command chosen from the Paths Palette, this type of path is commonly the basis for filled shapes, clipping paths, and new selections.

See Also

Appendix A (Special Tools: **Pen Tool**)
The Paths Palette
File: Export: **Paths to Illustrator**

Path Select (Arrow) Tool
(type "P")

The Path Select Tool, commonly referred to as the Arrow Tool, is used to move and manipulate the different parts of a path.

Common Uses

- **Selecting a point.** Click on a single point to independently select it. This displays the curve handles, if any have been extended. If desired, you can reposition the point by dragging it.

- **Selecting multiple points.** Hold down the Shift key and click a series of existing points. Or, drag a marquee with the tool—any points included in the box are selected when you release the mouse button. If desired, reposition multiple points by dragging them.

- **Selecting a path.** Hold down the (Option) [Alt] key and click the path. Or, drag a marquee around the entire path. If desired, reposition the entire path by dragging it.

- **Deselecting a path.** Click on the image, away from the path. The path remains visible, but no points are selected.

- **Repositioning a segment.** When you drag a straight segment, it moves along with the two points on either end. When you drag a curved segment, you either increase or decrease the curve—the points do not move.

- **Dragging a curve handle.** To change the shape of a curved segment, select a point to reveal its curve handles. Drag the handles to reshape the segment.

- **Duplicating a path.** Hold down the (Option) [Alt] key while dragging a path.

Special Notes

Hold down the (Command) [Control] key while using any of the path tools to temporarily access the Arrow Tool.

Add Point Tool
(type "P")

Use this tool to add a new point to a path. It cannot place new points to continue a path, like the Pen Tool—rather, you click on a path segment to insert a point where none existed before. Long segments have limited flexibility; this allows you to edit the shape of a path more accurately.

Special Notes

- If you add a point to a curved segment, Photoshop automatically extends the curve handles to maintain the segment's shape.

- To access the Add Point Tool while using the Arrow Tool, hold down the (Option-Command) [Alt-Control] key. Click on a segment to add a point.

Delete Point Tool
(type "P")

Use this tool to delete an existing point. If you delete a point by selecting it with the Arrow Tool and pressing the Delete key, you also remove the two segments on either side. By clicking a point with this tool, you remove it while leaving the segment intact.

Special Notes

To access the Delete Point Tool while using the Arrow Tool, hold down the (Option-Command) [Alt-Control] key. Click a point to delete it.

Convert Point Tool
(type "P")

After creating a path, use this tool to convert a point from one type to another.

Common Uses

- **Converting a corner point to a smooth point.** Drag from a corner point to reveal two locked curve handles.

- **Converting a smooth point to a corner point.** Click on a smooth point to hide the handles.

- **Converting a smooth point to a double-curve point.** Drag one of the curve handles of a smooth point. It moves independently of the other handle.

- **Converting a double-curve point to a smooth point.** Drag one of the curve handles of a double-curve point. The other handle snaps into a symmetrical position.

Special Notes

To access the Convert Point Tool while using the Arrow Tool, hold down the (Control-Option) [Control] key.

Type Tool
(type "T")

Use this tool to add type to an image. You can edit pixel-based type with the full range of Photoshop's tools, adjustment commands and filters. This allows you to generate effects that you simply cannot duplicate in other programs, such as semi-transparency, blurred edges, and soft drop-shadows.

Photoshop handles type differently than other graphics applications. Page layout and illustration programs have object-oriented type tools—once you add text to a document, they allow you to edit at will, similar to a word processing program. Photoshop, on the other hand, treats type like any other pixel-based image.

Special Tools

Common Uses

Refer to Appendix A for full descriptions of the following:

• Transforming type

• Creating semi-transparent type

• Creating a character mask

• Creating a type channel

• Transforming selection-based type

• Creating custom path shapes

Common Errors

• **Attempting to use the Type Tool without installing Adobe Type Manager.** This utility uses the output information stored in a font to render its shapes smoothly on-screen. Without it, the characters are jagged and unusable.

• **Simulating the type set with a page layout or illustration program.** Compared to those programs, Photoshop type has three limitations:

 – **Fixed resolution.** The resolution of object-oriented type is ultimately based on the output device. The resolution of pixel-based type depends on the image. Therefore, low-resolution files do not print well on high-resolution output devices.

 – **Fixed content.** Once you create type, you cannot change the words or formatting. You can only use standard image-editing tools.

 – **Limited formatting capabilities.** Formatting techniques such as curved baselines and finely-tuned typography are difficult at best in Photoshop. For that reason, many users create type in an outside program like Illustrator or Free-Hand before importing it into a Photoshop image. (See File: **Opening Vector-based Graphics** and File: Export: **Paths to Illustrator** for more information.)

Special Notes

- New type always appears in a separate image layer. The Preserve Transparency box is automatically checked, allowing you to edit the content of the characters without compromising the letter shapes. To change the inherent shape of the type with commands like the Blur or Distort filters, you must uncheck this box.

- The color of standard type is based on the current foreground color.

- If you use Adobe Type Manager, the ascenders and descenders of your type characters may appear clipped. By default, ATM's Preserve Line Spacing option is checked, which can negatively affect very tall or large fonts in Photoshop. Avoid this problem by selecting the Preserve Character Shapes option and restarting.

- For the best results, avoid the different Style settings. Instead of choosing Bold or Italic, use the appropriate font. For the remaining styles, apply a more flexible Photoshop technique after creating the initial type:

    - **Underline.** Use the **Line Tool**, which allows you to set different line widths and change the distance between the underline and the text.

    - **Outline.** Apply an Edit: **Stroke** value, which allows you to apply different colored strokes at varying widths.

    - **Shadow.** Create a soft drop-shadow, which allows you to create a soft-edged shadow, as well as control its position, color, and transparency. (See the **Layers Palette** (Chapter 20) for more information.)

The Type Tool Dialog

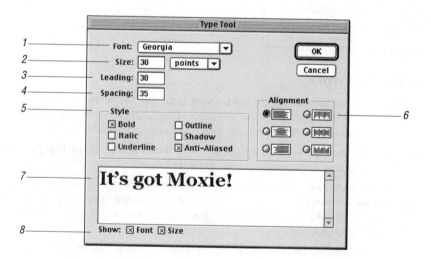

1. Font

All fonts currently available to your operating system appear in this pop-up. Unless you're using TrueType fonts, you must use Adobe Type Manager for the best results. Otherwise, your type appears jagged and formless on-screen.

2. **Size**

   Enter the desired size of the type in this field. Choose the desired unit of measurement from the pop-up menu:

   Points
   > The default setting, this option measures type in point sizes, regardless of the image resolution. Values can range from 4 to 1000 points.

   Pixels
   > This option measures type in image pixels. Therefore, the on-screen size of a specific value depends on the image resolution.

   The unit of measurement set in the Size pop-up applies to the Leading and Spacing values as well.

3. **Leading**

   This value determines the distance between baselines, or the invisible line a row of type sits upon. Values can range from 1 to 1000. Entering 0—or leaving the field blank—results in the default setting of 125% of the entered size.

4. **Spacing**

   This value determines the distance between letters, similar to tracking values in page layout or illustration programs. Values can range from –99.9 to 999.9. Negative values decrease the letter spacing; positive values increase it.

5. **Style**

   These settings represent the five standard type styles, and are applied in addition to any style variations built into the chosen font. Check the Anti-Aliased box to create smooth-edged type. By default, this option is turned on.

6. **Alignment**

   The three options on the left align the type horizontally. The three on the right align the type vertically. All six options use the spot you initially click as the alignment point.

7. **Text Box**

   In this field, enter the text you wish to convert into pixel-based type. Although you can highlight portions of the text, you can only edit the content—you cannot define multiple fonts or styles in one field.

8. **Show**

   Check these boxes to preview certain formatting elements in the Text Box. The Font box displays text in the currently selected font. The Size box displays the text at the specified size. When neither box is checked, the text appears in a small, unformatted default font.

See Also

Appendix A (Special Tools: **Type Tool**)
Type Outline Tool
The Line Tool
File: **Opening Vector-based Graphics**
File: Export: **Paths to Illustrator**
Edit: **Stroke**

Type Outline Tool
(type "T")

This tool does not result in pixel-based type. It accesses the same dialog as the standard Type Tool, but it pays no attention to the current foreground color. Instead, it places an active selection in the precise shape of the defined type. This selection behaves as if it was drawn manually; no new layers or floating selections are created. (See the **Selection Tools Overview** for more information.) Most often, this tool is used to create the basis for a layer mask.

This tool mimics the Type Tool of earlier versions of Photoshop. The only difference is that those tools resulted in an active selection filled with the foreground color.

Line Tool
(type "N")

Use the Line Tool to draw perfectly straight lines. The color of a line is based on the current foreground color. Constrain the lines to 45° angles by holding down the Shift key while dragging.

Common Uses

Refer to Appendix A for full descriptions of the following:

- Creating an editable line
- Creating a dotted line
- Creating a curved line
- Adding an arrowhead to an existing line
- Using a line as a measuring tool

Common Errors

Creating a non-editable line. Unless you create a new layer to contain a line, it is added to the current layer, replacing any existing underlying color.

Special Notes

This tool only creates straight, solid lines. Any variations like curves or dashes require additional tools.

Line Tool Options Palette

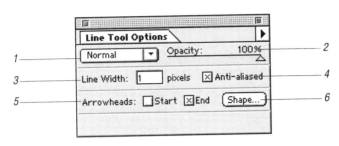

1. Brush Modes

When adding a line to an existing layer, these settings determine how its color combines with the underlying pixels. (See "Brush Modes" in Chapter 2 for more information.)

2. Opacity

When applying the Line Tool to an existing layer, this slider allows you to create a semi-transparent line.

3. Line Width

This option determines the thickness of the new line, measured in pixels. Unlike other programs, which allow you to measure in points, line thickness ultimately depends on the current resolution. For example, a 10-pixel line in a 72 ppi image is over 4 times wider than a 10-pixel line in a 300 ppi image.

4. Anti-aliased

Check this box to create a line with a soft, anti-aliased edge.

5. Arrowheads

This option allows you to create a line with arrowheads. Check one or both of the following boxes:

Start
This option adds an arrowhead at the beginning of a line, or at the point you initially clicked with the Line Tool.

End
This option adds an arrowhead at the end of a line, or at the point you release the mouse button.

6. Shape

Click this button to edit the shape of the arrowheads. The Arrowhead Shape dialog appears, where you set the following:

Width and Length

Enter a percentage between 10% and 5000%. These values are based on the current Line Width. For example, the default arrowhead is 500% wide, 1000% long. On a 4-pixel line, the arrowhead is 20 pixels wide and 40 pixels long. On a 10-pixel line, the arrowhead is 50 by 100 pixels.

Concavity

This value defines the shape of the arrowhead, and is also based on the current line width. Enter a value between –50% and 50%. Positive values result in a familiar, convex arrowhead. Negative values result in a diamond-shaped, concave arrowhead.

See Also

Appendix A (Special Tools: **Line Tool**)
Paint Tools Overview (**Brush Modes**)

Gradient Tool
(type "G")

Use this tool to create a *gradient*, or a progression of colors that blend gradually from one to the next.

To create a gradient, drag a line with the Gradient Tool. The start of the line represents the first color of the gradient; the end represents the last color. If a gradient consists of more than two colors, the remaining values are evenly spaced between ends of the line. Photoshop automatically inserts a series of tones between each defined color to create smooth transitions.

Common Uses

- **Filling a selection.** When a selection is active, only its contents are filled. If more than one area is selected, they are affected by the same progression.

- **Filling an entire layer.** When no selections are present, the entire active layer is filled, replacing any existing information.

- **Filling the contents of a layer.** By choosing a layer and checking the Preserve Transparency box, the gradient is only applied to the non-transparent pixels. This allows you to add a custom fill to information such as type.

- **Filling a mask channel.** Apply a gradient to a mask channel or an image in Quick Mask mode to create a diminishing selection. (See **The Channels Palette** and **Quick Mask Tools** for more information.)

Common Errors

Creating a gradient that is too long, resulting in shade-stepping. Any blend between two colors has a limited number of possible tones. For example, if you create a blend between black and white, up to 254 shades of gray can be generated between them. As you lengthen the gradient, you widen the individual tones. When a gradient extends too far, the tones become visible. The exact point at which banding occurs depends on two things:

- **The tonal difference between two colors.** For example, a black-to-white gradient can extend to approximately eight inches before banding occurs. A blend between two medium grays contains fewer tones, and can only extend a fraction of the distance.

- **The linescreen value of a printed image.** As you increase the linescreen of a printed image, you reduce the number of tones an output device can reproduce. If the linescreen exceeds a printer's recommended limit, banding will occur—and gradients are the first elements visibly affected.

Special Notes

- As an extra safeguard against banding, many users apply a low Filter: **Add Noise** value to long gradients, in addition to checking the Dither box. By entering a value of up to 10, you randomize the tones of the gradient without creating a visible noise texture.

- A gradient can contain up to 32 separate colors, plus transparent pixels.

- To restore the list of default gradients, you must choose Reset Tool from the Gradient Tool Options palette submenu.

Gradient Tool Options Palette

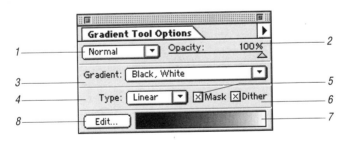

1. Brush Modes

When adding a gradient to an existing layer, these settings determine how its colors combine with the underlying pixels. (See "Brush Modes" in Chapter 2 for more information.)

2. Opacity

When applying the Gradient Tool to an existing layer, this slider allows you to create a semi-transparent gradient.

3. **Gradient**

This pop-up contains a list of all predefined gradients. The factory-installed settings appear first; any custom settings appear at the end.

4. **Type**

There are two styles of gradient:

Linear

This gradient proceeds in a straight line, following the angle of the line you drag with the Gradient Tool.

Radial

This gradient proceeds in a series of concentric circles. When you drag with the Gradient Tool, the start of the line represents the center of the gradient.

5. **Mask**

When you apply a gradient containing transparent or semi-opaque pixels, check this box to maintain those values. Otherwise, the gradient appears as 100% opaque.

6. **Dither**

Check this box to slightly randomize the distribution of colored pixels. This helps to prevent *banding*, or the visible shadestepping that occurs when too few tones are extended over too great a distance. Unless you have a specific reason to turn it off, leave this box checked for the best results.

7. **Gradient Preview**

This bar previews the effect of the currently selected gradient.

8. **Edit**

Click this button to access the Gradient Editor dialog, which allows you to define custom gradients.

The Gradient Editor

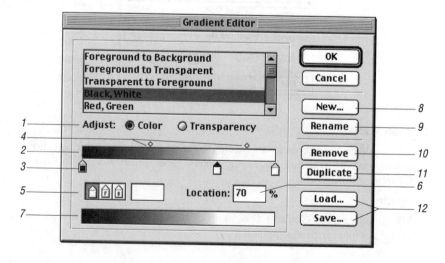

1. **Adjust**

   These buttons allow you to individually edit the two fundamental components of a gradient:

   Color
   The gradient's color content

   Transparency
   The gradient's transparency and opacity levels

   Both options use the same tools to generate their effects.

2. **Gradient Toolbar**

   This bar represents the line dragged with the Gradient Tool. It displays the current settings of your custom gradient, and acts as a guide as you edit the color and transparency values.

3. **Color Stops**

   These triangular markers are used to define the values and location of a gradient's key colors.

   Photoshop defaults to two color stops: one each at the beginning and end of the gradient. To add a new stop, click below the Gradient Toolbar. To remove a stop, drag it away from the Toolbar.

   Add a color to a gradient by changing the value represented by a color stop. After clicking once on the stop to select it, click the color swatch at the bottom of the dialog. The color picker appears, allowing you to define a new value.

4. **Midpoints**

   One diamond-shaped marker appears between every two color stops. These represent the color midpoint, or the point in the gradient where both colors are equally blended. Extend the impact of one color stop by moving the midpoint marker closer to the other color stop.

5. **Stop Types**

   These icons represent the three types of color stop. Regardless of the type of color stop you add, you can select it and change its color value.

   Flexible Color
   Add one of these to insert the color value currently visible in the color swatch.

   Foreground Color
   Add one of these to insert the current foreground color.

   Background Color
   Add one of these to insert the current background color.

6. **Location**

   This field displays the current position of a selected marker. When you reposition a color stop, the percentages represent positions across the Toolbar. When you move a midpoint marker, the percentages represent positions between two color stops.

7. **Gradient Preview**

   This bar previews the effect of the currently defined gradient.

8. **New**

   This button creates the basis for a new gradient. After naming the new item, it defaults to a two-color gradient, based on the current foreground and background color.

9. **Rename**

   This button allows you to apply a new name to an existing gradient.

10. **Remove**

    This button removes the selected gradient from the list.

11. **Duplicate**

    This button makes a copy of the selected gradient. This is useful when you want to change the color content of an existing gradient without replacing the original.

12. **Load and Save**

    If you frequently define a large number of gradients, you can save the entire list into a separate, organized file. Click the Load button to access a saved list.

See Also

The Paint Tools (**Brush Modes**)
Quick Mask Tools
Filter: Noise: **Add Noise**
The Channels Palette

Paint Bucket Tool
(type "K")

Although its title suggests otherwise, the Paint Bucket Tool is not a Paint Tool—it's a modified Fill command. This tool allows you to apply color by clicking on an image. A specific range of pixels are affected, controlled by the Tolerance setting in the Paint Bucket Tool Options Palette.

Starting from where you click, the Paint Bucket Tool affects only adjacent pixels that fall within the established Tolerance. For this reason, this tool has limited uses. If you're editing an image containing strongly defined solid colors, this tool works fairly well. Because of the method it uses to recognize pixels, however, it's a poor choice for coloring continuous tone images.

Special Notes

Using the Paint Bucket Tool, it's almost impossible to get accurate results on anti-aliased shapes—the edge colors are difficult to include in the Tolerance range without affecting additional pixels. Typically, in the time it would take to pinpoint

---

the exact range, you could create a selection outline and use Edit: **Fill**, a far more capable command.

Paint Bucket Options Palette

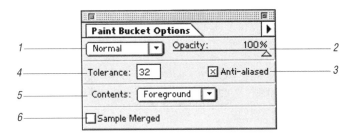

Make any changes to this palette *before* applying the Paint Bucket Tool. The following options have no effect on an existing fill area:

1. **Brush Modes**

   When filling an existing layer, these settings determine how its colors combine with the underlying pixels. (See "Brush Modes" in Chapter 2 for more information.)

2. **Opacity**

   When filling an existing layer, this slider allows you to create a semi-transparent gradient.

3. **Anti-aliased**

   Check this box to add a soft, anti-aliased edge to your fill color. If you are filling solid-colored areas that do not already have anti-aliased edges, turn this option off.

4. **Tolerance**

   This value determines the range of pixels affected by the fill. Choose a number between 0 and 255. A value of 0 changes only the exact color of the targeted pixel in the selection. Higher numbers gradually increase the range.

   Contrary to popular belief, the Paint Bucket Tool does not base a selection on color values. It measures the brightness values of the targeted pixel. The value you enter in the Tolerance field actually corresponds to the 256 possible tones in an 8-bit color channel. If the image is in RGB, CMYK, or Lab Color mode, it reads the value of each color channel.

   Photoshop defines the fill range by adding and subtracting the Tolerance from the brightness value of the targeted pixel. Assuming the Tolerance is set to its default of 32, clicking a pixel with a brightness value of 100 expands the range to paint all adjacent pixels between 68 and 132. If you select an RGB pixel with values of 160 red, 50 green, and 35 blue, the range includes all adjacent pixels with values between 128 and 192 red, 18 and 82 green, and 3 and 67 blue.

   This process makes the effect of this tool difficult to predict.

5. Contents

You can apply two types of fill:

Foreground
This option uses the current foreground color.

Pattern
This option uses the currently defined pattern. (See Edit: **Pattern** for more information.)

6. **Sample Merged**

This option allows the Paint Bucket Tool to recognize colors outside the currently active layer. When you click to add color, the Tolerance value considers all *visible* colors, regardless of their layer. The actual fill, however, is applied only to the current layer.

See Also

The Paint Tools (**Brush Modes**)
Edit: **Pattern**

Eyedropper Tool
(type "I")

This tool provides a simple method of defining new color values. Although many different dialogs contain eyedropper tools—Image: Adjust: **Curves** and Select: **Color Range** are good examples—they do not redefine the foreground or background colors. Rather, their use is restricted to the purpose of the specific dialog.

Common Uses

• **Defining a new foreground color.** Select the Eyedropper Tool and click on any color in an open image. If you hold down the mouse button, you can see the different colors cycling through the foreground color swatch.

• **Defining a new background color.** Hold down the (Option) [Alt] key and click on any color in an open image.

• **Paint Tool shortcut.** While using any Paint Tool, set a new foreground color by holding down the (Option) [Alt] key and clicking the desired color.

Special Notes

• At times, the Eyedropper Tool may appear to be working backwards. If the background color swatch is selected in the **Color Palette**, this tool defines the background color, and you must (Option) [Alt] click to define a new foreground color.

• The Sample Size settings influence the eyedroppers used by all dialogs. For the most accurate results—especially when sampling in color-specific dialogs—choose 3 by 3 Average.

Eyedropper Tool Options Palette

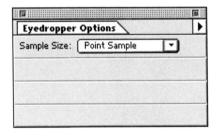

Sample Size

This option determines how the Eyedropper Tool reads the values of a sampled color:

Point Sample
Here, the tool reads the value of the single targeted pixel.

3 by 3 Average
Here, the tool reads the average color value of a nine-pixel square surrounding the targeted pixel.

5 by 5 Average
Here, the tool reads the average color value of a 25-pixel square surrounding the targeted pixel.

CHAPTER 4

The View Tools

The View Tools only affect the way Photoshop displays pixels inside the image window. They have no effect on the image itself.

These tools are closely related to the **View Menu** commands.

Hand Tool
(type "H")

With the Hand Tool, you drag to scroll an image within the image window. It is only effective when the image is larger than the window displaying it. Use this tool instead of the scroll bars on the right and bottom sides of the window.

Access the Hand Tool at any time by holding down the spacebar. Regardless of the currently selected tool, you can scroll the image by clicking and dragging. Release the spacebar to switch back to your original tool. The only time this doesn't work is while you are drawing a rectangular or elliptical marquee selection; then pressing the space bar allows you to reposition the selection outline.

Special Notes

The Hand Tool is much more flexible than using the scroll bars. Not only can you drag the image in any direction at will, but you can scroll when the image is in Full Screen View, which hides the scroll bars.

Hand Tool Options Palette

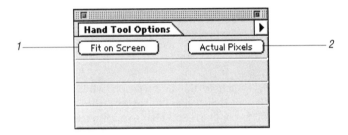

This palette contains two options:

1. **Fit on Screen**

   Click this button to expand the edges of the window to the perimeter of the screen, displaying the entire image at the largest possible size. This is the same as choosing View: **Fit on Screen**.

   Double-clicking the Hand Tool icon in the Toolbar applies the same command.

2. **Actual Pixels**

   Click this button to set the magnification of the image to 100%. This is the same as choosing View: **Actual Pixels**.

   Double-clicking the Zoom Tool icon in the Toolbar applies the same command.

See Also

View: **Fit on Screen**
View: **Actual Pixels**

Zoom Tool
(type "Z")

Use the Zoom Tools to increase or decrease the magnification percentage of the image window. The current percentage is displayed in the lower left corner of the window. (See "Magnification Box" in Chapter 14, *The View Menu* for more information.)

This tool defaults to the Zoom In Tool, which increases the magnification. Here, the cursor appears as a magnifying glass with a plus sign. There are two ways to zoom in:

- **Click on the image.** When you do, the point you click moves to the center of the image window. Starting from 100%, the automatic magnifications are 200%, 300%, 400%, 500%, 600%, 700%, 800%, 1200%, and 1600% (the maximum).

- **Drag a zoom box.** When you do, the contents of the box fill the window, regardless of the exact percentage. This allows you to precisely target part of an image for close-up editing.

Hold down the (Option) [Alt] key to access the Zoom Out Tool. The cursor changes to display a minus sign. Starting from 100%, the automatic percentages are 66.7%, 50%, 33.3%, 25%, 16.7%, 12.5%, 8.33%, 6.25%, and 5%. The smallest possible percentage ultimately depends on the width, height, and resolution of the open image. You cannot drag a zoom box to decrease the magnification.

Special Notes

• You can temporarily switch to the Zoom Tools while using any other tool. Hold (Command) [Control]-Spacebar to access the Zoom In Tool; hold (Option-Command) [Alt-Control]-Spacebar to access the Zoom Out tool.

• These tools mimic the View: **Zoom In** and **Zoom Out** commands. You can also set the magnification on the fly by adjusting the controls of the **Navigator Palette**.

Zoom Tool Options Palette

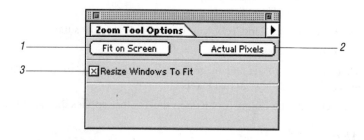

1. **Fit on Screen**

   Click this button to expand the edges of the window to the perimeter of the screen, displaying the entire image at the largest possible size. This is the same as choosing View: **Fit on Screen**.

   Double-clicking the Hand Tool icon in the Toolbar applies the same command.

2. **Actual Pixels**

   Click this button to set the magnification of the image to 100%. This is the same as choosing View: **Actual Pixels**.

   Double-clicking the Zoom Tool icon in the Toolbar applies the same command.

3. **Resize Windows to Fit**

   When this box is checked, the image window resizes to match the new magnification. When it's left unchecked, the window remains unchanged while you zoom.

See Also

Chapter 14, *The View Menu*
View: **Zoom In** and **Zoom Out**
View: **Fit on Screen**
View: **Actual Pixels**
The Navigator Palette

CHAPTER 5

The Color Controls

Every Photoshop user must define colors. Nearly every command and tool in the program exists to either manipulate existing colors or apply new values.

The magnitude of your color decisions depends on the type of work you're producing. If you scan line art for output, your colors are limited to black and white. If you scan and adjust halftones, you work with tints of black between 0% and 100%. If you create on-screen images, you can choose from millions of possible colors—but if you generate graphics for the Web, you may be limited to the 256 colors of an indexed palette. If you create full-color print images, you work with CMYK percentages—and the slightest variation may result in unexpected color shifts.

When you digitally acquire an image, the resulting colors depend on the quality of the scanner and the experience of the operator. Scanning has nothing to do with *defining* color, which takes place only when an image is opened in Photoshop. Regardless of your preferred medium, Photoshop's color controls allow you to properly define colors before applying them to an image.

Foreground Color Swatch

The foreground color is Photoshop's active color, similar to the paint an artist selects from her palette. When you apply a command that *adds* new color information, Photoshop uses the values defined in this swatch.

Photoshop always retains the last-applied foreground color. To define a new value, you must use one of the following methods:

- Click the swatch to access the **Color Picker** (see "The Color Picker" later this chapter).

- Use the **Eyedropper Tool** to sample a color from any open image.

- Manipulate the sliders of the **Color Palette** (see Chapter 17, *The Color Palette*) after selecting the foreground color swatch.

Common Uses

- Painting with the **Airbrush Tool, Paintbrush Tool,** or **Pencil Tool.**
- Using the **Paint Bucket Tool, Type Tool,** or **Line Tool.**
- Defining the starting color of a gradient using the **Gradient Tool.**
- Applying Edit: **Fill** or **Stroke** (although it's not required that you use the foreground color).
- Filling a selection or image layer by holding down the (Option) [Alt] key and pressing Delete.

Special Notes

Click the Default Colors button to set the foreground color to black. (See "Default Colors" later in this chapter.)

Background Color Swatch

The background color is Photoshop's passive color. It's similar to the color that remains when an artist scrapes her canvas with a palette knife: when you apply a command that *removes* existing color information, the values defined in this swatch are left behind.

Photoshop always retains the last-applied background color. To define a new value, you must use one of the following methods:

- Click the swatch to access the Color Picker (see "The Color Picker" later this chapter).
- Hold down the (Option) [Alt] key and use the **Eyedropper Tool** to sample a color from any open image.
- Manipulate the sliders of the **Color Palette** after selecting the background color swatch.

Common Uses

- Using the **Eraser Tool** on the background layer.
- Pressing the Delete key when a selection is active in the background layer.
- Using the Auto Erase feature of the **Pencil Tool.**
- Applying Edit: **Fill** or **Stroke** (although it is not required that you use the background color).
- Filling a selection or any image layer by holding down the (Command) [Control] key and pressing Delete.
- Defining the ending color of a gradient using the **Gradient Tool.**

Special Notes

- Although many filters use the background color in conjunction with the foreground color—Filter: Sketch: **Chalk & Charcoal** and **Photocopy** are two examples—no filters use only the background color value.

- Using the Eraser Tool or deleting a selection on an image layer results in transparent pixels instead of the background color.

- Click the Default Colors button to set the background color to white (see "Default Colors" later in this chapter).

Switch Colors
(type "X")

Click this icon to swap the foreground and background color swatches.

Default Colors
(type "D")

Clicking the Default Colors icon appears to set the foreground color to black and the background color to white. More specifically, it sets the lightest and darkest possible color values. The default colors for each color mode are as follows:

Bitmap
The foreground color is 100% black. The background color is 0% black.

Grayscale
The foreground color is 100% black. The background color is 0% black.

RGB
The foreground color is R: 0, G: 0, B: 0. The background color is R: 255, G: 255, B: 255.

CMYK
The background color is C: 0, M: 0, Y: 0, K: 0.

The default black of a CMYK image, however, depends on the Black Ink Limit and Total Ink Limit, both of which are established in the File: Color Settings: **Separation Setup** dialog.

The Black Ink Limit is the maximum allowable percentage of black. When this value is set to 100%, the black component of the default foreground color is also 100%. If it's lowered to 90%, the default black component is 90%.

The Total Ink Limit is the ceiling placed on the combined percentages of cyan, magenta, yellow, and black. To determine the CMY values of the default black, Photoshop subtracts the Black Ink Limit from the Total Ink Limit. The remaining CMY percentages add up to the remaining value, but in order to remain a neutral gray, the cyan percentage must be slightly higher than magenta and yellow.

For example, if the Total Ink Limit is 300% and the Black Ink Limit is 100%, the combined CMY percentages total 200: the default black is C: 75, M: 63, Y: 62, K: 100. If the Total Ink Limit is 280% and the Black Ink Limit is 90, the combined CMY percentages total 190: the default black is C: 72, M: 60, Y: 58, K: 90.

Lab Color

The foreground color is L: 0, a: 0, b: 0. The background color is L: 100, a: 0, b: 0.

Common Errors

Using different values for black in the same general area. This can cause visible artifacting. For example, if you apply a manually defined 100% black brushstroke to an area of enriched black, the lack of CMY inks make the brushstroke appear washed out after printing. Unless you have specific reasons to do otherwise, keep your black percentages consistent.

Special Notes

* The default black for RGB and Lab Color images are always the same. The black that results when you convert the image to CMYK, however, is based on the settings in the File: Color Settings: **Separation Setup** dialog.

* Default blacks in a CMYK image are always *enriched*, or comprised of all four process inks. This helps create a deeper black with better paper coverage. It also reduces the need for trapping four-color artwork containing black outlines. (See Image: **Trap Overview** for more information.)

See Also

File: Color Settings: **Separation Setup**
Image: **Mode Overview**
Image: **Trap Overview**

The Color Picker

The Color Picker is Photoshop's primary tool for defining color values.

Common Uses

Although it's strongly associated with defining the foreground or background color, the Color Picker is used for a variety of other purposes:

* **Defining endpoint target values.** Double-click one of the eyedroppers in the Image: Adjust: **Levels** or **Curves** dialogs.

* **Editing an indexed color.** Double-click one of the colors in the Image: Mode: **Color Table** dialog.

- **Defining a duotone color.** Click one of the swatches in the Image: Mode: Duotone dialog.

- **Editing the color of on-screen tools.** This includes the transparency pattern, gamut warning, ruler guides, grid, and Quick Mask overlay. The Color Picker appears when you click the appropriate swatch.

- **Defining a background color for an image burned to a color slide.** Click the Background button in the File: **Page Setup** dialog.

- **Defining multiple gradient colors.** Click the color swatch in the Gradient Editor.

- **Defining a new Printing Inks profile.** Open the File: Color Settings: **Printing Inks** Setup dialog. Choose Custom from the Ink Color submenu and click the appropriate swatch.

Common Errors

Attempting to use the Apple or Windows color picker. Both additional pickers lack the flexibility and power of the default Color Picker. Neither allows you to define output values, CMYK percentages, Lab colors, or colors from custom libraries. Also, you are not warned if you choose a color falling out of CMYK's reproducible gamut. They are adequate for only the most rudimentary color selections, and therefore are not recommended.

Special Notes

- Using the Color Picker in any dialog does not affect the current foreground and background color.

- When you need to apply specific CMYK values, wait until you convert the image to CMYK mode—otherwise, the values will change during conversion. If necessary, refer to process color swatchbooks like Trumatch or Pantone Process to select precise color values.

- The bit-depths of the color slider and field refer to the number of colors each option displays. Being 8-bit, the slider contains 256 (or 2^8) colors. Being 16-bit, the field displays 65,536 (or 2^{16}) variations of each color or tone selected in the slider. Multiply the two numbers to produce 16,777,216 (or 2^{24})—the precise number of colors your monitor is capable of displaying.

The Photoshop Color Picker

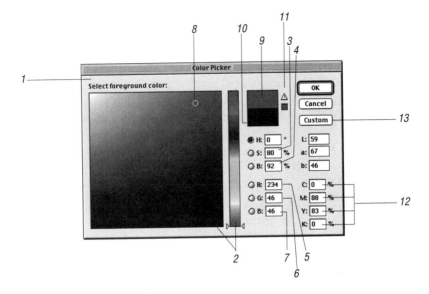

This is the default color picker, and by far the most powerful. It contains the following options:

1. **Task**

   The intended use of the new color appears in the upper left corner of the dialog.

2. **Color Field and Slider**

   The large color field and the vertical slider work together to provide access to over 16 million colors.

   Their contents depend on the radio buttons located directly to the right of the slider. Each option fills the slider with a particular 8-bit range and the field with an opposing 16-bit range. By manipulating the slider arrows and clicking somewhere in the field, you can properly target your desired color.

   For example, the button selected by default is H, or Hue. This fills the slider with the visible spectrum of colors, similar to the contents of the RGB/CMY color wheel. Move the arrows to select a particular hue, such as blue, yellow, or orange. The color field then displays all possible variations of the chosen hue: colors from left to right differ in *saturation*, or color intensity; colors from top to bottom differ in *brightness*, or tone.

   When you select a different radio button, you don't access a different range of colors. You simply change the way they appear in the field and slider.

3. **S (Saturation)**

This option fills the slider with the full range of possible saturation levels. The chosen hue appears fully saturated at the top of the slider, and progresses to fully desaturated, or gray, at the bottom.

In the color field, colors from left to right differ in hue. Colors from top to bottom differ in brightness.

4. **B (Brightness)**

This option fills the slider with the full range of possible brightness levels. The chosen hue appears at the top of the slider, and progresses to black at the bottom.

In the color field, colors from left to right differ in hue. Colors from top to bottom differ in saturation.

5. **R (Red)**

This option fills the slider with the full range of red, as it affects the currently selected color. The top of the slider displays the current color with the red level boosted to maximum (255). The bottom of the slider displays the current color with the red level reduced to the minimum (0).

In the color field, colors on the right contain maximum blue levels; colors on the left contain minimum blue levels. Colors on the top contain maximum green levels; colors on the bottom contain minimum green levels.

6. **G (Green)**

This option fills the slider with the full range of green, as it affects the currently selected color. The top of the slider displays the current color with the green level boosted to maximum (255). The bottom of the slider displays the current color with the green level reduced to the minimum (0).

In the color field, colors on the right contain maximum blue levels; colors on the left contain minimum blue levels. Colors on the top contain maximum red levels; colors on the bottom contain minimum red levels.

7. **B (Blue)**

This option fills the slider with the full range of blue, as it affects the currently selected color. The top of the slider displays the current color with the blue level boosted to maximum (255). The bottom of the slider displays the current color with the blue level reduced to the minimum (0).

In the color field, colors on the right contain maximum red levels; colors on the left contain minimum red levels. Colors on the top contain maximum green levels; colors on the bottom contain minimum green levels.

8. **Color Indicator**

This circular marker pinpoints the location of the current color in the color field. It moves when you click elsewhere in the field, click on the Gamut Alert swatch, click on the Previous Color swatch, or enter values in the Numerical Fields.

9. **Current Color**

   This swatch constantly changes to display the currently selected color. When you click OK, this color is defined for whatever reason prompted you to access the Color Picker.

10. **Previous Color**

   This swatch displays the color that existed before you accessed the Color Picker. For example, if you clicked the foreground color swatch to access the Color Picker, it displays the previously defined foreground color.

11. **Gamut Alert**

   The Gamut Alert triangle appears when you select a color that falls out of the reproducible range of process inks. The small swatch below the triangle represents the closest CMYK equivalent of the out-of-gamut color. Click on the triangle or the swatch to automatically select that value.

   While this feature seems helpful, it has limited uses. Its results depend on the current color mode of an image:

   - **CMYK.** The only advantage is the appearance of the foreground or background color swatch. Even if you apply an out-of-gamut color to the image, it applies the same values that appeared in the Gamut Alert swatch. However, if you add that color to the **Swatches Palette** for later use, you add the out-of-gamut color. Clicking the Gamut Alert swatch while defining the color allows you to apply the same values to the image as well as the Swatches Palette.

   - **RGB and Lab Color.** It's easy to believe that the values of the Gamut Alert swatch are the same as if you applied the out-of-gamut color, then converted the image to CMYK. That's not necessarily the case. When Photoshop determines the nearest CMYK equivalent, it refers to the File: Color Settings: **Printing Inks Setup** dialog to compensate for the expected dot gain. If you click on the Gamut Alert swatch, apply the color, then convert the image to CMYK, Photoshop compensates for dot gain again. The color doesn't change by much—only by one or two percentage points—but it's enough to cause a visible shift, especially when printing to a thermal wax or color laser printer.

12. **Numerical Fields**

   The numerical fields allow you to enter specific color values. Use these instead of the color slider and color field when you know the exact color you need to define. If desired, use the tab key to jump from one field to the next. (See Image: **Mode** for more information.)

13. **Custom**

   Click this button to access the Custom Colors dialog.

Custom Colors

Photoshop allows you to select colors from a series of predefined color libraries. Each library has a corresponding printed swatchbook, which you must purchase from either a graphic supply company or direct from the manufacturer.

- **Process colors.** Most predefined samples consist of CMYK percentages. The swatchbooks themselves are organized in different ways for different purposes, but the individual colors are all intended for four-color printing. When you choose a color from one of these libraries, you automatically enter the preset values in the CMYK fields of the standard Color Picker.

- **Spot colors.** You can also define spot colors, or solid inks. The Pantone library is the *de facto* standard for spot colors.

Common Uses

- **Selecting a color from a printed sample.** The swatchbooks allow you to do something that you cannot do with any of Photoshop's on-screen tools: define a color based on an actual printed sample. This is as close as you can get to predicting how a color will appear after printing—otherwise, you have to rely largely on memory, guesswork, and your knowledge of color theory when defining a specific color.

- **Creating spot-color duotones.** A duotone is the only image that allows you to define true spot colors without additional software. (See Image: Mode: **Duotone** for more information.)

- **Calibrating a non-standard ink system.** Occasionally, a process ink is replaced by a spot ink. To ensure proper separation, you must use a Pantone ink's Lab values, accessible only by defining the color in the Custom Color dialog. (See File: Color Settings: **Printing Inks Setup** for more information.)

Common Errors

Attempting to output spot colors from a Photoshop image. Unless you define a duotone or have a spot plate software package, Photoshop does not let you define and separate spot colors. If you try, Photoshop automatically converts the color to its closest CMYK equivalent—which contradicts the most common reasons to use spot colors in the first place.

Special Notes

- When you define a custom process color, your image must already be in CMYK mode. If you apply a custom color to an RGB or Lab Color image, its values are altered when you convert to CMYK. This is due to the settings in the File: Color Settings: **Printing Inks Setup** and **Separation Setup** dialogs.

- Although each Pantone spot color has a CMYK equivalent, only about 15–20% of the library can be accurately reproduced with process inks.

- Each supported library has a corresponding printed swatchbook. Unless you refer to one while choosing a color, your decisions are no more accurate than if you were using the standard Color Picker.

The Custom Colors Dialog

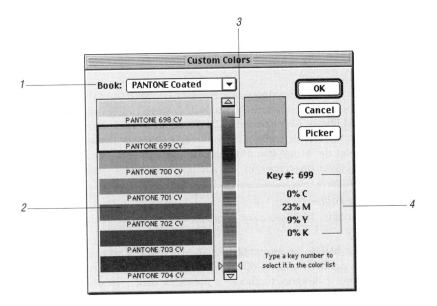

1. **Book**

Select your desired color library from this pop-up. Photoshop supports the following:

ANPA Color
    Short for *American Newspaper Publisher's Association*, this library contains the colors that reproduce most successfully on newsprint. This organization has recently changed their name to the Newspaper Association of America (NAA).

DIC Color Guide
    Short for *Dainippon Ink and Chemicals, Inc.*, this library is rarely used outside Japan.

FOCOLTONE
    From the United Kingdom, this library contains 763 CMYK combinations selected for their ability to form a *process bridge*, or share enough color components to reduce the need for trapping.

PANTONE Coated
    This contains the Pantone Color Formula Guide 1000. Select this option if the color will be printed to coated stock. Although inks from the Coated library have the same CMYK values as their Uncoated counterparts, they use a different naming convention, which can cause problems when you import the image into a different application. Also, these colors display slightly darker on-screen in an attempt to simulate their actual printed appearance.

PANTONE Process

This library contains over 3,000 CMYK combinations.

PANTONE ProSim

Short for *Process Simulation*, this library shows the printed effect of converting Pantone's spot color library to CMYK. This way, you can determine how closely a spot color's CMYK equivalent matches the actual ink.

PANTONE Uncoated

This contains the Pantone Color Formula Guide 1000. Select this option if the color will be printed to uncoated stock. Although inks from the Uncoated library have the same CMYK values as their Coated counterparts, they use a different naming convention, which can cause problems when you import the image into a different application. Also, these colors display slightly lighter on-screen in an attempt to simulate their actual printed appearance.

TOYO Color Finder

This is another Japanese color standard, rarely used outside that country.

TRUMATCH

This is a highly organized library of over 2,000 CMYK colors. Here, the range of printable color is divided into 50 different hues, each with 40 tints. This allows a designer to choose a lighter or darker version of a color with a minimal shift in color cast.

2. **Color List**

This scrolling list displays all the colors of the selected library. Type the title of your desired color to automatically scroll to its location.

3. **Color Slider**

The slider displays the hues of the currently loaded library. Reposition the slider arrows to move to another location in the library.

4. **Key Number and Color Information**

When you select a custom color, its title appears as the key number in the lower right of the dialog. Below that, the CMYK values for the selected color appear.

Additional Color Pickers

Photoshop lets you use two additional color pickers, one each for the Macintosh and Windows versions. To switch from the default Photoshop picker, you must open the File: Preferences: **General** dialog and select the second option from the Color Picker pop-up.

The Apple Color Picker

This is the standard color picker of the Macintosh operating system. Here, you can define colors based on the HSB or RGB color models. You cannot define output values, CMYK percentages, or Lab colors, and you are not warned if you choose a color falling out of CMYK's reproducible gamut.

The Windows Color Picker

This is the standard color picker of the Windows operating system. Here, you can choose from a series of basic colors, or you can define up to 16 custom colors based on the HSB or RGB color models.

CHAPTER 6

Quick Mask Tools

The Quick Mask tools allow you to graphically edit the shape of an active selection.

In Quick Mask mode, a selection appears as a semi-transparent overlay. As long as you remain in this mode, the overlay is the only information affected by your brushstrokes and adjustments. The altered overlay converts into a new selection outline as soon as you exit Quick Mask.

It's similar to editing a mask channel made by drawing a selection and choosing Select: **Save Selection**—both use an additional 8-bit channel to contain an editable selection, and both channels are visible in the **Channels Palette**. When you edit a mask channel, you can use paint tools, adjustment commands, and filters to alter the appearance of the selection before making it active again.

The capabilities of this method fall squarely between manual selections and mask channels. On one hand, you can create more complex selections than the selection tools allow. For example, you can add soft edges of varying widths and define partial selections, of which you can do neither with the **Marquee** or **Lasso Tools**. On the other hand, these selections are one-shot deals. They can't be loaded again unless you save them as a mask channel.

Quick Mask is a down-and-dirty technique, and the quality of its selections often show it. When the most precise selections are required, take the extra time to create a mask channel. If desired, you can edit a saved selection just like a Quick Mask.

Make Quick Mask Tool
(type "Q")

Click this button to switch into Quick Mask mode. When you do, a temporary mask channel, titled "Quick Mask," appears in the **Channels Palette**. As long as you remain in Quick Mask mode, your edits affect only the contents of this channel. Since its view button is checked in the Channels Palette, its contents appear on-screen as a semi-transparent overlay.

If a selection is active when you switch to Quick Mask mode, it changes to form the basis of the overlay. If you switch to Quick Mask mode without an active selection, no overlay appears at first. Either way, you can begin painting with any brush-based tool, using the existing image information as a guide.

Creating a Quick Mask is different than editing the regular image. Since you're really editing a Grayscale channel while in Quick Mask mode, the only colors you can define are black, white, and tones of gray:

Black
> Painting with black applies the overlay color. Black is really being applied to the Quick Mask channel. Depending on the Color Indicates option set in the Quick Mask Options dialog, areas painted with black are either fully selected or fully ignored when you click the Make Selection Tool.

White
> Painting with white removes the overlay color. White is really being applied to the Quick Mask channel. When you paint over a black area there, that part of the Quick Mask overlay is removed.

Gray
> Tones of gray result in partial selections. The actual percentage depends on the Color Indicates option set in the Quick Mask Options dialog. For example, if you paint with 25% black, the Selected Areas option results in a 25% selection. The Masked Areas option results in a 75% selection.

Common Uses

Refer to Appendix A for full descriptions of the following:

- Using an active selection in Quick Mask mode
- Cloning part of the overlay
- Transforming a selection
- Using Quick Mask in an individual channel
- Creating a mask channel from a Quick Mask selection
- Viewing a standard mask like a Quick Mask

Special Notes

- As long as you remain in Quick Mask mode, all colors defined with the Color Picker appear as a tone of gray. Most users paint in black or white—press the "D" key to automatically set the foreground color to black and the background color to white. To define precise gray values, use the Color Palette with Grayscale Slider chosen from the palette submenu. This way, you can target specific percentages when creating partial selections. (See Chapter 17, *The Color Palette* for more information.)

- Toggle back and forth between Masked Areas and Selected Areas by holding down the (Option) [Alt] key and clicking the Make Quick Mask Tool. The tool's icon displays the current option. If you toggle while in Quick Mask mode, the overlay reverses to reflect the change.

- When using any of **The Paint Tools**, hold down the (Option) [Alt] key to access the Eyedropper Tool. Click on the overlay color to set the foreground color to black. Click outside the overlay color to set the foreground color to white.

- When applying a gradient to the Quick Mask overlay, you must choose the Foreground to Background method in the Gradient Tool Options Palette. No other option works predictably in Quick Mask mode.

The Quick Mask Options Dialog

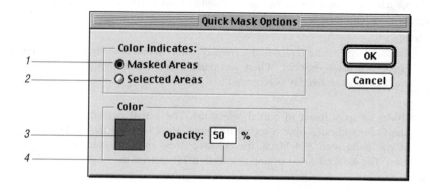

Double-click either Quick Mask button to access this dialog.

1. **Masked Areas**

   Photoshop defaults to this option. Here, all pixels not colored by the overlay are included in an active selection when you click the Make Selection Tool. As you paint the overlay, you cover the areas you don't want included in the selection. This method may be more intuitive if you have created opaque masks during conventional stripping or platemaking.

2. **Selected Areas**

   With this option, all pixels colored by the overlay are included in an active selection. As you paint the overlay, you cover the areas that you want included in the selection.

3. **Color**

   This box controls the color of the overlay. Photoshop defaults to red, emulating the opaque rubilith tape used to make conventional masks. If the overlay is too close to the colors in the image, click on this swatch and define a new color in the Color Picker. The color itself is only an on-screen reference; changing colors has no impact on the final selections.

4. Opacity

This value controls the opacity of the overlay. It's set to 50% by default, and there is little need to change this setting. If the opacity is too high, the image is obscured; too low, and the overlay is difficult to see.

Basic Quick Mask Techniques

In Quick Mask mode, you can use many common painting techniques to create a variety of selections:

- **Add to the overlay.** Set the foreground color to black and use any of the Paint Tools.

- **Subtract from the overlay.** Set the foreground color to white and use any of the Paint Tools.

- **Hard-edged selections.** Use the Pencil Tool, the only tool with hard-edged brushes, to create a selection without anti-aliased edges.

- **Anti-aliased selections.** Use any tool with anti-aliased brushes. The Paintbrush Tool and Eraser Tool are the most common examples.

- **Feathered selections.** Use the Paintbrush Tool or Eraser Tool with a very soft brush shape. Or, paint with a harder-edged brush and apply a Select: **Feather** value to the overlay.

- **Gradient selections.** Use the Gradient Tool, after setting the appropriate foreground and background colors.

- **Inverting a selection.** At any time, you can apply Image: Adjust: **Invert** to reverse the colors of the overlay.

- **Canceling a Quick Mask selection.** If you are not satisfied with the shape of your Quick Mask overlay, click the Make Selection Tool and choose Select: **None**. If desired, click the Make Quick Mask Tool and try again.

See Also

Appendix A (**Quick Mask Tools**)
Chapter 1, *Selection Tools*
Chapter 2, *The Paint Tools*
Image: Adjust: **Invert**
Select: **None**
Select: **Save Selection**
Chapter 17, *The Color Palette*
Chapter 21, *The Channels Palette*

Make Selection Tool
(type "Q")

Click this button to switch from Quick Mask back to normal editing mode. All areas masked by the overlay form the basis for the new selection. If no masked areas exist in the Quick Mask mode, no selection appears.

Special Notes

Once a selection is made active, you can turn it into a mask channel by choosing Select: **Save Selection**. Or, you can switch back to Quick Mask mode and continue refining the selection.

CHAPTER 7

The View Controls

The View Controls at the bottom of the Toolbar affect the display of the image window. These buttons have no effect on the image itself.

View Control Shortcuts

The following shortcuts apply to all three view modes:

- **Change views.** Scroll through all three options by repeatedly pressing the "F" key.

- **Hide all palettes.** Press the Tab key to hide all open palettes, including Toolbar. Press the Tab key again to reveal the palettes.

- **Hide all palettes except the Toolbar.** Hold down the Shift key and press the Tab key. Press Shift-Tab again to reveal the palettes, or press Tab to hide the Toolbar.

Window View

This is the default view for every image opened in Photoshop. It displays the image window, allowing access to the scroll bars, title bar, magnification box, and image data box. See the **View Menu Overview** for more information on these tools.

Special Notes

- This is the only view that allows you to see any underlying information, such as other open images, open applications, and the desktop.

- Different images can be set to different views. If the active image is in Window view, it sits in front of images in Full Screen view.

View Controls

Full Screen View (with Menu Bar)

This view hides the edges of the image window. The image rests on a solid gray background, which conceals all underlying information. This increases the total area that can be occupied by the image, which is especially useful when editing large graphics.

Special Notes

The menu bar and all of its commands remain visible. This view is often the choice of artists who want to maximize their workable space, but want constant access to all tools and commands.

Full Screen View

This view hides the menu bar and replaces the gray background with solid black. This increases the total area that be occupied by an image to include the entire screen.

Special Notes

- Even though the menu bar is hidden, you can still access a command by selecting its keyboard shortcut. To apply a menu command without a shortcut, you must switch to another view.

- This is primarily a display mode, especially with all the palettes hidden. The black background provides a high-contrast viewing area with no potentially influencing color bias. Also, if you're working on images that are exactly the same size as your monitor (for example, if you're creating CD-ROM graphics on a 640-by-480 screen), only this option allows you to see the image at 100%.

PART II

Menus

This section covers Photoshop's menus, from left to right.

When you first examine a menu, you see two things: commands and submenus. Each chapter lists these items in descending order of appearance. Each submenu lists its contents in the same order.

To help you navigate through the information in this book, we refer to each of these commands by its location in the menus. For example, the curves dialog is referred to as "Image: Adjust: **Curves**." When another item in the book mentions this dialog, it allows you to turn to the Table of Contents, quickly find the appropriate page number, and refer to this item for additional information.

Menus

CHAPTER 8

The File Menu

File: New
(Command) [Control]-O

Use this command to create a new image window.

Common Uses

- Creating a new canvas for original artwork generated using Photoshop's tools.
- Creating a temporary workspace for image information the user wishes to separately edit, then reincorporate into the original image.
- Creating a new, separate file for a selection copied from a larger image.

Common Errors

- **Failing to include additional image width and height to accommodate bleeds and trimming.** Add between 0.125 and 0.25 inches to each bleeding edge.
- **Entering a resolution too low for the image's intended use,** then attempting to raise the value after image editing has been completed. This method of increasing resolution is rarely successful.
- **Failing to Flatten an image that was originally created with a Transparent background.** Typically, this is noticed when the only file format available under the File: **Save As** dialog is the native Photoshop format.

Special Notes

- If a selection has been copied using Edit: **Copy** or **Cut**, then the values of the New dialog reflect the dimensions, resolution, and mode of that image information. If the intention is to create a new image out of a copied selection, choose

Edit: **Paste** after creating the new file. To ignore the contents of the Clipboard, choose (Option-Command) [Alt-Control]-N. This retains the last values entered in the dialog.

- To copy the dimensions of a currently open file, choose the file's title from the Windows menu while the New dialog is open.

- The default unit of measurement can be changed in two places—under File: Preferences: **Units & Rulers** or the pop-up in the lower-left of the Info Palette.

The New Dialog

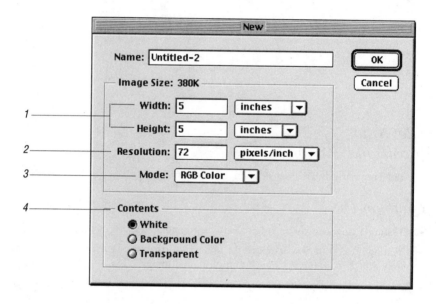

1. Width and Height

Before entering the image dimensions, select the preferred units of measurement from the Width and Height pop-up menus. Choices under both include pixels, inches, centimeters, points, and picas. The Width menu has an extra option called *Columns*. Here, you set the width of an image to a number of columns in your page layout (images with a width of two or more columns include a preset value for gutters). Establish these widths under File: Preferences: **Units & Rulers**.

2. Resolution

The Resolution value must match the target resolution requirements. Graphics for the World Wide Web or on-screen presentations rarely exceed 72 dpi, while print-destined images can range from 150 to 300 to 1200 pixels per inch.

3. Mode

The image mode determines the color type of an image: Bitmap displays only black and white; Grayscale displays 256 shades of gray; RGB, CMYK, and Lab all display in full color. Since color information can be lost or poorly translated when converting to another mode, the proper mode should always be selected when creating a new image. See Image: **Mode** for more information on Photoshop's color modes.

4. **Contents**

   Here, the user sets the pixels of the new image to be White, the current Background Color, or Transparent. Use the Transparent option if the new image will be composited with another image.

See Also

Appendix C, *Resolution Types*
Edit: **Copy**, **Cut**, and **Paste**
File: Preferences: **Units & Rulers**
Image: **Mode**

File: Open
(Command) [Control]-O

Most frequently, this command is used to open pixel-based images, such as stock and Photo CD files, scans made using proprietary software (like Scitex or Optronics), or any pre-existing Photoshop image. It can also be used to open vector-based artwork, from programs such as Adobe Illustrator, Macromedia FreeHand, or Adobe Dimensions (see "Opening Vector-Based Images," below).

Common Errors

- **Double-clicking on an image file not created in Photoshop**, resulting in either the wrong program opening or an "Application Not Found" message. Avoid this by opening files from within the program.

- **Existing files are difficult to find.** In lieu of a sound file management system, they'll often wind up in the Photoshop application folder or scattered over the Desktop. Keep all files in well-labeled job folders or image archives.

Special Notes

Make an Alias (Macintosh) or Shortcut (Windows 95) of Photoshop's application icon and place it on the Desktop. This way, files created in outside programs can be dragged onto it, simultaneously launching Photoshop and opening the images.

File Menu

The Open Dialog

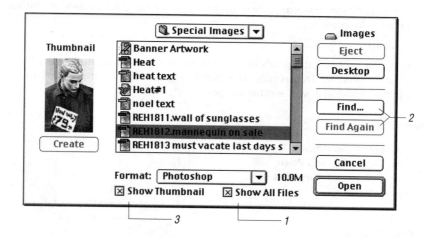

1. Show All Files

Photoshop recognizes a limited set of file formats (see File: **Save** for a detailed list). If the Show All Files box in the Open dialog is unchecked, only the files immediately recognized by Photoshop appear in the window. When images are moved from one platform to another, the files often lack the code Photoshop requires to "see" the image. Ordinarily, this problem is avoided if the image contains the proper suffix in its title—*.tif* for Tagged Image File Format and *.eps* for Encapsulated PostScript are common examples—but if it doesn't, Photoshop will not even know the file exists. Checking Show All Files allows the program to recognize *all* files on your hard drive. When you find your image and select it, you'll see an educated guess by the program in the Format pop-up (if necessary, you can choose a different format). If the file can be read, it opens into its own window when you select Open or press the Return key. If not—if you try opening a page layout document, for example—you receive an error message.

2. Find/Find Again

This option allows you to search for an image based on all or part of its file name. The search is very basic—only one file at a time is displayed in the Open window. Selecting Find Again lets you flip through the matching files until you find the one you need.

3. Show Thumbnail

Checking this option allows Photoshop to display a small preview of an image before you open it. This only works when QuickTime is running *and* the preview is saved into the image file (by checking Thumbnails under File: **Preferences: Saving Files**). If you attempt to preview a PICT image, it may be possible to generate a thumbnail by clicking the Create button.

See Also

File: **Opening Vector-Based Images**
File: **Save**
File: Preferences: **Saving Files**

Opening Vector-Based Images

Photoshop will open illustrations created in programs such as Adobe Illustrator, Adobe Dimensions, Macromedia FreeHand, Deneba Canvas, and CorelDRAW.

Illustrations are based on object-oriented paths—also known as Bézier curves— rather than pixels. To open one of these graphics as an editable Photoshop image, you must convert the shapes into pixels, a process known as *rasterizing*.

The term "rasterize" may seem new, but you've been exposed to the basic concept ever since the first time you printed a document. Every output device uses a RIP to process image information prior to printing. RIP stands for Raster Image Processor. Similar to changing a few multilayered objects into a flat canvas of pixels, a printer's RIP changes the multiple elements of a page layout into two-dimensional composites or color separations.

Common Reasons to Rasterize

- **On-screen graphics.** Although some vector-based programs allow you to con- vert illustrations to GIF, BMP or PICT images, none give you the flexibility of Photoshop's tools. If you want to use an illustration on the Web or in a multi- media presentation, open it in Photoshop first.

- **Photoshop effects.** Many effects, such as soft drop-shadows, semi-opacity, or high-end compositing, are only possible using Photoshop's tools and com- mands.

- **Customized type.** Photoshop's type capabilities are limited. Many users create customized lettering in a program with a powerful type tool, like Illustrator or FreeHand, then bring the graphic back into Photoshop for further editing.

Common Errors

- **Forgetting the differences between vector-based and pixel-based images.** If you rasterize an Illustrator graphic, you can no longer scale that image with reck- less abandon—not even if you save the image as a Photoshop EPS. The only way to get that back is to trace the image with paths, either manually (see **The Pen Tool**) or automatically, using a program like Adobe Streamline.

- **Attempting to blend images of different resolutions.** If you rasterize an Illustra- tor graphic at 72 ppi and drop it into a 300 ppi scan, the graphic appears dis- proportionately tiny. Since the Rasterize dialog always retains the last-applied resolution value, you should always double-check. Or, bypass the rasterize dia- log and import the image using File: **Place**.

File Menu

Special Notes

Photoshop successfully rasterizes images that contain imported graphics, whether vector- or pixel-based. Be aware that doing so can impair the image quality, particularly if the image will be reproduced on press:

- If the original graphic contains images of different resolutions (for example, a 300 ppi halftone and 1200 ppi line art), both images are interpolated to whatever resolution is entered in the Rasterize dialog. If it's too low, the line art loses important detail. Too high, and halftones may not output.

- If the original graphic contains images of different color modes (for example, a CMYK TIFF, a grayscale TIFF, and line art), they are all converted to the Mode selected in the Rasterize dialog. This can lead to altered color values, particularly if the graphic is translated into RGB mode first, then converted to CMYK.

- All components of a rasterized graphic, including any imported images, appear on a single layer. This makes it much more difficult to edit any one part independently of another.

If any of these pose a problem, the best solution is to combine the different parts of the graphic in Photoshop, rather than the vector-based software.

The Rasterize Generic EPS Format Dialog

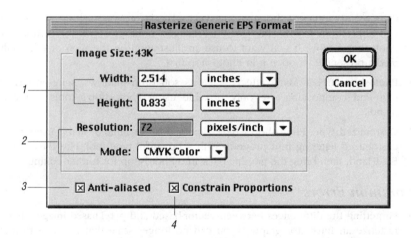

1. **Width and Height**

   These values reflect the actual size of the vector-based image. However, the illustration may not have been created at the proper size, and the values should be examined twice and changed if necessary.

2. **Resolution and Mode**

   Choose a Resolution and Mode consistent with the intended use of the image: a 72–pixel-per-inch RGB image is well-suited for the Internet, but that same image requires a 300 ppi CMYK file to reproduce on-press.

3. **Anti-aliased**

   Check this box to soften the edges of abutting shapes and colors, reducing any jagged appearances.

4. **Constrain Proportions**

   Check this box to constrain the Width to Height ratio, so any change made to one is consistently reflected in the other.

Once the image is opened, it appears in its own layer against a transparent background. It can be combined with another image, or edited, flattened, and saved into a usable file format.

See Also

The Pen Tool
File: **Open**
File: **Place**

File: Close
(Command) [Control]-W

This command tells Photoshop to close any active image window. If any changes have been made since the last Save, a prompt appears, asking whether to Save, Don't Save, or Cancel.

File: Save
(Command) [Control]-S

This command allows you to write the information contained in an image to a file on your hard drive.

Save images soon and frequently. When scanning images directly into Photoshop, save them before making any corrections, eliminating any need to rescan. When working on original images, save them just after creating the new image window. If translating graphics from a different program, save them just after opening them in Photoshop, overwriting the originals if they are no longer needed.

When you initially save an image, take the opportunity to place the file in its proper location. Once an image has been saved, selecting File: **Save** updates the current file without bringing up the Save As dialog.

Common Uses

- **Saving images**. It allows you to save your work as you go along, lowering the possibility of time-consuming frustration if your system crashes.

- **Placing files**. You can use the Save dialog to place saved images in the right place on your hard drives or removable storage media.

File Menu

Common Errors

- **The keyboard shortcut is chosen by accident.** The shortcut for Select: **None**— (Command) [Control]-D—is dangerously close to the shortcut for File: **Save**. Many users have accidentally saved a file when attempting to remove a selection outline. This would prevent you from reverting to the last saved version to reverse a series of commands.

- **Images are saved in the wrong file format.** Read "Supported File Formats" later in this chapter for more information.

- **Images are saved in the wrong color mode.** RGB files cannot be separated on an imagesetter, CMYK images cannot be imported into a multimedia presentation, and many Web graphics cannot be used unless they're switched to Indexed Color. See Image: **Mode** for more information.

- **Files are poorly named,** making it hard to locate the appropriate image. Several designers we know fall into the habit of creating multiple versions of an image, adding the numbers "2", "3", or "4" after each variation. Then they tag the word "final" at the end of their preferred file. If they make a series of last-minute edits, they wind up with file names containing "final FINAL," "REAL final," or "USE THIS ONE", which easily leads to the wrong graphic getting imported and used. File names should be as clear and simple as possible. Sometimes this means using a numerical job-tracking system for scans, but usually we name them after the focus or purpose of the image itself.

- **File names are not tagged with a three- or four-letter image code.** After typing in a file name, add a dot and the abbreviation for the file format you have selected: *Sparky's Portrait.eps, Hydrant.gif,* and *Angryman.tiff* are good examples. Doing so allows you to immediately see what types of image you have, which is beneficial if you need to troubleshoot problematic graphics. Also, Photoshop sometimes relies on the existence of this code when attempting to open an image from a different platform. You can tell Photoshop to automatically add a three-letter extension to every file by going to File: Preferences: **Saving Files** and choosing an option under Append File Extension.

Special Notes

- Save commands cannot be reversed by choosing Edit: **Undo**.

- Most users prefer File: **Save As** to File: **Save**, even when updating a previously saved image. The Save As dialog always appears, giving you the option of renaming the image or canceling the action. To simply update the image, save it to the same location without changing the name to replace the previous image file.

- Macintosh is the only platform that recognizes four-letter image codes. Windows, UNIX, and other platforms require the same three-letter codes that Photoshop applies automatically. For Mac users, this only becomes an issue when images are being prepared for distribution across platforms.

- While working on an image, leave it in the native Photoshop format. It's the only one that retains multiple layers. It also opens and saves more quickly than other formats, and that can make a big difference when editing 100 M. plus images. Save the image to the proper format when editing is complete.

- If you get tired of looking at obscure file formats that you never use in your Formats pop-up, delete the items from the File Format folder, in Photoshop's Plug-ins folder.

See Also

File: **Save As**
File: **Supported File Formats**
File: Preferences: **Saving Files**

File: Save As

This command allows you to save an additional copy of an image. It's similar to the first time you save. From the same dialog, you name the file, choose a file format, and place the new image somewhere on the hard drive. There's an important difference, however: this time, the original file is left untouched, and a new image containing all the most recent edits is written.

File: **Save As** uses the same dialog that appears when you choose File: **Save** for the first time. Photoshop automatically inserts the current file name in the Document Name field.

Common Uses

- **Determining a file format.** When your editing is complete, you can save the image into a file format appropriate for its intended use.
- **Preserving the original image.** Use this command when you need to create different variations of an image for later use. This often occurs when adding special effects to a color-corrected scan, such as a silhouette, drop shadow, or composite with another image.

Common Errors

- **Creating unnecessary multiple copies of an image.** Avoid this for two reasons. First, it leads to confusion about which image to finally use. Second, Photoshop images can be very large (a single 9-inch by 12-inch CMYK scan can exceed 40 Mb). Multiple copies can devour hard drive space, wasting the scratch disk space Photoshop uses to facilitate its commands.
- **Accidentally overwriting the original image** If you intend to create a separate file, you must change the name. Leaving the name unchanged and saving it to the same location as the original image overwrites the original with the new copy, just as if you'd chosen File: **Save**.
- **Saving a new copy to the wrong place.** If you assume that Photoshop automatically places the new copy in the right place, it may wind up in the Photoshop application folder, on the Desktop, a previous job folder, or any other location on your hard drive.

Special Notes

- Save commands cannot be reversed by choosing Edit: **Undo**.

- If you want to test a sequence of commands—but don't necessarily want to keep the changes—use the Image: **Duplicate** command to create an instant, unsaved copy of your image. If you don't want to keep the file, close it without saving, which conserves considerable time and hard drive space when working on large images.

See Also

File: **Save**
File: **Supported File Formats**
Edit: **Undo**
Image: **Duplicate**

Supported File Formats

Unless an image is saved in the right file format, it can't be used. The one you ultimately choose depends on the medium you're working in and the type of image you've generated. Although Photoshop supports many different formats, each major graphics industry—print, multimedia, and the Web—typically uses only two:

- Print graphics exist as either TIFF or EPS.
- Web graphics exist as either GIF or JPEG (although PNG is occasionally used).
- Multimedia graphics exist as either PICT (Macintosh) or BMP (Windows).

Photoshop

This option is Photoshop 4's native format. Images saved in this file format are readable only by Photoshop 3 or 4. It's the only format that saves every feature the program offers, such as multiple layers. Because you can save and reopen images much more quickly, use this format until editing is complete. Then flatten your layers, double-check your color mode, and save it into its appropriate file format. Unless you flatten the image, this is the only option available under the File Format pop-up.

Photoshop 2.0

This file format can be recognized by early versions of Photoshop, but cannot contain separate layers. Its safe to assume that nearly all Photoshop users have upgraded to version 3.0 or higher, so you can ignore it.

BMP

Short for Windows *Bitmap*, this format is compatible with Microsoft Paint, the bitmap editing program included with Windows 95. Use this format only in the following situations:

- When handing images over to someone who will continue editing using Paint or another Windows-based program

- If the images will be used in on-screen presentations using Windows-based software

CompuServe GIF

Because GIFs take up very little disk space—which means shorter download times—they've become the standard for on-screen web graphics. One of the reasons for their smaller size is their reduced color palette (always fewer than 256 colors), which you achieve by converting an image to Image: Mode: **Indexed Color**. The other is its compression scheme. Like TIFF files, GIFs use LZW compression, which results in no loss of image information. GIFs come in two forms:

- GIF87a, the default setting when you select CompuServe GIF from the File: **Save** dialog

- GIF89a, which supports transparent pixels (see File: Export: **GIF89a**)

Special Notes

- Because GIFs have such a limited color palette, they are best suited for images with areas of solid color, such as boxes, buttons, cartoon characters, corporate logos, and the like. For more continuous-tone images, use JPEG.

- Only an image with 256 colors or less can be saved as a GIF. So unless it exists in Bitmap, Grayscale, or Indexed Color mode, the CompuServe GIF file format is not available in the File: **Save As** dialog.

See Also

File: Export: **GIF89a**
Image: Mode: **Indexed Color**

Photoshop EPS

Along with TIFF, this is the only format used for print-related images. For the first time, Adobe is listing this file format as "Photoshop EPS" instead of simply "EPS." This was done to eliminate confusion with graphics from vector-based illustration programs like Illustrator or FreeHand. That artwork is comprised of PostScript-defined shapes, can be infinitely scaled, and has no specific resolution until it's either output or imported into Photoshop. Images edited in Photoshop, even if they originated as vectors, are always subject to pixel-based scaling and resolution requirements.

Common Uses

The only time an image is saved as an EPS file is when PostScript-based commands or behaviors are being built into the file. The most common examples include the following:

File Menu

- Clipping paths
- Duotone curves
- Custom screen angles
- Transfer functions (custom tone curves)
- Five-part DCS files

Common Errors

Attempting to recolor or trap EPS images in a page layout program. Images in this file format cannot be edited in another program, unlike TIFF files.

Special Notes

- If an EPS image is going to be used on a UNIX or Windows-based platform, you must set the encoding to ASCII. If this is the case, do not select a TIFF preview—these are binary, and will prevent the image from being recognized by the platform.

- When a Bitmap image is saved as an EPS, a button called Transparent Whites appears in the EPS Format dialog. Checking this button forces the white pixels to be transparent, as if the image was saved as a TIFF. Typically, the only reason to use this option is when you are importing a Bitmap image into a program that does not support TIFFs, such as early versions of Adobe Illustrator.

The EPS Format Dialog

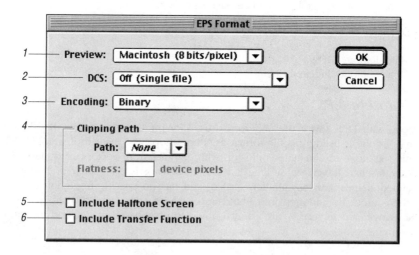

1. Preview

An EPS image is actually made up of two parts: the high-resolution information that's downloaded to an output device, and a low-resolution preview. This preview is the part of an image your page layout program imports. This is why

EPS images import so much more quickly than equally sized TIFFs, which force a preview to be generated on-the-fly by the software importing them. Mac users should select "Macintosh (8 bits/pixel)", which adds a 256-color PICT preview. Windows users should select "TIFF (8 bits/pixel)", which adds a 256-color TIFF preview. Selecting either a lower bit-depth or "None" results in a preview that's difficult at best to see on-screen, while saving only nominal disk space in return.

2. **DCS**

When saving a CMYK image, you can create a *Desktop Color Separation* file. Originally introduced by Quark, this process splits the image into five separate files: the low-resolution preview, plus the individual channels containing the cyan, magenta, yellow, and black information. Typically, this process is used by service bureaus or print shops who perform high-end scanning services for their clients. Rather than transport potentially enormous files back to their page layouts, clients take the previews, which are only about 10% of the original file size. These files are imported, scaled, and rotated as FPO (For Position Only) graphics, then the layout files are taken back to the service bureau for processing. The imported previews are relinked to the high-resolution files just prior to output. If a designer has scanning done in-house, this feature is probably not required. In fact, ignore this option unless you have a good reason for using it. Without the high-resolution parts, the preview cannot be edited in Photoshop, and if any one of the five image files are accidentally deleted, the graphic is worthless.

3. **Encoding**

This option indicates how the code representing the image file is written to the disk. All major graphics software supports Binary (the default selection), which results in smaller file sizes, quicker imports, and faster downloading times than ASCII. Anyone still using a PostScript Level 1 output device may have better luck using ASCII encoding, but those printers have become scarce indeed. The JPEG compression selections should be avoided at all costs. True, they result in much smaller file sizes, but it always comes at the expense of image quality. It's easy to get away with that on the Web, but hardly ever in print.

4. **Clipping Path**

Select the path you wish to use as a PostScript-defined mask when you import the graphic into a page layout. (See Chapter 22, *The Paths Palette*, for more information). We prefer to use the Clipping Path command under the Paths Palette because we can double-check our work in case the image contains more than one path.

5. **Include Halftone Screen**

By clicking the Screen button under File: **Page Setup**, you can enter custom screen angles and halftone dot shapes. Unless you check this button, you can't override the Printer's Default settings. Any image using Photoshop's predefined set of Duotone Curves must include the halftone screens.

6. **Include Transfer Function**

By clicking the Transfer button under File: **Page Setup**, you can create tone curves that lighten, darken, or add contrast to images on output. Unless you check this button, the output device does not know to apply the curve.

File Menu

See Also

File: Supported File Formats (TIFF)
File: Save and Save As
File: Page Setup: Screen
File: Page Setup: Transfer
Image: Mode: Duotone
Chapter 22, *The Paths Palette*

Filmstrip

Adobe Premier, the industry-standard QuickTime movie editing suite, cannot edit individual movie frames—its commands only control fades, edits, merges, sound synching, and the like. Filmstrip files consist of a vertical series of movie frames, each one editable using any of Photoshop's tools or commands (except Image: Image Size and Canvas Size, which render the file unreadable by Premier). Editing a sequence of frames is known as *rotoscoping*.

JPEG

JPEG (short for Joint Photographic Experts Group, the developers of the format) offers powerful compression for Photoshop images by averaging the color values of groups of adjacent pixels. Because it always comes at the expense of image quality, it should never be used on images destined for print reproduction—artifacting and pixelization invariably occurs. If images are going to be used over the Web, JPEG is perfect. Here, the smaller a file is, the better—even if quality takes a hit. For example, a 3-by-3-inch, 72-ppi RGB image takes up 136K of disk space. Downloading at 1 or 2K per second, the average modem could take over two minutes to retrieve this image. Using JPEG compression, you can reduce the file size to under 20K, allowing it to download in seconds.

Special Notes

JPEG images work best for tone-sensitive images like photographs and flesh tones. Images containing solid colors become blocky and pixelized—for these, consider using the GIF file format.

The JPEG Options Dialog

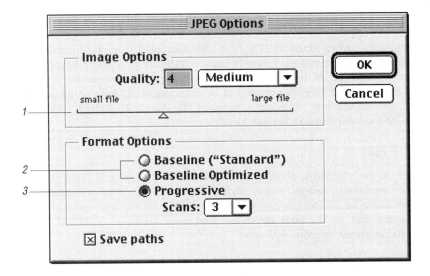

1. **Quality Slider**

   How small you make a file depends on the amount of image quality you want to retain. This slider allows you to set a Quality value from 0 (lowest quality, smallest size) to 10 (highest quality, largest size). Many users decide upon one preferred value for all of their images—we've found that a value of 4 or 5 avoids most of the visible artifacting while producing a satisfactory file size.

2. **Baseline**

   JPEGs saved under this option appear in your browser one line at a time, from top to bottom. Baseline Optimized uses a different encoding that slightly reduces the file size. Baseline JPEGs are used by fewer web designers these days because of the additional time it takes for a viewer to see the entire image.

3. **Progressive**

   These images appear in a series of passes, giving the viewer a rough-and-ready idea of a graphic before it's fully refreshed. Determine the number of passes by selecting a number from the Scans pop-up. Higher numbers begin refreshing sooner, but take longer to complete. For consistency, set all graphics used in a web site to the same value.

PCX

Images in this format are similar to BMP files, but the PCX extension indicates the image is compatible with *PC Paintbrush*, an ancient DOS-based paint program still in widespread use. Older versions of this file format had only one color channel, used for indexed color, grayscale, or line-art images. Current versions support 16 million colors.

File Menu

PDF

Adobe's Portable Document Format allows you to create images or page layouts viewable by anyone using Adobe Acrobat, regardless of whether they're using a Macintosh or PC. Usually, these files originate as QuarkXPress or PageMaker documents, then are exported to PDF files and distributed over the Internet or CD-ROM. Photoshop, however, can only make a PDF out of a single image—it can't create multiple pages, it offers no control over the JPEG compression it supports, and it cannot read PDF files created in other programs. Anyone wishing to create PDF files should start off using a program like Adobe PageMaker, which ships with Adobe's Acrobat and Acrobat Distiller.

PICT File

Used on the Macintosh platform, the PICT file format is used primarily for on-screen multimedia images. Occasionally, PICTs are used in print because they're more likely to be compatible with lower-end software like word processing programs, but they should never be used in a document intended for high-resolution output or color separation.

Common Uses

- Images for interactive applications
- CD-ROM images
- Still images for video
- Slide show presentations

Common Errors

Attempting to separate a color PICT file. Although you can set the resolution of a PICT to 300 ppi and above, color PICTs can only exist in RGB or Indexed Color mode, neither of which will output successfully. Use TIFF or EPS for any print-related image.

Special Notes

PICTs should only exist at 72 ppi—anything more only slows down the software used to import the image.

The PICT File Options Dialog

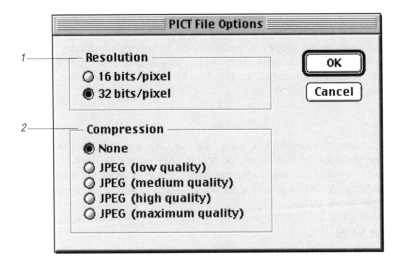

1. **Resolution**

   Select either 16 or 32 bits/pixel, which determines how much color information can be contained in the file. Choosing 16 bits/pixel gives a slightly smaller file with fewer colors. It imports and displays more quickly in your multimedia applications, but banding and posterizing may occur in your blends and continuous tones. 32-bit PICTs not only retain photographic tones, they allow you to save an additional color channel into the file (many video editing suites, for example, require an alpha channel for masking purposes).

2. **Compression**

   If QuickTime is installed on your system, you can save a 32-bit PICT using JPEG compression. Bear in mind that this is QuickTime's version of JPEG, not Photoshop's. The quality of compression is a little worse, and opening and re-saving these PICTs leads to an image being compressed multiple times, trashing additional image data. If you wish to create a JPEG file, use the JPEG format—otherwise, leave the option alone.

PICT Resource

This format is used by on-screen images accessed by the Macintosh operating system. The most common appearances of PICT Resource files are application splash screens, images saved in the Scrapbook, and system startup screens. (To create a startup screen, see Appendix A.)

Special Notes

To import PICT Resources from sources containing more than one, like applications or the Scrapbook file, see File: Import: **PICT Resource**.

Pixar

If you've watched Disney's computer-animated movie *Toy Story*, you've seen the type of work created by Pixar. Although they create versions of their 3-D rendering software for the more common graphics platforms, the ultra–high-end work you see in the movies is generated on their own proprietary workstations. Even so, Photoshop can open individual frames rendered by Pixar software. RGB and grayscale images saved in this format can be incorporated into a Pixar rendering.

PNG

Portable Network Graphics (or "ping") files are a rising alternative to CompuServe GIFs for designers of web graphics. So far, they have only limited support from the major browser manufacturers. Stronger support is expected soon, since PNG compatibility can be built into a software package without its developers paying royalties—unlike GIFs.

Special Notes

- As far as image size and quality go, PNG falls somewhere between JPEG (which are smaller due to compression) and GIF (which have a smaller color palette). This makes them a better choice for images that are smaller in width and height but contain important details and tones, like highly stylized buttons or online advertisements.

- PNG files can contain an additional masking channel that allows the image to be part opaque, part transparent. By manipulating the gray levels of the mask, you create semi-transparent pixels in your web graphics.

The PNG Options Dialog

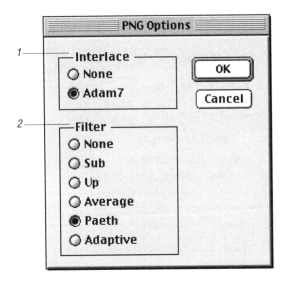

1. Interlace

   Although the choices are between None and "Adam7", it's actually a choice between On and Off. Select Adam7 if you want the graphic interlaced. When accessed by a browser, the graphic will refresh on-screen in seven passes.

2. Filter

   PNG files have their own compression scheme. To truly determine which option creates the smallest file, you'd have to save a copy of the image under each one and compare. The differences are minor, and are often unnoticeable when the graphic is set up online. Just choose Adaptive, know that the file is compressed, and move on.

Raw

A relatively rare file format, raw images exist only as strings of code. There are no colors, no channels, no pixels, nothing you've learned to recognize as an image component. Typically, information like this is downloaded from mainframe computers—a platform not known for its high-end imaging capabilities—or older proprietary systems with image types Photoshop doesn't recognize.

File Menu

The Raw Options Dialog (when saving a Raw image)

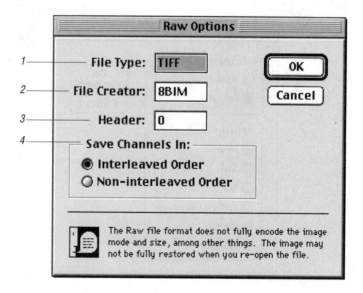

1. **File Type**

   Presumably, you enter the four-letter image code—PICT or TIFF, for example—in this box. Only Macintoshes pay any attention to it, though, so ignore it if the file is headed for another platform.

2. **File Creator**

   This value is used to specify which application created the image. It defaults to "8BIM", Photoshop's four-digit code. Leaving or changing the code has little if any impact on the file.

3. **Header**

   The header is the data written at the start of the code that the computer uses to identify the image type and contents. This box is asking for the byte-size of the header. Setting a value higher than 0 (the default) means you'd have to use third-party code editing software to actually create the header.

4. **Save Channels In**

   Interleaving has to do with how the color data is stored in the file. Remember, every single pixel in the image is defined by a length of code. Since each pixel in an RGB file, for example, has three different values (red, green, and blue), there are two different ways the file can communicate them to a computer. Choosing Non-Interleaved means that all the red pixels are listed first, then all the green, then all the blue. Choosing Interleaved means that all three RGB values for the first pixel are listed, then all three for the second pixel, and so on. Interleaved graphics should open more quickly, but the platform receiving them must be able to recognize the command.

The Raw Options Dialog (when opening a Raw image)

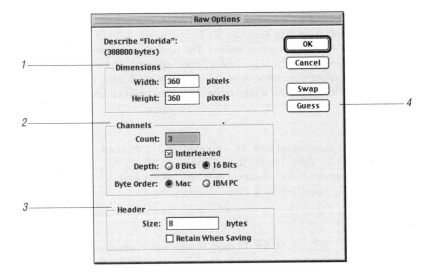

1. **Dimensions**

   If the width and height of the image has been provided, enter them here. The Swap button on the right of the dialog switches these values back and forth.

2. **Channels**

   The Count value alerts Photoshop to the number of channels an image is supposed to contain—grayscale images have one, RGB images have three, CMYK images have four. To know if you should check Interleaving (described previously), you must determine whether the image information was originally saved in that form. Depth refers to the number of bits contained in each color channel. The vast majority of graphics contain 8 bits per channel, but graphics from more obscure platforms may contain 16. If this option is chosen, you must select Mac or PC to determine the Byte Order.

3. **Header**

   Here, enter the byte-size of the file's header (described above), so Photoshop will not attempt to open that portion of the data as an image.

4. **Guess**

   If you lack any of the specs listed above, click the Guess button in the upper left of the Raw Options dialog. Photoshop takes a half-hearted stab at discerning the necessary information, but it's rarely successful. A better bet is to contact the creators of the file, or at least someone who can read the image on its original platform.

File Menu

Scitex CT

Many service bureaus and printers use high-end Scitex scanners and workstations, which provide powerful image acquisition, editing and correcting capabilities. Most often, a Photoshop user sees this file format in the form of a raw scan, ready for adjusting on a color correcting station. The only time to save an image in this format is if it's going to be opened on a Scitex system—and even then, double-check with the system's operator. Scitex systems can read other formats, and operators may prefer to import the image using their own color tables.

Targa

Images saved in this format can be imported and combined with digital video sequences driven by video boards from TrueVision, Media 100, and Radius. These images often contain a chroma-key color (to be masked out and replaced by video, like the big maps behind a TV weatherman) or an additional alpha channel.

TIFF

Along with EPS, TIFF (short for Tagged Image File Format) is the primary file format used for outputting an image to paper or film. Unlike Photoshop EPS files, which communicates complex PostScript commands as well as pixels to an output device, TIFFs handle only pixel-based information.

Special Notes

- TIFFs are the most widely used print-oriented format, fully compatible with Macs and PCs alike.

- Although line art and grayscale TIFFs import as black-and-white images into your page layout programs, you can apply a different color to them in your page layouts. EPS files cannot be recolored.

- Some trapping commands, such as those found in QuarkXPress or Adobe Trap-Wise, can affect the contents of an imported TIFF. EPS files are closed to these commands, and must be trapped using the original software.

- TIFFs use LZW Compression. Unlike JPEG, LZW reduces file size without destroying image data. It does this by abbreviating lengths of repetitive pixel values. If 200 consecutive pixels share the same color, an uncompressed file lists all 200 of those values. LZW lists the value of the first pixel, then inserts a character essentially stating, "the next 199 pixels are the same color as this one." Because of this, LZW works better on images containing fewer colors. Line art, only consisting of two colors, compresses to as low as 10% of the original file size. Grayscale images have more tonal variation, but are limited to 256 possible shades. With less potential for repetitive values, files will typically reduce to 40–50% of original size. Full color images hardly reduce at all, since the chances of repetitive values are remote.

File: Save a Copy

This command allows you to write a copy to the hard drive without flattening, duplicating, or otherwise changing the open image.

When you choose this command and open the Save a Copy dialog, Photoshop automatically appends the word "copy" at the end of the current file name, preventing any attempt to overwrite an open file. Name the file and choose the desired file format, just like choosing File: **Save** or **Save As**.

Common Uses

- **Saving a usable copy of an image while preserving the original.** For example, you may use the same high-resolution montage as a resource for a print catalog, Web graphics, and CD-ROM presentation.

  Each style of graphic has different resolution, color, and file format requirements, but saving copies from the original prevents you from having to backtrack or rescan.

- **Saving individually edited animation frames.** If you want to use Photoshop to create step-by-step cels of an image being affected by a series of commands, use Save a Copy to save files one at a time. For easier importing, name the files with sequential numbers ("000", "001", "002").

Special Notes

- Unlike File: **Save** or **Save As**, the new image does not remain open in Photoshop. The current image remains open, unaffected by the save command, while the new file is written to the hard drive.

- Even if the current image contains multiple layers or additional channels, you can select a file format that does not support them. If necessary, Photoshop alters the new image, either by flattening or discarding channels.

- When saving a copy of an image, you cannot choose any file format incompatible with the image's current color mode.

The Save a Copy Dialog

```
┌─────────────────────────────────────────────────────────────┐
│                                                               │
│          [🔍 Special Images  ▼]          📁 Images           │
│        ┌──────────────────────────┐┌──┐   ┌───────────────┐  │
│        │ 🖼 Banner Artwork        ▲││▤│   │    Eject       │  │
│        │ 🔲 Heat                  │└──┘   └───────────────┘  │
│        │ 🔲 heat text             │       ┌───────────────┐  │
│        │ 🖼 Heat#1                │       │   Desktop      │  │
│        │ 🔲 noel text             ▼│       └───────────────┘  │
│        └──────────────────────────┘       ┌───────────────┐  │
│                                           │ 📁  New       │  │
│        Save a copy in:                    └───────────────┘  │
│        ┌─────────────────────────────┐   ┌───────────────┐  │
│        │ Behavior                    │   │    Cancel      │  │
│        └─────────────────────────────┘   └───────────────┐  │
│                                           │               │  │
│        Format: [ Photoshop      ▼ ]       │     Save      │  │
│                                           └───────────────┘  │
│  1──── ☐ Flatten Image      ☐ Don't Include Alpha Channels ──2│
│                                                               │
│        Image Previews:   ☐ Icon  ☐ Thumbnail  ☐ Full Size    │
│                                                               │
└─────────────────────────────────────────────────────────────┘
```

1. Flatten Image

   This box is automatically checked whenever you select a file format that does not support multiple layers—meaning, any format other than native Photoshop. Remember that the original image retains all of its layered information.

2. Don't Include Alpha Channels

   If the image includes additional channels used for masking or finely edited selections, Photoshop discards them when you select a file format that does not support them. The only formats that accept alpha channels are native Photoshop, CompuServe GIF, PICT, PICT Resource, PNG, Raw, Targa, and TIFF.

See Also

File: **Save** and **Save As**
Layer: **Flatten Image**
Chapter 21, *The Channels Palette*

File: Revert

This command tells Photoshop to reload the most recently saved version of a file, clearing any edits made since then. Successful reverting requires that you save an image at the stage you want to be able to get back to, such as after color correcting or after creating a series of layers. At the very least, save an image whenever making a change you know you want to keep permanently.

Common Uses

- **Reversing a test series of commands.** Many users save an image before attempting a long series of commands. Since Photoshop has only one Undo level, this allows you to reverse a long chain of effects.

- **Reverting back to an original scan.** A common technique of scanner operators is to save an image immediately after scanning, so they can revert back to the original scan if they perform an incorrect adjustment. Failure to save would mean the image has to be rescanned.

Common Errors

Failing to save an image at the proper time. To successfully use this command, you must be aware of the last time you chose File: **Save**. After reverting, you cannot choose Edit: **Undo**.

Special Notes

- If a file isn't saved at least once, File: **Revert** is not available.

- Choosing File: **Revert** only reloads the entire image, but other tools and commands allow you to revert smaller portions of the image to the last saved version.

- Rather than use File: **Save** and **Revert** to test a series of commands, many users create a quick copy of an image using Image: **Duplicate** and try the commands there.

See Also

The Eraser Tool
The Rubber Stamp Tool
Edit: **Undo**
Edit: **Fill**
Image: **Duplicate**

File: Place

This command allows you to import the contents of an EPS graphic.

After choosing a graphic in the Place dialog, a low-resolution preview appears in a bounding box. Scale the graphic by dragging the corner points of the box, rotate it by dragging the cursor outside the box, and position it by dragging the box or using the arrow keys. Double-clicking on the box or pressing the Return key tells Photoshop to permanently apply the artwork.

Common Uses

- **Importing and rasterizing vector-based EPS files.** This command bypasses the Rasterize EPS dialog and uses the dimensions of the active image.

File Menu

- **Importing Photoshop EPS images.** This command will not recognize a Photoshop image in any other file format.

Common Errors

- **Failing to account for different color modes.** For example, if you place a CMYK file into an RGB image, the CMYK percentages are converted to RGB brightness values. If you later convert the image to CMYK, the resulting colors will differ from the original values.

- **Over-transforming a placed pixel-based image.** Excessive scaling and rotation, particularly when combining graphics of different resolutions, quickly degrades the quality of the added image.

Special Notes

- The color mode and resolution of the placed graphic automatically convert to match the active image.

- A placed graphic always appears on a new layer.

- When the bounding box is present, you can cancel the Place command by pressing the Escape key. Immediately after you apply the command, you must choose Edit: **Undo** to reverse the effect.

See Also

File: **Opening Vector-Based Images**
Edit: **Undo**
File: **Import**

File: Import

The File: **Import** options allow you to access graphics from external sources, such as scanners and digital cameras. You can also acquire images from software formats that Photoshop doesn't immediately recognize, like system resources containing multiple graphics. The import commands are based on different plug-ins, only a few of which are present when Photoshop is installed. Whenever a third-party input device like a scanner or camera is connected to a workstation, you must install the plug-in that ships with it into the Plug-ins' Import/Export folder. Choosing the plug-in from the submenu launches the software interface that allows you to capture or transfer images into an editable Photoshop form.

Anti-Aliased PICT

Use this command only if you use a less-powerful vector-based drawing program, like the ones found in integrated software packages like Microsoft Works, Claris Works, or certain word processors. Although native files from these programs are not recognizable by Photoshop, their graphics can be saved as PICT files. Simply opening these graphics via File: **Open** gives you a 72-ppi image with the same width and height as the original graphic. By importing it, Photoshop attempts to anti-alias the edges of the shapes, gently blending them into their surrounding pixels.

Special Notes

- The PICT opens at 72 ppi, but you can change the size of the resulting image by increasing or decreasing the width and height. Checking Constrain Proportions locks the ratio between the two values. To create a file of higher resolution than 72 ppi, increase the width and height to double or triple the actual size, then increase the resolution under Image: **Image Size** while leaving the Resample Image box unchecked.

- This command only does an adequate job. You get a much higher quality image when placing or opening vector-based artwork existing in true EPS form. If you find yourself importing these types of PICTs often, consider investing in a more powerful software package, like Adobe Illustrator or Macromedia FreeHand.

See Also

File: **Open**
File: **Place**
Image: **Image Size**

PICT Resource

Using this import command, you can tap into a file (usually an application) containing multiple PICT images. A scrolling dialog appears, allowing you to browse through the different graphics, select one you want, and import it into an active Photoshop window.

Common Uses

- **Acquiring application-specific graphics.** Images like cursors, splash screens, and icons are often difficult or time-consuming to grab using a screen-capture program. Select File: Import: **PICT Resource**, find the application you desire, and click open. After scrolling through the selections in the PICT Resource dialog, click Open to access the desired image in Photoshop.

- **Browsing through images saved to the Scrapbook.** Many screen-capture programs like Capture or Snapz save images to the Scrapbook file, and many frequently used Photoshop images are placed there as well. After taking your screen shots, you can scroll through the PICT Resource dialog to open images one at a time.

Special Notes

- Not all applications will contain the images you desire. Some, like Macromedia Director, have over 200. Others, like Adobe PageMaker, have only two.

File Menu

- Adobe Photoshop is the only application that cannot be tapped into using the PICT Resource dialog. This is to prevent application and system crashes—telling any program to open itself invariably leads to trouble.

- Rather than save screen-captures to the Scrapbook, we use a different method. Since most of our screen-captures are going to be printed, we save them all as TIFFs to one specific folder. This way, we can open many images at once, edit them, and automatically have the proper file format selected when we save them again.

Quick Edit

Quick Edit allows you to open a selected portion of a large image, edit it, and seamlessly insert it back into the original file using File: Export: **Quick Edit Save**. This command is only useful if your workstation is not powerful enough to open very large images—many users cannot afford the large amounts of RAM and hard drive space Photoshop needs to efficiently edit these files, which easily consume dozens of megabytes apiece.

Special Notes

- Since this command is used predominantly on high-resolution images, Quick Edit only recognizes TIFF (with no LZW Compression) and Scitex CT images, two formats often used for print-related work.

- If you change the color mode, resolution, or size of the smaller image portion, you cannot successfully reinsert it into the larger file.

Twain Acquire

TWAIN is a multi-platform scanner interface. It dates back to 1990, before scanners came bundled with their own interface in the form of a Photoshop plug-in. Back then, a scanner's interface shipped as a kind of stand-alone application (or source module) you'd have to launch, use, and close before being able to edit the scans in Photoshop. The biggest problem was the lack of standardized controls. They looked and acted differently for each scanner, there was seldom a preview window for pre-scanning, and the process itself was non-intuitive. By linking a program like Photoshop to a connected scanner's source module, TWAIN offers users a predictable and more user-friendly interface.

Common Uses

Refer to Appendix A for a full description of the following:

- Connecting to a scanner

Common Errors

Attempting to connect without the proper TWAIN module. Windows NT and Windows 95 require 32-bit TWAIN source modules (Photoshop is 32-bit). They do not work with the same scanner software used in earlier versions of Windows. To use Photoshop with an older version of the TWAIN32 module, copy the *Twain32.8ba* file to Photoshop's Plug-ins folder and copy the *Twain32.dll* file to the Windows folder. To use TWAIN under the Windows 3.1 operating system, also load the *Share.exe* file before starting Windows. If this doesn't work, contact the scanner manufacturer about the availability of compatible TWAIN source modules.

Special Notes

- TWAIN is still used by many professionals who either use scanners without a Plug-in interface, or who prefer the TWAIN interface to the one provided by the manufacturer. The vast majority of scanners shipping today are TWAIN-compatible, but the manufacturer of the input device must provide a Source Manager and TWAIN Data source for your device; otherwise, it will not work. Photoshop supports the current TWAIN, TWAIN32, and TWAIN_32 standards for scanning.

- TWAIN was developed by Hewlett-Packard and initially promoted by such companies as Aldus, Caere, Logitech, and Kodak. According to legend, TWAIN stands for *Technology Without An Impressive Name*, or *Toolkit Without An Interesting Name*. More realistically, Logitech claimed it was named after the relationship it developed between input devices and applications, and how they were finally able to meet "*in the 'twain.'*"

Twain Select

This option is used to select an active TWAIN device to access from within Photoshop. Since only one device can be active at a time, this command must be chosen whenever you need to focus Photoshop's attention onto a different one. See File: Import: **TWAIN Acquire** above for more information.

File: Export

Export information from Photoshop when you need to access a specific image feature in a different application, such as making certain GIF pixels appear transparent in a browser, or being able to edit Photoshop paths in Adobe Illustrator. This function also lets you write a smaller image into a larger file, as part of Photoshop's Quick Edit feature. The export commands are based on different Plug-ins, only a few of which are present when Photoshop is installed. Whenever certain third-party products are installed in a workstation, you must install the plug-in that ships with it into the Plug-ins' Import/Export folder. Choosing the plug-in from the submenu allows Photoshop to create the appropriate files. For example, Kodak's PCS 100 color correcting system, still in use by many companies, allows production specialists to make accurate color adjustment decisions when editing RGB images on a rigidly calibrated monitor. Rather than use Photoshop's RGB to CMYK conversion tables, users must apply values stored on a special video board installed in their workstation. When editing is complete, they access a PCS 100 Plug-in and export the image into a Photoshop EPS file.

GIF89a Export

This command allows you to export an Indexed Color or RGB image to a GIF89a file, an option not found under the File Format pop-up of the Save As dialog. The two types of GIF files—GIF87a and GIF89a—are essentially the same. Both have reduced (or Indexed) color palettes, both use LZW Compression, and both are standards for web graphics because of their smaller file size. The major difference: GIF89a files, because of their ability to save an additional masking channel, can display transparent pixels. Transparent GIFs are built in order to see through part of a web graphic to the underlying information. This typically happens when you want to place an irregularly shaped object, like a rounded button or cartoon character, on a colored or patterned background.

GIF87a files (generally called "GIFs") are created when an Indexed Color image is saved in the CompuServe GIF file format. GIF89a files (generally called "transparent GIFs") require that you export the file after defining the transparent area. When exporting an RGB image, this command uses the transparent areas of an image layer to form the necessary alpha channel. Indexed Color images cannot contain multiple layers, so you must define the transparent area manually.

Common Uses

Refer to Appendix A for full descriptions of the following:

- Creating a transparent GIF from an Indexed Color image
- Creating a transparent GIF from an RGB image

Common Errors

- **Exporting an Indexed Color image with a conflicting background color.** If the background shares a color with any part of the image, there is no way to differentiate between the two areas. If you manually designate the background as transparent, part of the image will be transparent as well. You must do one of the following: change one of the colored areas to a unique value, select the background and create your own alpha channel, or convert to RGB and isolate the image on a separate layer.

- **Exporting an RGB image before isolating an image on its own layer.** This command uses the transparent pixels of the layer as the basis for the alpha channel—if no such pixels are present, you cannot produce a transparent GIF.

Special Notes

- You can access two different GIF89a Export dialogs, depending on whether the image is in Indexed Color or RGB mode. No other mode can be exported.

- Exporting an RGB image offers more flexibility, since you can anti-alias or feather the edges of a layer's contents, resulting in semi-transparent web graphics.

- Images with anti-aliasing contain far more colors in the indexed palette of the GIF89a dialogs. You can reduce the number of colors—and therefore the file size—by not anti-aliasing the contents of the image, or by reducing the number of tones with a command like Image: Adjust: **Posterize**.

The GIF89a Export Dialog (Indexed Color)

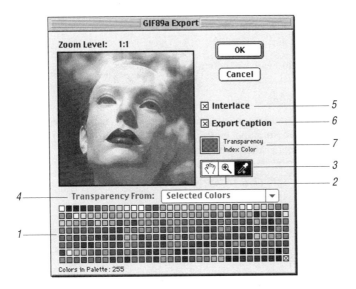

1. **Color Palette**

   This index displays all color values contained in the image. The maximum number of colors is 256, but the specific number was determined when the image was initially converted to Indexed Color. Here, the swatches are used only to define transparent areas—to change the actual values, cancel the command and choose Image: Mode: **Color Table**.

2. **Viewing Tools**

   Use the Hand Tool and Zoom Tool to navigate the preview window. Like their counterparts in the Toolbar, you can access them while the Eyedropper is selected. Hold down the space bar to access the Hand Tool. Hold down the (Command) [Control] key and the space bar to access the Zoom In Tool. Hold down (Option-Command) [Alt-Control] and the space bar to access the Zoom Out Tool.

3. **Eyedropper**

   Use this tool to define the transparent area. You can click on a specific color in the preview window, or you can choose a swatch directly from the Color Palette. Either way, the color in the preview turns gray and the appropriate Palette swatch highlights, indicating its transparency. To remove the transparency designation, hold down the (Command) [Control] key and click the color in the preview window or Color Palette.

4. **Transparency From**

   If the Indexed Color image contains an alpha channel or an active selection, select it from this pop-up. Otherwise, you must use the eyedropper to set transparency.

5. **Interlace**

   Check this box to export an interlaced GIF.

6. **Export Caption**

   This box is only available when you have added a caption to the image using File: **File Info**.

7. **Transparency Index Color**

   This color is used to indicate transparent areas in the preview window. The default value is Netscape gray, or R: 192, G: 192, B: 192. Change this value only if it conflicts visually with another color in the image.

The GIF89a Export Dialog (RGB)

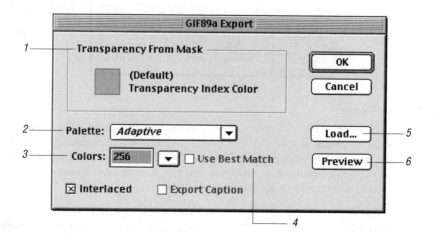

1. **Transparency from Mask**

   The color defined in this swatch is used to indicate transparent areas when you click the Preview button. This swatch is only available when an image is surrounded by transparent pixels in an image layer.

2. **Palette**

   Since this command converts the RGB image to Indexed Color, you must select a palette from this pop-up. There are three options (see Image: Mode: **Indexed Color** for more information):

   Exact

   This palette is only available when there are 256 colors or less in the image. For example, if you've converted an Indexed Color image to RGB to take

---

advantage of the layer-based transparency technique, choose Exact to retain the original color values.

Adaptive

This option creates a color palette based on the most frequently occurring values in the image.

System

This option uses the colors of the Macintosh or Windows system palette, depending on the operating system in use when you choose this command.

3. **Colors**

This field displays the number of colors contained in the image's palette. When Exact is chosen from the Palette pop-up, you cannot edit this number. When Adaptive or System is chosen, you can specify the exact number of colors.

4. **Use Best Match**

This box is only available when System is chosen from the Palette pop-up. Check it to ensure that the system colors used in the exported GIF match the original colors as closely as possible.

5. **Load**

This button allows you to load a color palette saved from the Image: Mode: **Color Table** dialog.

6. **Preview**

Click this button to see a preview of the exported GIF. Although the Color Palette appears at the bottom of the window (similar to the GIF89a Export dialog for Indexed Color images), you cannot make any changes.

See Also

Appendix A (File: Export: **GIF89a Export**)
File: Supported File Formats (**GIF**)
Image: Mode: **Indexed Color**
Image: Mode: **Color Table**
Image: Adjust: **Posterize**
Layer: **New**
Chapter 21, *The Channels Palette*

Paths to Illustrator

Use this command to export paths created with the **Pen Tool** (see Chapter 3, *Special Tools*) into an Adobe Illustrator file. From there, you can open the files in Illustrator or FreeHand and continue editing. Later, if desired, the stroked and filled shapes can be rasterized using File: **Open** or imported into a Photoshop image using File: **Place**.

Common Uses

Refer to Appendix A for full descriptions of the following:

File Menu

- Positioning customized type
- Editing a manually traced Photoshop image

Common Errors

- **Attempting to export multiple paths from the same image.** Photoshop can only export one path at a time. If you've created more than one individually named path, combine them into one path by cutting the different shapes and pasting them into one Path level.

- **Deleting the crop marks that are automatically placed in the Illustrator file.** The crops reflect the dimensions of the original Photoshop image, and this is what maintains the path's original position. If you don't change the crops or move the path, you can place the new graphic back in its original position.

Special Notes

- Paths exported from Photoshop have no stroke or fill color. When opened in Illustrator or FreeHand, they're not visible unless the Preview mode is turned off. In Illustrator, choose (Command) [Control]-E to switch to Artwork mode. In FreeHand, choose (Command) [Control]-K to switch to Keyline mode. After color has been applied, turn Preview back on to continue editing the shapes in color.

- If you use Illustrator, you can copy Photoshop paths and paste them directly into an Illustrator document. If you use FreeHand, you cannot paste Photoshop paths, but you can open the Illustrator file containing the exported path.

- An item called Document Bounds is listed in the Write pop-up in the Export Paths dialog. Choose this option to export object-oriented crop marks matching the width and height of the image.

See Also

Appendix A (File: Export: **Paths to Illustrator**)
The Pen Tool
File: **Open**
File: **Place**
Chapter 22, *The Paths Palette*

Quick Edit Save

After a small portion of a larger image has been edited using the File: Import: Quick Edit command, choosing Quick Edit Save is the only way to insert the image back into the original file. After the command is applied, close the open image without applying any additional save commands.

File: File Info

This feature allows you to annotate your images with creator information, category tags, tags, copyright details, even captions and web site addresses. It's never required to use this feature, but many professionals, like photographers and digital illustrators, routinely create original graphics. These are often sent to newspapers, ad agencies, stock image distributors, and other large production facilities. If that's the case, then this feature builds necessary information right into the image, avoiding the need to send handwritten documents or READ ME files.

Common Uses

Annotating a file for cataloging software. Many file retrieval applications are used to search for key textual information built into a file.

Common Errors

Adding information not used by the end receiver. Not all locations receiving digital images make it an official practice to refer to this built-in information. Be sure to inquire ahead of time, at least until this feature becomes more widely used—*if* it ever does. It's rather ironic; you use this feature to cut down on extra documentation, but you still have to supply extra documentation to let people know the feature has been used.

Special Notes

If you have a series of images that share File Info, you can save each section into a small text file. Choosing Load and opening that file relieves you from having to type the information again. Or, choose Append, find an image that contains the same information, and import it into the section.

The File Info Panels

Caption
You can insert up to 2,000 characters in the Caption field. If you output an image from Photoshop, this information prints beneath the image if you check the Caption box under File: **Page Layout**. If the image must be handled or treated in a specific way, enter a description under Special Instructions.

Keywords
Here, enter any number of words associated with the image, so search software can seek and find it at the user's command.

Categories
Many publishing organizations use codes to describe different categories of information. If you know a specific code, enter it here, along with any supplemental categories that may apply. If instructed to enter how time-sensitive an image is, choose an option from the Urgency pop-up.

File Menu

Credits

Enter the name of the image creator, his/her title, any acknowledgment to another person or company, and the person or company that owns the image.

Origin

Here, describe the image's history, including file name, creation date, and the location of production.

Copyright and URL

Add the desired copyright notice, and determine if that information displays in browser or catalog software. You can also list a web site address that applies to the image, such as one containing additional work by the same artist. Anyone clicking on the Go to URL button will automatically connect to the listed address.

File: Page Setup
(Command-Shift) [Control-Shift]-P

In one sense, the Page Setup dialog is where you fine-tune the output behavior of a file before downloading the information to a printer. More realistically, this dialog is used to build certain customized output commands into a file before it's saved, imported into a page layout program, and *then* output. For reasons we discuss under File: **Print**, you'll rarely output images from Photoshop, even though the application has a range of printing commands.

The top half of the Page Setup dialog contains the same information found in most other applications: paper size, orientation, selected printer, and so forth. The ones that ultimately appear depend on your type of output device and the print driver installed in your operating system.

The remaining options are specific to Photoshop. Most of these functions only apply to images output directly from the program. The Screens and Transfer buttons, however, contain commands you can build into an image, ready to be applied when printed from another application. Therefore, these are the most commonly used features in the Page Setup dialog.

Screens

Halftoning is the method used to reproduce the smooth, continuous tones of your images on press. In it, a grid of different sized dots is used to create an illusion. For an easy example, examine a grayscale image printed on your laser printer: dark areas are reproduced using large dots; light areas are reproduced using small dots. The varying dot sizes combined with the white spaces between them create what the eye perceives to be tone.

Reproducing full-color images takes this concept one step further. Since it has only four different inks (cyan, magenta, yellow, and black) to reproduce millions of on-screen colors, the printing process overlays four different grids of halftone dots. Process inks are transparent, so whenever dots of different colors are printed on top of each other, they blend to form new colors. Using this method, you can reproduce thousands of different colors—not enough to reproduce all the colors you see on-screen, but enough to adequately reproduce most high-quality photographic images.

For print-oriented work, then, the entire purpose of Photoshop is to prepare these tone-rich images for translation into halftone dots. You'll use other tools for adjusting the image's color content. The Screens dialog is used to adjust the structure and behavior of the halftone dots themselves, independent of the colors they represent.

Before making any changes, understand that in most cases you don't have to touch this dialog. Photoshop defaults to a setting called Use Printer's Default Screens. If you leave the Screens dialog untouched, the screen values are based on two different sources: the output device (which contains its own screening information) and the page layout program (which allows you to set the linescreen value for the entire document).

Common Uses

- **Creating duotones.** There are two ways to create a duotone, and both require changing the screen angles. You can define your own duotone curves or use the pre-defined curves that Adobe supplies with Photoshop. Either way, consult with the person running the job on press. Many print shops prefer a specific set of duotone angles for their presses. (See Image: Mode: **Duotone** for more information.)

- **Triggering stochastic screens.** Imagesetters that support *stochastic* (or randomized) screens need to be told when to discard standard screening for an image. Usually, an obscure linescreen value, like 102 or 108, is used to trigger the new screens. In this case, you don't need to change the screen angles—they will be ignored.

- **Embedding images of a different linescreen.** When a page layout file contains images reproducing at a different frequency than the rest of the document, those values must be entered in the Screens dialog.

Common Errors

- **Failing to make consistent changes to every color plate.** If you make only one change under Screens, you must make sure that the rest of the information is correct. For example, if you enter custom screen angles but do not set the linescreen to the desired value, the image prints with the correct angles at the incorrect frequency (and the default is about 47 lines per inch, meaning the dots will be about twice as large as those found in the average newspaper).

- **Entering inappropriate screen angles.** If the angles for a multicolor image are incorrect, a moiré pattern will result on-press. If there is any question about which angles to use, consult with your printer.

Special Notes

- Whenever you make any alterations to the Screens dialog, you have to make sure that your page layout program can understand the changes. The only way

File Menu

to do this is to save the image as an EPS file, and check the Include Halftone Screen box in the EPS Options dialog.

• To change the default settings, first make the desired changes. Then (Option) [Alt]-click the Save button. Before you click, you'll notice that its title changes to Default. (Option) [Alt]-click the Load button to restore the original factory-installed defaults.

The Screens Dialog

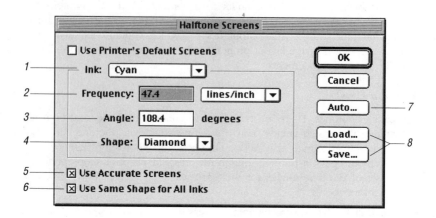

1. **Ink**

   Set values one color at a time. If you're changing a grayscale image, the only option is black. If it's a duotone, choose the first or second color ink. Full-color images let you edit cyan, magenta, yellow, and black separately.

2. **Frequency**

   Enter a linescreen value. Unless you're creating some sort of visible effect, these values remain constant for all color plates. Be careful—setting a value for one color does not automatically set the rest.

3. **Angle**

   Every color must output at a different screen angle. The only time to deviate from the default setting is when you have it on good authority—meaning the person who will be running the job on press—what the preferred screen angles should be. Identical screen angles result in muddy, low-quality reproduction, and incorrect angles result in *moiré*, a blotchy pattern formed by conflicting halftone grids.

4. **Shape**

   The universal default dot shape is elliptical. The majority of printed materials use these dots because they are predictable, time-tested, and effective. In rare cases, some people use square or diamond-shaped dots, believing the crisper shapes capture more of an image's fine details. Also, many designers use custom screens to create a special effect, such as reproducing an image with line-shaped dots at a low screen value.

5. **Use Accurate Screens**

   This option allows you to use the new screen angle technology available on PostScript Level 2 printers when making color separations. This only applies when outputting images directly from Photoshop.

6. **Use Same Shape for All Inks**

   Checking this button ensures that once a dot shape is changed on one ink, it automatically changes the remaining ink. It does not affect any other values.

7. **Auto/Auto Screens**

   This is a shortcut to use only when you want to change the screen frequency on all color plates at once. In the dialog, enter the resolution of your output device and your intended linescreen value. Clicking OK applies the screen frequency to all colors.

8. **Load and Save**

   When applying the same changes to multiple images, save the changes made to the first image and load them into the remaining ones to automatically apply the same values.

See Also

File: **Print**
Image: Mode: **Duotone**
Image: Mode: **CMYK**

Transfer

The Transfer button refers to *transfer functions*. This feature allows you to create tone curves similar to the ones encountered in the Image: Adjust: **Curves** dialog. Unlike those curves, a transfer function does not change the color values of an image's pixels—rather, the change is applied by the RIP when the image is output.

Common Uses

* **Applying a tonal adjustment without affecting the original image.** Since the curve is applied during output, you can make adjustments without changing the original tones and colors. Often, a curve is created to compensate for dot gain.

* **Using the same corrected image in a variety of reproduction methods.** In the print industry, it usually means inserting a correcting curve that compensates for different presses and paper stocks. For example, an image printed on coated stock at 150 ppi using a finely tuned digital press will not reproduce identically to the same image printed on a 70-year-old Heidelberg on uncoated paper. If you're aware of the capabilities of the different presses—which requires making contact with the print shop—you can attempt to compensate for the areas that will darken or lighten.

File Menu

Common Errors

- **Attempting to apply finely detailed adjustments.** The Transfer Curve is less precise than the Image: Adjust: **Curves** dialog, and it is difficult at best to preview the changes. For the most important adjustments (and any color correcting), use the standard Curves dialog. If necessary, create a duplicate of the original image.

- **Loading a Transfer curve into the Image: Adjust: Curves dialog to preview its effect.** In a perfect world, you could save the curves from the Transfer Functions dialog, load them into the Curves dialog, and temporarily apply them to test the results of the transferred curve. This only works on composite curves, which equally affects all channels. Unfortunately, the Curves dialog often misinterprets curves intended for specific color channels as being meant for the entire image, which doesn't help at all.

Special Notes

It's important to realize that building transfer functions into full-color images requires direct contact with the service bureau outputting the files and the printer reproducing the images. All decisions must be based on profiles of the printing presses in question, and the predicted behavior of different combinations of line-screen, paper stock, and ink densities.

The Transfer Functions Dialog

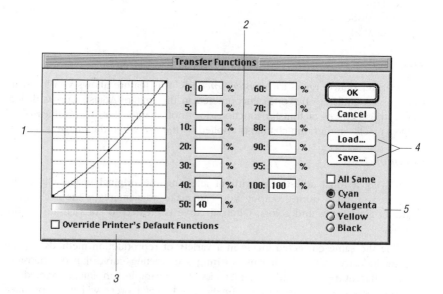

1. The Curve

This panel is a graph that plots pixel values against final output values. Ordinarily, an area of pixels colored 30% black outputs as a 30% screen. The curve, which starts as a diagonal line, changes the relationship between on-screen color and the output value without editing the actual image.

For example, if you want to lighten the midtones of a grayscale image to compensate for dot gain while leaving the original image untouched, you might consider editing the transfer curve.

2. **Percentages**

   Use these boxes to enter your desired changes numerically instead of manually. To lighten the midtones of a grayside image, enter "40" in the field labeled "50". Leave the other fields blank if they are not being specifically changed—entering a number anchors the curve to that value, and the ability to smoothly add changes may be compromised.

3. **Override Printer's Default Functions**

   This button forces the image to ignore any transfer functions already built into an output device. When you're making your own transfer curve, it seems like the right thing to do, but bring it to the attention of your service bureau nonetheless. Clicking this button may also override all of their imagesetter's calibration data, leaving the ultimate quality of the image up to fate and chance.

4. **Load and Save**

   To apply the same transfer curve to multiple images, save the values of the first and load them into the subsequent files.

5. **Color Buttons**

   An option only when editing full-color images, they allow you to create separate curves for each channel. To edit all channels at once, leave the All Colors box checked.

See Also

Appendix A (File: Page Setup: **Transfer**)
File: **Print**
Image: Adjust: **Curves**

The Page Setup Dialog

The remaining check boxes only apply to images being output from Photoshop, and are seldom used in print publishing.

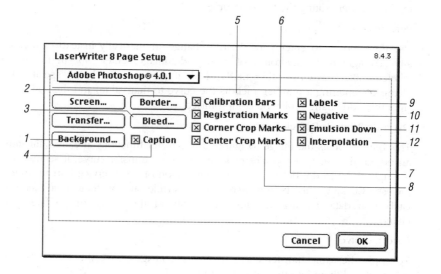

1. **Background**

   This button brings up the Color Picker. Here, define a value to be used as a background color when an image is shot to slides using a film recorder. It does not affect the original image—the color is only applied during printing.

2. **Border**

   Also intended for film recorders, this command adds a black border to the image at a width you specify.

3. **Bleed**

   This command only applies to images being separated directly from Photoshop. It allows image areas to be printed beyond standard page sizes, which are then trimmed, giving the appearance of an image printing all the way to the edge of a page. Most offset printing requires at least an eighth of an inch of bleed (9 points), but other press types require a little more. If an image is being printed from a page layout program, don't worry about this command. Create bleeds simply by placing an imported image over a page's boundary.

4. **Caption**

   This option prints the caption entered under File: File Info: **Caption** under the image. It's not intended for any design purposes, and the position, typeface, and type size cannot be altered.

5. **Calibration Bars**

   This option adds a strip of 10 gray squares, ranging from 10% black to 100% black in 10% increments. These bars are output alongside any separated image or page layout file, and they are used to test the accuracy of an imagesetter's halftone dot values.

6. **Registration Marks**

These marks are crosshairs that print in the exact same position on each film separation. Strippers—the prepress professionals responsible for imposing plate separations into usable flats—use these marks to properly align page films. In this case, however, the only time they'd be of any use is if you printed some raw film separations from Photoshop for a color proof (a process where we still prefer to use QuarkXPress or Adobe PageMaker). This option also places two *star targets*. These are used to measure image resolution while a press plate is burned, and to indicate the integrity of the plate during printing.

7. **Corner Crop Marks**

Crops mark the page boundaries of a printed image. They tell the person trimming the pages where to cut. This option places crops in each corner of the image.

8. **Center Crop Marks**

This option places crosshairs marking the center of each side of an image.

9. **Labels**

Checking this box prints the title of an image above it, in the same typeface as the Captions option.

10. **Negative**

Check this box to invert the printed image. As with most traditional separations, white pixels are represented by black areas, and black pixels are represented by white (or, if printing to film, clear) areas. If printing the image as a composite to a color printer, this option will invert the color values.

11. **Emulsion Down**

Emulsion refers to the silver halide emulsion that coats one side of lithographic film. This is the material that is exposed to a finely focused beam of light. This box determines which direction the image will face upon output: right-reading up or right-reading down. Leaving the box unchecked results in film printing with the emulsion up.

12. **Interpolation**

This option will anti-alias a low-resolution graphic by resampling the image to twice the original size and resizing back to 100%. It only works on PostScript Level 2 printers, and it doesn't even work there that well.

See Also

File Info: **Caption**
File: **Print**

File: Print
(Command) [Control]-P

This command allows you to output a single image to a printer or to your hard disk.

Although Photoshop has quite an array of printing options (see File: **Page Setup**), you'll rarely print final, separated color from the program. Why? Because other programs do it faster, better, and more predictably. Photoshop is rarely used in a vacuum—without fail, it's always part of a larger suite of software, regardless of your industry. For publishers, this includes a page layout program (like Quark or PageMaker), an illustration program (like Illustrator or FreeHand), and other sundry utilities and system extensions. Photoshop is part of a larger process, and should never be considered its own closed loop.

Common Uses

- Outputting a single image to a laser printer or color output device
- Separating a single image on an imagesetter
- Converting a single image into a PostScript file

Common Errors

Attempting to mimic a page layout or illustration program. In terms of output, Photoshop has some serious limitations:

- You cannot adjust the position of a printed graphic.
- It becomes more difficult to incorporate graphics and text from other programs.
- You cannot reproduce crisp, PostScript-defined lines, like artwork created in Illustrator or type set in Quark.

Special Notes

Designers occasionally output separations from Photoshop to check the color of an image in progress. If you do this, the screen frequency must be set appropriately in the File: Page Setup: **Screen** dialog; otherwise, the values default to roughly 47 lpi, far too low to get an accurate representation of the final printed image. Also, the dot shape must be set to the same one you'll ultimately use—different halftone dot shapes can slightly alter your perception of an image's color. For the most predictable results, print test separations from the same program using the same values you'll use to output the final project. This way, you duplicate the final output environment.

The Print Dialog

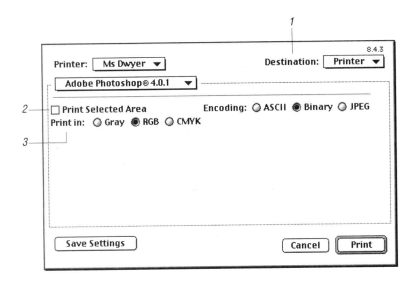

The information in the top half of the dialog is the same found in most other applications—here, you determine the number of copies to print, the paper source, the printer type, and so forth. The options ultimately depend on the print driver installed in your operating system.

1. **Destination**

   From this pop-up, choose whether the image information will be downloaded to a printer or a PostScript file on your hard drive.

2. **Print Selected Area**

   Checking this option tells Photoshop to output only what is currently selected with the rectangular Marquee Tool. If you have an image too large to be printed on one page, this is the only way Photoshop can tile it.

3. **Print in Gray/RGB/CMYK**

   These options only apply to composite (non-separated) printouts output to a color output device. Checking Gray tells Photoshop to send a grayscale version of the image, regardless of the image's color mode. If sending an RGB image to print, you have two options: check RGB and let the printer convert the RGB data to CMYK, or check CMYK and let Photoshop do it. Telling Photoshop to do it cuts down on processing time and printer errors.

See Also

File: **Page Setup**
File: Page Setup: **Screens**

File: Preferences
(Command) [Control]-K

Every major graphics application has a vast and complex interface. Because there are so many variables and so many different uses for the program, there are certain elements that can be altered to better suit your working environment. These are called *Preferences*, or default settings, and can be changed on-the-fly whenever Photoshop is open.

These preferences are stored in the Adobe Photoshop Preferences file, located in the Preferences folder in the System folder. To reset all the Preferences at once, delete the file and let Photoshop create a new one the next time the program is launched. Also, if the program begins acting inconsistently—certain values keep resetting, or colors keep changing—deleting the preferences file will often solve the problem.

There are eight Preferences panels (where we specifically prefer a setting, we've included it after the title of the preference):

General

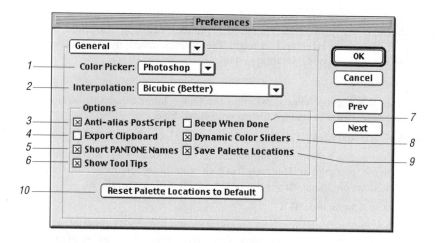

1. **Color Picker (Mac):** *Photoshop*

   Choose between Photoshop's built-in picker or the one developed by Apple. Apple's is found in many other programs, but only defines RGB and HSB (Hue, Saturation, Brightness) colors. Photoshop's picker also defines Lab and CMYK colors, displays a gamut warning, and allows you to select custom colors supported by different swatch book systems (see Chapter 5, *The Color Controls* for more information).

2. Interpolation: *Bicubic*

   When Photoshop resizes an image or the information in a transform box, it must figure out how to rearrange the pixels. It does this by comparing pixel values to get an educated guess about what to do. This is called interpolation. The highest-quality option is *Bicubic*, the factory default, because it looks at the highest number of pixels before making its decision. *Nearest Neighbor* offers the lowest quality, not attempting to interpolate the pixels at all. *Bilinear* falls in the middle (see Image: **Image Size**).

3. Anti-alias PostScript: *On*

   When importing vector-based images, this option tells Photoshop to automatically anti-alias the edges of the shapes. It has no impact on opening or pasting these graphics, since anti-aliasing is always an option by clicking a check box (see File: **Place**).

4. Export Clipboard: *Off*

   This option tells your computer to hold copied information in memory when you quit the program—although it is unlikely you will paste it into another program (see Edit: **Copy**).

5. Short Pantone Names: *On*

   When Pantone names are selected as part of a duotone (the only way to define a spot color in Photoshop), the short version of the name—PMS 506 CV rather than Pantone 506 CV is a good example—is used. The short names are used by almost all print-related graphics software (see Chapter 5, *The Color Controls*).

6. Show Tool Tips: *On*

   This option displays a tiny, single-letter keyboard shortcut when the cursor is placed over a tool or palette.

7. Beep When Done: *Off*

   This option tells Photoshop to sound an alert whenever a command is finished processing.

8. Dynamic Color Sliders: *On*

   This option displays an active preview of colors formed using the sliders in **The Color Palette**.

9. Save Palette Locations: *On*

   This option forces Photoshop to remember where you place the floating palettes on-screen.

10. Reset Palette Locations to Default

    If a floating palette is positioned off-screen or any other inconvenient area, clicking this button restores their position to the factory default.

File Menu

Saving Files

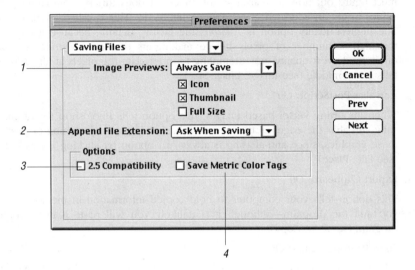

1. **Image Previews**

    Previews are small renderings of an image that Photoshop creates when saving a file. Checking Icon creates a 32 × 32 pixel image used as the image's icon, presumably for visual identification. Checking Thumbnail creates the small preview referred into the Open dialog. Checking Full Size builds in an actual-size 72 ppi preview—this allows the image to be imported more quickly into another program, but it also slightly increases the file size.

2. **Append File Extension:** *On*

    This option tells Photoshop whether or not to automatically add the three-letter code for an image's file format at the end of the title. Although it uses the Window-style method of file extensions, it's always preferable to include the extension, whether you do it automatically or manually (see File: **Save**).

3. **2.5 Compatibility:** *Off*

    Checking this box creates the illusion that Photoshop 3 and 4 images are compatible with Photoshop 2.5. In truth, Photoshop simply writes an additional flattened version of the image that the older software, which can't recognize layers, can read. Leaving this off saves considerable file size when saving images in the native Photoshop format.

4. **Save Metric Color Tags:** *Off*

    Check this box only if using the EFIColor calibration system. It helps a saved file better communicate the information of EFI's color tables to QuarkXPress, the only compatible page layout program.

Display & Cursors

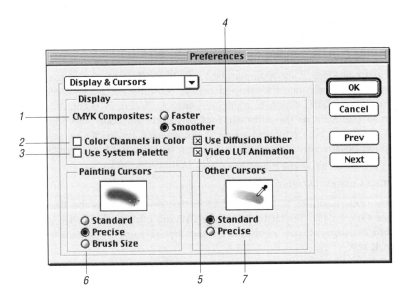

1. **CMYK Composites**

   This option controls how Photoshop displays CMYK information using your RGB monitor. People involved in color-sensitive print work should select Smoother. This dynamically converts CMYK information into RGB values, displaying a little more slowly but a little more accurately on-screen—provided the monitor is calibrated. Everyone else can select Faster to disable this function.

2. **Color Channels in Color**: *Off*

   This option colorizes the separate channels in a color image with the same colors they are supposed to represent. The colors are only visible when you view an individual channel by clicking it in the **Channels Palette** (see Chapter 21). This can reduce the possibility of editing the wrong channel, but the colored versions display with less contrast and clarity than their Black counterparts.

3. **Use System Palette**: *Off*

   For users of 8-bit (256 color) monitors, this option tells Photoshop to refer to only one color palette when editing multiple open images, expediting display times. Web designers and cross-platform multimedia developers in particular will want to leave this off.

4. **Use Diffusion Dither**: *On*

   For users of 8-bit (256 color) monitors, this option tells Photoshop to use a more randomized pixel diffusion method as it attempts to mimic a monitor with more colors.

5. **Video LUT Animation:** *On*

Video LUT, or Look-Up Table, allows you to evaluate your color and tone adjustments much more quickly by changing the appearance of the entire screen instead of just the image pixels. This slightly hinders color accuracy, but when you need to see the actual pixel values, just click the Preview button.

6. **Painting Cursors:** *Precise*

When using any Paint tool, Standard tells Photoshop to display the descriptive but wholly inaccurate tool-shaped cursor. Selecting Precise replaces the cursor with a crosshair, which is more accurate, to a certain point. When using a brush tool such as the **Airbrush Tool** or **Paintbrush Tool**, selecting Brush Size uses a round cursor the exact size of the selected brush. We prefer the Precise option because the Brush Size feature can be activated by depressing the Caps Lock key, giving us easy access to both options on the fly.

7. **Other Cursors:** *Standard*

This option applies to rest of the tools that do not access the **Brushes Palette** (see Chapter 19). Similar to use of the Painting Cursors above, we choose Standard because we can easily access the Precise tools by depressing the Caps Lock key.

Transparency & Gamut

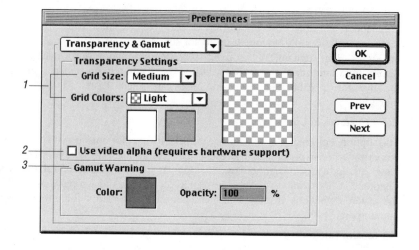

1. **Transparency Settings**

In order to illustrate the transparent pixels Photoshop uses when you start working with multiple layers, Adobe devised a checkerboard pattern that only appears where there are no color values whatsoever (not even white). Here, select the size of the grid and the color of the tiny squares. Change the colors by using the pop-up, the two color pickers below, or by clicking and (Option)

[Alt]-clicking anywhere on an open image. To be honest, we prefer the default settings, but changing this information hurts nothing.

2. **Use Video Alpha**

   This option is for anyone using a video board supporting chroma-key functions. Checking this box allows a television signal to display in any transparent area.

3. **Gamut Warning**

   Clicking on this box opens the color picker, where you choose the color that the View: **Gamut Warning** command uses to highlight colors that are out of the reproducible CMYK gamut. Lowering the opacity value turns the highlight color semi-transparent.

Units & Rulers

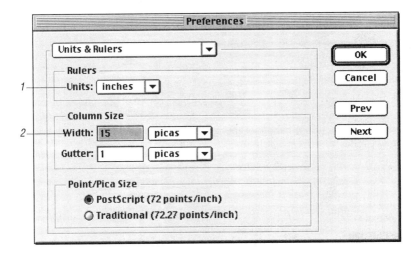

1. **Rulers**

   Select the preferred units from the pop-up. Web and multimedia designers tend to use Pixels, while most print publishers use Picas or Points (see View: **Rulers**).

2. **Column Size**

   This option is referred to in the File: **New** dialog when Columns is chosen as a Width value. It's asking for the width of a column used in a page layout, as well as the gutter, or the space in between columns. Now, when you enter a number of columns as an image width, the proper size, gutters included, is created.

File Menu

Guides & Grid

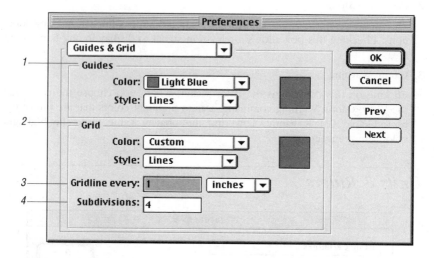

1. Guides

   Use the pop-up menu, the color picker, or clicking anywhere in an open image to choose a color for the horizontal and vertical ruler guides. From the Style pop-up, choose whether the guides will be solid or dotted lines (see View: **Guides**).

2. Grid

   Use the pop-up menu, the color picker, or (Option) [Alt]-clicking anywhere in an open image to choose a color for the grid. From the Style pop-up, choose whether the grid will be solid or dotted lines (see View: **Grid**).

3. Gridline Every

   This value determines the distance between the gridlines displayed over an image.

4. Subdivisions

   This value determines how many thinner lines are placed between the gridlines. For example, if you have gridlines every inch with a subdivision of four, the result is a crisscross pattern of quarter-inch increments that Photoshop uses to align selections and layers.

Plug-ins & Scratch Disk

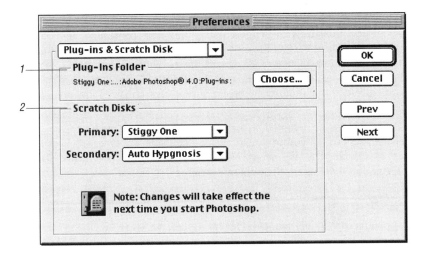

1. Plug-ins Folder

The Choose button allows you to select a different folder for Photoshop to read this information from. The only time to change that folder is when you use other applications that support plug-ins, like Fractal Design Painter or CoSa After Effects. If so, you may consider creating one central Plug-ins folder that each program is told to read. This way, each program has access not only to its own plug-ins, but to all the rest as well (see Appendix A for a full description).

After clicking the Choose button, you must highlight the desired folder and click the Select button at the bottom of the navigation window. Pressing Return or Enter will not automatically choose the folder.

Some power users may have hundreds, if not thousands, of plug-ins. Loading this many modules when launching the software can take a prohibitively long time, especially on older model computers. If so, consider dividing your plug-ins into multiple folders, rather than one primary folder. This way, if you hold down the (Option-Command) [Alt-Control] keys while launching Photoshop, you can select your desired Plug-ins Folder on the fly.

2. Scratch Disks

When Photoshop runs low on available RAM, it temporarily uses available space on the hard drive, a process known as *virtual memory* (See View: Overview for more information). If you only have one hard drive, Photoshop automatically uses that as a scratch disk, searching out the largest free chunk of drive space and using it to help process the commands you apply. If you have multiple drives, Photoshop defaults to the startup drive.

Because anyone creating Photoshop files can easily run short on megabytes, many users have a large capacity, high-speed external hard drive for storage

File Menu

and scratch disk space. To select this external drive as the new scratch disk, choose that drive's name from the Primary pop-up. Select the drive with less available space from the Secondary pop-up, should the primary scratch disk run out of room.

Photoshop only uses the largest contiguous (not containing any fragmented files) space for its scratch files. To keep this space constant, consider creating a 100 Mb partition on one of your hard drives. This partition will appear in the Primary pop-up, just like a separate hard drive. As long as no files are ever copied into this partition, the space will always remain contiguous and fully available.

Many people are tempted to use removable storage media for scratch disk space. We can tell you from experience that using a SyQuest, Zip, or Bernoulli as a scratch disk is inconvenient, unreliable, and potentially dangerous. Regular hard drives are the only safe choice.

See Also

Appendix A (File: Preferences: **Plug-ins & Scratch Disk**)
View: **Overview**

Image Cache

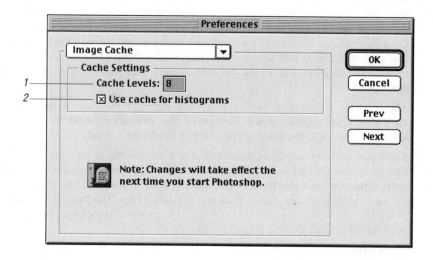

Image caching is a scheme that speeds the on-screen redraw of high-resolution images. When it's enabled, Photoshop uses lower resolution versions of an image to update the image on-screen when performing operations like transformations, compositing, and color adjustments.

1. Cache Levels

   Setting a Cache Levels value determines the number of different sized low-res previews that Photoshop holds in memory. The default is 4, which means previews for four zoom percentages from 100% on down are maintained in RAM. The image redraws faster when editing at these zoom percentages, but it comes at a cost: Photoshop requires more RAM. Therefore, users with large amounts of RAM (48 Mb and above) can safely increase the Cache Levels to 8, the maximum. Workstations with less RAM should reduce the value.

2. Use Cache for Histograms

   Checking this box tells Photoshop to use the information of one of its cache levels to generate the histograms found in the Image: Adjust: **Levels** and Image: **Histogram** dialogs. The information won't be totally accurate, but histograms are rarely used for anything more than a general overview of an image's tonal range. Because leaving this option on uses a bit more RAM, turn it off if the Cache Level is set below 4.

See Also

Image: Adjust: **Levels**
Image: **Histogram**
View: **Zoom In** and **Zoom Out**

File: Color Settings

The Color Settings commands serve two purposes: they control the colors that appear on your monitor, and they control the conversion of RGB colors to CMYK output values.

These commands apply primarily to the print publishing industry.

Monitor Setup

Using this panel, you attempt to create the most accurate source for Photoshop to refer to while it makes its internal decisions on how CMYK colors should display in RGB color space.

Common Uses

- **Making Photoshop aware of your monitor's parameters.** This allows Photoshop to address its specific mechanics.

- **Compensating for the amount of ambient light in your workspace.** Different levels of light affect how your eye perceives color, which impacts your color correcting decisions.

File Menu

Common Errors

Assuming that these setting result in a "calibrated" monitor. Adjusting the Monitor Setup values is often called monitor calibration, but that's only true in a sense. True calibration requires that additional tools, such as a calibration cup or accelerator card, be used every day to ensure that your monitor displays those colors as consistently as possible.

Special Notes

Changing these settings does not affect how RGB colors appear on your monitor, but it does affect the display of CMYK (and Lab) colors. It also affects the values that result when you change an image from RGB to CMYK mode. Photoshop refers to the values you enter in this dialog, determines the colors you see on the monitor, and attempts to recreate those same colors as they exist in CMYK space.

The Monitor Setup Dialog

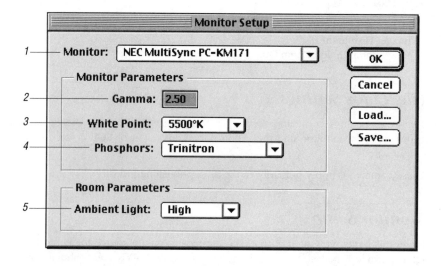

1. **Monitor**

   Selecting your monitor from this pop-up automatically sets the proper Monitor Parameters values. If your exact monitor isn't there, select another one only if you are certain that its parameters are identical to your own. Otherwise, refer to the literature that accompanied your monitor for the necessary information. Leave the setting on General and enter the parameters manually.

2. **Gamma**

   Essentially an overall correction to a monitor's contrast, the gamma value depends on the work you do as much as the monitor you use. The standard for print-oriented work is 1.8. Workstations connected to an NTSC-compatible video screen work in a slightly darker color space, which usually requires a higher gamma of 2.2.

3. **White Point**

Here, choose the temperature of the light your work is viewed in. Doing so determines the brightness of monitor pixels displaying as white.

Light is measured by the Kelvin scale. Zero degrees Kelvin is absolute zero, the point at which all molecular motion ceases. The temperature of light ranges from 1900° K for weak candlelight to 7500° K for bright daylight. Rather than attempt to determine the ultimate viewing conditions for all printed pieces, print publishers typically use a single lighting standard. In the U.S., it's 5000° K.

4. **Phosphors**

Phosphors are the chemicals that coat the glass of a monitor. Setting this to the appropriate choice determines how the most saturated reds, greens, and blues appear on-screen.

5. **Ambient Light**

This option refers to the general amount of lighting in a room. If the room is dark, setting the pop-up to Low will slightly brighten an on-screen image upon conversion to CMYK. This compensates for the lighting without having to reset all the monitor parameters. Selecting High from the pop-up causes no change at all, and is the required setting for anyone using an external calibration system.

Printing Inks Setup

This dialog, along with Separation Setup, determines the output values created when an image is converted from RGB to CMYK. Photoshop also refers to the Printing Inks Setup when displaying CMYK colors on-screen in an attempt to predict the printed result.

Common Uses

- Making Photoshop aware of the ink standard used to reproduce an image
- Profiling a non-standard ink (refer to Appendix A for a full description)
- Setting a dot gain value

Common Errors

- **Choosing the incorrect ink set.** Different ink sets have different proofing requirements. Correcting a proof based on Toyo before printing in SWOP offers no realistic ground for your decisions.
- **Failing to reset any changes for future images.** Settings in the Printing Inks Setup dialog are not specific to a single image; they remain in effect until they are manually changed.

File Menu

Special Notes

- Profiles of several color printers are included in the Ink Colors pop-up, but they should only be accessed when an image will output solely to one of those devices.

- Dot gain is measured in percentages, and occurs most severely in the midtones. When you say "20% Dot Gain", you say that a 50% dot increases by 20% of its size, to 60%.

The Printing Inks Setup Dialog

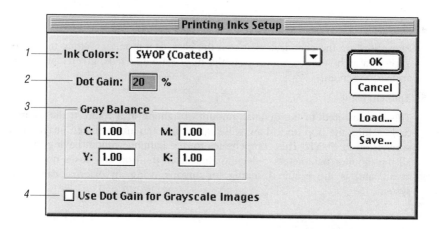

1. Ink Colors

Selecting an ink set allows Photoshop to refer to an internal model of how those particular printed inks appear. Photoshop's default is the North American standard—SWOP (Specifications for Web Offset Printing)—but it's not universal. For example, Japan uses the Toyo set and Europe uses Eurostandard. If there is any question about the type of ink used to reproduce an image on-press, consult your printer. Each standard has a setting for coated paper, uncoated paper, and newsprint. Selecting one over the others alters the Dot Gain value.

2. Dot Gain

Dot gain is the tendency of printed halftone dots to expand slightly as the ink is absorbed into the paper. If ignored, dot gain darkens any halftone reproduced on-press. The amount of the darkening depends on the absorbency of the paper—coated paper absorbs the least, uncoated paper a little more, and newsprint the most.

Selecting an ink standard automatically enters a value for dot gain. When a full-color image is converted to CMYK from RGB, you don't see this change—but when the separations are output, they are lightened slightly to compensate for the gain on-press. The amount depends on the ink standard and paper type.

This value can be changed independently of the Ink Colors pop-up, so consult your printer to determine the expected amount to dot gain.

3. **Gray Balance**

These values affect the appearance of neutral gray, and should only be changed on the advice of your printer.

Gray balance refers to the CMYK combinations that produce tone unaffected by a color bias. This is easy in RGB color space: equal brightness values create neutral grays. Flaws inherent in process inks make that same approach impossible when printing full color images. In theory, equal amounts of cyan, magenta, and yellow match the same percentage of black. Because of imperfections in the inks, the amount of cyan must be slightly increased. If it's not, your printed images have a colored cast. Photoshop understands this relationship and acts accordingly when an RGB image is converted to CMYK.

4. **Use Dot Gain for Grayscale Images**

Grayscale images are also subject to dot gain. Clicking this button tells Photoshop to attempt to display the projected change. It's only an on-screen change, however; the idea is that you can correct the darkened image, compensating for the darkening the image will receive on-press. Unless your monitor is extremely well-calibrated, this option does little good and should be left off.

See Also

Appendix A (File: Color Settings: **Printing Inks Setup**)
File: Color Settings: **Separation Setup**

Separation Setup

This dialog has the greatest impact on RGB-to-CMYK conversion, and therefore the reproduction of these images on-press. It controls two functions: the total ink is used to reproduce an image on-press, and the information written to the black channel of a CMYK image.

Common Uses

Refer to Appendix A for a full description of the following:

• Setting up RGB to CMYK conversion profiles

Common Errors

Failing to reset any changes for future images. Settings in the Separation Setup dialog are not specific to a single image; they remain in effect until they are manually changed.

Special Notes

• The Black Generation setting impacts the use of CMYK information throughout Photoshop. For example, the default black of an image in CMYK mode is

File Menu

directly based on the current setting. (See The Color Controls: **Default Colors** for more information.)

• As abstract as they may seem, you must apply a UCR or GCR value when converting an RGB image to CMYK. By doing so, you determine that equal values of cyan, magenta, and yellow—which form gray—are replaced with black ink. This cuts down ink density, material costs, and drying time.

The Separation Setup Dialog

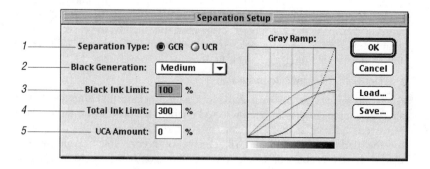

1. Separation Type

This command controls the generation of black information. Two methods are available:

UCR

UCR stands for Under Color Removal, because color is literally being removed from under a gray area. UCR dictates that cyan, magenta, and yellow are replaced with black only in neutral areas—so when CMY combine to make gray, it's replaced with a black screen. For example, a color consisting of C: 20, M: 20, and Y: 20 is replaced with K: 20. This typically removes unneeded ink in the shadows, but leaves the remaining image full of CMY ink. This makes images affected by UCR more difficult to control on-press.

GCR

GCR stands for Gray Component Replacement, which takes UCR one step further. It replaces all of the gray it can, swapping any areas consisting of gray combinations with black information. For example, a color consisting of C: 50, M: 30, and Y: 20 could become C: 30, M: 10, and K: 20. This is more powerful, but can be destructive to the image. If you replace every single gray with black ink, the human eye begins to notice the difference in the lightest tones. To counter this effect, use the remaining controls.

2. Black Generation

This setting determines the black highlight, or where substitution will begin. For example, choosing Light from the pop-up sets the starting point at 40%, meaning all tones under 40% are left unchanged. The values for each option are as follows:

- **None**: no black is generated, resulting in a CMY image

- **Light**: black generation starts at 40%

- **Medium**: black generation starts at 20%

- **Heavy**: black generation starts at 10%

- **Maximum**: black is substituted for all colors.

Choosing Custom from the pop-up allows you to set a custom black genera-tion curve. Edited similarly to the curves used to correct color, use it to manually determine the extent that black replaces the remaining CMY compo-nents. Typically, these are created for difficult-to-print *high-key* images like white, snowy mountain tops or *low-key* images, like dark cityscapes. High-key images, with little information, tend to lack color. Low-key images tend to be too rich in black. Use the Image: **Histogram** dialog to evaluate image key.

3. **Black Ink Limit**

This value states the darkest percentage of black that Photoshop allows to exist. Where Black Generation was used to define the black highlight, this value determines the black shadow. Typically, the only time to reduce this value is when you're reducing the total ink limit. Otherwise, leave it at 100%. Any necessary changes can be made during color correction.

4. **Total Ink Limit**

This value sets the maximum amount of ink laid down on-press. This decision is based on the type of press being used as well as the material receiving the ink. Too much ink, and it shows through the material. Too little, and the colors are not as rich as they could be. If the amount is set to below Photo-shop's default—we actually recommend that anyone unsure of their press requirements set this value to 280%—it is wise to reduce the Black Ink Limit to 90%.

5. **UCA Amount**

Short for Under Color Addition, it compensates for the rather severe effects of GCR. UCA replaces some of the black removed from neutral shadow areas. Even at the highest value, it only affects tones darker than 50%, so you still receive the benefit of reduced ink coverage. Typically, only 10–20% of UCA is required.

See Also

Appendix A (File: Color Settings: **Separation Setup**)
File: Color Settings: **Printing Inks Setup**
File: Color Settings: **Separation Tables**
Color Controls: **Default Colors**
Image: Mode: **RGB** and **CMYK**
Image: **Histogram**

File Menu

Separation Tables

After you've established settings in the Printing Inks Setup and Separation Setup dialogs, this command allows you to save those changes as a separation table for future use.

When you have a similar project in the future, load the table and all the settings in all the dialogs reset automatically.

File: Quit
(Command) [Control]-Q

This commands forces the operating system to discontinue running Photoshop. If any open images are unsaved, you're prompted to Save, Don't Save, or Cancel.

CHAPTER 9

The Edit Menu

Edit: Undo/Redo
(Command) [Control]-Z

Undo works the same as in any other program: selecting it reverses, or "undoes," the last applied command. Unlike other graphics programs, Photoshop has only one Undo level, so only the very last command can be reversed. Choosing Undo again reapplies the command. Toggling back and forth between Undo and Redo is the only way to see the before-and-after effects of a command on an entire image.

Common Errors

- **Attempting to undo a command after choosing Select: None.** After applying a command or filter to a selection, many users click on-screen to make the selection disappear. If you try to undo the command, you can't—the selection path just reappears. Clicking to make a selection disappear is the same as choosing Select: **None**, an impossible command. To temporarily hide a selection from view, choose View: **Hide Edges**.

- **Attempting to undo multiple commands.** If you're about to apply a series of commands to an image, the following precautions allow you to compensate for Photoshop's lack of multiple Undo levels:

  - Save the image before applying the next suite of commands. You can always select File: **Revert** if you're dissatisfied with the results.

  - Make a copy of the image using Image: **Duplicate** and apply the commands here. If dissatisfied, close the copy without saving. If satisfied, close the original, save the copy, and continue editing.

  - Take a snapshot of the image using Edit: **Take Snapshot**. The **Rubber Stamp Tool** (see Chapter 2, *The Paint Tools*) and Edit: **Fill** command can later refer to this information.

Special Notes

- Use Filter: **Fade** to partially undo the effect of a command. There, you can move a slider to blend an applied command from zero (total Undo) to 100% (no Undo) with the previous image.

- Edit: **Undo** applies to all paint, selection, and palette-based commands. Commands that can't be reversed include the following:

  - Commands that create or manipulate information on the hard drive, such as File: **Open, Close, Save, Import,** and **Export.**

  - Splitting and merging channels from the **Channels Palette** (see Chapter 21) submenu.

  - Deleting the contents of RAM using the Edit: **Purge** commands.

  - Edit: **Take Snapshot**—this way, you can apply a command, take a snapshot, then undo the command.

See Also

The **Rubber Stamp Tool**
Edit: **Fill**
Edit: **Take Snapshot**
Select: **None**
View: **Hide Edges**

Edit: Cut
(Command) [Control]-X

Edit: **Cut** deletes image information from view while copying it to the Clipboard. Later, you can reapply the information using Edit: **Paste.** This command is only available when an open image contains an active selection, or when text in a field is highlighted.

Common Errors

Using Edit: **Cut** instead of Edit: **Copy.** Copying leaves the selected information intact; cutting removes it from the image.

Special Notes

- Edit: **Cut** only works on the current layer. To copy information on multiple layers to the Clipboard, use Edit: **Copy Merged.**

- Cutting and pasting a selection is the same as choosing Layer: New: **Layer Via Cut,** but with one big difference—cutting and pasting places the new image in the dead center of a new layer; Layer Via Cut maintains the selection's original position.

See Also

Edit: **Copy**
Edit: **Copy Merged**
Edit: **Paste**
Layer: New: **Layer Via Cut**

Edit: Copy
(Command) [Control]-C

Edit: **Copy** saves a selected area to the Clipboard, a section of "short-term" memory that applications use as an invisible holding area. You can apply that information to the same image or a new image using Edit: **Paste**. Although this command is called *copy*, that term only applies to the act of copying to the Clipboard. To create a copy of a selected image area on-screen, you must select a paste command after copying to the Clipboard. Unlike Edit: **Cut**, copied information is not removed from the image.

Common Errors

Leaving large amounts of information in the Clipboard. If you copy an image larger than the amount of RAM available to Photoshop, then the application is forced to use virtual memory, considerably slowing the computer. This can happen when copying large portions of print-specific graphics, which easily grow to dozens of megabytes in size. Unless your machine has RAM to spare, select Edit: Purge: **Clipboard** after copying and pasting large images.

Special Notes

- Edit: **Copy** only works on the current layer. To copy information on multiple layers to the Clipboard, use Edit: **Copy Merged**.

- Information copied to the Clipboard is dynamic, meaning active RAM is required to store it. After pasting the contents of the Clipboard, the information remains in memory until one of two things happens:

  – Another selected area is copied, replacing the previous one.

  – The contents of the Clipboard are purged (or deleted) using Edit: Purge: **Clipboard**.

- Copy a selection from one open image to another by holding down the (Command) [Control] key and dragging. The selection will be placed into a new layer. Watch out, though—if you don't hold down the key, you only drag the selection path to the second image, not the selected pixels.

Edit: Copy Merged
(Command-Shift) [Control-Shift]-X

Where Edit: **Copy** only copies the information in the current layer, this command copies all the visible information in an active selection, regardless of the number of layers involved. The individual layers are not maintained; when you paste the information into a new layer or new image, everything is reduced to one "merged" layer.

Edit: Paste
(Command) [Control]-V

Pasting places the contents of the Clipboard into the active image.

Common Uses

Refer to Appendix A for full descriptions of the following:

- Pasting pixels into the same image
- Pasting pixels into a second image
- Pasting shapes from Adobe Illustrator
- Pasting info from other pixel-based applications
- Pasting text from one field to another

Common Errors

- **Failing to account for different color modes.** When pasting pixels from a different mode, they assume the mode of the image being pasted into. For example, RGB colors convert to process percentages if pasted into a CMYK file, or convert to a limited palette when pasted into an Indexed Color file.

- **Failing to account for different resolutions.** When copying and pasting from images of different resolutions, the results can be surprising. For example, if you paste an inch-wide selection from a 72-ppi image into a 300-ppi image, it pastes as 0.24 inches wide. On the other hand, if you paste a 300-ppi selection into a 72-ppi image, it appears so large that it may not fit in the image window. This is because Photoshop maintains the exact number of pixels in the selection rather than attempt to create new pixels.

- **Attempting to paste type from Illustrator without converting to paths.** Before copying type in Illustrator, always convert it to outlines using Illustrator's **Type: Create Outlines** command. If you fail to convert the type, you can't Paste as Paths, even though Photoshop appears to go through the motions. Converted type also renders more accurately when you Paste as Pixels.

Special Notes

- To automatically place the contents of a selection into a new layer without using Copy or Paste, choose Layer: New: **Layer Via Copy** or **Layer Via Cut**. The info in each new layer retains its original position.

- Photoshop will not paste into an existing layer. To achieve this effect, select the existing layer in the Layers palette before choosing Edit: **Paste**. Immediately after the new layer appears, choose Layer: **Merge Down**. The new layer combines with the one underneath.

- Text copied from another program retains no formatting when pasted into Photoshop. If you want to paste formatted type, create it in Adobe Illustrator.

See Also

Appendix A (Edit: **Paste**)
Edit: **Cut**
Edit: **Copy**
Layer: New: **Layer Via Copy** and **Layer Via Cut**

Edit: Paste Into
(Command-Shift) [Control-Shift]-V

This command allows you to paste the contents of the Clipboard into an active selection. This is really an alternative method of creating a layer mask. Here, the selection acts like a mask, letting only a portion of the information you paste show through. When you choose this command, two things happen: the pasted selection is placed into a new layer, and the selection is automatically converted to a layer mask.

Special Notes

- By holding down the (Option) [Alt] key while applying this command, you invert the mask, creating the impression of pasting behind the active selection.

- Depending on how you manipulate the **Layers Palette**, you can move the pasted information in two different ways:

  If you activate the link between the image and layer mask thumbnails, you can reposition the image as well as the mask. If you deactivate the link, you can reposition the image without moving the mask.

Edit: Clear

Choosing Edit: **Clear** is the same as pressing the Delete (or Backspace) key.

Special Notes

- Clearing a selection on an image layer with Preserve Transparency unchecked fills the selection with transparent pixels.

Edit Menu

- Clearing a selection on the background layer or on a layer with Preserve Transparency checked fills the selection with the Background Color.

Edit: Fill

This command fills a selection or layer with colored pixels. The fill information can be based on the foreground or background color, a pattern defined using Edit: **Define Pattern**, a snapshot defined using Edit: **Take Snapshot**, or the last saved version of the file. All of these options can be applied at different opacities and blend modes.

Common Uses

- **Filling an active selection.** The most common use of the Fill command, it allows you to accurately determine which portion of an image will be filled and which will left alone.

- **Filling a layer without a selection.** Applying the Fill command with no active selection fills the entire layer.

- **Filling a layer with Preserve Transparency checked.** If you have a portion of an image residing in a separate layer, you can fill its exact shape without creating a selection.

Refer to Appendix A for full descriptions of the following:

- Filling with saved information
- Filling with a snapshot
- Ghosting
- Creating resizeable ghosts

Common Errors

Using the Black option to fill an area in a CMYK image. Filling with Black in a CMYK image creates a total ink density of 400—far too high for any printing process. If you need to fill part of an image with black, select the default black (which gives you lower percentages of C, M, and Y) and fill with the foreground color.

Special Notes

- For the most part, the Opacity option is a holdover from earlier versions of Photoshop. The problem is, once you apply a semi-opaque fill, you can't increase the opacity later on. You have more control if you fill at 100% Opacity, then use the slider in the **Layers Palette** (see Chapter 20) to reset the value.

- Even though you can select a blend mode from the Fill dialog, we recommend filling with Normal and applying a blend mode from the **Layers Palette** (see Chapter 20). This way, you can preview the blend before setting it in stone.

- Normally, you don't fill with Black, 50% Gray, or White for the visible color effect. These are neutral colors, used in conjunction with the blend modes applied in the **Layers Palette** (see Chapter 20). For example, if you fill a layer with 50% Gray and apply the Soft Light blend mode, the neutral color is hidden from view. However, if you edit that layer with filters and adjustments, the new tonal variations affect the underlying layers (see Layer: New: **New Layer** for more information).

- Try using the following Fill shortcuts:

    - **Access the Fill dialog.** Press Shift-Delete.

    - **Fill with background color.** Press (Command) [Control]-Delete.

    - **Fill with background color, preserving transparency.** Press (Command-Shift) [Control-Shift]-Delete.

    - **Fill with foreground color.** Press (Option) [Alt]-Delete.

    - **Fill with foreground color, preserving transparency.** Press (Option-Shift) [Alt-Shift]-Delete.

    - **Fill a selection with transparent pixels.** Make a selection on an image layer and press Delete. (If the selection is on the background layer, pressing Delete fills with the background color.)

The Fill Dialog

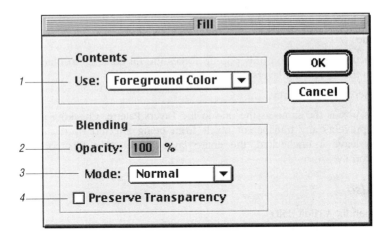

1. **Use**

    The options in this pop-up determine the information used to fill a selection or layer:

    Foreground Color
    This option fills with the current foreground color.

    Background Color
    This option fills with the current background color.

Pattern

This option fills with a repeating tile that you create using the Edit: **Define Pattern** command. It is not available unless you've already defined a pattern.

Saved

This option fills with the last saved version of a file.

Snapshot

This option fills with image information captured using Edit: **Take Snapshot**. It is not available unless you've already taken a snapshot.

Black

This option fills with the darkest possible color. In a grayscale image, the value is K: 100. In an RGB image, it fills with R: 0, G: 0, and B: 0. In a CMYK image, choosing Black fills with 100% of each component color.

50% Gray

This option fills with a neutral value of exactly half of the darkest possible color. In a grayscale image, that value is K: 50. In an RGB image, it's R: 128, G: 128, B: 128. In a CMYK image, it fills with 50% of each component color.

White

This option fills with the lightest possible color.

2. **Opacity**

By lowering this value, you decrease the opacity of the fill, letting the underlying information show through.

3. **Mode**

Selecting a mode from this pop-up forces the fill contents to blend differently with the underlying layers.

4. **Preserve Transparency**

This box is the same as the one in the **Layers Palette**. Checking it before you fill prevents any transparent pixels from being affected by the command. If you leave it unchecked, the entire layer or selection fills completely and uniformly.

See Also

Appendix A (Edit: **Fill**)
Edit: **Take Snapshot**
Edit: **Define Pattern**
Layer: New: **New Layer**
The Layers Palette

Edit: Stroke

When you stroke part of an image, you apply a colored border of a specified width. Edit: **Stroke** applies that border two different ways:

• Around the edge of an active selection

• Around the outer edge of an image layer (no selection required)

Common Uses

Refer to Appendix A for full descriptions of the following:

- Stroking a selection edge
- Stroking the contents of a layer
- Framing an entire image
- Creating outlined type

Common Errors

Applying a stroke with Preserve Transparency checked. If the box is checked in the Stroke dialog or the **Layers Palette**, the Center and Outside options do not apply properly.

Special Notes

- When editing the background layer, Edit: **Stroke** is not available unless you have an active selection.

- Photoshop can only apply a 16-pixel stroke. For wider strokes, divide the value in half and apply three strokes: one inside, one outside, and one centered. The center stroke compensates for the anti-aliased fringe that occurs between the first two.

- When you apply an odd-numbered pixel width, Photoshop cannot precisely center the stroke over the selection path. The extra pixel is always placed inside the selection. For example, a centered stroke width of five pixels places two pixels outside the selection, three pixels inside. This is only noticeable in low-resolution images.

The Stroke Dialog

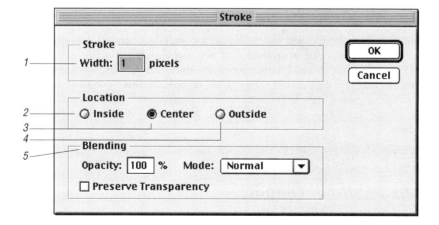

1. **Stroke**

   Apply a stroke thickness in the Width field. In other programs, you enter stroke values in point sizes. In Photoshop, you must enter a number of pixels. Therefore, a five-pixel stroke appears much thicker in a 72-ppi web graphic than in a 300-ppi print graphic. Often, the only way to determine the right thickness of a stroke is to apply a series of different values, choosing Edit: **Undo** after each one, until the correct value is found.

2. **Inside**

   This option applies a stroke inside the selection path or layer.

3. **Center**

   This option applies a stroke that straddles the selection outline or layer.

4. **Outside**

   This option applies a stroke outside the selection path or layer.

5. **Blending**

   The Opacity, Mode, and Preserve Transparency options function the same as the Edit: **Fill** dialog, described previously in this chapter.

Edit: Create Publisher

Available only on the Macintosh platform, Publish and Subscribe allows you to create a dynamic link between Photoshop and the images you import into another application. Using this feature, multiple users access (or Subscribe to) image files made available over a network. When a graphic is updated, the changes automatically appear in every document containing it.

It never caught on, mainly because it appeals to a very specialized use: editing information embedded in documents shared over a network, using a suite of software that supports this feature. Even then, you'd have to be willing to redefine your work habits to accommodate what is, at best, an unnecessarily complex process.

Publish and Subscribe will never impact its intended market—fast-paced print-publishing systems like magazines and newspapers—but it could enjoy a small resurgence on Mac-driven intranet networks. Here, different users within the same company can update text and images used by time-sensitive corporate documents stored on a central server. These documents remain available electronically to the rest of the company, and whenever one is opened, all the new changes are present.

If your work does not specifically call for this feature, ignore it.

Edit: Publisher Options

In this dialog, you determine whether a published edition is updated manually or automatically upon saving. By default, it updates automatically. When you specify

---

manual updating, the edition is updated only when you click Send Publisher Now in the Publisher Options dialog.

To cancel the edition and simply use the original Photoshop image, click Cancel Publisher. The edition is removed from the hard drive.

Edit: Define Pattern

Use this command to turn a rectangular Marquee selection into a pattern, or a repeating series of tiles.

Defining a pattern is simple: draw a rectangular marquee around the area you wish to use as a pattern, and choose Edit: **Define Pattern**. The pattern is stored in RAM—ready to use—until you define a new pattern, delete the current pattern from RAM by choosing Edit: Purge: **Pattern**, or quit Photoshop.

Common Uses

Refer to Appendix A for full descriptions of the following:

• Loading a predefined pattern

• Defining a pattern with non-adjacent edges

• Defining a non-continuous pattern

• Defining a simple seamless texture

• Defining seamless image patterns

• Defining seamless patterns using third-party software

• Defining patterns containing transparent pixels

• Defining a custom pattern for web graphics

Common Errors

Attempting to define a pattern with the incorrect selection tool. Patterns are defined only with an unfeathered rectangular selection. If you use any other selection tool, the command is not available.

Special Notes

• Patterns can be accessed by three tools or commands: Edit: **Fill**, which can fill a layer or selection with a pattern; the **Rubber Stamp Tool**, which can paint with a pattern; and Image: Mode: **Bitmap**, which can use a pattern as a custom halftone screen when you convert an image from Grayscale to Bitmap.

• Before you create a pattern, you must have some sense of how it's going to be used. As evidenced by the number of available techniques, one simple pattern does not satisfy all purposes.

Edit Menu

See Also

Appendix A (Edit: **Define Pattern**)
The Rubber Stamp Tool
Edit: **Fill**
Edit: Purge: **Pattern**
Image: Mode: **Bitmap**

Edit: Take Snapshot

A snapshot is a copy of the entire visible image, at the same resolution, stored in RAM for future reference. Using snapshots, you can undo a series of commands by restoring all or part of an image to its last saved version.

Using snapshots is similar to filling with information from the last saved version of a file, but is much more flexible. You can take a snapshot at any time, without saving or additional editing.

Common Uses

* **Filling a selection or layer with previously affected color information.** In the Fill dialog, select Snapshot from the Contents pop-up.

* **Retouching an image using previously affected color information.** In the **Rubber Stamp Tool** Options Palette, choose From Snapshot from the Options pop-up.

Special Notes

In an image containing multiple layers, Edit: **Take Snapshot** records the selected layer. To take a snapshot of all visible layers, see Edit: **Take Merged Snapshot**.

See Also

The Rubber Stamp Tool
Edit: **Fill**
Edit: **Take Merged Snapshot**
Edit: Purge: **Snapshot**

Edit: Take Merged Snapshot

Beyond the ability to take a snapshot of multiple layers, snapshots created using this command are identical to the ones made using Edit: **Take Snapshot**. To prevent any layer from being included in the snapshot, hide them from view before selecting the command.

Edit: Purge

Whenever you copy any information to RAM, it takes up space. If too much active RAM is occupied, Photoshop uses virtual memory, or megabytes from the hard drive, to compensate. This seriously hinders the performance of your workstation, so make it a point to purge the contents of RAM when you no longer need that information.

Undo

Photoshop always retains a copy of an image as it existed before the last command. Whenever you choose Edit: **Undo**, Photoshop merely replaces the visible image with this invisible Undo image. Selecting Edit: Purge: **Undo** removes this image from RAM, but it will be replaced as soon as the next command is applied.

Clipboard

Purging the Clipboard deletes any information placed there by the Edit: **Cut** or Edit: **Copy** commands.

Pattern

Purging the Pattern deletes any information created using Edit: **Define Pattern**.

Snapshot

Purging the snapshot deletes any information created using the Edit: **Take Snapshot** or Edit: **Take Merged Snapshot** commands.

CHAPTER 10

The Image Menu

Image: Mode Overview

In a Photoshop image, color is defined by two things:

- **Its color model.** This is a predetermined range of color used by Photoshop to generate a color image.

- **Its color mode.** This, on the other hand, provides a file structure that allows that range of color to be displayed, edited, and—if necessary—printed.

Photoshop Color Models

Color models are only used to generate full-color images. In an attempt to compensate for our very subjective perception of color, two- or three-dimensional models are used to mathematically represent a color's position in a particular space. This method ensures that color information is accurately communicated between your computers, software, and peripheral devices.

In Photoshop, images with 256 colors or less—including Bitmap, Grayscale, Duotone, and Indexed Color images—are not represented by any particular model.

The RGB (and CMY) Model

The RGB model is used to reproduce the spectrum of visible light. Any object that transmits, filters, or reads light—your monitor, your scanner, and the human eye are good examples—is based on this model.

RGB color has one major strength and one major flaw. On one hand, this model is extremely useful for full-color image editing; it has a wide range of colors, and you can adjust RGB images using nearly all of Photoshop's 24-bit color commands. Unfortunately, RGB is a *device-dependent* model, meaning that regardless of the mathematical definition of a color, the way it appears on-screen depends on the hardware used to display it. A variety of environmental factors, including a monitor's age and the amount of ambient light in the room, make consistent color from device to device impossible.

RGB is also known as the *additive primary* model. Primary, because red, green, and blue are the dominant, or primary, colors of the visible spectrum. Additive, because black is the absence of all light—you must add higher levels of red, green, and blue to create lighter colors.

The model opposite RGB is CMY, or the *subtractive* primary model. The CMY model pertains to reflected light, or the colors manifest in printed inks, photographic dyes, and colored toner. It's a subtractive model, because in this case, black is the full presence of all colors—you must subtract levels of cyan, magenta, and yellow to create lighter colors.

Because RGB and CMY are the inverse of each other, they have a special relationship. If you turn this information into a color wheel, the colors alternate between RGB and CMY (See Figure 10-1). If you combine two RGB colors, you get a CMY color. If you combine two CMY colors, you get an RGB color. For example, red is described in the CMY model as the combination of magenta and yellow; magenta is described in the RGB model as the combination of red and blue.

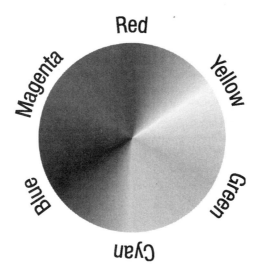

Figure 10-1: RGB-CMY color wheel

Refer again to the color wheel. When you combine two colors of one model to create a color in another, there is one color left over. This is known as the new color's *complement.* For example, magenta and yellow combine to form red—cyan, therefore, is the complement of red.

Understanding component and complementary colors is useful when scanning or adjusting a color image. When scanning an object that you perceive to be too yellow, you can adjust the scanning software to reduce the amount of yellow information in the scan. Problem is, RGB scanners have no yellow controls—only red, green, and blue. You can do one of two things:

- Yellow is a combination of red and green. Reducing those two colors is the same as reducing yellow.

- The complement of yellow is blue. Increasing blue is the same as decreasing yellow.

If an RGB image is destined for print, you must convert its additive color values to CMY, a purely subtractive model. This model has a much smaller range of colors, and Photoshop must compensate for certain on-press imperfections by adding a fourth color: black.

The CMYK Model

The CMYK color model represents the four colors used to reproduce full-color images: cyan, magenta, yellow, and black. Since all printed colors reflect light, this model is based on the subtractive primary colors, described above. In theory, CMY inks are sufficient to reproduce the full range of colors—in fact, color photography is *trichromatic*, meaning that only cyan, magenta, and yellow dyes are used. This is impossible in print. CMY inks invariably contain slight impurities, and different types of paper stock absorb different levels of light, affecting your perception of color. As a result, combining 100% levels of CMY inks produces a muddy brown color instead of black. To compensate, black ink is added to balance the range of colors.

In the CMYK acronym, black is represented by a "K" because it was originally referred to as a "Key" color. Traditionally, black ink was the first color laid down on paper, providing the basis for registering the remaining inks.

Because CMYK represents a much smaller range of color than RGB, it is impossible to reproduce all the colors that appear on your monitor. Therefore, when you convert an RGB image to CMYK in order to reproduce the colors in print, many of the tones are altered.

The Lab Model

The Lab color model is often referred to as "CIE Lab," because it was created by the *Commission Internationale d'Eclairage* (CIE). Two features make this model stand out:

- In theory, this model represents the entire range of color discernible by the human eye.

- This model is device-independent, allowing you to maintain accurate color information across different platforms and hardware setups.

It's not based around combinations of specific colors, like RGB or CMYK. Instead, image color is defined by its actual appearance, as determined by three factors: the overall lightness values, all color components ranging from green to red, and all color components ranging from yellow to blue.

This approach gives the Lab color space a wider range of colors than RGB and CMYK. Unfortunately, Lab is also complex and non-intuitive. Few individuals prefer to work in this model, but its wide range makes it the choice of many high-end color specialists and color management systems. Lab is frequently used for stock images on Photo CD, where the end user converts the image to RGB or CMYK, depending on the ultimate use of the image.

The HSB Model

This model is not represented by a color mode. Rather, the HSB color space defines color using three criteria that people often intuitively use when describing color—hue, saturation, and brightness (see Figure 10-2):

Hue

    Hue is a particular color, such as blue or red. If you picture HSB space as a three-dimensional cylinder, the visible spectrum of colors encircle its circumference. Each color is assigned an angle. Red is positioned at 0°, and the remaining colors are arranged the same as the RGB/CMY color wheel: cyan, the complement of red, is at 180°. Yellow is at 60°, green is at 120°, blue is at 240°, and magenta is at 300°.

Saturation

    Saturation is the intensity of a color. The difference between a soft, pastel orange and the blaze orange of a hunter's cap is the amount of saturation. In the cylindrical model, saturation increases as a color is positioned closer to the outer edge. In this model, a saturation value of 0 *desaturates* the color, or reduces it to a value of gray. Which level of gray that is depends on the color's brightness level.

Brightness

    Brightness is the tone of a color, or how light or dark that color is. Decreasing the brightness darkens a color, or creates what you perceive to be a deeper tone. Refer again to the cylindrical model: at one end, the brightness is at full value; at the other, all colors are reduced to black.

This system is primarily referential, as opposed to the RGB or CMYK spaces. Those color models are actually instructions that tell a monitor or printer how to construct a color, while HSB controls are available in every color mode. They are accessed in the Color Picker, the Image: Adjust: **Hue/Saturation** dialog, and the Image: Adjust: **Replace Color** dialog.

Color Gamut

The range of a color model is also referred to as its *gamut*. Of the models described above, Lab color has the largest gamut, encompassing all the possible values of RGB color space. RGB, in turn, displays many more colors than CMYK, the smallest gamut.

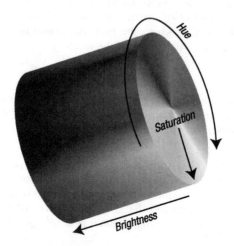

Figure 10-2: The HSB model

Differences between color gamuts are always apparent when you convert an image from Lab or RGB to CMYK space. When you convert to CMYK, you ask Photoshop to describe the former pixels with a combination of CMYK values based on the information established in the File: Color Settings: **Separation Setup** dialog. If a color falls outside the CMYK range and cannot be described, it's pushed back to the closest color on the borderline. Unfortunately, this means two things:

- Many shades and subtle differences in tone are lost. Two slightly different RGB colors can even be changed to the same CMYK color.

- You only get one chance to move between color spaces. Once the colors are clipped by converting to CMYK, you cannot regain them by switching back to the previous model.

A color gamut should not be confused with the number of tones its mode can mathematically reproduce. An image in Lab space, the largest color gamut, is capable of displaying six million different colors. Even though RGB has a smaller gamut, an image in this mode can display 16.7 million colors. And a CMYK image, with the smallest gamut, is mathematically capable of displaying 100 million colors. These extreme numbers are just abstract side effects of the file structure required to display a particular color space.

Color Depth

A color mode is actually a file structure. Different types of color image can be displayed only if a file contains the appropriate components. This boils down to two things: an image's pixel depth and the number of color channels.

Pixel depth describes the color potential of a single pixel. In any Photoshop image, each pixel can be only one color. As far as your computer is concerned, color is defined by binary data, or strings of ones and zeros. Each character is called a *bit*. The more bits used to describe a pixel, the more possible colors that pixel can be:

1-bit Color
The most common example of 1-bit color is black and white line art. Its pixels are one of only two colors: black or white. Here, black pixels are described with a "1", white pixels are described with a "0". There are fewer than 256 colors, so only one color channel is required.

Since so little information is required to display these colors, 1-bit images have the smallest relative file size.

8-bit Color
The perfect example of 8-bit color is a Grayscale image. Here, each pixel is described with eight bits of information. There are 256 possible combinations of ones and zeros in a string of eight characters, so there are 256 possible levels of gray. This is the maximum amount of information that can be contained in a single color channel—to display full color, an image requires additional channels.

Eight-bit images contain eight times the amount of information as a 1-bit image. Therefore, a similarly configured image is eight times as large.

24-bit Color
An RGB image is made of three internal Grayscale channels, each one representing a different color. Now each pixel is described by three 8-bit values—or 24 total bits.

Containing three times the amount of information as a single-channel, 8-bit image, 24-bit images are three times as large.

Pixel depth should not be confused with the bit depth of a scanner. An RGB image may be limited to 8 bits of information per color channel, but many scanners acquire up to 16 bits per channel (which translates into a 48-bit scanner). This extra information is not written directly into the file, but it almost always results in a higher-quality scan.

Establishing Color Mode

An image never automatically appears in the appropriate color mode. After understanding the differences between Photoshop's supported color models, you must first determine the appropriate mode, then create it.

Consider the following factors when determining an image's mode:

- **The ultimate use of the image.** Just as an image must be saved in the right file format, it must also exist in the right mode. RGB files, for example, cannot separate on an imagesetter; CMYK images cannot display on the Web.

- **The number of available colors.** One-color images require a mode that displays only one color. On the other hand, when working with full-color images, you usually edit in a mode with a wide range of colors (like RGB) before converting to a smaller gamut (like CMYK).

- **The editing tools available to that mode.** Not all commands are available to all modes. This largely depends on the number of colors in an image. If you're editing an RGB image, which can contain 16.7 million colors, you have access to all filters and color adjustment tools. If you're editing a Bitmap image, which contains only one color, you can't use any of those commands.

Image: Mode: Bitmap

Images in Bitmap mode are 1-bit color, so pixels are either black or white. Most often, Bitmap images are used to reproduce solid black line art in print.

Common Uses

• Creating line art for print

• Generating specialized, one-color effects

• Creating small-sized, one-color web graphics

Common Errors

• **Mistakenly saving line art as EPS files.** When line art is saved as a TIFF and imported into another program, the white pixels are transparent. If the same file is saved as an EPS, the pixels appear white unless Transparent Whites is checked in the EPS dialog. Unless you have a specific reason for saving as an EPS—for example, you're using an older version of Adobe Illustrator, which does not support TIFF images—save all line art as TIFFs.

• **Using the Halftone command to produce an actual halftone screen.** Despite the name, this method should not be used in lieu of an actual halftone screen. When printing a Grayscale image, screens are automatically applied by the output device and controlled by either Photoshop's File: Page Setup: **Screens** dialog or the program printing the file. Halftone dots with a frequency above 65 lpi must be comprised of extremely tiny printer dots (at least 1200 dpi, but most imagesetters today output at 2400 dpi). Unless a Grayscale image is scanned at an ultra-high resolution—which produces unwieldy file sizes and limited control—this option cannot effectively reproduce a frequency above 53 lpi.

Special Notes

• Only Grayscale images can be converted to Bitmap mode. To convert a color image to Bitmap, convert to Grayscale first, then to Bitmap.

• Depending on the artwork involved, Bitmap line art offers several print-oriented advantages over modes containing more tones or color:

They're not halftoned. Every pixel in a line art file is printed directly to an output device, so no information is lost due to screening. This allows you to print finely detailed, crisp edges. It also means that line art for print must exist at much higher resolutions (up to 1200 ppi) to avoid visible pixelization.

They can be recolored in a page layout program. Black is not your only color option for line art. As long as it's saved as a TIFF, you can apply a different color to it in your page layout program.

Black line art doesn't have to be trapped. If black line art is placed on top of a colored background in page layout program, it automatically overprints, removing the need for trapping.

The Bitmap Dialog

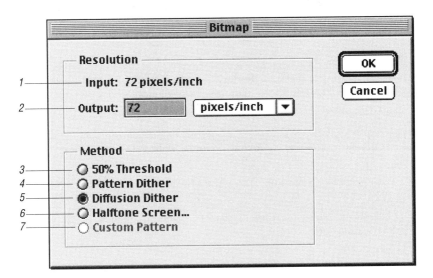

1. Input

    This value is unchangeable; it states the current image resolution in pixels per inch.

2. Output

    By changing the value in this field, you re-interpolate the image resolution when you click OK to convert the image. This option is nowhere near as effective as it sounds. In theory, you can convert a low-resolution Grayscale image to a high-resolution line-art image, concealing the jagged edges by greatly reducing pixel size. Setting a higher value indeed raises the resolution, but the relative pixel size remains the same. The jagged edges remain, but each one is simply made up of more pixels. For best results, ignore this setting and use a higher resolution when creating the original image.

3. 50% Threshold

    This conversion method changes all image tones into pure black or white. It makes no attempts to shade or simulating tone, producing the same effect as a 1-bit line art scan. It does this by applying a *threshold*, or a dividing line, at 50% black. All tones above 50% become black, all tones below become white. This method is appropriate for artwork containing bold, solid areas or ultra-fine details.

    If you're looking for this type of effect but don't want to change the color mode, use Image: Adjust: **Threshold**. It allows you to reposition the 50%

threshold, changing the number of tones that become black or white—and the image retains its original mode.

4. **Pattern Dither**

By *dithering* pixels, Photoshop scatters them in an attempt to simulate the tones of a Grayscale image. The Pattern method uses a predefined geometric pattern that produces awkward, blotchy results, similar to the patterns used in the earliest paint programs. Those of you wishing to simulate tone in a 1-bit image should use Diffusion Dither.

5. **Diffusion Dither**

Instead of using a pattern, this method randomizes the individual pixels to simulate tone. This method is ineffective at resolutions above 300 ppi.

6. **Halftone Screen**

This method reduces the tones of gray to a series of halftone dots. After choosing this option, set the following in the Halftone Screen dialog:

Frequency
This value determines the size of the simulated halftone dots.

Angle
This value determines the angle of the screen frequency, or the rotation of the halftone grid.

Shape
Select a halftone dot shape from this pop-up menu: Round, Diamond, Ellipse, Line, Square, or Cross.

These options only produce a simulated halftone screen, and should only be used as a special effect. If you want the appearance of halftone dots, consider applying Filter: Pixelate: **Color Halftone** to a Grayscale image, which changes the tones to smooth, anti-aliased dots without converting the color mode. The only available shape is Round, however—any other shape must be created with this dialog.

7. **Custom Pattern**

This option uses a pattern already defined using Edit: **Define Pattern** to create a customized screen. The same idea of the 50% Threshold applies here; the information is reduced to black and white, but the repeating pattern only appears in areas darker than 50% black.

See Also

File: Page Setup: **Screens**
Edit: **Define Pattern**
Image: Mode: **Grayscale**
Image: Adjust: **Threshold**
Filter: Pixelate: **Color Halftone**

Image: Mode: Grayscale

Grayscale images are also known as 8-bit color, meaning each pixel is one of 256 possible tones of gray. Once you start working with this many tones, there are two ways to interpret the information: as brightness values or output values. The method you use typically depends on whether an image is going to be used on-screen or printed.

Pixels in a Grayscale image are given a value between 0 (no brightness, or black) and 255 (full brightness, or white). The higher the value, the lighter gray the pixel is. When your monitor displays a Grayscale pixel, it's actually displaying equal values of red, green, and blue, which gives the appearance of different gray levels. Most Grayscale images, however, are intended for output and printing. To assist you, the tones are presented as output values, or halftone dot sizes from 0% (white, or no ink) to 100% (black, or full ink coverage).

Common Uses

- Generating halftones for print
- Converting a color image to be used as a printed halftone
- Creating the appearance of a black-and-white photograph for a web or on-screen graphic
- Converting a 1-bit image to a mode you can edit with a wider range of tools
- Converting a color image, en route to Bitmap mode

Common Errors

Producing a quadtone by converting a Grayscale image to CMYK. The most successful way to make this type of image is to convert to Image: Mode: **Duotone**. Otherwise, the CMYK image is larger and much less flexible than its Duotone counterpart. There are only two reasons to bypass the Duotone mode:

- If you prefer to have access to individual color curves in the Image: Adjust: **Curves** dialog when editing a quadtone.
- If you're going to be changing some part of the image to a more vivid color, which isn't possible in a duotone.

Special Notes

- Every other Photoshop mode can be converted directly to Grayscale. Conversely, a Grayscale image can be converted to any other mode.
- To reduce a color image to the appearance of a Grayscale image without changing modes, choose Image: Adjust: **Desaturate**. By applying this command to a selected area, you can reduce smaller portions of an image to gray tones.
- When you convert a color image to Grayscale, Photoshop attempts to maintain the relative brightness of the colored pixels. Since different colors can share the same brightness level, some colors may convert into the same tone of gray.

Because of this, you can't always expect a satisfactory Grayscale version of a color image. Usually, you'll need to adjust the image using Image: Adjust: **Levels** or Image: Adjust: **Curves**.

- Before converting to Grayscale, a common technique is to examine the individual color channels. Occasionally, one channel looks better than the Grayscale image that results from converting the entire file. If you choose a channel and select Image: Mode: **Grayscale**, the brightness values of that one channel are used, while the others are discarded.

The Grayscale Dialog

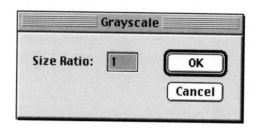

This dialog appears when you convert a Bitmap image to Grayscale.

Size Ratio

Photoshop defaults to a size ratio of 1. This means the new Grayscale image is exactly the same size as the original Bitmap. Any number higher than this produces a smaller image: a ratio of 2 reduces to 50%, a ratio of 3 reduces to 33%, 4 reduces to 25%, and so forth. You cannot enter a value less than 1 to generate a larger image.

See Also

Image: Mode: **RGB** and **CMYK**
Image: Adjust: **Levels**
Image: Adjust: **Curves**
Image: Adjust: **Desaturate**

Image: Mode: Duotone

Duotones are created to expand the tonal range of a printed halftone. The average printing press is able to reproduce 40–60 different tones of a single color ink—far less than the 256 levels for each color that Photoshop supports. In a duotone, multiple inks are used to reproduce a halftone. This broadens the number of reproducible tones, adding depth and range to the printed image.

Duotones can be made of process or spot inks, but they must begin as a Grayscale image. There are no multiple color channels; rather, the duotone retains the brightness values of the original Grayscale image. This mode simply tells output devices to print the image differently, much like the File: Page Setup: **Transfer** command. So make sure the image is adjusted and sharpened as needed before you convert.

Common Uses

Refer to Appendix A for full descriptions of the following:

- Using multiple inks to reproduce a halftone
- Controlling the application of duotone inks
- Loading Photoshop's preset duotone curves
- Renaming duotone ink colors

Common Errors

- **Incorrectly renaming a Pantone ink.** When selecting a different Pantone color, don't just change the name. Enter the color picker and define a new color, and the name will change automatically. Photoshop must know the relative brightness values of the new color in order to separate it properly.

- **Saving a duotone incorrectly.** Regardless of the type of duotone you create, two things must happen before you can import and output the image:

  If you used a duotone preset, these angles are automatically set. If you set your own curves, you must set your own screen angles in the File: Page Setup: Screens dialog. Otherwise, they all output at the same angle, ruining the image. If unsure of which angles to use, consult your printer.

  Make sure the Include Halftone Screens box is checked in the EPS options dialog. Otherwise, the colors separate at the same angle.

Special Notes

- Define the darkest color in your duotone as Ink 1—it reproduces most of the shadow detail. Ink 2 colorizes the image, providing most of the highlight information. When additional inks are added, Ink 3 warms the image by affecting the midtones, and Ink 4 primarily focuses on the three-quarter tones.

- The only time you can define a Pantone ink for output is when you create a duotone. The only alternative is a third-party plug-in like In Software's *PlateMaker.*

- The maximum number of inks in a duotone is four. Even though many designers create projects consisting of five, six, or more colors, the Duotone Options dialog cannot combine that many inks.

Image Menu

The Duotone Options Dialog

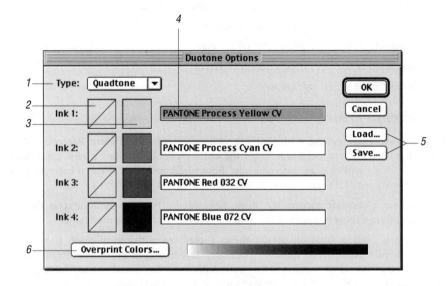

1. Type

By choosing an option from this pop-up, you determine how many inks are used to reproduce the image:

Monotone

Monotones use only one ink, typically a Pantone color, to reproduce a halftone.

Usually, there's no need to create a monotone in Photoshop. If you save a Grayscale image as a TIFF and import it into a page layout program, you can recolor it with any color defined in the program.

The only reason to make a monotone is if you want to recolor a halftone, but you have to save it as an EPS. This happens for one of two reasons: if you import the image into a program that doesn't support TIFF images, or if the image already contains a PostScript command, such as a transfer function or clipping path.

Duotone

Although Photoshop refers to all images in this mode as duotones, that term really describes images reproduced with two inks. The majority of duotones use black as one of the two colors.

Tritone

Tritones use three different inks to reproduce a halftone.

Quadtone

Quadtones use four inks. The majority of them use combinations of cyan, magenta, yellow, and black to reproduce a halftone, although combinations of spot inks are possible.

2. Curve

The distribution of each ink is controlled by a gamma curve, which works the same as File: Page Setup: **Transfer** or Image: Adjust: **Curves**. Since two or more colors are going to be combined, they must be combined intelligently. If you don't adjust the curves, equal amounts of both inks are printed in all areas of the image, causing it to shift and darken significantly. Manually adjusting duotone inks is a complex science—they are difficult at best to proof, and standard color correcting techniques do not apply. To assist you, Adobe provides a series of preset curves for a great variety of duotones. They can be manipulated to suit most of your needs, and we recommend using them instead of attempting to set your own curves.

3. Swatch

Clicking this box accesses the Custom Color picker. For a duotone containing spot colors, choose the appropriate PMS ink from this list. To select a process color—for example, if you're making a black and cyan duotone as part of a four-color job—click on the Picker button to switch to the standard color picker.

4. Color Name

Once you select a color and click OK, its name appears in this field. If you've chosen a spot color, make sure the name matches the name in your page layout program. Using the incorrect spot color name results in an additional color plate during output.

If you choose a process tint as a color, no name appears in the field. You must enter a name manually in order to apply the curves to the image.

5. Load and Save

Using these buttons, you can save the information in the Duotones options dialog to load and apply to another image. Most frequently, these buttons are used to load the preset duotone curves that ship with Photoshop.

6. Overprint Colors

Duotones create tonal depth by overlapping different inks. In an attempt to display this effect on-screen, this option lets you change the colors that result when your inks combine. Clicking on any swatch accesses the color picker, allowing you to define a new color. This only affects the on-screen appearance of the active duotone, and Photoshop's first guess is usually about as accurate as it gets. Unless your monitor is rigidly calibrated, changing these values accomplishes little.

See Also

Appendix A (Image: Mode: **Duotone**)
File: Supported File Formats (**EPS**)
File: Page Setup: **Screens**
File: Page Setup: **Transfer**
Image: Adjust: **Curves**

Image: Mode: Indexed Color

When you convert an image to Indexed Color, you reduce the number of colors it can display to 256 or less. By doing so, you reduce the amount of information contained in the file, which results in a smaller file size. For this reason, all web graphics saved as CompuServe GIFs have indexed color palettes. Also, multi-media designers often use Indexed Color graphics because of their faster display times. Print professionals, however, have no use for this color mode.

When you convert to Indexed Color, Photoshop creates a *color table*, or a small index that describes the image's few remaining colors. Only the colors present there appear in the image. Although the color table can contain 256 colors, you'll usually specify a lower number to further reduce the file size. Photoshop attempts to recreate the original range of colors as closely as possible, based on the final number of colors you choose.

Common Uses

• Creating small-sized, quick-loading web graphics

• Creating small-sized, quick-loading multimedia graphics

Common Errors

• **Creating double-dithered graphics.** Although the Diffusion dither option may look best on your monitor, it may not be the best choice for your web graph-ics. The vast majority of people using the Internet use 8-bit monitors, which use their own dithering scheme to display colors on-screen. An image dithered twice—once by the Indexed Color dialog, once by the viewer's monitor—suf-fers in quality. Choosing None as a dithering option at least results in the most predictable quality.

• **Converting to Indexed Color before editing is complete.** Make sure your editing is completed before you convert an image to Indexed Color. The lost colors cannot be regained by converting back to RGB, and most editing functions—including filters, Image: **Adjust** commands, anti-aliasing, and feathering—are not available in this mode.

Special Notes

• The only color mode you can convert to an indexed palette is RGB. If you wish to index the colors of a Lab or CMYK image, convert first to RGB, then to Indexed Color.

• After you convert an image to Indexed Color, you can further edit its color pal-ette under Image: Mode: **Color Table**. There, you can increase or decrease the number of colors, as well as change the color values.

• In Photoshop versions 3.0, 3.0.5, and 4, the Windows system palette is incor-rect: the color R: 128, G: 128, B: 128 (neutral gray) is repeated twice. The miss-ing color is R: 192, G: 192, B: 192 (Netscape's default gray). To correct this, select Image: Mode: **Color Table** and choose Windows System from the Table pop-up. Click on the second repeating gray and enter 192 in all three RGB fields. Save the table to load for future use.

- Often, the difference between 7 and 8 bits/pixel is visually negligible. You can usually cut the number of available colors down to 128 without noticing any additional image degradation—and save considerable file size in the process.

- Since Grayscale images contain 256 tones or less, the Indexed Color dialog does not appear when you convert to that mode. Instead, it automatically applies the Exact palette. To access the dialog, switch the Grayscale image back to RGB before converting to Indexed Color.

The Indexed Color Dialog

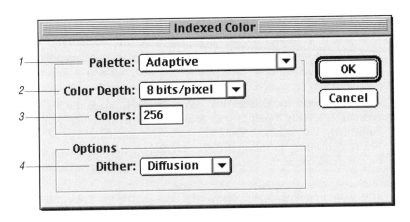

1. Palette

Select a palette type from this pop-up:

Exact
This palette is automatically chosen when the original image contains 256 colors or less, such as a screen shot, logo, or highly posterized image. It also appears if the original image was Grayscale. It means that Photoshop uses precisely the same colors that appear in the image to construct the color table. If the original image contains more than 256 colors, this option is not available.

System (Macintosh) and System (Windows)
This option uses the default color palette of your operating system. Macintosh and Windows may use many of the same colors, but they are arranged in different orders. Therefore, use this palette if you're sure the image will only be viewed on the same platform as yours. Most often, the System palette is applied to graphics that enhance the operating system itself. For example, someone creating specialized icons or Finder-level graphics for the Macintosh should select the System (Macintosh) option.

Web

This palette represents the 216 colors recognized by most major web browsers. When a browser displays a color not included in this palette, it must dither the color on-screen, or combine colored pixels in an attempt to simulate the color. This results in visible artifacting, which most web designers prefer to avoid. Many designers load these colors into the **Swatches Palette**, so they can refer to them directly when designing web graphics.

Uniform

This palette contains an evenly stepped sampling of colors from the RGB spectrum. Initially, it's the same as the web palette (216 colors), but it has a touch more flexibility—you can reduce the number of colors to as low as eight.

Adaptive

This palette generates a color table based on the colors most frequently appearing in the original image. Less frequently used colors are discarded, and their original values are changed to the indexed colors they most closely match.

You may need to redirect the color decisions made by the Adaptive method, especially if part of your image is tone-sensitive and you're using a particularly low number of colors. Select the important part of the image before converting to Indexed Color. Photoshop bases the new color table on the tones within the selection.

Custom

This option automatically opens the Image: Mode: **Color Table** dialog, where you can import a previously saved color palette. This can be useful when creating a series of on-screen graphics for a multimedia project, but it's of little use for creating web graphics.

Previous

Selecting this option automatically applies the last-used color palette. This is useful if you are applying the same values to a series of images, whether it's a 3-bit Adaptive palette or an extensively edited custom table. This option is only available when at least one image has been converted to Indexed Color since the last time Photoshop was launched.

2. **Color Depth**

Here, you can determine the number colors an indexed image can display. This option is only available when Uniform or Adaptive is selected from the Palette pop-up. Each option under the Color Depth pop-up results in a different number of potential colors:

3 bits/pixel

Adaptive Palette: 8 colors. Uniform Palette: 8 colors.

4 bits/pixel

Adaptive: 16 colors. Uniform: 8 colors.

5 bits/pixel

Adaptive: 32 colors. Uniform: 27 colors.

6 bits/pixel
Adaptive: 64 colors. Uniform: 64 colors.

7 bits/pixel
Adaptive: 128 colors. Uniform: 125 colors.

8 bits/pixel
Adaptive: 256 colors. Uniform: 216 colors.

Other
This item automatically appears in the pop-up whenever you manually enter a number in the Colors field.

3. **Colors**

This field serves two purposes. First, it displays the number of colors generated in the new color table, based on your selections in the Palette and Color Depth pop-ups. Second, it allows you to enter your own value for the Uniform and Adaptive palettes. By doing so, you override the specified bit-depths in the Color Depth pop-up. This way, you can create a color table with fewer than eight colors. Or, you can enter arbitrary numbers to achieve a more satisfactory distribution of colors.

4. **Dither**

The dither method determines how the indexed colors are distributed throughout the image:

None
With no dithering selected, Photoshop simply changes each image pixel to its closest equivalent in the color table. In images with more continuous tones, this usually results in harsher color transitions and visible banding. This option does result in smaller GIFs, since LZW compression works best with contiguous color areas.

Pattern
This method is only available when System (Macintosh) is the selected palette. It uses a predefined pattern to redistribute the colors, attempting to compensate for the lost tones. It does a poor job, and should not be used.

Diffusion
This method randomizes the colored pixels, creating the illusion of additional colors.

See Also

File: Supported File Formats (**GIF**)
File: Export: **GIF89a Export**
Image: Mode: **Color Table**
The Swatches Palette

Image: Mode: RGB Color

RGB is the most commonly used color mode. All scanners acquire images in RGB, even if some scanning software automatically converts them to CMYK.

An RGB file consists of three Grayscale color channels: one red, one green, and one blue. Like a standard Grayscale image, each channel uses 8 bits of data per pixel to display color, which translates into 256 brightness levels per channel. Therefore, each image pixel is defined by three brightness values from 0–255, one for each color. When all three values are 0, the color is black. When all three are 255, it's white. When all three are equal numbers between 0 and 255, it's some shade of gray.

Common Uses

* **Editing a scan before converting to CMYK.** Since RGB contains a much wider range than CMYK, the first round of editing is usually performed in RGB mode. This ensures that as much information as possible is present in the image. It's then converted to CMYK, a mode containing much less color information, for proofing and printing.

* **Editing a graphic before converting to Indexed Color.** All web and multimedia graphics are viewed on RGB monitors, even if they don't necessarily remain in RGB mode. By editing them in RGB, you have more control over how they ultimately display.

Common Errors

Converting from RGB and back. Once an RGB image is converted to another mode, it may not be wise to convert back for further editing. You cannot regain any lost color information by converting back to RGB.

Special Notes

RGB values are never displayed as output values, since the mode does not exist in a printable form. However, Photoshop already knows how it will convert an image to CMYK at any given moment. Show both RGB and the relative CMYK values by selecting Palette Options from the Info palette submenu. There, set First Color Readout to RGB, and Second Color Readout to CMYK.

See Also

Image: Mode: **Indexed Color**
Image: Mode: **CMYK**

Image: Mode: CMYK Color

Images in CMYK mode contain the information necessary to produce four-color process separations. Each image consists of four Grayscale channels, one each for the cyan, magenta, yellow, and black information. When you separate a CMYK image, the color channels output as four individual halftones. For that reason, all CMYK colors are read as output values, or percentages from 0 to 100.

Usually, color images are edited in RGB or Lab Color mode and then converted to CMYK just prior to printing.

Image Menu

Common Uses

- **Preparing a full color image for print.** CMYK is the standard mode used to produce color separations on a laser printer, imagesetter, or digital press.

- **Making additional adjustments to a CMYK image.** Some high-end scanning software automatically converts RGB scans to CMYK. If your service bureau provides a color proof with their scans, then those images are converted to CMYK. Also, if you rasterize a CMYK-colored vector-based graphic, you'll continue editing in this mode. Never switch to another mode to make additional edits.

Common Errors

- **Failing to correct the color of high-resolution scans.** Accurately adjusting and reproducing color is one of the most complex tasks in the print publishing industry. Although an image may look acceptable on-screen, proper color correcting requires a calibrated monitor, an understanding of the Image: Adjust: Curves dialog, and the ability to read the output percentages in the **Info Palette.**

- **Failing to adjust the Separation Setup settings.** The File: Color Settings: **Separation Setup** dialog controls the way Photoshop converts an RGB image to CMYK values. These settings must be tailored to match the anticipated press conditions.

- **Defining out-of-gamut colors.** There are three ways to identify RGB and Lab colors that fall out of CMYK's gamut. The first two, the **Info Palette** and the color selection window in the Color Picker, display an exclamation point when an out-of-gamut color is targeted. The third is the View: **Gamut Warning** command, which temporarily masks out-of-gamut colors.

Special Notes

- CMYK images are only destined for print—therefore, they are saved as either TIFF or EPS.

- Before converting an RGB image to CMYK, Photoshop internally converts to Lab color first. This helps ensure that only the colors falling out of CMYK gamut are changed.

See Also

File: Supported File Formats (**EPS** and **TIFF**)
File: Color Settings: **Separation Setup**
Image: Adjust: **Curves**
View: **Gamut Warning**
The Info Palette

Image: Mode: Lab Color

Understanding the information in the individual channels of a Lab image can be difficult, since people are generally accustomed to dealing with color as the product of a device, not as an independent entity.

The L channel represents Lightness, or how bright a color is. Values in the Lightness channel range from 0, which is black, to 100, which is the full intensity of the color. The a and b channels represent the location of the color on the standard color wheel. The a channel represents the colors between green and magenta, which are directly opposite each other on the color wheel. 0 is the exact center of the color wheel. Values between 1 and 100 are towards the center of the magenta spectrum of the color wheel, and values between −1 and −100 are toward the green center of the spectrum. Similarly, the b channel represents the colors between blue and yellow.

Common Uses

- Outputting to IRIS printers (or similar devices)
- Correcting color images on color management systems that support Lab Color

Special Notes

- PostScript Level 2 output devices can print Lab Color images directly to CMYK separations. However, most users prefer editing in CMYK. If an image already exists in CMYK mode, you gain nothing by converting it to Lab Color before outputting.

- When you examine the individual a and b channels, they make no intuitive sense. The shades of gray do not represent brightness or output values, but locations on the color wheel. Darker values in the b channel indicate more blue and less yellow. Lighter values in the a channel represent more magenta, less green.

- While device-independent color is nice in theory, it is actually less useful than RGB or CMYK color, since you almost always create images in Photoshop for on-screen display or print, rarely for a device-independent purpose.

See Also

Image: Mode: **RGB**
Image: Mode: **CMYK**

Image: Mode: Multichannel

An image in Multichannel mode simply contains multiple channels. Unlike the other color modes, no relationship exists between them, regardless of how many there are. This mode has no composite view. There are two ways to convert an image to Multichannel:

- **Select Image: Mode: Multichannel while a color image is open.** This removes the relationship between the color channels, allowing them to simply exist within the structure of a single image. If an RGB or Lab Color image is converted, then the Multichannel image contains three channels. If a CMYK image is converted, it has four.

- **Delete one of the channels in a color image.** This forcibly destroys the relationship between the color channels, since removing one of them alters the basic structure of the mode. Rather than attempt to deal with this type of effect on-screen, Photoshop converts the image (and the remaining channels) to Multichannel.

Special Notes

- Other than making it easy to exchange color channels or dealing with it as an intermediary step, there is little use for this mode.

- Only images containing more than one channel can be converted to Multichannel mode.

See Also

The Channels Palette

Image: Mode: 8 Bits/Channel

This command is used to convert 16 bit-per-channel images—such as those generated by certain scanners and digital cameras—back down to standard 8 bits. Sixteen-bit graphics can only be acquired with special plug-ins that ship with those input devices. These files contain twice as much color information as an average file, so the user has more latitude when making adjustments. Convert to this setting when you have completed the editing of the file.

Special Notes

- Nothing is gained by converting an 8 Bits/Channel image to 16 Bits/Channel. It does not give you any additional color data, nor any more flexibility in editing.

- A checkmark appears next to this command to indicate an image's status as 8 Bits/Channel.

Image: Mode: 16 Bits/Channel

Although you're able to convert any Grayscale or RGB image to 16 Bits/Channel, you have no need to do so. This command exists to indicate whether a digitally acquired image contains that much image data. If it does, it must be converted to 8 Bits/Channel before the final image is saved and used.

Special Notes

Because these images contain twice as much color data as 8 bit images, the relative file sizes are twice as large.

Image: Mode: Color Table

Once you've converted an image to Indexed Color, there are two ways to edit the existing values.

- Convert back to RGB to access the 24-bit spectrum. Unfortunately, converting back and forth between the two modes can result in additional image degradation.

- Edit the image's color table using the Image: Mode: **Color Table** dialog.

This command is only available when an image is in Indexed Color mode. Once you open the dialog, there are two ways to edit the color palette: select a predefined palette or edit colors individually.

Common Uses

Refer to Appendix A for full descriptions of the following:

- Editing an indexed color value
- Creating a custom color table gradient
- Saving a custom palette

Special Notes

Most often, indexed graphics are saved using the Adaptive palette option. To make any changes to these custom palettes, you must selectively edit individual color values in the Color Table dialog.

The Color Table Dialog

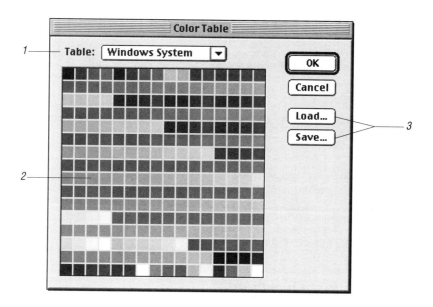

1. Table

If desired, select a custom palette from this pop-up:

Custom

This appears whenever any other palette except System (Macintosh) or System (Windows) was selected in the Indexed Color dialog. The colors specific to your settings appear in the swatches below.

Black Body

This palette is supposedly based on the colors emitted by a superheated slab of black iron—they exist as a gradient from black, to red, to yellow, to white. While this table can be applied to interesting effect on an indexed Grayscale image, the results of this table are unpredictable, and the values do not necessarily translate over the Internet. It's rarely used for anything useful.

Grayscale

This option only appears if you've converted a Grayscale image to Indexed Color. Otherwise, selecting it remaps the colors of the image to the 256-level gray scale. You have little control over which colors are converted to which grays, so it's a poor technique to convert a colored Indexed image to gray levels. Do this more effectively by converting an image to Grayscale mode before converting to Indexed Color.

Macintosh System

This option appears if you selected System (Macintosh) in the Indexed Color dialog.

Spectrum
The colors of this option appear as gradient between the primary hues of the spectrum. Again, the results of applying this table are unpredictable at best.

Windows System
This option appears if you selected System (Windows) in the Indexed Color dialog.

2. **The Color Palette**

This grid contains all the colors of the indexed file. To edit a specific value, click once on the color.

3. **Load and Save**

These buttons allow you save and reload a customized color palette.

See Also

Appendix A (Image: Mode: **Color Table**)
Image: Mode: **Indexed Color**

Image: Adjust Overview

The Image: **Adjust** commands allow you to *remap* pixel values, or selectively target colors to change them from one to another. These commands are used for two purposes:

- **To adjust the tones and colors of scanned images.** Due to limitations of scanning technology, every halftone or color image requires some degree of correction. Traditionally, this was true only of print-oriented images. Today, now that multimedia and the Web have matured, the Image: **Adjust** tools are more widely used than ever.

- **To generate special effects.** Rather than use these commands to make small corrections, you can use them to radically alter color content.

Adjusting color is arguably the most complex and demanding Photoshop-driven process in the graphic arts. Even though Photoshop measures color with scientific models and precise numerical values, individual perception of color is highly subjective. To make matters worse, the act of correction itself quickly reduces the amount of color information in an image—so you have only a small degree of latitude when making adjustments.

Color correction actually involves many different tools and commands, most of which are found in the Image: **Adjust** submenu. As you become more familiar with the process, it pays to develop a consistent workflow strategy. A colleague of ours put it best: adjusting color without a plan is like cutting hair with an electric clipper and no comb. Fixing one section usually throws another one out of whack. Fixing that one impairs another. Soon, you have nothing left but an irreparably bad haircut.

Image Adjusting Guidelines

Use the following list as a basis for developing your own approach to color editing. Refer to each specifically mentioned command for more information.

- *Step 1:* **Evaluate the original image and determine its purpose.** Will it be printed or displayed on-screen? Are the colors critical, or do they simply need to be balanced and appealing? This usually involves meeting with the client or art director of a project.

- *Step 2:* **Preview, measure, and perform any adjustments to the image using your scanner's software.** These options ultimately depend on the make and quality of your scanner and its interface.

- *Step 3:* **Scan the image.** Open it in Photoshop if your scanner interface doesn't do it automatically.

- *Step 4:* **Evaluate the scan.** Make sure the image was adequately captured by the scanner by reading the values in the Image: **Histogram** or Image: Adjust: **Levels** dialogs. If not, scan again. If so, save the image.

- *Step 5:* **Prepare the RGB to CMYK separation settings.** These values are found in the File: Color Settings: **Printing Inks Setup** and **Separation Setup** dialogs. (Print-oriented color graphics only.)

- *Step 6:* **Repair any obvious image flaws.** These are the big ones, like a tear in the negative or an element that must be removed from the image.

- *Step 7:* **Sharpen the image.** For best results, use Filter: Sharpen: **Unsharp Mask**.

- *Step 8:* **Retouch the smaller image flaws.** These include scratches, dirt, and other small imperfections.

- *Step 9:* **Evaluate and adjust the endpoints for press.** This prevents the lightest image areas from burning out and the darkest details from filling in during printing. These values are controlled by Image: Adjust: **Levels**, **Auto Levels**, or **Curves**. (Print-oriented graphics only.)

- *Step 10:* **Adjust the tones**, or the image's overall lightness, darkness, and contrast. Image: Adjust: **Levels** and **Curves** are the most powerful tools.

- *Step 11:* **Adjust the overall color content of the image.** Although you can use such commands as Image: Adjust: **Levels** or **Color Balance**, the **Curves** command is by far the most powerful color adjusting tool.

- *Step 12:* **Convert the image from RGB to CMYK mode.** (Print-oriented color graphics only.)

- *Step 13:* **Proof.** Readjust the image if necessary.

Common Image: Adjust Options

Most Image: **Adjust** dialogs share the following options.

Previewing Adjustments

You can preview the effects of most Image: **Adjust** commands before they are applied. The only exceptions are Auto Levels, Desaturate, Invert and Equalize—

these only produce one effect, so they don't need to be previewed. There are two ways to preview:

- **Leave the Preview box unchecked.** Here, Photoshop uses the computer's own graphics card to generate previews using the card's video color lookup table (VLUT). The effect is applied to the entire screen, not just the image. Since the preview is hardware-based, it's much faster—but it's a less accurate representation of the final adjustment. Temporarily turn off the hardware preview by clicking the title bar of the dialog box.

- **Check the Preview box.** Here, Photoshop itself generates the preview. Only the part of the image being adjusted is affected by the preview. It takes longer to generate than the hardware-based preview, but it provides an exact representation of the final adjustment.

Accessing Previously Used Settings

Any Image: **Adjust** command with an editable dialog recalls its last-entered values when you hold down the (Option) [Alt] key while selecting the command. If there is a keyboard shortcut, such as (Command) [Control]-L for Image: Adjust: **Levels**, then hold down the (Option) [Alt] key in addition to the standard shortcut.

Numerical Field Shortcuts

Many Image: **Adjust** dialogs use sliders to edit color content or tonal values. Every slider has a field that displays the associated numerical values. To bypass the slider, insert the cursor in the field (press the Tab key to scroll through them). (Option) [Alt]-click the up and down arrows to increase or decrease the values in increments of one. Shift-click to increase or decrease in increments of 10.

Cancel/Reset

Clicking Cancel closes the dialog, leaving the image unchanged. However, holding down the (Option) [Alt] key changes the Cancel button into the Reset button. Clicking this button restores the original settings without closing the dialog.

Save and Load

If an Image: **Adjust** command has multiple settings, they can be saved into a separate file and reloaded later. This is useful when the same settings must be applied to multiple images, or to multiple layers of the same image.

Depending on the situation, using the **Actions Palette** may be more efficient than saving and loading settings. If you're batch processing, or applying the same commands to a number of images in quick succession, then record an Action. If you intend to use the settings again at some unspecified time in the future, then save them.

Image: Adjust: Levels
(Command) [Control]–L

This command allows you to remap the brightness values of an image by manipulating controls representing its shadows, midtones, and highlights. By repositioning the Levels sliders and referring to a graph that displays the image data, you compress, expand, or clip the existing tonal range.

Common Uses

Refer to Appendix A for full descriptions of the following:

- Evaluating the tonal range.

- Identifying endpoints.

- Setting and applying endpoints for print.

- Simple image enhancing.

Common Errors

- **Attempting delicate or complex image adjustments.** Image: Adjust: **Curves** offers much more powerful and accurate tools.

- **Over-adjusting the tonal range.** Whenever a tonal range is expanded, no new values are created—the existing tones are simply spaced farther apart to cover a broader range. When a range is expanded by too much, visible shade-stepping occurs.

- **Setting endpoints using the Output Values sliders.** Doing so is similar to setting endpoints for print, but with two problems. First, the tones are displayed as brightness values, instead of print-specific output percentages. Second, your adjustments are applied evenly—you have little control over which pixels are affected. For the best results, use the eyedroppers.

Special Notes

This command only controls pixel brightness, or values ranging from 0 to 255—unlike the Curves dialog, which has the option of displaying output percentages. Accuracy ultimately depends on your understanding of this system.

The Levels Dialog

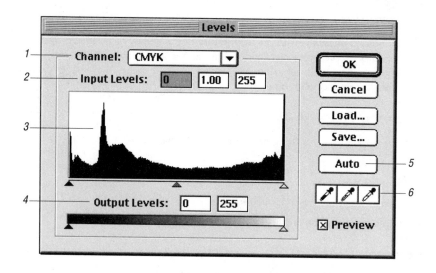

1. Channel

This pop-up allows you to edit the individual channels of a color image, or edit a composite representing all channels at once. When you select a different channel, the histogram displays its specific content.

2. Input Levels

The left and right fields respond to two things. They allow the user to enter values for the shadow and highlight areas, or they display the changes made when you adjust the black and white sliders. For example, if the shadow value is raised from 0 to 45, all pixels with brightness values of 45 and below become black. Similarly, lowering the highlight value from 255 to 210 turns every pixel with a value of 210 or more to white.

The middle field controls *gamma*, in this case the brightness value of neutral gray. This value always starts at 1.00, even if it was changed in a previous edit. Gamma values can range from 0.1 to 9.99—any changes up or down darken or lighten the tones of an image without changing the white or black points.

Readjusting the midpoint expands one part of the tonal range while compressing the other. For example, raising the gamma from 1.00 to 2.00 remaps the brightness value of 64 to 128. The values between 0 and 64 are expanded to range from 0 to 128, while the values between 64 and 255 are compressed to range from 128 to 255.

3. The Histogram

This graph plots the tonal range of an image or a channel, similar to Image: Histogram. It contains up to 256 vertical lines, each one representing a brightness level from black to white. If a particular value colors a larger number of pixels, the line appears taller; if it colors a smaller number of pixels, the line is shorter. Areas where no lines exist are tones not present in the image.

4. **Output Levels**

The Output Values restrict the darkest and lightest possible tones. For example, setting the shadow value to 40 remaps all pixels so the darkest value is 40 (85%), rather than black. Likewise, setting the highlight value to 230 (10%) remaps the pixels so the lightest value is 230. This is a more obvious form of tonal compression—as the endpoints are pushed closer together, the number of possible tones decreases, causing the image to lose contrast.

5. **Auto**

Click this button to reposition the tonal endpoints of an image. It's the same command as Image: Adjust: **Auto Levels**. The values it follows are set using the eyedroppers.

6. **The Eyedroppers**

Use the black and white eyedroppers to manually set the endpoints of a half-tone image.

The gray eyedropper is only available in color images, and is used to establish neutral gray. In theory, you would include a swatch of neutral gray (one of the Pantone Cool Grays, for example) with a scan—when you click that swatch with the gray eyedropper, it removes any color bias, bringing it (and the remaining image grays) into neutral spec. In practice, it provides only a cursory adjustment with unpredictable results.

See Also

Image: Adjust: **Curves**
Image: Adjust: **Auto Levels**
Image: **Histogram**

Image: Adjust: Auto Levels
(Command-Shift) [Control-Shift]-L

Selecting this command is the same as clicking as the Auto button in the Image: Adjust: **Levels** and **Curves** dialog. It remaps the highlight and shadow value, based on the values set by double-clicking the black and white eyedroppers.

Special Notes

- Keep the clip value low—from 0.5% to 1.5%—for the best results.

- Even though this command is automatic, you still have some control over the pixels it targets. In either the Levels or Curves dialog, hold down the (Option) [Alt] key. The Auto button changes to Options.

The Auto Range Options Dialog

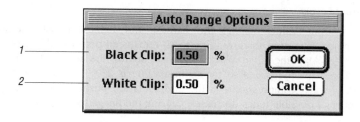

1. Black Clip

This option lets you ignore a certain percentage of the darkest pixels before applying the changes. This way, a few extreme pixel values don't throw off the effects of the command. Enter a value between 0.5% and 9.99%. The higher the percentage, the more severe the effect.

2. White Clip

This option functions the same as Black Clip, but it pertains to the adjustment of the highlight dot.

Image: Adjust: Curves
(Command) [Control]-M

This command is Photoshop's most powerful tool for remapping pixel values. Unlike Image: Adjust: **Levels**, you can change the value of one pixel to virtually any other.

Common Uses

Refer to Appendix A for full descriptions of the following:

- Adjusting a halftone for contrast
- Adjusting an on-screen image for contrast
- Adjusting a halftone for dot gain
- Identifying and adjusting a color cast
- Adjusting neutral tones
- Half cast removals

Common Errors

- **Applying curves that are too steep.** When color correcting, even changes of 2–3% are noticeable.

- **Applying too many curves.** Each change reduces the number of tones, and the image eventually becomes washed out or posterized.

Special Notes

- (Option) [Alt]-click anywhere in the graph to change the grid to 10% increments. (Option) [Alt]-click again to switch back to 25%.

- When you click on the tone gradient to change to output percentages, the gray ramp reverses. Because brightness and output values are the opposite of each other, the curve must now be edited in the opposite direction.

- If unsure of a particular color or tone value, move the cursor onto the image. It changes to an eyedropper. When you click on the image, a small circle appears, indicating its location on the curve. When editing a color channel—cyan, for example—the circle indicates the cyan component of whatever color you've selected. This is very useful when making color corrections, but it does not work when the composite channel is selected.

- As many as fourteen points can be added to a single curve, in addition to the endpoints. Remove a point by dragging it off the graph.

The Curves Dialog

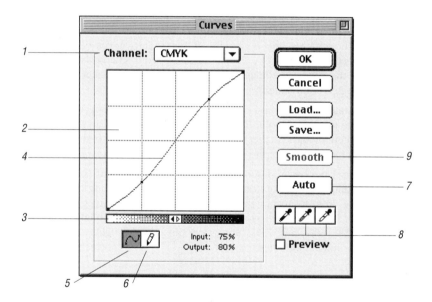

1. **Channel**

   The Channel pop-up allows you to edit individual channels in a color image, or edit a composite representing all channels at once. When a single color is selected, you edit the Grayscale values of that color's channel. When the composite is selected, you edit all channels simultaneously.

2. **Tone Graph**

   The Tone Graph is the heart of the Curves dialog. Here, two forms of color information are plotted against each other. The horizontal axis represents *input levels*, or the color values that existed before you opened the Curves dialog. The vertical axis represents *output levels*, or color values that will exist after you apply a curve.

By default, the graph is divided into a four-by-four grid. This makes it easier to target the primary image tones: highlights, quarter tones, midtones, three-quarter tones, and shadows.

3. Tone Gradient

The bar at the bottom of the graph is a gray ramp, displaying all the values from black to white. By looking at this, you know which end of your curve represents shadows and which represents highlights.

The tone gradient also determines whether the dialog measures in brightness values or output percentages. Photoshop defaults to brightness values, which many users prefer for reading RGB color. Most print professionals, however, prefer reading color in terms of halftone dot sizes. Click once on the gradient to change the measurement values.

4. The Curve

Make your adjustments by manipulating the diagonal line bisecting the graph. This line represents all the possible tones from lightest to darkest, even though your image may contain a shorter range. This command is called "Curves" because although this line is straight, it bends into a curved shape as you make corrections. This curve helps distribute your changes more smoothly throughout the rest of the image, avoiding more jarring results like posterizing and unexpected color shifts.

Make adjustments by placing and repositioning points along the curve. Click on the curve to insert a point. Drag this point above or below its original position to lighten or darken the tones of the image. Refer to the Input/Output values in the lower right of the dialog to track your changes.

Curve points have two different uses. They adjust tone and color, as happens when you drag a point from one point to another, remapping the values. Also, you can use them to anchor the curve, allowing you to target one part of the tonal range. For example, if you only want to edit the highlights, click to add points at 25%, 50%, and 75%. Now, you can edit the lightest values without affecting the remaining tones.

5. The Point Tool

This option is Photoshop's default, and allows you to click-drag points, as described above.

6. The Pencil Tool

Here, you can manually draw curves on the graph. Usually, this option is casually dismissed as just another special effect. While it's true that you can create off-the-wall color adjustments, you can also switch to the pencil tool to make discreet edits that may be more difficult with the point tool.

7. Auto

The Auto button applies the same command as Image: Adjust: **Auto Levels**. See Image: Adjust: **Levels** for a full description.

---

8. **Eyedroppers**

The eyedroppers are used to define and apply endpoint values. See Image: Adjust: **Levels** for a full description.

9. **Smooth**

Use the Smooth button to convert a manually-drawn curve to one based on points. Clicking the button again slightly flattens the adjustments made to the curve. Continued clicking ultimately straightens the curve completely.

See Also

Appendix A (Image: Adjust: **Curves**)
Image: Adjust: **Levels**
Image: Adjust: **Auto Levels**

Image: Adjust: Color Balance
(Command) [Control]-B

This command allows you to adjust colors by changing their position in the RGB/CMY color wheel. Similar to the color controls of your scanner's software, you make adjustments in one of three ways:

- **Add a color by moving its slider toward it.** For example, add yellow by moving the bottom slider toward Yellow.

- **Subtract a color by moving its slider away from it, or toward its complement.** For example, subtract yellow by adding blue.

- **Add or subtract a color by adjusting its two components.** Referring to the RGB/CMY color wheel, you can subtract yellow by adding red and green.

Common Uses

- Removing a color cast from an image

- Tweaking the color of an on-screen image

Special Notes

Although easy to use, this tool has limited function—its edits are not based on exact color values, and you cannot target specific tones to correct. If anything, this tool is best suited for adjusting on-screen images. Print images require the precision of Image: Adjust: **Levels** or **Curves**.

The Color Balance Dialog

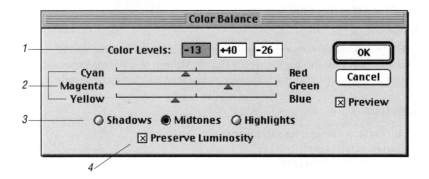

1. **Color Levels**

   From left to right, these fields display the values of the top, middle, and bottom color sliders. If desired, enter the values manually.

2. **Color Sliders**

   Each slider in the dialog pairs a color with its complement on the color wheel. The values of the sliders default to 0, but range from –100 to 100. Unless you're creating a special color effect, keep your adjustments small. Any changes more than 3–5 units above or below 0 are likely to create another color cast.

3. **Tone Buttons**

   Here, you target the part of the tonal range you wish to adjust: Shadows, Midtones, or Highlights. Each option actually affects the entire range of the image—but by choosing one of these options, you determine which portion receives the brunt of the changes. The Shadows option primarily affects tones above 75%. Midtones primarily affects tones between 25% and 75%. Highlights primarily affects tones below 25%.

4. **Preserve Luminosity**

   Check this button to preserve the luminosity, or the overall lightness values, of the image. If you edit with this button unchecked, the tonal balance is affected along with the color content.

See Also

Image: Mode: Overview (**The RGB/CMY Model**)
Image: Adjust: **Levels**
Image: Adjust: **Curves**

Image: Adjust: Brightness/Contrast

This command may be the most intuitive adjustment tool, but it's also the least useful. It suffers from two major drawbacks: its effects are applied to all channels simultaneously, and it provides no precision beyond oversimplified curve adjustments.

The Brightness/Contrast Dialog

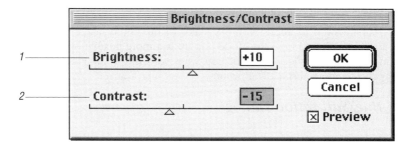

1. **Brightness**

   Moving this slider to the right lightens the overall image. It has the same effect as opening the Curves dialog and moving the shadow straight toward the highlight value. Moving the slider to the left darkens the overall image, creating the same effect as dragging the highlight point straight toward the shadow value.

2. **Contrast**

   Moving this slider to the right exaggerates the difference between the lighter and darker image tones. It has the same effect as opening the Curves dialog and moving the highlight and shadow endpoints horizontally toward 50%— light information becomes white while dark information becomes black. Moving this slider to the left reduces contrast, producing the same effect as dragging the endpoints vertically toward 50%. All tones eventually turn gray.

Image: Adjust: Hue/Saturation
(Command) [Control]-U

This command allows you to edit colors based on the HSB color model (see "The HSB Model" earlier in this chapter). Rather than use specific color values, you change the position of one or more colors in the HSB spectrum.

Common Uses

- Adjusting color using HSB-based controls
- Colorizing a black and white image

Special Notes

- Most Hue/Saturation corrections are made to edit specific colors, not tones. Tonal edits are far more accurately performed using Image: Adjust: **Levels** or **Curves**.

- When editing an image in Lab Color mode, you only have four color options: yellow, green, blue, and magenta. These correspond to the color ranges represented by the a and b channels.

- When you select the Colorize option, Photoshop automatically applies the highest saturation level. The Saturation slider is altered to read only from 0 to 100, meaning you can only reduce the saturation.

- If your intent is to apply only one color to the entire image, using Edit: **Fill** with Color selected from the Mode pop-up is a more flexible option. Here, you can specifically define the color you want with the Color Picker, rather than depend on more abstract HSB values.

The Hue/Saturation Dialog

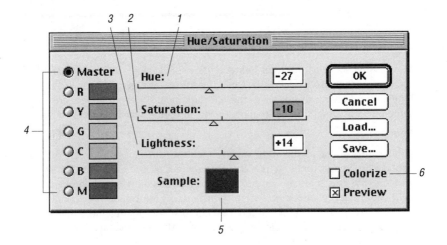

1. **Hue Slider**

   Hue pertains to a color's location on the RGB/CMY color wheel. The values you see when moving this slider are actually degrees; moving the slider all the way to the left or right places the color halfway around the color wheel, or 180 from its original position. For example, if you adjust red by moving the slider 60 to the right, the color becomes yellow. Sixty degrees to the left, it becomes magenta. Adjusting this slider, then, is like moving any color in a perfect circle around the color wheel.

2. **Saturation Slider**

   Moving this slider affects the intensity of a color, or its distance from the center of the color wheel. Lowering the saturation value moves the color closer to the center of the wheel, or reduces it closer to gray. Raising the saturation moves a color closer to the edge of the wheel, a color's brightest point.

3. **Lightness Slider**

    This slider affects brightness levels, similar to the Brightness slider in Image: Adjust: **Brightness/Contrast**. Here, adjustments move colors closer to one end or the other of the cylindrical HSB model. Moving the slider to the left gradually darkens the overall image tones, eventually turning them black. Moving it to the right gradually lightens the tones, eventually turning them white.

4. **Color Buttons**

    Photoshop always defaults to the Master setting, which results in all color values being adjusted in equal amounts. To target a more specific color, select one of the additional color buttons: R for red, Y for yellow, G for green, C for cyan, B for blue, and M for magenta—or, as you may have noticed, the six primary colors of the RGB/CMY color wheel.

    When editing one of these colors, the Hue slider only has a range from –60° to +60°, or the distance between the selected color's two components on the color wheel. For example, if you select Red and adjust the Hue slider, you change red values to anything between magenta and yellow—the degree of change is apparent in the small swatch next to the color's button. You can also use the Saturate slider to affect only the colors containing red.

    Selecting individual colors is more flexible than editing with Master selected. You can apply different values for each color, allowing for relatively specific edits.

5. **Sample**

    This swatch previews the effects of the command on one specific color. If only one color is present or selected in the image when you open the Hue/Saturation dialog, that color appears as the sample. To select a particular color, you must move the cursor over the image (it changes to an eyedropper) and click somewhere.

6. **Colorize**

    Checking this option does two things. First, it removes all the color from an image or selection while retaining the brightness levels. This is also known as *desaturating.* Then, it applies one hue to the entire image.

    The effect here is different from creating a monotone (using Image: Mode: **Duotone**) or recoloring a halftone in another program. The deepest tones remain black, but all lighter brightness values are tinted with one color. When you move the Hue slider, that one color cycles through the different stages of the color wheel.

    This option is commonly used to colorize different portions of a Grayscale image, an effect similar to antique, hand-tinted photographs. The image must be converted to a color mode in order to access the command, and the best results are achieved in RGB. From there, use the selection tools to isolate different portions of the image. Each time, open this dialog, choose Colorize, and apply your desired color.

See Also

Edit: **Fill**
Image: Mode: Overview (**The HSB Model**)

Image: Adjust: Desaturate
(Command-Shift) [Control-Shift]-U

This command reduces the saturation of all colors to 0, creating the effect of a Grayscale image without changing modes. The result is the same as selecting Image: Adjust: **Hue/Saturation** and moving the Saturation slider all the way to the left.

Special Notes

Converting JPEG images to Grayscale mode often results in small, black artifacts. This is especially common with certain CD-ROM stock images. This is a flaw in the conversion scheme resulting from the compression used on the images. Avoid this problem by applying Image: Adjust: **Desaturate** before converting them to Grayscale.

Image: Adjust: Replace Color

With this command, you target a range of colors and change their values using Hue, Saturation, and Lightness controls. Colors are targeted by clicking on the image or a thumbnail with a series of eyedroppers, avoiding the need for potentially complex selections.

Common Uses

Editing continuous tones, blends and gradients, or areas of subtly varying color, such as fleshtones.

Special Notes

This command is strikingly similar to making a selection using Select: **Color Range** and editing color using Image: Adjust: **Hue/Saturation**. On one hand, it saves time because only one command is used instead of two. On the other, it offers only a pared-down version of the Hue/Saturation tools. The only advantage to using Replace Color is the lack of active selections.

The Replace Color Dialog

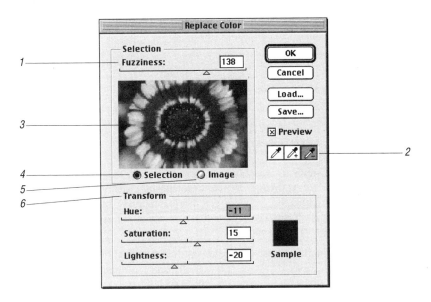

1. **Fuzziness**

   This slider determines the range of targeted colors. Lower values include fewer colors in the selection; higher values include more. A fuzziness value of 0 means only the exact color you click on can be changed.

2. **Eyedroppers**

   Use the three eyedroppers to define the editable colors. The plain eyedropper simply selects a particular color. Clicking elsewhere selects a different value. To add values to the selection, use the plus-eyedropper or hold down the Shift key while selecting with the standard eyedropper. To subtract values from the selection, use the minus-eyedropper or (Option) [Alt]-click with the standard eyedropper.

   Drag with one of the eyedroppers to add or subtract a wider range of tones.

3. **Image Map**

   Use this thumbnail to facilitate your color selection. If there is an active selection, only that information appears in the image map. If no selection exists, then the entire image appears.

4. **Selection**

   This mask displays the currently selected colors. The portions of the image editable with the Transform options appear white, and the unselected areas remain black.

5. **Image**

   This displays a full-color version of the image.

6. **Transform Options**

These include the same three Hue, Saturation, and Lightness sliders found in the Image: Adjust: **Hue/Saturation** dialog. The Sample swatch displays any color encountered by the eyedropper tools.

See Also

Image: Adjust: **Hue/Saturation**
Select: **Color Range**

Image: Adjust: Selective Color

This command attempts to simplify color correcting by adjusting CMYK values with sliders, similar to the Image: Adjust: **Color Balance** dialog. Rather than target specific process percentages, you correct more intuitively by focusing on Reds, Blues, Yellows, and so forth. The idea is that you make adjustments the same way you would evaluate a color proof.

Although this command is based on a good idea, it falls short of being an effective color editing tool. It relies too much on on-screen appearances and guesswork to be considered accurate, and you have no reliable method of measuring your color changes.

Special Notes

Although this command is available in RGB mode, it is most effective when applied to a CMYK image. RGB images must still be converted to CMYK, and those values ultimately depend on the settings under File: Color Settings: **Printing Inks Setup** and **Separation Setup**.

The Selective Color Dialog

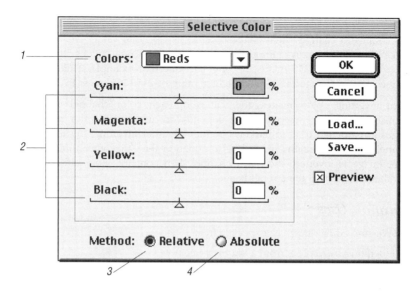

1. **Colors**

   Select a general tonal range from this pop-up. For example, if you notice a yellow cast in the red tones, select Reds and edit the Yellow slider. Also included are options for Whites (for editing the diffuse highlight), Neutrals (for the gray tones), and Blacks (for shadows).

2. **CMYK Sliders**

   One slider exists for each process component. By manipulating them, you either add or subtract ink from a chosen range. Don't be fooled by the numerical fields—although they measure in percentages, they do not refer to output percentages. Their meaning depends on the option selected under Method.

3. **Relative Method**

   This method evaluates the range you've chosen to adjust and attempts to apply your changes proportionately. In theory, if you wanted to make the Reds 5% more magenta, Photoshop would determine the actual red values and then add 5% magenta. There are two problems with this method, however. First, you have no say in what Photoshop determines to be "red"—you have to take the program's word for it. Second, this command may use multiple components to make the change, especially with larger percentages. You're not only unaware of which pixels are being edited, you have no idea what's being done to them until you click OK and check the Info palette.

4. **Absolute Method**

   This method is no less confusing. Changes are based on a percentage of the actual values. For example, if you lessen an area containing 75% magenta by 25% magenta, the result is 56% (twenty-five percent of 75 is 18.75. Subtract that from 75% to get 56%).

Image: Adjust: Invert
(Command) [Control]-I

This command changes each image pixel to its opposite value, creating an effect similar to a film negative. Photoshop determines the new values by changing a pixel's brightness to 255 minus the original value. For example, a dark pixel with a value of 40 is changed to a much lighter value of 215 (255−40=215).

When inverting color images, the values of each color channel are reversed. Because of this, the inverted result depends on an image's color mode. CMYK images in particular tend to darken considerably after inverting, because the black channel typically contains much less information than the other three. When the entire image is inverted, the black channel then contains more information than the others, darkening the overall image.

Common Uses

- Reversing color values as a special effect
- Generating true colors from a scanned negative
- Reversing image components such as selection masks and layer masks, thereby reversing their effect

Common Errors

Double-inverting a feathered selection. Although you can safely reapply the command to an entire image without suffering any degradation, inverting a selection twice leaves artifacts around feathered or anti-aliased selections. If you change your mind about inverting a selection, choose Edit: **Undo** rather than invert again.

Special Notes

When inverting all or part of a CMYK image, invert only the cyan, magenta, and yellow channels. This way, the image is not compromised by a sudden influx of black information.

Image: Adjust: Equalize

This command redistributes an image's tonal range by maximizing the values of the lightest and darkest pixels. When applied, it does two things. First, it locates the lightest and darkest pixels in the image. Second, it remaps those pixels so the lightest becomes white and the darkest becomes black. The remaining tonal range is expanded to accommodate the new endpoints.

Common Uses

Refer to Appendix A for a full description of the following;

- Generating a map of your flatbed scanner

Common Errors

Attempting to color correct with this command. While it is somewhat similar to the Image: Adjust: **Auto Levels** command, Equalize only looks at a couple of factors, and provides no adjusting.

Special Notes

When you Equalize a color file, the results may be unexpected. Since this command is applied to the individual color channels, the colors black and white do not necessarily appear in the image. In a CMYK image, for example, the cyan or magenta of a pixel may maximize to white, but the remaining components may still contain gray values.

The Equalize Dialog

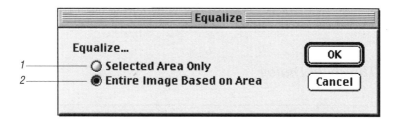

This dialog only appears when an active selection exists.

1. **Selected Area Only**

   This option applies the command only to the selected area.

2. **Entire Image Based on Area**

   This option applies the command to the entire image, based on the color values found within the selection.

See Also

Appendix A (Image: Adjust: **Equalize**)
Image: Adjust: **Auto Levels**

Image: Adjust: Threshold

This command reduces an image to two colors: solid black and solid white. It has the effect of converting an image to 1-bit color—similar to scanned line art—without converting to a different image mode. A *threshold* is the dividing line between the tones that become black or white. This command allows you to easily reset the threshold to any value.

Common Uses

Refer to Appendix A for full descriptions of the following:

- Preparing detailed line art
- Creating solid black masks

Common Errors

Failing to convert line art to Bitmap mode. If you apply this command to a Grayscale image, you must convert it to 1-bit color to have it output properly.

Special Notes

When you apply this command to a color image, you may see a range of colorful splotches before you click OK. This is just a side effect of the Video LUT Animation preference, and it displays Photoshop's attempt to apply the same threshold level to each color channel. Avoid the colors by turning the Preview option on. Or, duplicate the colors you see by manually applying the command on each channel.

The Threshold Dialog

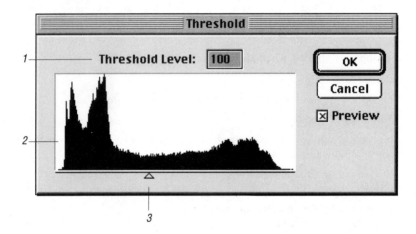

1. **Threshold Level**

   This field indicates the current threshold value. It can range from 1 to 255—a level of 1 turns all pixels white, and a level of 255 turns all pixels black. When you first select the command, the level defaults to 128, or the midpoint between black and white. In the future, the dialog retains the last applied value. If desired, you can manually enter a threshold value.

2. **Histogram**

Similar to Image: Adjust: **Levels** and Image: **Histogram**, this graph represents the entire range of image tones. It acts as a loose guide while determining the location of the threshold.

3. **Threshold Slider**

Move this slider to reposition the threshold. Moving it to the left results in a lighter image, to the right results in a darker image. The threshold is reflected in the Threshold Level field, above the histogram.

See Also

Appendix A (Image; Adjust: **Posterize**)
Image: Mode: **Bitmap**
Image: Adjust: **Levels**
Image: **Histogram**

Image: Adjust: Posterize

The Posterize command reduces the number of tonal levels in an image. Unlike Image: Adjust: **Threshold**, which reduces only to black and white, Posterize averages the 256 tone levels of each color channel into the number of levels you specify.

Common Errors

- **Using this command to reduce the number of colors for a web graphic.** For this technique, use Image: Mode: **Indexed Color**.

- **Applying a Levels value of 2 to create line art.** For this effect, use Image: Adjust: **Threshold**, then convert to Bitmap.

Special Notes

Although this command is primarily used to create a silkscreen-style special effect, it can be used to simplify an image before converting it to vector-based artwork. This gives you more control over specific image areas—especially if you're using an automatic tracing program like Adobe Streamline.

The Posterize Dialog

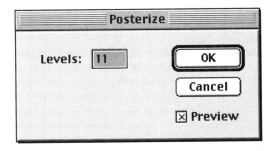

Levels

To posterize an image, enter a value from 2 to 255. Lower values result in obvious banding, or identifiable patches of color. Higher levels result in less apparent changes. The image previews dynamically as you enter different values in the dialog, giving the best indication of the final effect. The lowest value you can enter is 2, since a value of 1 would render the image either all white or all black. A value of 255 leaves the image unchanged.

See Also

Image: Adjust: **Threshold**
Image: Mode: **Indexed Color**

Image: Adjust: Variations

This command combines the tools found in the **Brightness/Contrast, Hue/Saturation,** and **Color Balance** commands. These are controlled by an expansive interface that displays a series of small previews. Each preview represents a possible color correction, and you click on the desired effect to change the image.

The advantage to using Variations is that you can edit the colors of an image while watching the direct result of your actions. This is an intuitive and dynamic method of adjusting color. The disadvantage is that you have no direct control over the actual color values. Since the dialog takes up nearly the entire screen, your decisions are based on very small, low-resolution thumbnails—hardly an accurate indication of subtle color changes. For this reason, this command is best used for adjusting on-screen images.

Special Notes

• Since the image thumbnails are so small, previewing smaller selections is difficult at best. Also, you are unable to see any changes in relation to the rest of the image. Therefore, this command is best used on the entire image.

• The tone controls that appear when editing a color image are similar to the Saturation slider in the Image: Adjust: **Hue/Saturation** dialog, but the end result may be slightly different. This command adjusts saturation without changing any brightness values, so the colors may appear deeper and more intense than those edited with Hue/Saturation.

• After clicking OK to apply an adjustment, make it a practice to double-check the new values by choosing Edit: **Undo** and **Redo** while examining different portions of the image with the Info palette. There is no other way to evaluate the degree of change.

The Variations Dialog (Grayscale)

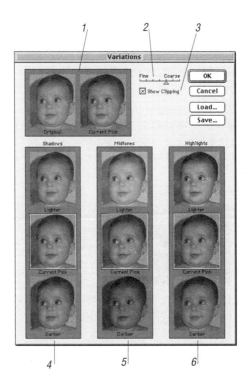

1. Status Thumbnails

The thumbnail marked Original represents the image that existed before you opened the dialog. Click on this image at any time to restore the original values. The thumbnail marked Current Pick represents the current status of the image, with all the new changes. Clicking on this image does nothing.

2. Intensity Slider

This slider controls the amount of change that occurs each time you click one of the tone-correction thumbnails. A Fine setting results in very small changes, or an approximate 1% increase or decrease per click. A Coarse setting results in very large changes, or an approximate 35% increase or decrease per click. It defaults to the midpoint.

3. Show Clipping

If this box is checked, any color that is pushed beyond black or white is colored with a gray mask in the Preview thumbnails. This is done to alert you that the command is generating patches of solid black or white. Once you click OK, the mask is not applied to the image.

4. Shadows

This column adjusts shadows, or the values between 75% and 100%. Lighten the shadow tones by clicking the Lighten thumbnail. Darken the shadows by clicking the Darken thumbnail. The degree of change is determined by the Intensity slider as well as the number of times you click.

5. **Midtones**

This column adjusts the midtones, or the values between 25% and 75%. Again, lighten or darken this range by clicking on the appropriate thumbnail. Changes to the midtones have the most visible effect on the image.

6. **Highlights**

This column adjusts the highlights, or the values from 0% to 25%. Be aware that overlightening the highlights quickly results in large areas of burnout, or 0% black.

The Variations Dialog (Color)

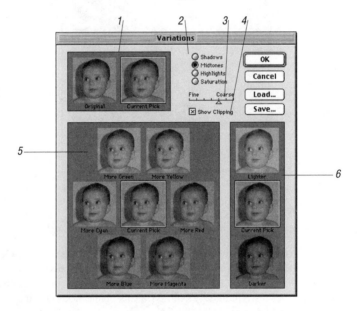

1. **Status Thumbnails**

Similar to the Grayscale option described above, these represent the Original image and current status. Click on Original at any time to restore the original image values.

2. **Tone Selections**

Choosing the Shadows, Midtones, or Highlights button focuses the command on that portion of the tonal range. You can select and edit more than one area while the dialog is open.

There is also a button for Saturation. When this is selected, there are only three thumbnails available: Less Saturated, which lessens the overall color intensity; More Saturated, which increases the overall color intensity; and Current Pick, which displays the current status.

3. **Intensity Slider**

   This slider works the same as in the Grayscale-editing dialog, described above.

4. **Show Clipping**

   Turning this option on acts as a gamut warning. If you begin making extreme adjustments, you'll notice bizarre, unexpected colors appearing in the thumbnails. These inverted values represent values that have extended beyond the available gamut, indicating that certain colors will not display accurately when you click OK. If you apply the adjustment, the colors simply appear flatter than you may expect.

   Many users find the gamut warning a nuisance, and leave the option turned off. At the very least, you can continue using the thumbnails to make basic color decisions.

5. **Hue Thumbnails**

   These buttons are similar to the color sliders in the Image: Adjust: **Color Balance** dialog. Arranged in the same order as the RGB/CMY color wheel, you edit color content by clicking the appropriate hue. Add color by clicking the color you want to add. Subtract a particular color by clicking on its complement, or the opposite button. For example, to add yellow to an image, click More Yellow. To subtract yellow, click More Blue.

   When you click a color button, the Current Pick thumbnail reflects the new edit. The remaining thumbnails are altered to show the new possible changes.

6. **Brightness Thumbnails**

   Use these buttons to lighten or darken the tonal content of the image, while leaving the hue and saturation untouched.

See Also

Image: Adjust: **Color Balance**
Image: Adjust: **Brightness/Contrast**
Image: Adjust: **Hue/Saturation**

Image: Duplicate

This command creates an unsaved copy of the open image.

Special Notes

- This command is most useful when you want to test a series of commands on an image. Simply duplicate the image and edit the copy. This provides the unique opportunity to compare the altered image with its original. If you want to keep the changes, then save the copy, close the original, and continue editing. If you don't want the changes, close the copy without saving.

- Bypass the Duplicate Image dialog by holding down the (Option) [Alt] key while selecting the command. This shortcut leaves all multiple layers unmerged.

The Duplicate Image Dialog

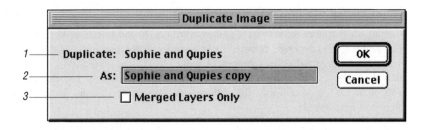

1. Duplicate

   This non-editable field displays the name of the image being duplicated.

2. As

   This editable field allows you to name the duplicate image. It defaults to the name of the original file with the word "copy" tagged on the end. You don't need to rename the new image, but it keeps things organized when making multiple duplicates. Naming a new image is not the same as saving it—if you want to keep a duplicate, you must select File: **Save** to write it to your hard drive.

3. Merged Layers Only

   This option is available only when duplicating an image with multiple layers. Checking the box flattens all the layers in the new image. Leaving the box unchecked creates an identical duplicate.

Calculations Overview

Image: **Apply Image** and Image: **Calculations** are largely holdovers from early versions of Photoshop. Before this program had advanced channel-editing tools and multiple layers, these commands were the only way to composite images from different files. If you wanted to create a montage back then, you had to forcibly merge the pixel values of one image (the source) with the active image (the target). Today, with very few exceptions, every technique they're capable of can be performed using other, more intuitive tools.

While these commands are certainly powerful, they contain three serious limitations:

- They possess the most non-intuitive interface found in Photoshop. Often, it's impossible to predict the results of your settings.

- They only work on images sharing the exact width, height, and resolution.

- Once an effect is applied, it cannot be further adjusted or "tweaked." The result typically has all the flexibility of a flattened image.

If you're new to image compositing, there's little to be gained by mastering these commands. Your time is much better spent working with the **Layers Palette** (see Chapter 20) and the **Channels Palette** (see Chapter 21). If you're more comfortable with the ideas involved there, you may be intrigued by the ability of both commands to produce complex combinations of masking channels.

Image: Apply Image

This command combines the contents of layers or channels to create composite images. It reads information from either one or two equal-sized images.

Special Notes

It can be difficult to preview the image if a color channel is selected as the target. Ordinarily,. when you select a channel from the Channels palette, the remaining colors are hidden—unless you click the View eyeball next to the composite channel *after* you select your desired color channel. Now, when you open the Apply Image dialog, you can preview the overall effect of targeting one color channel.

The Apply Image Dialog

1. Target

   Located in the center of the dialog, this lists the image and layer affected by the command. To target an image layer, select it from the Layers palette before choosing the command. To affect one particular channel, select it from the Channels palette. Once the dialog is opened, this information cannot be altered—so make sure the appropriate layer or channel appears in parentheses. All other options determine how this information is changed.

2. **Source**

    This pop-up lists all available open images. It defaults to the target image, or the image that was active when you opened the dialog. Select the image you want to pull information from.

3. **Layer**

    This pop-up lists all the available layers in the selected source image. If no multiple layers exist, then Background Layer is the only choice. To blend the target image with a specific layer, select the layer from this list. Choose Merged from the list to treat all visible layers as one.

4. **Channel**

    From the source image, you can access either one specific channel or the overall composite. This allows for a variety of effects, depending on the channels selected in the target image (RGB mode is used for the following examples):

    Target Image: *RGB;* **Channel Pop-Up:** *RGB*
    The red, green, and blue channels of both images are combined.

    Target: *RGB;* **Channel:** *Red, Green, or Blue*
    The one color channel is applied equally to the red, green, and blue channels of the target image.

    Target: *Red, Green, or Blue;* **Channel:** *RGB*
    A composite Grayscale version of the source image is combined in that one channel.

    Target: *Red, Green, or Blue;* **Channel:** *Red, Green, or Blue*
    The contents of those two channels are combined.

    Depending on the contents of the source image, four additional options may appear in the Channels pop-up:

    Masking Channels
    If the source image contains any saved selections, their numbers appear in the pop-up.

    Selection
    If the source image contains an active selection, choosing this item results in a mask channel based on the selection.

    Transparency
    If the source image contains transparent pixels, this item results in a mask channel based on the transparent areas.

    Layer Mask
    If the source image has a layer mask attached to it, this item results in a mask channel based on the layer mask.

5. **Blending**

    This pop-up controls the method used to combine the source image with the target image. Twelve of the standard blend modes are available, including Add and Subtract, which are only available here and under Image: **Calculations**.

The effects of these blend modes are simple: Add essentially lightens the result, while Subtract darkens.

6. **Opacity**

   The opacity value affects the source image as it combines with the target image. It's functionally identical to the Opacity slider in the Layers palette.

7. **Preserve Transparency**

   If the target image contains any transparent pixels—for example, an object on its own layer, like a placed EPS graphic—checking this box tells the Apply Image command to ignore the transparent pixels. Compositing only occurs on the colored pixels, similar to a layer mask.

8. **Mask**

   By checking this box, you can use part of the source image as a mask when you combine it with the target image. It can be an active selection, layer mask, or even a regular color channel. For example, if the source image contains an active circular selection, you can use it to mask the rest of the image. Only information inside the selection appears in the target image.

   The dialog expands, displaying another Source, Layer, and Channel menu. Source and Layer work together—use them to choose the image and particular layer you want to use as a mask. From Channel, select your desired color channel. Like the first Channel pop-up, selections, transparency, and layer masks will appear on this list when available.

   Check the Invert button to reverse the effect of the mask.

9. **Result**

   This pop-up menu only appears when you hold down the (Option) [Alt] key while choosing Image: **Apply Image**. It lists possible destinations for the blended information:

   Current Target
   Same as the default, it writes the information into the target image.

   New Document
   This writes the information into a new, unsaved image.

   New Layer
   This creates a new layer within the target image.

   New Channel
   This creates a new masking channel within the target image.

   Selection
   This results in an active selection in the target image, based on the blending of the source image and the target image.

See Also

Image: **Calculations**
Chapter 20, *The Layers Palette*
Chapter 21, *The Channels Palette*

Image: Calculations

This command is nearly the same as Image: **Apply Image**. The primary difference is that Apply Image is used to combine two source *images* into a target image—Image: **Calculations** is used to combine two source *channels* into a target channel.

Common Uses

See Appendix A for full descriptions of the following:

- Creating a replacement for an existing color channel
- Creating a new selection channel
- Creating a new Grayscale image

The Calculations Dialog

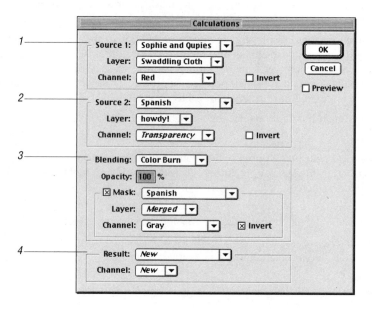

1. **Source 1**

   Here, define your first image. Choose the file name from the Source pop-up. Choose your desired layer from the Layer pop-up. Finally, choose the channel you want to blend from the Channel pop-up. Click Invert to reverse the channel's values.

2. **Source 2**

   Here, define your second image. As with Source 1, choose the appropriate file name, layer, and channel from the pop-up menus. Click Invert to reverse the channel's values.

3. **Blending**

To further affect the compositing of the two channels, select a blend mode from the Blending pop-up. Both the blend modes and the opacity value affect Source 1, as if it was in a layer above Source 2. If desired, choose a third channel to act as a mask between the two sources. Such a mask affects the Source 2 channel. Click Invert to reverse the effect of the mask.

4. **Result**

These pop-ups determine the location of the new channel. To create a new Grayscale image, choose New from the Result pop-up. To replace a color channel in an existing image, select the image from the Result pop-up and choose the appropriate color from the Channel pop-up. To create a new masking channel in an existing image, select the image from the Result pop-up and choose New from the Channel pop-up.

See Also

Appendix A (Image: **Calculations**)
Image: **Apply Image**

Image: Image Size

Resizing an image in Photoshop is different than scaling an image in a page layout program. There, you can only change the width and the height, with no control over the number of image pixels. With Image: **Image Size**, you can dictate exact values for all three image dimensions: width, height, *and* resolution.

Common Uses

- **Resizing an image.** Here, you change the width and height, but not the number of image pixels. Similar to a page layout program, the resolution increases if you make the image smaller, and decreases if the image is made larger. Because the number of pixels remains constant, the file size stays the same. This technique is useful for converting a large low-resolution image into a small print-oriented image.

- **Resampling an image.** This is the most common use of Image: **Image Size**. Here, you force Photoshop to change the number of image pixels, either by *down-sampling*, or decreasing the resolution, or by *upsampling*, or increasing the resolution. This can be done while leaving the width and height untouched, or by setting them to disproportionate values.

See Appendix A for full descriptions of the following:

- Reducing moiré in a scanned pre-screened image
- Repurposing a print-oriented image for the Web

Common Errors

Upsampling by too much. Photoshop downsamples with virtually no image degradation, since it only removes unnecessary pixels. Upsampling, however, makes

Photoshop add pixels where none existed. The program is not very good at guessing, and the result appears pixelated. If you must upsample a scan, you're better off rescanning. To upsample placed artwork, import it again at a higher resolution. If you created the image in Photoshop, you must upsample at your own risk.

Special Notes

- Once an image has been imported into a page layout, it should not be scaled by more than 20%. If you need to make the image smaller, downsample it to a smaller size using Image: **Image Size**. If you need to enlarge it, the best option is to have the image rescanned at the proper dimensions.

- To automatically apply the dimensions from another open image, open the Image Size dialog and choose the other image from the Window menu.

- The default Resample Image option can be changed by selecting another interpolation method under File: Preferences: **General**. Think hard before doing this, however—there is rarely any reason to switch from Bicubic.

The Image Size Dialog

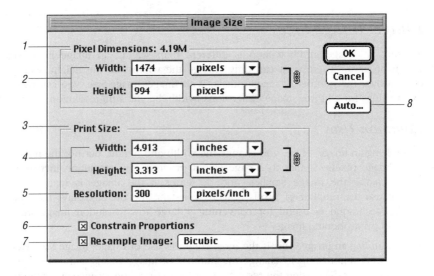

1. **Pixel Dimensions**

   This displays the current file size. As you change the values in the dialog, this number changes to reflect the new size, while putting the original size in parentheses.

2. **Pixel Width and Height**

   These values display the current width and height in terms of pixels. Use these fields to resize images to a specific pixel value, such as monitor widths for multimedia presentations. If desired, select Percent from the pop-up to reduce or increase the image size by percentages. If the Resample box is unchecked, these values cannot be edited.

3. **Print Size**

   These values represent the printable image size, or the image dimensions as they apply to importing, printing, and output.

4. **Print Width and Height**

   By default, these two values are constrained—if you change one, the other changes to maintain the original proportions. Choose a unit of measurement from the pop-ups: percent, inches, centimeters, points, or picas. Just like the File: **New** dialog, the Width pop-up has an option for Columns, which allows you to set a new image width based on the values defined in File: Preferences: **Units & Rulers**.

5. **Resolution**

   This field represents the current image resolution. Entering a different value sets a new resolution, but the method used to apply it depends on the remaining settings. If the Resample Image box is checked (or if Constrain Proportions is unchecked), changing the resolution either downsamples or upsamples the image. If Resample Image is unchecked, the resolution is constrained to the Width and Height values.

6. **Constrain Proportions**

   Checking this box connects certain values in order to maintain the original image proportions. If Resample Image is checked, Width and Height are constrained. If Resample Image is unchecked, Width, Height, and Resolution are constrained. Unchecking this box allows you to edit all three values independently.

7. **Resample Image**

   When you resample an image, Photoshop must use one of three interpolation methods to calculate the new pixels:

   Bicubic
   This method takes the longest, but it results in the highest quality distribution of pixels.

   Bilinear
   This takes less time, but it does a poor job.

   Nearest Neighbor
   This option uses no interpolation at all. It simply adds or discards pixels without averaging any new values.

8. **Auto**

   Theoretically, this option optimizes image resolution for print. Clicking the Auto button brings up the Auto Resolution dialog, where you enter the target linescreen. Based on this value and your selected Quality setting, Photoshop enters a new resolution in the Image Size dialog. For example, if your target linescreen is 150 lpi, clicking Draft sets a value of 150 pixels per inch (lpi × 1). Good sets a value of 225 ppi (lpi × 1.5). Best sets a value of 300 ppi (lpi × 2).

In practice, this option is of little use. If your image was scanned at the appropriate resolution, it does not need to be changed. If the original resolution is too low for print, then Photoshop would have to upsample the image, hindering its quality.

See Also

Appendix A (Image: **Image Size**)
File: Preferences: **General**
File: Preferences: **Units & Rulers**

Image: Canvas Size

This command changes an image's width and height. Unlike Image: **Image Size**, it does this without affecting the resolution.

Common Uses

• **Cropping an image.** Lowering the width and height clips existing pixels, resulting in a smaller image window. When you crop an image this way, an alert appears warning you that pixels are going to be clipped from the current image; click Proceed to apply the new measurements.

• **Expanding the canvas.** Increasing the width and height adds pixels around the existing image, resulting in a larger image window.

Special Notes

• If an image only contains a background layer, then the new pixels appear as the current background color. To add transparent pixels instead, duplicate then delete the background layer in the Layers palette. Then apply Image: **Canvas Size**.

• Occasionally, filter or transformation-based edits place image information off the canvas. To avoid clipping part of your image, undo the command and use Image: **Canvas Size** to temporarily enlarge the image window. If necessary, use Image: **Image Size** or Layer: Transform: **Scale** to reduce the image back to its original dimensions.

The Canvas Size Dialog

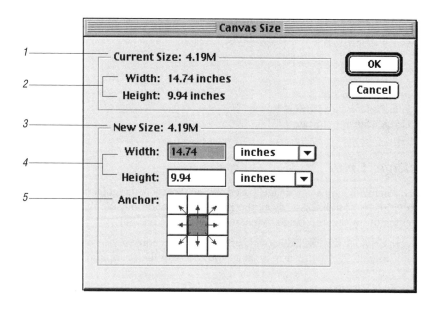

1. **Current Size**

   This displays the current file size.

2. **Width and Height**

   These display the current width and height in terms of pixels.

3. **New Size**

   This displays the higher or lower image size that will result from the new dimensions.

4. **Width and Height**

   Enter new values in these fields to change the width and height of the current image window. Units of measurement include percentages, inches, centimeters, points, and picas. Like the File: **New** dialog, the Width pop-up has an option for Columns, which allows you to set a new image width based on the values defined in File: Preferences: **Units & Rulers**.

5. **Anchor**

   With this grid, you determine the placement of the current image in the new window.

   If cropping the image, the anchor grid allows you to preserve a specific portion of the image. For example, if you reduce the height by one inch and click the top center square, the inch is cropped from the bottom of the image. If you click the center square, a half-inch is removed from the top and bottom.

If expanding the canvas, this grid determines the position of the original image in the larger window. For example, if you add two inches to the width and height and click the center square, one inch is added all the way around the image. If you click the upper left square, two inches are added to the right and two inches are added to the bottom.

See Also

Image: **Image Size**
File: Preferences: **Units & Rulers**
Layer: Transform: **Scale**

Image: Crop

This command crops an image based on an active rectangular selection. When you crop, Photoshop discards all the image information outside the selection area, resetting the width and height while maintaining the resolution.

Image: **Crop** is not available with any other selection shape. Also, you cannot rotate or easily resize the crop area, as you can with the Cropping Tool.

Special Notes

By choosing Select: **All** and applying Image: **Crop**, you discard any layer information that extends beyond the image boundaries.

Image: Rotate Canvas

Unlike the Layer: **Transform** options, which can rotate selected areas, these commands rotate the entire canvas.

180°

This option rotates the entire image 180°, or halfway around a circle.

90° CW

This option rotates the entire image 90° to the right.

90° CCW

This option rotates the entire image 90° to the left.

Arbitrary

This option rotates the entire image by an amount you define, either to the left or right. Since Photoshop only displays images in upright-rectangular windows, the canvas size is increased to accommodate the tilted corners.

Special Note

If your image only contains one layer, applying an arbitrary rotation fills the new canvas area with the background color. Avoid this by duplicating and deleting the background layer before rotating the image. The new pixels now appear as transparent areas.

Flip Horizontal

This option flips the image on a vertical axis, providing a horizontal mirror-image.

Flip Vertical

This option flips the image on a horizontal axis, providing a vertical mirror-image.

Image: Histogram

This histogram is Photoshop's most thorough and accurate graph of an image's tonal values. It does not perform any specific commands—it's used only to evaluate existing information.

Although this dialog gives very detailed information about an image, most of it is simply academic. Indeed, knowing the exact number of pixels in an image is of little help when making tonal corrections.

Common Uses

- **Checking the distribution of image tones captured by a scanner.** If any gaps exist, or if certain tones such as shadows or highlights were not acquired, rescan the image before applying any corrections.

- **Determining image key.** Certain images have a naturally higher concentration of light or dark colors. For example, a scan of a snow-covered field is considered *high-key*, because it consists primarily of quarter- and highlight-tones. A scan of a cityscape at night is *low-key*, consisting mainly of three-quarter and shadow-tones. This information helps you create a better color correcting strategy.

- **Checking the status of an image during correction.** As you apply Image: **Adjust** commands, you consistently remove levels of information from the image. If the number of tones is reduced by too much, the image appears grainy and posterized. Checking the histogram channel lets you know how much information remains in each channel.

Special Notes

If the image contains an active selection, only those values are represented in the histogram.

The Histogram Dialog

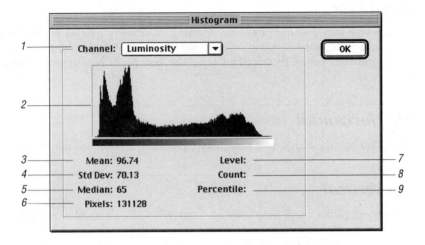

1. Channel

Choose the channel you wish to review from this pop-up. To see a composite of all color channels, select Luminosity. If the active image is in Grayscale mode, to pop-up is replaced by a single option: black.

2. The Histogram

From left to right, this graph displays the darkest to lightest pixel values. The vertical lines each represent one of 256 possible tones. The higher the line, the more of that particular tone exists in the image.

The histogram for the Luminosity channel is particularly useful. This displays the overall range of the image, allowing you to determine the distribution of light and dark tones.

This graph differs from the histogram found in Image: Adjust: **Levels**. There, the composite histogram overlays the values of all color channels. For example, a value of 255 means at least one of the channels contains all-white information—regardless of the values of the remaining channels. The Image: **Histogram** composite averages the values of all channels before graphing them. Now, a value of 255 only occurs when *every* color channel is maxed.

3. Mean

This value is the average brightness level for all image pixels. It's based on two things: the range from endpoint to endpoint and the tonal emphasis. For example, a high-key image may share the same tonal range as a low-key image, but since it has an abundance of lighter tones, the mean value is higher.

---

4. **Std Dev**

   Short for Standard Deviation, this value represents the difference in brightness of the average pixel from the Mean.

5. **Median**

   This value represents the value in the exact center of the existing tonal range. For example, if a Grayscale image contains brightness values from 10 to 240, the Median is 125. With color images, a different value typically applies to each channel.

6. **Pixels**

   This value is the total number of image pixels.

7. **Level**

   To target the brightness value of an individual point on the histogram, position the cursor over it and click. The value appears under this option. If you click-drag to highlight a range of values, the darkest and lightest points appear here, separated by an ellipsis.

8. **Count**

   When you click on the histogram to see a brightness value under Levels, this value displays the number of image pixels containing that value.

9. **Percentile**

   This value displays the percentage of existing image pixels possessing a value darker than the selected value.

See Also

Image: Adjust: **Levels**

Image: Trap Overview

Trapping is a time-honored conventional prepress technique, and applies only to images containing more than one ink color. To compensate for any misregistration that may occur on-press, the color of one object is slightly expanded into its adjacent color. By creating this thin overlap, you prevent tiny gaps from appearing between colored objects in your printed piece.

Although trapping is an important part of any print job, the question is whether or not you need to use this particular command. The vast majority of CMYK images are one of two types:

- Continuous tone images, like scanned photographs, containing a wide and varied range of cyan, magenta, yellow, and black inks.

- Artwork or logos with colors that share multiple CMYK components.

Ninety-five percent of the time, these images do not need to be trapped. This is due to a *process bridge*, which essentially states that two adjacent colors sharing at least 20% of one component do not need to be trapped. Should misregistration occur, that color prevents any gaps from showing.

Most often, the only time you need to use Image: **Trap** is when an image consists of colors that do not share a process component. For example, a pure cyan shape abutting a pure black shape needs to be manually trapped, since they share no components.

Trapping Imported Vector-Based Artwork

Whether or not imported graphics need to be trapped depends on the content of the image and the techniques that were used in creating it. First and foremost, an illustration created using process colors must be imported as a CMYK image. Importing it as RGB and then converting to CMYK alters all the color values. Beyond that, most trapping needs can be taken care of before the image is imported:

- If the shapes in the image share a process bridge, they do not need to be trapped.

- If you added trap to a vector-based illustration before importing it into Photoshop, those color commands translate into the new image.

- If the image contains black outlines—like a cartoon character or a box with a frame—set them to Overprint before importing the image.

Image: Trap

This command allows you to apply a trapping value to any CMYK image.

Once applied, Image: **Trap** seeks out all abutting colors and traces them with a thin, colored line. Since trapping consists of one color expanding into another, this command uses the following guidelines:

- All colors expand into black.
- Lighter colors expand into darker colors.
- Yellow expands into cyan, magenta, and black.
- Pure cyan and pure magenta expand into each other equally.

Common Errors

Trapping a continuous-tone image. Doing so may visibly distort the tones in the cyan, magenta, and yellow channels.

Special Notes

- If you apply your own traps, always contact your printer for advice on appropriate trap widths. Different press types and printing methods all have unique requirements.

- Image: **Trap** is only available when editing an image in CMYK mode.

The Trap Dialog

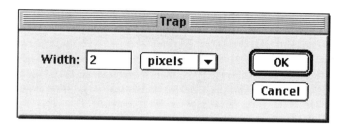

Width

Here, you determine the width of the overlapping line. Choose points, pixels, or millimeters as a unit of measurement. Other programs with trapping functions use points, so this may be the most intuitive unit.

See Also

Image: Mode: **CMYK**

CHAPTER 11

The Layer Menu

Layers allow you to work with image elements as if they were on a series of transparent overlays.

Without layers (which debuted in version 3.0), you could only edit one flat canvas of pixels. To make a focused adjustment, you had to draw a selection outline to isolate the targeted area. When creating image composites or montages, you were mostly limited to complex channel techniques and the Image: **Calculations** commands.

With layers, the effect is similar to working in a page layout or illustration program. There, you treat each element as an independent entity. By selecting one item, you can make changes without affecting the others. You can easily rearrange an item, placing it above or below the rest at will.

There are three types of layer: background, image, and adjustment.

The Background Layer

The background layer is Photoshop's default layer. It's fully opaque, similar to the single canvas used by early versions of Photoshop, or any other pixel-based editing software that does not support multiple layers. Background layers automatically appear in the following images:

- **Scans.** When you use a scanning Plug-in to acquire an image while Photoshop is open, the sampled data appears on a background layer.

- **Images saved in any file format other than native Photoshop.** Only native Photoshop images can contain multiple layers. Images saved as a GIF, EPS, or any other file format can only contain a single layer.

- **New images with non-transparent contents.** When creating a new image with the File: **New** dialog, setting the Contents to White or Background Color results in a background layer.

- **Flattened images.** Applying Layer: Flatten Image converts all multiple image layers to a single background layer.

Common Errors

Confining all your edits to the background layer. A background layer is not required to continue editing. As soon as you require additional layers, the restrictions of the background layer can prove cumbersome:

- A background layer cannot possess transparent pixels or an opacity value of less than 100%.
- A background layer cannot be repositioned in the Layers Palette.
- If a portion of the background layer is selected and deleted, the selected area is filled with the current background color.
- Increasing the image dimensions using Image: **Canvas Size** fills the new pixels in the background layer with the current background color.

Special Notes

- An image can only contain one background layer. In the **Layers Palette**, it is always titled *"Background"*.
- An image layer cannot be converted to a background layer, but you can create a new background layer using the Layer: New: **Layer** dialog.
- Avoid the limitations of the background layer by converting it to an image layer:
  - **Double-click the background layer in the Layers Palette.** After entering a new name in the Make Layer dialog and clicking OK, it appears as an image layer.
  - **Duplicate the background layer.** Either choose the background layer and select Duplicate Layer from the Layers Palette submenu, or drag the background layer item onto the New Layer control button. The copy appears as an image layer, allowing you to hide or delete the original background layer.

See Also

File: **New**
Layer: New: **Layer**
Image: **Canvas Size**
The Layers Palette

Image Layers

Image layers are created in addition to the background layer, allowing you to isolate an image element smaller than the entire window. Each layer appears as a separate item in the Layers Palette, giving you independent control over their position and front-to-back arrangement. Since these layers support transparent pixels, you can see the image data contained in underlying layers.

When you choose Layer: New: **Layer**, the result is an empty, fully transparent layer. This allows you to paint, fill, or otherwise add new color to an image without affecting any existing pixels. More often, however, new layers are based on existing image information.

Once an image contains multiple layers, you can only apply changes to the layer currently chosen in the Layers Palette. There are three exceptions to this rule:

- Changing the color mode of an image.

- Applying a Layer: **Transform** command to a linked layer. See the **Layers Palette** (Chapter 20) for more information on linking layers.

- Changing the width, height, or resolution of an image using Image: **Image Size** or **Canvas Size**.

Special Notes

- A single image can contain up to 100 separate layers.

- As long as an image is open in Photoshop, it can contain multiple layers—even if the image was originally saved in a file format that doesn't support them. However, once an image contains anything but a background layer, it can only be saved in the native Photoshop file format. To save an image containing multiple layers into a different file format, you must choose one of the following commands:

  Layer: Flatten Image. This combines all visible layers into a single background layer, allowing you to save the image into any available file format.

  File: Save a Copy. This allows you to save a separate, flattened copy of the open image into any available file format.

See Also

File: Save a Copy
Image: **Image Size**
Image: **Canvas Size**
Layer: New: **Layer**
Layer: **Transform**
Layer: **Flatten Image**
The Layers Palette

Adjustment Layers

An adjustment layer contains no image data—rather, it contains the values of one of the Image: **Adjust** commands. It acts as a sort of lens, affecting the appearance of any underlying information.

The adjustments appear as if they were applied directly from the Image menu, but there are two key differences. Instead of affecting a single layer, an adjustment layer affects the pixels of all underlying layers. Also, the effect of an adjustment layer is a *preview*, not a permanent adjustment—no pixels are permanently altered until the image is flattened or layers are merged.

When you create an Adjustment Layer, an additional mask item is listed in the **Channels Palette** (see Chapter 21). By editing the contents of this channel, you can limit the area affected by an adjustment layer:

- **Make a selection before creating an adjustment layer.** When you examine the new layer's thumbnail in the **Layers Palette**, the contents of the former selection are white, and the remaining areas are black. The adjustment only affects the white areas.

- **Use a Paint Tool to edit the contents of an adjustment layer.** When an adjustment layer is active in the Layers Palette, you can only define black, white, or tones of gray as the foreground or background color. Areas painted black are not affected by the adjustment layer, similar to editing a Quick Mask, layer mask, or mask channel. Painting with gray partially reduces the effect of the adjustment layer, similar to lowering its opacity.

Special Notes

Since you do not apply visible color to the image, it may be difficult to apply precise brushstrokes. Use the following shortcuts to facilitate this process:

- Hold down the (Option) [Alt] key and click the adjustment layer thumbnail to display the contents of the mask. (Option) [Alt]-click again to return to the normal editing mode.

- Hold down the (Option-Shift) [Alt-Shift] keys and click the adjustment layer thumbnail to view the mask as a semi-transparent overlay, similar to the one used by the **Quick Mask Tools**. (Option-Shift) [Alt-Shift]-click again to hide the overlay.

See Also

Layer: New: **Adjustment Layer**
Layer: **Adjustment Options**
The Layers Palette
The Channels Palette

Transparency

When a single element is added to an image layer, it is surrounded with transparent pixels. These pixels contain no color information, and allow you to "see through" the unused portions of a layer to the underlying information. This is sometimes referred to as a *transparency mask*.

Photoshop displays a checkerboard pattern to indicate transparency values. This pattern does not print or appear in any other application—it is only used to differentiate transparent areas from any other colors. The pattern is visible when the background layer has been removed or hidden from view, or when no color information appears on a specific portion of all visible layers.

Special Notes

- Most Photoshop commands only affect *existing* color information—the Image: **Adjust** commands are good examples. Transparent pixels can only be affected by actions that add *new* data.

- Since transparent pixels contain no image data, they do not contribute to the overall file size. Only colored pixels increase the file size.

Opacity

When a layer is 100% opaque, its contents completely conceal any underlying information. When you reduce the opacity of a layer, you create the appearance of fading the image, allowing the underlying colors to show through. At 75% opacity, 75% of the visible information is contained in the visible layer, and 25% comes from the layers beneath. When the opacity is set to 50%, the active layer and the underlying layers appear at equal intensities. Most often, layer opacity is set with the opacity slider in the **Layers Palette** (see Chapter 20).

Special Notes

- Setting opacity only affects the appearance of a layer. It does not permanently alter the pixel values until you apply either Layer: **Merge** or **Flatten Image**.

- When you lower the opacity of an adjustment layer, you decrease the impact of its adjustment values.

See Also

Layer: **Merge**
Layer: **Flatten Image**
The Layers Palette

Layer: New

Each option under this submenu adds a new item to the **Layers Palette**.

New: Layer

This command adds a new image layer to the **Layers Palette**, placing it above the currently active item.

Common Uses

- Creating a new, blank image layer
- Filling a new layer with a blend mode's neutral color

Special Notes

Many filters, such as Filter: Render: **Lens Flare** or **Lighting Effects**, cannot be applied to the transparent pixels of an empty image layer. By choosing a blend mode and checking Neutral Color for Blend Mode, you can affect this new layer without permanently altering any underlying color values. This technique offers three distinct advantages:

- You can continue editing the underlying information, independent of the filter's effect.

- You can adjust the intensity of the effect by manipulating the layer's opacity slider, or by choosing different blend modes that share the same neutral color.

- You can reposition the effect, since it resides on a separate layer.

The New Layer Dialog

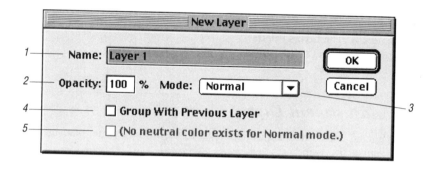

1. **Name**

   Photoshop automatically enters a name in this field, loosely based on the number of layers that already exist. If desired, enter a new layer title of up to 32 characters.

2. **Opacity**

   The value in this field sets the opacity slider of the new layer. This value isn't permanent—you can always reset the slider at any time during editing.

3. **Mode**

   This pop-up allows you to apply any of the 17 available blend modes to the new layer. This setting isn't permanent—you can always choose a new blend mode at any time during editing. Most often, a specific blend mode is chosen from this dialog to take advantage of the Neutral Color for Blend Mode option, described later in this list.

   If the current image does not contain a background layer, an additional listing appears at the bottom of the pop-up: *Background*. Choose this item to add a new background layer. You cannot enter a new title in the Name field when *Background* is chosen.

4. **Group with Previous Layer**

Check this box to create a clipping group between the new layer and the item directly beneath it in the Layers Palette. If the underlying layer is already part of a group, this option adds the new layer to the existing group.

5. **Neutral Color for Blend Mode**

When certain blend modes are set in the Mode pop-up, checking this box fills the new layer with their *neutral color*, or the tone that results in no visible effect on the underlying information. The available neutral color depends on the blend mode set in the Mode pop-up:

- **Black**. The neutral color for Screen, Color Dodge, Lighten, Difference, and Exclusion.

- **White**. The neutral color for Multiply, Color Burn, and Darken.

- **50% Gray**. The neutral color for Overlay, Soft Light and Hard Light.

See Also

Appendix A (**The Layers Palette**)
Layer: **Group with Previous**
The Layers Palette

New: Adjustment Layer

This command adds a new adjustment layer to the **Layers Palette**, placing it above the currently active item.

Special Notes

It is important to select the proper command as you create the adjustment layer. This is the only option that cannot be changed once the layer is added to the Layers Palette—to set a new adjustment command, you must discard the item and create a new adjustment layer.

The New Adjustment Layer Dialog

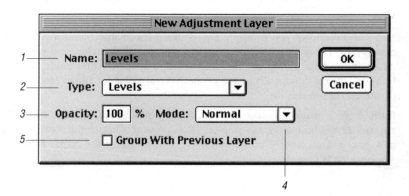

1. **Name**

   Photoshop automatically enters the name of the command chosen from the Type pop-up. If desired, enter a new layer title of up to 32 characters. Many users enter a brief description of the applied adjustment.

2. **Type**

   Choose the type of adjustment you wish to apply from this pop-up. Every available command also appears under the Image: **Adjust** submenu—for full descriptions of their use, refer to the appropriate item in the **Image Menu** (see Chapter 10). When you click OK to close the New Adjustment Layer dialog, Photoshop automatically opens the dialog of the selected command.

3. **Opacity**

   The value in this field sets the opacity slider of the new layer. Unlike image layers, adjustment layers contain no visible pixels. Here, lowering the opacity reduces the effect of the adjustment. This value isn't permanent—you can always reset the slider at any time during editing.

4. **Mode**

   This pop-up allows you to apply any of the 17 available blend modes to the new adjustment layer.

   This setting isn't permanent—you can always choose a new blend mode at any time during editing. When you set a blend mode, the result colors may appear wildly unpredictable. In reality, the effect is the same as if you did the following:

   – Duplicate the underlying image layer.

   – With the duplicate layer active, apply an adjustment command from the Image Menu.

   – Set the blend mode.

   Leave the Mode pop-up set to Normal to apply only the new adjustment values to the underlying layers.

5. **Group with Previous Layer**

   Check this box to group the new layer with the active item in the Layers Palette. Do this to restrict the effect of an adjustment layer to a single image layer, instead of all underlying layers.

See Also

Image: **Adjust**
The Layers Palette

Layer Via Copy
(Command) [Control]-J

Choose this command to place the contents of an active selection into a new image layer, similar to making a selection and choosing Edit: **Copy** and **Paste**. The base layer is untouched, and the contents of the new layer maintain their original position.

Special Notes

Hold down the (Option) [Alt] key while choosing this command to access the Make Layer dialog. It is identical to the New Layer dialog, without the Fill with Neutral Color option. (See Layer: New: **Layer** for more information.)

See Also

Edit: **Copy**
Edit: **Paste**
Layer: New: **Layer**

Layer Via Cut
(Command-Shift) [Control-Shift]-J

Choose this command to place the contents of an active selection into a new image layer, similar to making a selection and choosing Edit: **Cut** and **Paste**. The contents of the new layer maintain their original position, but the base layer is affected: if the information came from an image layer, the selection area is filled with transparent pixels; if the information came from a background layer, the selection area is filled with the current background color.

Special Notes

Hold down the (Option) [Alt] key while choosing this command to access the Make Layer dialog. It is identical to the New Layer dialog, without the Fill with Neutral Color option. (See Layer: New: **Layer** for more information.)

See Also

Edit: **Cut**
Edit: **Paste**
Layer: New: **Layer**

Layer: Duplicate Layer

This command creates a copy of the currently active layer.

Common Uses

• Duplicating a layer to the same image or another open image

• Creating an entirely new, unsaved image from a layer

Special Notes

• Regardless of the image a layer is duplicated to, the new item is listed above the active layer in the Layers Palette.

- If the color mode of the destination image is different than the source image, the color values of the duplicate layer convert to match the destination image.

- When copying a layer from one image to another, it's not necessary to access the Duplicate Layer dialog. Drag the appropriate item from the Layers Palette in the source image onto the image window of the destination image. When a black border appears around the image window, release the mouse button. The item appears in the Layers Palette of the second image.

The Duplicate Layer Dialog

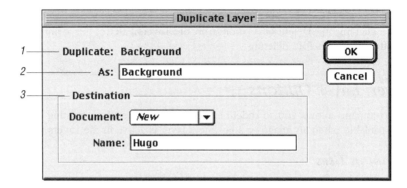

1. Duplicate

   This non-editable field contains the name of the original layer.

2. As

   This field contains the name of the new layer. When duplicating the layer into the same image, Photoshop automatically enters the original layer name with "copy" added at the end. When sending the new layer to another image, the automatic name is loosely based on the number of existing layers. If desired, enter a new title of up to 32 characters.

3. Destination

   The options in this pop-up determine the location of the new layer:

   Document

   This pop-up lists all open images, and defaults to the image containing the original layer. To duplicate the layer to another image, select its name from the pop-up. To convert the duplicate into a new image, select New from the pop-up.

   Name

   When New is selected in the Document pop-up, this field allows you to title the new image. Entering a name here does not automatically save the image—you must still choose File: **Save**.

See Also

File: **Save**
Chapter 20, *The Layers Palette*

Layer: Delete Layer

This command permanently removes the active layer from a multilayer image. When an image contains only one layer, this command is not available.

Special Notes

Unlike clicking the Delete Layer button in the **Layers Palette**, this command does not offer an alert before deleting.

Layer: Layer Options

This command allows you to redefine the characteristics of an existing layer. It is only available when an image or adjustment layer is active in the Layers Palette.

Common Uses

• Renaming a layer

• Blending the contents of multiple layers

Special Notes

Access the Layer Options dialog by double-clicking any image layer.

The Layer Options Dialog

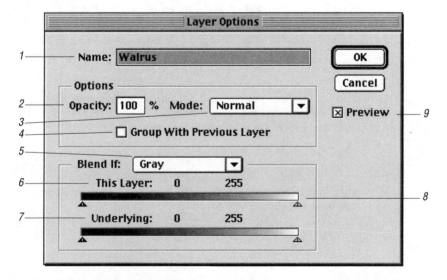

---

1. **Name**

   If desired, enter a new name for the layer in this field.

2. **Opacity**

   Setting a new opacity value here is the same as manipulating the opacity slider of an existing layer.

3. **Mode**

   Choosing a new blend mode here is the same as applying a mode from the Layers Palette pop-up.

4. **Group with Previous Layer**

   Checking this box is the same as choosing Layer: **Group with Previous** or (Option) [Alt] clicking between items in the Layers Palette to create a clipping group.

5. **Blend If**

   This pop-up allows you to isolate the blend command to a specific color channel.

   When editing an RGB or CMYK image, choose Gray from the pop-up to include all color channels in the blend. This designation is inconsistent with the rest of Photoshop's controls, which refer to this composite channel as "RGB" or "CMYK." No composite is available when editing a Lab Color image. When editing layers in a Grayscale image, Black is the only available option.

6. **This Layer**

   This bar represents the brightness values of the active layer. When the two sliders are positioned at 0 and 255, all colors in the layer are visible. By repositioning a slider, you hide a range of visible brightness values. For example, moving the right slider from 255 to 200 forces all values between 201 and 255 to become transparent.

7. **Underlying**

   This bar represents the brightness values of the underlying image information. The effect is the opposite of the This Layer bar: by repositioning a slider, a range of underlying colors becomes visible through the active layer, regardless of the active layer's brightness values. For example, moving the left slider from 0 to 30 forces the active layer to reveal all underlying values between 0 and 29.

8. **Smooth Transition Sliders**

   If the layers contain continuous tones, moving the blend sliders can result in harsh transitions between the visible and hidden color values. By holding down the (Option) [Alt] key and dragging one side of a slider, it splits in two. This adds a range of increasing semi-opacity between the hidden and visible colors, creating a smoother transition.

   For example, moving the left slider of the bar to 20 and (Option) [Alt]-dragging its right half to 40 creates a smooth transition. When applied to the This Layer bar, values between 0 and 19 are transparent, values between 20 and 39 gradually increase in opacity, and values above 40 are fully opaque. When applied to the Underlying bar, values between 0 and 19 are fully opaque,

Layer Menu

values between 20 and 39 gradually increase in transparency, and values above 40 are not visible.

Once you have separated the two sections of a slider, you can reposition them without holding down the (Option) [Alt] key.

9. **Preview**

Check this box to see the effect of your adjustments on-screen while the Layer Options dialog is still open.

Layer: Adjustment Options

This command opens the Image: **Adjust** dialog defined in an adjustment layer, allowing you to further manipulate its settings.

Layer: Add Layer Mask

A layer mask uses the contents of a temporary channel to partially conceal the contents of a layer. Although this channel can be accessed in the **Channels Palette**, it also appears as a thumbnail in the layer's item in the **Layers Palette**. To edit the layer's contents, click the image thumbnail. To edit the layer mask, click the mask thumbnail.

This channel has the same properties of any other 8-bit color or mask channel. You can only add tones of gray, which dictate how the contents of the image layer are revealed. Black areas mask the image, and white areas expose the image. Gray values result in semi-opacity, depending on the value. For example, an area painted with 75% gray exposes 25% of the image layer's color values.

Common Uses

Refer to Appendix A for full descriptions of the following:

- Using the Paint Tools to create soft image transitions
- Creating custom image frames
- Viewing the contents of a layer mask

Common Errors

- **Unintentionally breaking the layer mask link.** The layer mask is linked to the image layer by default, as indicated by the three-link chain between the two thumbnails. If you click the icon to break the link, you can independently reposition the image and the mask.
- **Editing the image instead of the mask.** It's easy to edit the image when you intend to work in the layer mask. The line around the thumbnails thickens to indicate whether the image or its mask is being edited. This line is black—the same color as our mask, making it difficult to see. Pay attention to the Status box for the selected layer in the Layers Palette. If a paintbrush appears in the Status box, you can edit the image layer. If a dotted circle appears, you can edit the layer mask.

Special Notes

- Aside from choosing Layer: **Remove Layer Mask**, there are two ways to delete a layer containing a layer mask. In the Layers Palette, dragging the image thumbnail to the Delete button removes the entire layer, mask and all. Dragging the mask thumbnail to the Delete button opens an alert, which gives you the option of removing the mask or permanently applying it to the image.

- Clicking the Add Layer Mask button in the **Layers Palette** has the same effect as choosing Layer: Add Layer Mask: **Reveal All**. If an active selection exists, it has the same effect as Layer: Add Layer Mask: **Reveal Selection**.

See Also

Appendix A (Layer: **Add Layer Mask**)
Layer: **Remove Layer Mask**
The Layers Palette
The Channels Palette

Reveal All

This command adds a layer mask completely filled with white, allowing you to gradually hide the image by painting the layer mask with black.

Hide All

This command adds a layer mask completely filled with black, allowing you to gradually reveal the image by painting the layer mask with white.

Reveal Selection

This option creates a layer mask based on the active selection. Areas inside the active selection are filled with white. Areas outside the active selection are filled with black. Feathered or anti-aliased selection edges result in gray tones.

Hide Selection

This option creates a layer mask based on the active selection. Areas inside the active selection are filled with black. Areas outside the active selection are filled with white.

Layer: Remove Layer Mask

This command removes a layer mask. An alert appears, asking, "Apply layer mask before discarding?" Select Apply to make the changes permanent. Select Discard to remove the layer mask without applying any changes.

Special Notes

This command is available regardless of which thumbnail is selected in the **Layers Palette**.

Layer: Disable/Enable Layer Mask

Choose this command to turn off the effects of the mask without discarding the layer. In the Layers Palette, the mask thumbnail appears with a red X through it. If the layer mask is disabled, selecting Enable activates it again.

Layer: Group with Previous/Group Linked
(Command) [Control]-G

A *clipping group* is a masking technique. Instead of using a temporary mask channel (like a layer mask does), a clipping group uses the contents of one layer to mask the contents of another. Photoshop uses the transparent pixels of the lower layer as the basis for masking the upper layer. When the layers are grouped, the information of the upper layer only appears wherever non-transparent pixels exist in the base layer.

To create a clipping group, select a layer in the **Layers Palette**. If the layer is not linked to another, Group with Previous appears in the Layer Menu. If the layer is linked to any adjacent layers, the Group Linked command appears in the Layers menu.

Layer: **Group with Previous** creates a clipping group between the active layer and the layer directly beneath it. Layer: **Group Linked** joins all adjacent linked layers into a linked Clipping Group. The bottom linked layer becomes the clipping layer, regardless of which layer was selected.

Special Notes

*   Duplicate the effect of this command in the Layers Palette by holding down the (Option) [Alt] key and clicking the dotted line between two layers.
*   Ungrouped layers dragged into clipping groups become part of the clipping group.
*   Clipping groups are not automatically linked. To link the relative position of the grouped layers, you must link them manually.

Layers: Ungroup
(Command-Shift) [Control-Shift]-G

This command splits a clipping group into ordinary layers. All grouped layers revert back to their unclipped state.

Layer: Transform

Use the Transform commands to scale, rotate, skew and otherwise distort a selection or layer.

Common Errors

- **Over-manipulating the transformation box.** It is possible to move the handles of the transformation box to such a degree that the mathematics of re-interpolating the image become impossible for Photoshop to calculate. When this happens, the lines of the bounding box change from solid to dotted, indicating that you are asking Photoshop to do the impossible. To correct this, move the handles until the dotted lines become solid again or cancel the transformation and begin again.

- **Applying multiple transformations individually.** Every time you transform an image, you force Photoshop to recalculate the data for every pixel. While Photoshop does an excellent job at this, some information will be lost. Typically, this means a loss of detail, resulting in a slightly blurred image. This increases with every transformation. Apply all your transformations at once to minimize this loss of detail information.

Special Notes

- Background layers cannot be transformed, but selected parts of the background layer can.
- The **Info Palette** displays the status of any active transformation.
- To switch from one command to another while the transformation box is active, use the context-sensitive menus. Control-click (Macintosh) or right-click (Windows) inside the transformation box to bring up a complete list of available transformations.

See Also

Chapter 16, *The Info Palette*

Layer: Free Transform
(Command) [Control]-T

This command allows you to access all dynamic transformations simultaneously.

As with other dynamic transformations, Free Transform uses a transform box to preview the changes. Holding the Command, Option, or Shift keys is necessary to apply certain changes.

Move

Click and drag inside the transform box to reposition of the selection.

Scale

Drag any handle to change the height and width of the selection.

- Hold down the Shift key while dragging corner handles to scale proportionately.

- Hold down the (Option) [Alt] key to scale symmetrically from the center.

- Hold down the (Option-Shift) [Alt-Shift] keys to scale symmetrically and proportionally from the center.

Flip

To flip the image, drag a handle past a handle on the opposite side of the transform box.

- **Flip Horizontally.** Drag a handle on the left-hand side of the transform box past a handle on the right-hand side.

- **Flip Vertically.** Drag a handle from the top of the box past one on the bottom.

- **Flip Proportionally.** Hold the Shift key down while dragging a corner handle to keep things in proportion.

- **Flip Proportionally from the Center.** Hold the Option and Shift keys down while dragging a corner handle to flip proportionally from the center.

Rotate

Move the pointer outside of the transform box and drag clockwise or counterclockwise to change its angle. Hold the Shift key while dragging to constrain the rotation to 15° increments.

Distort

Hold down the (Command) [Control] key and drag any handle in any direction. Distort symmetrically from the center of the transform box by holding down the (Option-Command) [Alt-Control] keys and dragging any handle.

Skew

Hold down the (Command) [Control] key and drag any handle to skew the image.

Apply Perspective

Hold down the (Option-Command-Shift) [Alt-Control-Shift] keys and drag a corner handle to apply perspective.

Scale

Scale allows you to change the height and width of a selection or layer.

- Drag the top or bottom center handles to increase or decrease the height.

- Drag the left or right center handles to increase or decrease the width.

- Drag the corner handles to change both the height and width simultaneously.
- To change the height and width proportionally, hold down the Shift key while dragging the corner handles.
- To flip the image while scaling, drag any handle past the anchor point.

Layer: Transform

All layer transformation commands except for Free Transform are located under the Layer: **Transform** menu.

Layer Menu

Rotate

This command allows you to change the angle of the selection or layer.

Rotate is the only dynamic transform command that does not use the handles to make changes. Instead, click and drag anywhere outside the transformation box. Hold down the Shift key while dragging to rotate in 15° increments. Double-click inside the image to apply the rotation.

Special Notes

Don't use the rotate tool for straightening crooked scans. It increases the canvas size and still requires the extra step of cropping the image. Instead, use the **Cropping Tool** (see Chapter 1, *Selection Tools*) to simultaneously rotate and crop the image.

Skew

This command constrains the movement of the handles to the same direction of the lines of the transformation box. You can only drag the handles in one direction at a time.

Special Notes

- (Option) [Alt]-dragging a corner handle is the same as dragging a center handle.
- (Option) [Alt]-dragging a center handle skews the image while anchoring the two adjacent center handles.

Distort

Distort allows you to move any handle in any direction. As with any dynamic transformation, moving a center handle moves the entire side of the transformation box.

Special Notes

• Hold the Shift key to constrain the distortion, similar to Skew.

• Hold the (Option) [Alt] key while dragging to make the opposite handle mirror the new position.

Perspective

This command constrains the movement of the handles to the direction of the lines of the transformation box. When one corner handle is dragged, the opposite handle moves an equal distance in the opposite direction.

Numeric
(Command-Shift) [Control-Shift]-T

This command allows you to apply transformations based on precise numerical values.

Special Notes

• The Distort and Perspective options are not available with this command.

• Since dynamic transformations are not recorded by the **Actions Palette**, Numeric Transformations are the only way you can record scaling, skewing, and rotating.

The Numeric Transform Dialog

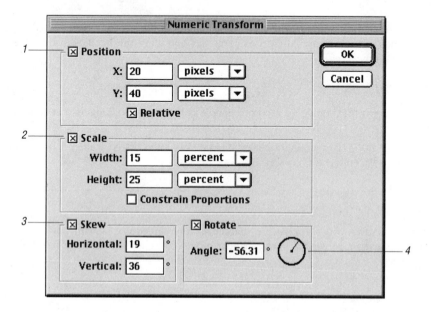

1. **Position**

   Use this option to reposition a selection or image layer. You can move it relative to its current position or to specific XY coordinates. Check the Relative button beneath the XY values to move an item the specified distance from its starting position. Uncheck the button to move the item according to the XY coordinates of the entire image. This location is based on the upper-left corner of the image layer or selection.

   Enter values in the X and Y fields. Positive values move the image to the right and up, negative values move it to the left and down.

   By default, this option measures in pixels. To use a different unit, select from the Unit pop-up.

2. **Scale**

   Use this option to scale a selection or layer. Check the Constrain Proportions box to keep the height and width proportional.

3. **Skew**

   Use this option to skew a selection or layer. Positive values in the Horizontal field skew on the Y axis toward the left, as measured from the lower left corner. Negative values skew to the right. Positive values in the Vertical field skew upwards on the X axis, as measured from the lower left-hand corner. Negative values skew downwards.

4. **Rotate**

   Use this option to rotate a selection or layer. Enter a value from -360 to 360 in the Angle field, or drag the arm of the rotate circle beside the field to rotate the selection or layer by that degree.

See Also

The Actions Palette

Rotate 180˚

This command turns the active selection or layer upside-down.

Rotate 90˚ CW

This command turns the active selection or layer onto its right-hand side.

Rotate 90˚ CCW

This command turns the active selection or layer onto its left-hand side.

Flip Horizontal

This command turns the image over from left to right, like flipping a transparent colored overlay.

Special Notes

Use Image: Rotate Canvas: **Flip Horizontal** to perform this correction on an image consisting solely of a background layer, or when all image layers need to be rotated.

See Also

Image: **Rotate Canvas**

Flip Vertical

This command turns the image over from top to bottom like flipping a transparent colored overlay. At the same time, it rotates the image 180%.

Special Notes

Use Image: Rotate Canvas: **Flip Vertical** to perform this correction on an image consisting solely of a background layer, or when all image layers need to be rotated.

See Also

Image: **Rotate Canvas**

Layer: Arrange

Use the Arrange commands to change the order of layers in the **Layers Palette**. These options are not available when the background layer is active.

Bring to Front
(Command-Shift) [Control-Shift]-]

In the **Layers Palette**, this command moves the active layer above the top layer.

Special Notes

- If the active layer is an image layer, its contents appear in front of the pixels in all other layers.
- If the active layer is an adjustment layer, all underlying layers are affected by its command.

- If the active layer is in a clipping group (and the topmost layer is not part of the group), the layer is removed from the clipping group. If the top layer is part of the clipping group, only the order of the grouped layers changes.

Bring Forward
(Command) [Control]-]

In the **Layers Palette**, this command moves the active layer over the item immediately above it.

Special Notes

- If the active layer is an adjustment layer, the layer above it is then affected by its command.
- If the active layer is part of a clipping group (and the layer above it is not part of the group), it is removed.
- If the active layer is beneath a clipping group, it is added to the group.

Send Backwards
(Command) [Control]-[

In the **Layers Palette**, this command places the active layer under the item directly beneath it.

Special Notes

- If the active layer is the bottom layer of a clipping group, the entire group is moved.
- If the active layer is above a clipping group, it is added to the group.
- If the selected layer is an adjustment layer, the effects of the adjustment will be removed from the layer directly beneath it.

Send to Back
(Command-Shift) [Control-Shift]-[

In the **Layers Palette**, this command moves the active layer to the lowest position possible. If the image has no background layer, the active layer becomes the bottom layer. If the image has a background layer, the active layer is placed immediately above it.

Special Notes

- If the active layer is the bottom layer of a clipping group, the entire group is moved.

- If the selected layer is an adjustment layer, its effects will only apply to the Background layer. If there is no background layer, the adjustment layer will no longer apply to anything.

Layer: Merge

This command combines multiple layers into a single image layer. Unlike Layer: **Flatten Image**, Merge only applies to specified layers. You can apply Merge to as few as two layers. Merged layers can still retain most of Photoshop-native attributes, such as transparent areas and adjustable opacity.

Common Uses

- **Reducing file size.** Although transparent areas of layers do not increase file size, the images do. Merging layers together reduces file size wherever images overlap each other.
- **Simplifying navigation.** Problems with multiple layers include keeping track of them all, finding a specific layer, and scrolling through dozens of layers. Merging layers when you are done editing reduces confusion.
- **Restricting the effects of an adjustment layer.** Adjustment layers apply to all layers beneath them. While this can be restricted to certain areas, you must avoid moving layers between Adjustment Layers and the layers you intend for them to affect. Merging adjustment layers with image layers applies the adjustments and then removes the Adjustment Layer, thus simplifying layer relationships.
- **Adding layers.** Since it is only possible to have 99 layers, you need to merge layers if you wish to add new layers once an image contains 99.
- **Simplified editing.** Many Photoshop functions, such as filters, can only be applied one layer at a time. To apply the same function to multiple layers, you must run the same function with the same settings to each layer—or, you can merge the layers and apply the command once.

Common Errors

Merging prematurely. Before merging, ask yourself the following questions:

- Are the opacity settings exactly the way you want them?
- Are you finished editing any layer masks?
- Are the adjustment layers properly set?
- Are the blend modes properly set?
- Are the layers properly positioned?

Special Notes

Adjustment layers cannot be merged exclusively with other adjustment layers. Also, layers can't be merged when there is an adjustment layer as the bottom layer, unless Merge Linked is used. Since adjustment layers can only affect layers beneath them, Photoshop assumes you are making a mistake if you try to do this, and prevents you from doing it.

Layer: Merge Down
(Command) [Control]-E

This command appears when the active layer is neither linked nor part of a clipping group. You can merge either two image layers or one adjustment layer and one image layer.

Special Notes

- Hold down the (Option) [Alt] key when choosing this command to copy the contents of the selected layer into the layer below it, leaving the active layer unmerged and unchanged.

- This command cannot merge a layer outside a clipping group with one inside a clipping group.

- This command cannot merge an image layer with an adjustment layer if the adjustment layer is beneath the image layer.

Layer: Merge Group
(Command) [Control]-E

This command appears when the active layer is part of a clipping group. The bottom layer of the group must be selected in order to merge.

Special Notes

- Grouped layers will not merge if any layer inside the group is linked to a layer outside the group.

- Hold down the (Option) [Alt] key when choosing this command to copy the contents of all grouped layers into the bottom layer, leaving the upper layers untouched.

Layer: Merge Linked
(Command) [Control]-E

This command appears when the active layer is linked to another, but is not part of a clipping group.

Special Notes

Hold down the (Option) [Alt] key when choosing this command to copy the contents of all linked layers into the selected layer, leaving the linked layers untouched.

Layer: Merge Visible
(Command-Shift) [Control-Shift]-E

This command merges all visible layers, regardless of which one is currently active.

Special Notes

- Layers merge into the bottom-most visible layer.
- Layers will not merge if the bottom visible layer is an adjustment layer.
- Hold down the (Option) [Alt] key when choosing this command to copy the contents of all visible layers and merge them into the selected layer, leaving other layers untouched.

Layer: Flatten Image

This command converts all visible layers to a single background layer. All layer masks and adjustment layers are applied and discarded.

If there are any layers hidden when the image is flattened, an alert appears, asking "Discard hidden layers?" Click Discard to eliminate the layers. Click Cancel to close the alert, leaving the image unchanged.

Special Notes

Images with multiple layers cannot be saved as any format other the native Photoshop. Using File: **Save a Copy**, you can save the image into different formats. The saved copy is automatically flattened.

See Also

File: **Save**
File: **Save a Copy**

Layer: Matting

Occasionally, when you place an anti-aliased selection into an image layer, the edge pixels retain color values from the original image. The matting commands can sometimes help this problem. They are often ineffective, though, because they only apply to anti-aliased edges that result from a solid background color. Also, they fill the edge pixels with sampled colors rather than making them semi-transparent, which would allow for true anti-aliasing with the underlying layers.

Defringe

This command replaces the pixels at the edge of a floating selection or image layer with pixels sampled from the adjacent pixels inside the selection or image layer.

Defringe should only be used when there is an obvious problem with the edge pixels of an image layer or floating selection. Otherwise, it will have no apparent effects on the image layer or floating selection.

Remove Black Matte

This command removes black edge pixels in a floating selection or image layer and fills them with colors sampled from adjacent pixels inside the selection or image layer.

This command is intended for images selected from a solid black background. Renderings from 3-D modeling programs are often created with such black backgrounds. Otherwise, it has little or no effect.

Remove White Matte

This command removes white edge pixels from a floating selection or image layer and fills them with colors sampled from adjacent pixels inside the selection or image layer.

This command is meant to be used exclusively on images selected from a solid white background. Objects on clip art CD-ROMs are frequently photographed on solid white backgrounds. Otherwise, it has little or no effect.

CHAPTER 12

The Select Menu

Select: All
(Command) [Control]-A

This command creates a selection around the entire image window. The selection path surrounds the border of the image, and every visible pixel is included. If an image only contains a background layer, this command selects all the available image information.

Common Errors

Using Select: All to select the contents of a layer. Only the visible pixels of the active layer are included in the selection—any image pixels positioned off the canvas are not included. If you move the selection, the visible pixels separate from the hidden portion. To move or change the contents of an entire layer, activate the layer but create no selections.

Special Notes

Select all visible nontransparent pixels by holding down the (Command) [Control] key while clicking a layer in the **Layers Palette** (see Chapter 20). This technique does not work on the background layer.

See Also

The Layers Palette

Select: None
(Command) [Control]-D

This command removes all active selections from an image. Select: **None** allows you to remove a selection without touching the image, greatly reducing the possibility of human error.

Common Errors

- Confusing this command with Select: Hide Edges. After making a selection and applying an adjustment, you may want to evaluate its effect by removing the selection from view. If you choose Select: **None**, then you cannot undo the adjustment—the selection path simply appears again. Select: **Hide Edges** hides the selection edges while leaving the selection active.

- Opting to remove a selection by clicking on-screen. Many users—particularly those who have used earlier versions of Photoshop—prefer clicking somewhere on-screen to remove a selection. This poses the following problems:

   - It only works if the Marquee Tool or Lasso Tool is selected. It works with the Magic Wand Tool only if you click directly on the selection.

   - If you accidentally drag while you click, you'll reposition the selection path. If you happen to be holding down the (Command) [Control] key, the contents of the selection move as well.

   - If any other tool is active while you click—the Paintbrush Tool, for example—you may accidentally edit the contents of the selection.

Special Notes

While working with a series of small selections, you may attempt to use a Paint Tool or filter only to find it has no effect on the image. This is common when working at high zoom ratios or on small monitors. If a selection remains active somewhere else in the image, no other tool can be used outside its boundaries. Choose Select: **None** and try again.

See Also

Edit: Undo
Select: Hide Edges

Select: Inverse
(Command-Shift) [Control-Shift]-I

This command creates the *inverse* of an active selection, or the exact opposite of the original. The effect of this command is the same as applying Image: Adjust: **Invert** to a mask channel before reloading it as a selection.

Common Uses

Refer to Appendix A for a full description of the following:

* Creating a silhouette

Special Notes

When you invert a selection, the diminishing opacity values of a feathered edge are inverted as well. To determine the new value, Select: **Inverse** increases the current opacity value to the maximum (100%) and subtracts the original value. Therefore, if part of a feathered edge has an opacity value of 40%, it changes to 60% after applying this command.

See Also

Appendix A (Select: **Inverse**)

Select: Color Range

This command creates selections based on a specified color range. Instead of manually-drawn shapes, selections are based on targeted values.

Common Uses

* **Selecting fine details.** Good examples are hair, lace, or blades of grass—anything too complex to select by hand. This command is most successful when the colors surrounding the target image are in high contrast.

* **Selecting subtly varying tones and color.** This command excels at selecting a range of closely related colors, like fleshtones or the blue of a sky.

Refer to Appendix A for a full description of the following:

* Removing red-eye from a scanned photograph

Common Errors

Using Select: Color Range for standard selections. As a tool for assisting in delicate and subtle color adjustments, Select: **Color Range** is unparalleled. As a tool for creating standard selections, it falters. It does not use anti-aliasing, so changes like fills, extreme color adjustments, and filters can exaggerate the jagged selection edges.

Special Notes

* This command can be applied to an entire image layer or to the contents of an active selection. If a selection is active when you choose this command, only the selected pixels appear in the dialog. When you target colors in this area, the remaining pixels are removed from the active selection.

* While the Color Range dialog is open, you can still change the current image view. Hold down the spacebar and drag to scroll the image; hold (Command)

[Control]-spacebar to access the Zoom In Tool; hold (Option-Command) [Alt-Control]-spacebar to access the Zoom Out Tool. When combined with different preview options, these shortcuts allow you to target colors with much more precision.

- Press the (Command) [Control] key to toggle between thumbnail view options. For example, when the thumbnail is set to Selection, you can hold down the (Command) [Control] key to display the Image option. After using the eyedropper to affect the selected range, release the (Command) [Control] key to switch back.

The Color Range Dialog

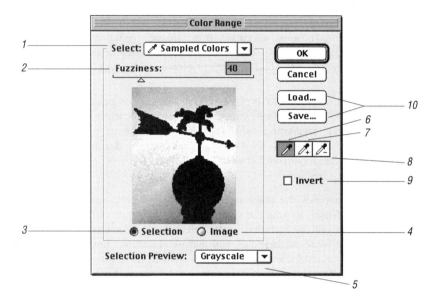

1. Select

Specify the range of colors you wish to target from this pop-up.

Sampled Colors

Photoshop defaults to this option. Here, the ultimate selection area depends on the color you initially *sample*, or target with the eyedropper tools. This range is increased or decreased using the Fuzziness slider and the plus/minus eyedroppers.

Predefined Colors

This option targets color by measuring a pixel's color intensity. For example, choose Cyan from the pop-up. The full intensity of cyan is 100%. A pixel colored 100% cyan is 100% selected. A pixel containing 60% cyan results in a 40% transparent selection. Pixels containing no cyan are left untouched.

If you're editing an RGB image, the colors are based on brightness values. Intensities of Reds, for example, are compared to a value of R: 255. If a pixel contains R: 128—50% of full intensity—it results in a 50% transparent selection.

When choosing an option that differs from the current color mode, Photoshop creates an average based on the RGB/CMY color wheel. For example, choosing Reds while editing a CMYK image affects pixels containing magenta and yellow. Likewise, choosing Cyans while editing an RGB image affects pixels containing green and blue.

Since these options are based on pre-existing color content, the eyedroppers and Fuzziness slider are not available. The selection preview cannot be edited.

Tonal Range

These options base a selection on an image's tonal content. Highlights targets the average tones from 0 to 25%, Midtones targets average tones from 25% to 75%, and Shadows targets average tones over 75%.

Out of Gamut

This option targets all RGB colors falling outside the printable spectrum of CMYK inks. In theory, you can use this setting to select and adjust those colors before converting to CMYK, leaving in-gamut colors untouched. Unless the adjustments are very subtle, however, this technique quickly leads to visible tonal shift between the two sets of colors.

2. **Fuzziness Slider**

Fuzziness determines the color range of a targeted area, based on the originally sampled color. Raising the value increases the range of colors throughout the image that will be included in the selection. In a continuous-tone image, this creates a more widespread and diffuse selection. Lowering the value decreases the range of colors, resulting in a smaller, more focused selection.

Fuzziness gets its name from the method it uses to include additional colors to a selection. Only the colors that you click or Shift-click with the eyedroppers are completely selected. The expanded range controlled by the Fuzziness slider is only partially selected, as evidenced by the gray values in the Selection preview. This creates a more evenly blended selection.

3. **Selection**

This option highlights the selected range of color. Similar to a masking channel, the selected areas are white, the unselected areas are black, and partially selected areas are different tones of gray. Whether you click on the actual image or directly on the thumbnail, the gray tones change to reflect the new selection area.

4. **Image**

This displays a small preview of the actual image. If the Selection Preview is set to any option other than None, this provides the only full-color representation of the image. If you click on this thumbnail, the only way to preview the selection is to check the actual image, behind the dialog.

5. **Selection Preview**

These options control how the selection is previewed in the original image.

None

This displays the original image, with no indication of the selected range. Choose a preview of None when you need to target very precise details or colors with the Target Eyedropper.

Grayscale

This matches the image thumbnail in Selection view. This option is usually the intuitive choice for users familiar with masking channels.

Black Matte

Instead of previewing the selected areas, this option previews the selected colors. Before any colors are targeted, this preview fills the images to black. As colors are added to the selection, the black levels are reduced to display the selected colors on-screen. The effect is the same as if the currently selected colors were copied and pasted onto a black background.

White Matte

The effect of this option is similar to Black matte, except that the preview image is filled with white before any colors are targeted. As colors are added to the selection, they are displayed on-screen.

Quick Mask

Similar to the Quick Mask feature found in the Toolbar, this option previews a selection with a semi-transparent colored overlay. Uncolored areas indicate the currently selected range, while colored areas reflect unselected pixels. By default, the overlay is a 50% opaque red. If the default is too close to colors in the image, you can reset the color off the overlay. Double-click one of the Quick Mask buttons in the Toolbar and set a new color in the Quick mask Options dialog.

6. **Target Eyedropper**

This tool is used to target the initial color in a selection. The color that you click with this eyedropper is 100% selected. The surrounding tones, as determined by the Fuzziness slider, are partially selected. With this eyedropper, only one color can be targeted at a time.

7. **Add Eyedropper**

To target more colors, use this eyedropper or hold down the Shift key while using the Target Eyedropper. Each additional color is 100% selected, and their surrounding ranges are also determined by the Fuzziness slider. To add a range of colors at once by dragging across the image or image preview.

8. **Subtract Eyedropper**

To remove colors from a selection, use this eyedropper or hold down the (Option) [Alt] key while using the Target Eyedropper. Remove a range of colors by dragging.

9. **Invert**

Checking the Invert box reverses the currently targeted areas. The result is similar to applying Select: **Inverse** to an active selection.

10.Save and Load

These buttons allow you to save targeted color ranges into a separate file.

This is useful for targeting similar areas in a series of images. For example, an entire roll of film can be affected by the same problem, such as over-exposure or red-eye, which can be narrowed down to a specific range of color.

Target the colors for one image using Select: **Color Range**, then click the Save button to save the settings to your hard drive. When this file is loaded into the Color Range dialog of another image, the same range of colors are targeted without using the eyedroppers.

See Also

Appendix A (Select: **Color Range**)
Select: **Inverse**

Select: Feather
(Command-Shift) [Control-Shift]-D

This command softens the edges of a selection. Rather than have a sharp distinction between selected and unselected pixels, feathering creates a fringe of increasing transparency. It's similar to anti-aliasing, which blends the contents of a selection with its surrounding pixels. There, however, the blend is only one pixel thick. By feathering a selection, you can increase the blend by up to 250 pixels.

Common Uses

Refer to Appendix A for full descriptions of the following:

• Creating a soft transition between selected and unselected pixels
• Creating a glowing effect

Common Errors

Attempting to use a low feather value in lieu of anti-aliasing. Anti-aliasing is intended to produce an invisible effect, creating a seamless blend between a selection and the remaining image. Even at its lowest values, feathering is a special effect, and its results are always visible to the eye.

Special Notes

If the Feather Radius is set high enough, you may see an alert claiming that "No pixels are more than 50% selected." This means the feathered edges have increased to the point of overlapping, and cover the entire selected image. Since Photoshop only displays selection paths when a selection is less than 50% transparent, this alert is telling you that the image will remain selected, but it will not display the outlines. To view the effect of the selection, change to Quick Mask mode and evaluate the colored overlay.

The Feather Selection Dialog

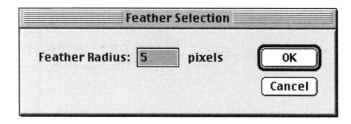

Radius

This value determines the width of a feathered selection edge.

Although the Feather Radius is specified in pixels, that value does not accurately reflect the width of the feathered area. Photoshop uses a formula called the Gaussian Bell Curve to determine how the selection fades into the unselected areas. To prevent harsh transitions between the feathered and unfeathered portions, this formula slightly increases the distance of the blended area. The effect is more appealing to the eye—without this formula, the transitions appear mechanical and obvious. As a result, feathering affects about five times the number of pixels entered as the Feather Radius.

Select Menu

Select: Modify

The Modify commands are used to edit the shape of an active selection. These changes are always based on the selection's original shape.

Border

This command traces the edge of a selection with a new selection of a specified width. The original selection is discarded.

Like Select: **Feather**, this command creates a selection that fades into the surrounding pixels. Unlike Select: **Feather**, it does not use a Gaussian Bell Curve, and the transition is awkward and poorly executed. This greatly reduces the usefulness of this command.

Special Notes

This command can be applied to anti-aliased or feathered selections. Those values are ignored, however—Photoshop simply traces the edge of the visible selection path.

The Border Dialog

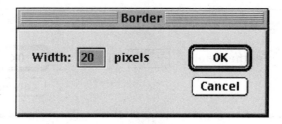

Width

Enter a value from 1 to 64 pixels. This represents the distance of the fade. Since the border is created both inwards and outwards from the original selection edge, the total width of the border is twice the entered pixel value. Only the two pixels on either side of the original selection edge are 100% selected.

Smooth

This command reduces any jagged areas or sharp edges from a selection outline.

Special Notes

When this command is applied, the only thing Photoshop examines is the shape of a selection. Therefore, you have no control over which colors or tones are affected by the command.

The Smooth Dialog

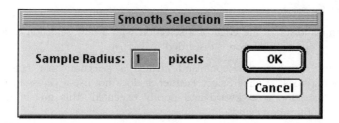

Sample Radius

This command works by rounding off any corners that exist in a selection path. The Sample Radius determines the amount of rounding that occurs. Enter a value from 1 to 16. Unlike Select: Modify: **Border**, this value does not affect any existing anti-aliasing or feathering.

Expand

This command increases a selection by expanding its edges outward.

Special Notes

This command cannot increase the selected area beyond the canvas.

The Expand Dialog

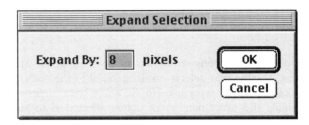

Expand By
> Enter a value between 1 and 16 to expand the selection by that amount. To increase the selection by more than 16 pixels, apply this command repeatedly. Anti-aliasing and feathering are unaffected by this value.

Contract

This command reduces a selection by contracting its edges inward.

Common Uses

Refer to Appendix A for a full description of the following:

* Removing the edge pixels from a layer's contents

Special Notes

This command cannot contract selection edges that run along the edge of the canvas, but will contract the remainder of the selection.

The Contract Dialog

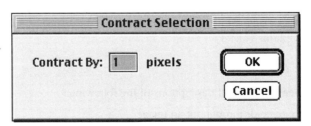

Contract By

Enter a value between 1 and 16 to contract the selection by that amount. To decrease the selection by more than 16 pixels, apply this command repeatedly. Anti-aliasing and feathering are unaffected by this value.

See Also

Appendix A (Select: Modify: **Contract**)

Select: Grow

This command increases a selected area by including a wider range of similar colors.

Select: **Grow** bases its decisions on the Tolerance value in the Magic Wand Tool Options Palette. A value of 1 selects pixels identical to the colors of the selected area. A value of 255 selects every pixel in the active layer. Unfortunately, the only way to determine the exact number of colors affected is to simply apply the command. If necessary, choose Edit: **Undo** and enter a new value.

Special Notes

• This command only recognizes colors adjacent to the current selection.

• Select: **Grow** is useful for expanding a selection to include an image of subtly-varying colors, such as a piece of fruit or a high-contrast backdrop surrounding a product shot. If you want to select colors that occur throughout an image, use Select: **Color Range** or Select: **Similar**.

• Apply Select: **Grow** more than once to continue adding pixels to the active selection. Each time, the tolerance increases by the value in the Magic Wand Tool Options Dialog.

See Also

The Magic Wand Tool
Select: **Color Range**
Select: **Similar**

Select: Similar

This command is similar to Select: **Grow**, but colors from the whole image are added to a selection—they do not need to be adjacent. The range of colors affected by this command are determined by the Tolerance value of the Magic Wand Tool Options Palette.

Common Uses

Refer to **Appendix A** for full descriptions of the following:

• Selecting one color throughout an image

• Selecting a range of colors throughout an image

See Also

Appendix A (Select: **Similar**)
Select: **Grow**

Select: Load Selection

This command creates an active selection based on currently existing image information.

Common Uses

- **Creating a selection based on a mask channel.** When a selection is saved, it's written to a mask channel. You can view and edit this channel by clicking its thumbnail in the Channels Palette. This command allows you to reload the saved selection. If a second open image contains any mask channels, they can be loaded as selections in the first image—as long as the two images have identical proportions.

- **Creating a selection based on an image layer.** This effect is the same as holding down the (Command) [Control] key and clicking a layer in the Layers Palette.

Special Notes

- This command is not available unless the current image contains a mask channel or multiple layers. This command is also available when an image of the same width, height, and resolution is open and contains a mask channel or multiple layers.

- An image in Bitmap mode cannot be loaded as a selection, regardless of its dimensions—neither can color channels from RGB, CMYK, and Lab images. A separate Grayscale image—because its structure is identical to a mask channel—can be loaded as a selection, as long as its width, height, and resolution match the current image.

- When creating selections based on channels or layers in the same image, the following shortcuts allow you to bypass the Load Selection dialog:

  - **New Selection.** Hold down the (Command) [Control] key and click the appropriate channel in the Channels Palette. Or, hold the (Option-Command) [Alt-Control] keys and type the number of the desired mask channel.

  - **Add to Selection.** Hold down the Shift and (Command) [Control] keys and click the appropriate channel in the Channels Palette.

  - **Subtract from Selection.** Hold down the (Option-Shift) [Alt-Shift] keys and click the appropriate channel in the Channels Palette.

  - **Intersect with Selection.** Hold down the (Option-Command-Shift) [Alt-Control-Shift] keys and click the appropriate channel in the Channels Palette.

The Load Selection Dialog

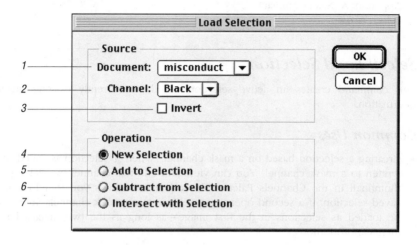

1. **Document**

   Choose the source image from this pop-up. If no other image meets the Load Selection requirements, only the current image appears here.

2. **Channel**

   This pop-up lists all available channels, depending on the image chosen in the Document pop-up. Mask channels are listed by their number. Matching Grayscale images are listed as Black.

   If the currently active layer contains transparent pixels, it appears as a Transparency option (for example, Layer 1 Transparency or Layer 3 Transparency). Choose this option to create a selection based on the non-transparent layer pixels.

3. **Invert**

   Checking this box reverses the final selection. The effect is the same as applying a regular selection and choosing Select: **Inverse**.

4. **New Selection**

   This option replaces any existing selection with a new one, based on the Source information.

5. **Add to Selection**

   This option adds the new selection to the current selection. The effect is similar to making a new selection while holding down the Shift key. Use this option to combine two saved selections into one active selection.

6. **Subtract from Selection**

   This option removes the area of the new selection from the current selection. The effect is similar to using a selection tool while holding down the (Option) [Alt] key.

7. **Intersect with Selection**

This option results in a selection based on the overlapping areas of the current and new selections.

See Also

Select: **Inverse**
Select: **Save Selection**
The Channels Palette
The Layers Palette

Select: Save Selection

This command allows you to save a selection for future use. This has nothing to do with saving the *contents* of a selection—rather, the outline and edge-softness of the selection itself is saved. The most efficient way to save this type of information is to make a *mask*, or a graphic representation of the selection outline. Photoshop does this by creating an additional item in the **Channels Palette** that reflects the nature of the selection.

When the selection is made active again using Select: **Load Selection**, Photoshop refers to the information in this channel. White areas result in full selections, different levels of gray result in partial selections, and black areas are ignored.

Common Uses

- **Creating a selection you can load repeatedly.** It takes time to generate a complex selection. If there is a chance you might require that selection again, save it. This way, it can be restored with a single command, instead of creating the same selection again.

- **Graphically editing a selection.** Since a selection is saved graphically, it can be edited using Photoshop's tools, adjustment commands, and filters. This simply cannot be done with selection tools alone. A basic selection can be modified extensively before being reloaded. Photoshop simply bases the selection on the existing gray values.

- **Creating an alpha channel.** Certain types of graphics require an additional masking channel. When creating a transparent GIF using File: Export: **GIF89a Export**, this channel determines which pixels are ignored in a Web browser. Also, many video editing suites use a masking channel to simulate a blue-screen effect.

- **Creating a layer mask.** This command can be used to create or replace a layer mask.

Special Notes

This command is only available when an image contains an active selection.

The Save Selection Dialog

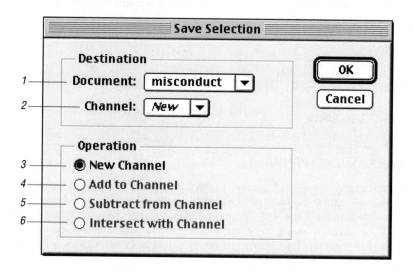

1. **Document**

   The Document pull-down menu lists all possible images a selection can be saved into:

   Current Image
   > By default, the name of the active image appears in this pop-up. Leave this option alone to save the selection as a new channel in the same image.

   Open Images
   > Only open images sharing the same width, height, and resolution as the current image are listed here. Choosing one of these saves the selection as a mask channel in the second image.

   New
   > This option saves the selection as a separate Grayscale image. The content is the same as if it had been saved as a mask channel. As long as the new image is open, it can easily be reloaded into the original image. This allows users with less-powerful workstations to save selections without increasing the file size of the current image.

2. **Channel**

   This pop-up determines where a saved selection is placed within the destination image:

   New Channel
   > This option saves a selection as a new channel, listed as a separate item in the Channels Palette. Mask channels are always named numerically, by their order of appearance in an image.

Existing Mask Channels

If an image already contains one or more mask channels, their numbers appear in the Channels pop-up. If you select an existing channel, you can replace it with the new selection or combine the two, depending on the chosen Operation setting.

Layer Mask

If an image layer is active when you choose Select: **Save Selection**, this option appears in the Channels pop-up. It allows you to create a layer mask based on the current selection, similar to making a selection and choosing Layer: **Add Layer Mask**. If the active image layer already has a layer mask, you can replace it with the new selection or combine the two, depending on the chosen Operation setting.

3. **New Channel**

This option is the only one available when New or Layer Mask is selected in the Channel pop-up. The selection is either saved as a new channel without affecting any other image information or applied as a layer mask.

4. **Add to Channel**

This option combines the contents of the existing and new mask channels. If a mask channel is chosen from the Channel pop-up, this option changes to Replace Channel, which allows you to replace the selected mask channel.

5. **Subtract from Channel**

This option removes any area in the existing channel that is overlapped by the new selection. This information is simply filled in with black, which prevents that area from becoming an active selection when the channel is reloaded.

6. **Intersect with Channel**

This option modifies the existing channel so it displays only the areas that intersect with the current selection. The areas that do not overlap are filled with black, preventing them from loading as active selections.

See Also

File: Export: **GIF89a Export**
Layer: **Add Layer Mask**
Select: **Load Selection**
The Channels Palette

CHAPTER 13

The Filter Menu

Filters are automated global image editing tools. They are named after photographic filters, the devices placed over a camera lens to correct bad lighting conditions or create special effects.

Like camera filters, Photoshop filters fall into two categories:

- **Production filters.** These filters prepare images for printing or for display in Web or Multimedia projects. They help correct deficiencies in the image, such as blurriness, film grain, noise, scratches and other problems. When using Production filters, the goal is to create an image that appears in print or on screen as close to the original photograph as possible, or to enhance a specific quality of the image.

- **Creative filters.** These filters substantially alter the image in order to create a completely new and different result. Some creative filters recreate the image as though it were created using traditional media such as ink or charcoal. Others change the positions of pixels to make them appear as if they were distorted by glass. Others alter the image in ways that aren't easily classified. The goal of creative filters is to create a new image rather than improving the quality of an existing image.

The Former Aldus Gallery Effects

The Artistic, Brush Strokes, and Sketch filters (as well as a few scattered throughout the remaining categories) are part of the former Aldus Gallery Effects suite. Adobe acquired these tools when it merged with Aldus. Even though some of these filters have barely changed since they debuted in Photoshop 2.0, they have been included as part of the standard filter set.

While these filters can certainly create some interesting effects, each one suffers from one or more of the following drawbacks:

- **Bad or nonexistent anti-aliasing.** Anti-aliasing blends the colors of pixels together to provide smooth transitions between colors. Without anti-aliasing, transitions are harsh, with the obvious square pixels clearly identifying an image as computer-generated. This defeats the Artistic, Brush Strokes, and Sketch filters attempts to emulate natural media and typically produces images of unsatisfactory quality.

- **Meaningless values.** The Artistic, Brush Strokes, and Sketch strokes are all controlled by numerical values. However, these values are only relevant to the field itself—they do not relate to color values of the pixels, or to pixel distances. They don't even relate to values in other fields. A value of 0 that produces no effect in one field can produce a substantial effect in another. The only meaning they have is that a higher setting produces a different effect from a lower setting.

- **Incomplete options.** Nearly all the filters are missing a key element. Rough Pastels, for example, has settings for stroke length, stroke detail, texture, even for lighting, and yet it has no setting to change the angle of the brush stroke from 45°.

- **Superfluous functionality.** Many filters contain settings that blur, sharpen, adjust brightness and contrast, and perform other commands found in more useful forms elsewhere in the program.

- **Limited color modes.** These filters only function in RGB and Grayscale color modes.

Filter: Last Filter
(Command) [Control]-F

This command applies the last filter used, repeating the same settings.

Special Notes

Hold down the (Option) [Alt] key when choosing this command. This opens the dialog of the last filter used, allowing you to change the settings before applying the filter again.

Filter: unfilteredFade Filter
(Command-Shift) [Control-Shift] F

This command must be chosen immediately after a filter has been applied. Fade Filter fades the filtered image into the previous, unfiltered image. This can be used to reduce the intensity of the effect of a filter. The effect is identical to duplicating an image layer, applying the filter to the duplicated layer, then reducing the opacity. If desired, fade the filter using an available blend mode, which affects how the filtered image combines with the unfiltered version.

Special Notes

This command can also be used to fade the effects of the Image: **Adjust** commands.

Filter: Artistic

These filters claim to reproduce an image as though it had been created using a traditional artistic technique. The Artistic filters all function on the same basic principal: they define areas of similar colors, then average or blur them together to form areas of solid color.

Colored Pencil

This filter makes the image appear as if cross-hatching were applied over the original image using a pencil the color of the background color. It also finds edges and blurs the image within the edges.

The Colored Pencil Dialog

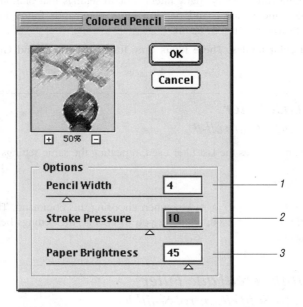

1. Pencil Width (1 to 24)

   This setting controls the density of the cross-hatching. A value of 1 covers the image with fine hatch marks. Higher settings produce large patches of solid foreground color and few hatch marks.

2. Stroke Pressure (1 to 15)

   This setting controls the total quantity of the hatch marks. At 1, there are so many strokes that the resulting image is solid background color. At 15, the image is thoroughly cross-hatched, but still retains enough of the original image to be identifiable.

3. **Paper Brightness (1 to 50)**

This setting darkens or brightens the crosshatching color. A value of 1 darkens the color to black. A value of 50 brightens the color substantially.

Cutout

This filter recreates the image as though it were created from torn pieces of construction paper. Similar to an Image: Adjust: **Posterize** command with edge detection, it selects large areas of the image based on color similarity and reduces the color range within those areas. Unlike the Posterize command, edges are anti-aliased by the Cutout filter.

The Cutout Dialog

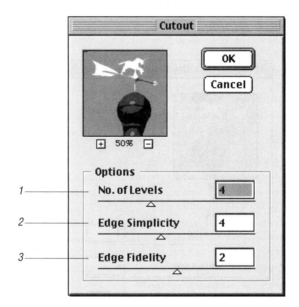

1. **No. of Levels (2 to 8)**

This value determines the number of color levels.

2. **Edge Simplicity (0 to 10)**

This setting determines the number of edges found by the filter. A value of 0 finds many edges, creating an image resembling the original image. Settings above 5 reduce detail to a point where only abstract shapes remain of the original image. A value of 10 reduces the image to a single solid color that is the average value of the selected colors.

3. **Edge Fidelity (1 to 3)**

   This setting determines how closely the edges of the solid colors match the edges of the original image. A value of 1 follows the edges of the original image very loosely, and a value of 3 attempts to match the edges as closely as possible.

Dry Brush

Traditional dry brush technique paints with liquid water colors without dipping the brush in water, producing dense areas of pure pigment. This filter attempts to reproduce this effect by repainting the image with small areas of solid color. It defines areas based on the similarity of the colors, then fills those areas with the average color values. It defines many more areas than other Artistic filters, creating a more detailed image.

The Dry Brush Dialog

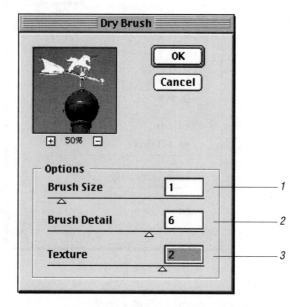

1. **Brush Size (0 to 10)**

   This value sets the relative size of the area of color averaged into an area of solid color. 0 creates many small colored areas, and 10 defines fewer, larger areas.

2. **Brush Detail (0 to 10)**

   This setting determines the quantity of edges found. A value of 0 captures the least detail, but it still captures enough detail information for the image to be recognizable as the original. A value of 10 finds the most edges, producing the highest number of colored areas and an image closely resembling the original.

3. **Texture (1 to 3)**

This setting determines the amount colored areas are lightened or darkened from their original colors. A value of 1 keeps the original, averaged values. A value of 3 darkens and lightens pixels to the point where there are many stray black and white pixels scattered over the image.

Film Grain

Film grain often exists in enlarged photographs taken with high-speed film. Typically, it appears as a soft noise over the entire image. This filter attempts to recreate photographic film grain by randomly lightening and darkening pixels. Because the grain it adds is too blocky and pixelated, it produces nothing resembling film grain at any setting. The filter has the additional feature of lightening the image before applying the grain.

Special Note

To create more realistic film grain effects, use the Noise: **Add Noise** or Texture: **Grain** filters.

The Film Grain Dialog

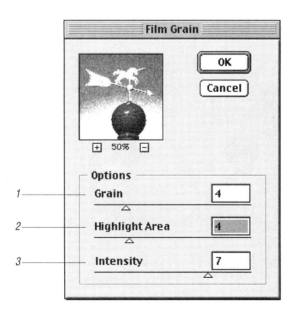

1. Grain (0 to 20)

   This setting controls the amount pixels are randomly lightened or darkened. Low settings add slight noise to the image. Higher settings obliterate the image entirely.

2. **Highlight Area (1 to 20)**

   This value defines areas to be made lighter. The higher the setting, the greater the range of colors lightened. A value of 1 lightens only the lightest areas of the image. A value of 20 lightens all colors.

3. **Intensity (0 to 10)**

   This setting determines how much the range of colors defined by Highlight Area is lightened. A value of 0 does not lighten the image. A value of 10 produces a very light image, with most information lightened to white.

Fresco

Fresco, a technique renowned for its beauty and durability, involves painting drying plaster with water color paints. This filter produces nothing remotely resembling a true fresco. Rather, it defines areas based on the similarity of the colors, then fills those areas with the averaged color values. It groups the new areas of solid color together based on a wider range of color similarity, and outlines them with thick black or gray lines. The effect is more reminiscent of coloring books than of frescos.

The Fresco Dialog

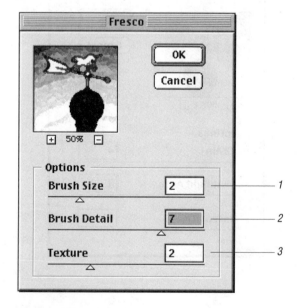

1. **Brush Size (0 to 10)**

   This setting controls the size of the colored areas changed to the same color. A value of 10 produces the largest colored areas and the least detail in the resulting image.

2. **Brush Detail (0 to 10)**

   This amount controls how many areas of similar color are defined before being averaged together. Higher settings define more areas, resulting in a more detailed image. This setting is virtually identical to Brush Size, only the values have the opposite effect. A value of 0 and a Brush Detail of 10 will produce the most detailed image.

3. **Texture (1 to 3)**

   This value increases the contrast of the colors in the image. A value of 1 fills areas with the original, averaged values. Settings above 1 makes fill colors darker or lighter.

Neon Glow

This filter emulates the appearance of an object lit by the flash of a neon light at night. Neon Glow replaces shadows with the foreground color, midtones with the background color, and highlights with a third color specified in the Neon Glow dialog. The Neon Glow filter produces the most realistic results when the foreground and background colors are set to the default black and white.

The Neon Glow Dialog

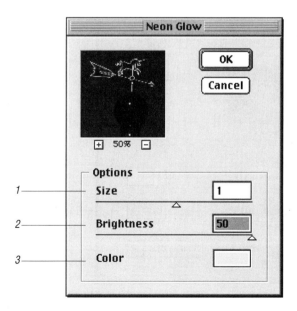

1. **Size (-24 to 24)**

   Size is the range of colors considered to be highlights. These colors are changed to the color specified in the Color setting. Negative values invert the image. The closer the amount to 0, the greater the highlights.

2. **Brightness (0 to 50)**

   Brightness determines if it is twilight or night. A value of 50 equals twilight, dark enough for colors to desaturate, but light enough so the glow from a neon light has no impact. At this setting, the image is defined completely by the foreground and background colors. Lower settings emulate darker night. More of the image is colored by the neon light, but the image is darker overall. At 0, it is too dark for the neon to light anything, producing an image of solid foreground.

3. **Color**

   Clicking the Color box opens the Color Picker, where you choose the color of the neon light assigned to highlights.

Paint Daubs

This filter creates nothing resembling daubs of paint. Rather, it defines an area based on color similarity, then blurs the area. The result is a blurry image that still retains edges where colors are substantially different. Additional blurring and sharpening effects can be performed using the Brush Type settings.

The Paint Daubs Dialog

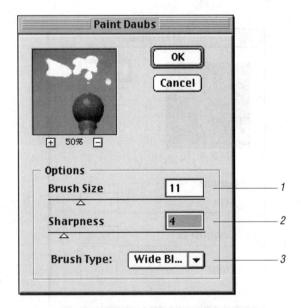

1. **Brush Size (1 to 50)**

   This setting controls the relative size of colored areas. The lower the number, the greater the quantity, providing more color variations and more detail in the image.

2. **Sharpness (0 to 40)**

   Sharpness determines how much sharpening is done to the image after the blurring has occurred. (see Filter: **Sharpen** for details on sharpening).

3. **Brush Type**

   Brush Types add additional blurring, lightening, darkening or sharpening to the image:

   Simple Brush
   This option makes no additional changes.

   Light Rough
   This option lightens and sharpens the image after the initial blurring.

   Dark Rough
   This option darkens and sharpens the image after the initial blurring.

   Wide Sharp
   This option sharpens the image after the initial blurring.

   Wide Blurry
   This option blurs the image after the initial blurring.

   Sparkle
   This option picks out the lightest of the highlights and lightens them even more, until they are substantially brighter than the rest of the image.

Filter Menu

Palette Knife

Traditional palette knife technique paints an image with a hard palette knife instead of a brush, producing, large, solid strokes of even color. This filter defines colored areas based on their similarity, averages the values, and fills the area with the averaged color. Colored areas are limited to roughly the same size and shape, as if created with a palette knife.

The Palette Knife Dialog

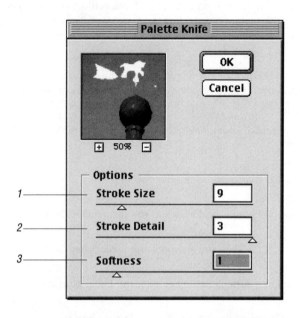

1. **Stroke Size (1 to 50)**

   This setting determines the size of the colored areas. The larger the size, the larger the area. A value of 1 produces a pixel-sized stroke, producing no change in the image. At 50, strokes are so large nothing is identifiable from the original image. Values from 2 to 5 substantially alter the image while retaining enough detail for the original image to be recognizable.

2. **Stroke Detail (1 to 3)**

   This value sets the roughness of the colored areas. A value of 1 results in smooth, rounded areas, while 3 produces very rough edges.

3. **Softness (0 to 10)**

   This setting determines how much blurring occurs at the edges where colors meet. At 0, there is no blurring. At 10, the edges blend together slightly.

Plastic Wrap

This filter makes an image appear as though it were wrapped in heat-shrink plastic.

The Plastic Wrap Dialog

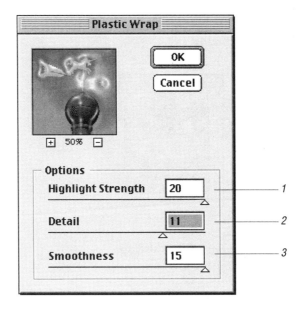

1. **Highlight Strength (0 to 20)**

   This value represents the intensity of the light shining on the plastic, creating the reflection. A value of 0 is ambient light, producing no reflections. A value of 20 resembles a bright spotlight shining on the image.

2. **Detail (1 to 15)**

   This setting determines how tightly the highlights follow the contours of the image. A value of 1 follows the contours loosely, while a value of 15 follows them closely.

3. **Smoothness (1 to 15)**

   A better label for this setting would be glossiness or shininess. This setting determines how much light is reflected by the plastic. A value of 1 reflects very little light. A value of 15 hides the image almost completely, showing little but shiny plastic.

Poster Edges

This filter reduces the number of tones, similar to Image: Adjust: **Posterize**, giving the image a flat, silk-screened appearance. The filter then traces the edges between more extreme differences in color with dark lines. It posterizes the colors more faithfully to the original colors than the Posterize command, and unlike Posterize, colors are anti-aliased. Unfortunately, there is no way to turn off the edge tracing, and no way to set a precise number of levels of posterization, limiting the usefulness of the filter.

The Poster Edges Dialog

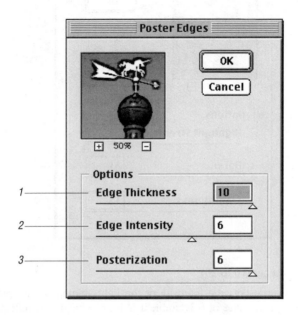

1. **Edge Thickness (0 to 10)**

   This setting determines the thickness of the dark lines the filter draws between colored areas. A value of 0 produces a thin line, and a value of 10 produces a very thick line.

2. **Edge Intensity (0 to 10)**

   This setting determines the number of edges that will be traced. A value of 0 only traces edges where colors are substantially different. A value of 10 traces the edge of nearly every area, producing an image thoroughly covered with black.

3. **Posterization (0 to 6)**

   This setting determines the relative number of levels of color. A value of 0 compresses the image into very few levels of color. A value of 6 produces an image with a color range almost identical to the original image.

Rough Pastels

This filter streaks over the image with irregularly-shaped clumps of color. The colors of the streaks are saturated colors sampled from the image. Strokes only occur at a 45% angle.

The Rough Pastels Dialog

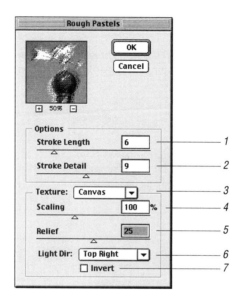

1. **Stroke Length (0 to 40)**

   This setting determines how far the saturated sampled colors are smeared from their original colors. A value of 0 leaves the sampled colors in patches shaped by the selected texture over the original colors in the image. A value of 40 smears the colors over a distance long enough to produce obvious strokes.

2. **Stroke Detail (1 to 20)**

   This setting is the amount that the filter saturates the sampled colors when it applies them to the image. A detail setting of 1 does not change the color values. A value of 20 pushes the saturation of the colors to their maximum values.

3. **Texture**

   Strokes are roughened according to the pattern of the texture. Any file saved in the Photoshop format can be used as a texture by choosing Load Selection. An Open dialog appears, allowing you to select a file. When the selected texture is smaller than the image, it is tiled to cover the entire image. When the selected texture is larger than the image, it crops to fit.

4. **Scaling (50 to 200)**

This setting changes the size of the texture before applying it to the image, from half to twice its original size.

5. **Relief (0 to 50)**

This setting determines how much of the texture is filled in. The higher the number, the more the texture is filled.

6. **Light Dir**

This setting makes the image appear to be lit from the specified direction.

7. **Invert**

Checking the Invert box inverts the lightness values of texture before applying the filter, producing an inverted texture. It does not invert the image or the color values of the brush strokes.

Smudge Stick

Smudge sticks are used to smear charcoal on paper. This filter considers the darkest pixels in the image to be charcoal and smears them over lighter pixels at a left diagonal, leaving lighter pixels unsmudged.

The Smudge Stick Dialog

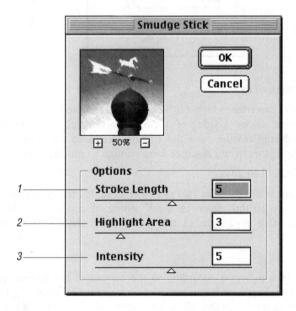

1. **Stroke Length (0 to 10)**

This setting controls the distance that dark pixels are smudged over light pixels. Higher settings result in longer smudges. A value of 0 still produces substantial smudging.

2. **Highlight Area (0 to 20)**

The filter can lighten pixels slightly before smudging occurs. Highlight Area determines the range of pixels to be lightened. A value of 0 produces no lightening of pixels. Low settings lighten only the lightest pixels. A value of 20 lightens all but the darkest pixels.

3. **Intensity (0 to 10)**

This setting determines how much the pixels in the Highlight Area will be lightened. A value of 0 does not lighten the image at all. When you set a high Highlight Area setting, a value of 10 lightens the image considerably.

Sponge

This filter emulates the effect of applying a damp sponge to a painting. Detail disappears, and the colors are reduced to random, irregular shapes. Sponge defines large areas of color based on the similarities of color, then blurs the contents while preserving the edges. It varies the shape of the areas and the fill color more than other Artistic filters, so that the shapes and color follow the original image very loosely.

The Sponge Dialog

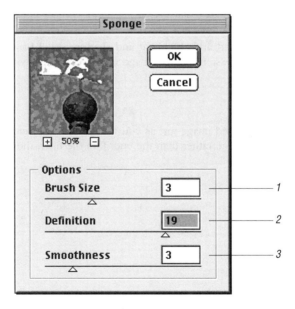

1. **Brush Size (1 to 10)**

   This setting controls the size of the colored areas. The higher the size, the larger the areas. The filter blurs the image so much there is very little difference between 1 and 10, though 10 preserves slightly more detail from the original image and creates slightly smaller sponge pore shapes.

2. **Definition (1 to 25)**

   This setting controls the darkness of sponge pore shading. A value of 1 produces slight mottling. A value of 25 looks like military camouflage painted over the image.

3. **Smoothness (1 to 15)**

   This setting controls the amount of blending between the image and the sponge pore shadows. A value of 1 produces very rough-edged sponge pore shadows. A value of 10 blends the pores with the image, adding blurring to the image and creating large, diffused sponge pores.

Underpainting

In traditional painting, underpainting roughs out the general colors and shape of the subject before detail information and shading is added.

This filter does a decent job of recreating the appearance of an underpainting. It lightens and blurs the image, destroying all detail information and producing a very diffuse image.

Then it moves pixels and adds highlight and shadow detail based on a selected texture, giving the impression that the image was roughed out with oil paints on a textured canvas.

Special Notes

Use an Undercolor filtered image just as you would a true undercolor painting, as the beginning of an image rather than the end. Run the filter, then add detail over the filtered image.

The Underpainting Dialog

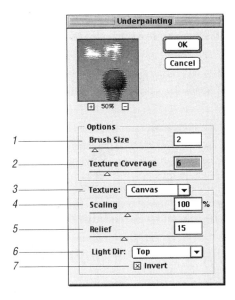

1. **Brush Size** (0 to 40)

   This setting determines the amount of blurring the filter does before it applies the texture. A value of 0 obliterates all detail information from the image, but leaves enough of the original color information to resemble the original image. A value of 40 shifts colors and distorts shapes, leaving a vague outline of the original image.

2. **Texture Coverage** (0 to 40)

   This setting determines the distance pixels are moved (displaced) into the shape of the texture. With a value of 0, pixels move very little. At 40, the image appears thoroughly mashed into the texture.

3. **Texture**

   The filter uses the lightness values of the texture for adding highlight and detail information, and for displacing pixels. When you select Load Texture, Photoshop an Open dialog appears, prompting you to select a Photoshop file to use as a texture. The texture will be tiled if it is smaller than the image, or cropped if it is larger.

4. **Scaling** (50% to 200%)

   This setting alters the size of the texture before it is applied to the image, from half to twice its original size.

5. **Relief** (0 to 50)

   This setting determines the amount of highlight and shadow the texture adds to the image. This detail is based on the highlight and shadows of the texture file. A value of 0 adds no texture at all. At 50, all pixels are pure black or white. Settings from 3 to 7 produce the most realistic texture.

6. **Light Dir**

   The options in this pop-up make the image appear to be lit from a specific direction.

7. **Invert**

   Check this box to invert the values of the texture image.

Watercolor

Watercolor paint dries from the edges, drawing more pigment to the edges of colored areas. This filter defines colored areas based on their similarity, averages the colors together, then fills the defined area with the new value. Then it darkens the edge pixels of those areas to produce a watercolor-like outline. Completely uncharacteristic of watercolors, the filter inexplicably saturates colors and adds dark shadows.

The Watercolor Dialog

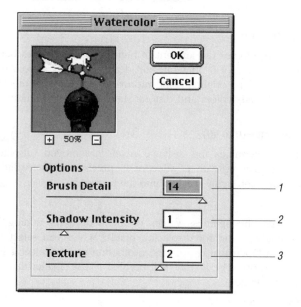

1. **Brush Detail (1 to 14)**

   This setting defines the range of similar colors to be averaged together and turned into an area of solid color. The lower the number, the wider the range, resulting in larger areas and less detail. A value of 14 produces an image fairly close to the original. A value of 1 obliterates most information, leaving a rough outline of the original image.

2. **Shadow Intensity (1 to 10)**

This setting controls the amount edge pixels and shadows are darkened. Any setting above 1 darkens all but the very lightest pixels to the point where most of the image is black.

3. **Texture (1 to 3)**

The texture setting increases the contrast of colors. Settings above one result in lighter lights and darker darks.

Filter: Blur

The Blur filters soften images. They work by analyzing the image and determining hard edges and areas of sharp color differences. Then, they average the colors of the pixels in those areas together to eliminate the sudden color differences.

Blur filters can be used as both production and creative filters. At low settings, they can hide noise and grain in an image. At higher settings, they can be used to create drop shadows and produce motion effects.

Special Notes

- Blur filters produce significantly different results when used on a selected or unselected image layer. When the image layer is selected, pixels at the edge of the selection become partially transparent, but pixels outside the selection are unchanged. This leaves a sharp edge roughly 50% transparent at its most transparent point. When blur filters are applied to unselected image layers, transparent pixels at the edge of the image become semi-transparent, so the image fades into complete transparency. For most purposes, applying the filter to an unselected image layer produces much more satisfactory results than selecting the image layer.

- The Blur filters function in RGB, CMYK, Grayscale and Lab modes.

Blur

This filter calculates areas in the image where color differences are most extreme, then averages the edge pixels between the areas of different color. Unlike Blur: **Gaussian Blur**, there is no way to determine the amount of blur and no way to preview the effect. This filter is only suitable for situations where speed is more important than image quality.

Blur More

This filter is identical to Blur, but has 4 to 5 times the effect.

Gaussian Blur

This filter averages the colors of adjacent pixels together to reduce detail. Gaussian Blur is one of the most important Photoshop filters, used for everything from eliminating moiré patterns to creating drop shadows. The Gaussian Blur filter is superior to other Blur filters for two reasons: it can be set to precise values, and it blurs according to the Gaussian Bell Curve distribution. The Gaussian Bell Curve distribution fades the amount of blurring unevenly over a distance to create a more natural, aesthetically pleasing blur. The human eye is very sensitive to changes in color. When a blur fades steadily, it is noticeable and appears computer-generated. By varying the amount of blur, this filter emulates blurring found in nature, such as the edges of shadows.

Special Notes

- The filter provides a full-image preview that dynamically shows what the effects of the filter will be before the filter is applied. To take full advantage of this preview, the view must be set to 100%, or Actual Pixels. This previews the image most accurately on screen. Other resolutions can blur the image preview slightly, which can lead to under-blurring.

- When blurring for corrective purposes, such as removing a moiré pattern, view each color channel individually before blurring. Moiré patterns and other flaws often exist only in one or two channels. Blurring one channel preserves more detail and results in a higher quality image.

The Gaussian Blur Dialog

Radius (0.1 to 250 pixels)

This setting controls the amount of blurring. Radius is the distance from the center of each pixel that pixels are averaged together. The higher the Radius, the greater the amount of blurring. A pixel radius of 0.1 produces little visible blurring. A value of 250 obliterates the image. Pixels bordering transparent areas are averaged with the transparency.

The exact amount that one pixel is averaged with another depends on the Gaussian Bell Curve distribution. Pixels within the first third of the radius closest to the center pixel are blurred the most. These pixels receive about 80% of their color from the pixel at the center of the radius.

The remaining 20% comes from the original pixel color. The amount of blurring fades about 60% across the next third of the radius. Over the last third, it fades 20%, until pixels are not blurred together.

The color from one pixel is actually averaged further than the radius specifies. For example, with a Radius value of 1, pixels immediately adjacent to the pixel at the center of the radius are averaged so that roughly 70 percent of their color comes from the center pixel and 30 percent from their original color value.

Adjacent pixels are blended with their new color, and so on. Even though the Radius is set to one pixel, color from a single pixel can be spread as far as five pixels.

Filter Menu

Motion Blur

This filter creates the effect of an image in motion, blurring pixels in a specified direction over a specified distance. As with other Blur filters, Motion Blur is created by averaging the color values of pixels together. Colors are averaged not according to their differences, but according to the direction and distance of the blur. The amount colors fade increases further from the original pixels.

Unfortunately, the Motion Blur occurs both in the direction specified and in the opposite direction, as if the image were vibrating back and forth very quickly, rather than moving quickly in the specified direction.

The Motion Blur Dialog

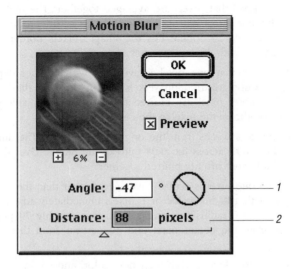

1. Angle (-90° to 90°)

   This setting specifies the angle of the blur. The blur occurs in the direction specified and in the opposite direction.

2. Distance (1 to 999 pixels)

   This setting determines the distance pixels are blurred.

Radial Blur

This filter blurs an image outward from a center point. The image is increasingly blurred further from the center. This is useful for creating a feel of vertigo or focusing attention on a specific area. Radial Blur possesses no preview capabilities and is slow on even the most powerful computers.

The Radial Blur Dialog

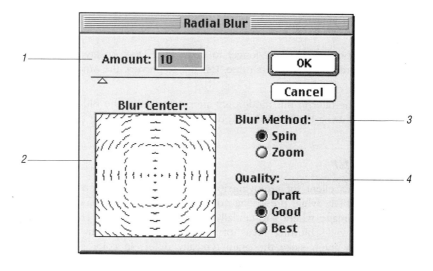

1. **Amount (1 to 100)**

   This setting controls the intensity of the effect. A value of 1 produces slight blurring. A value of 100 obliterates the image, leaving only streaks of color, except for pixels at the center of the blur which are only slightly changed.

2. **Blur Center**

   The blur radiates from the blur center. Click within the square to position the blur center. The Blur Center box is always square regardless of the shape of the selection. Unless you have made a perfectly square selection, you must make an educated guess as to where the center of the blur is relative to your image.

3. **Blur Method**

   Choose a blur method from this pop-up:

   Spin

   Spin applies the Radial Blur in concentric circles radiating from the center. The circles increase in frequency and blur more intensely the further they are from the center.

   Zoom

   Zoom applies the Radial Blur in lines radiating from the center. The blur increases in intensity the further it gets from the center.

4. **Quality**

   Quality settings help compensate for the lack of an image preview. Preview the effects of the filter by running the filter at lower settings, choose Edit: Undo, then run the filter at its best setting.

Draft

This option applies the filter quickly, but produces a low quality blur with much noise and no smoothness. This is good for previewing the position of the Blur Center.

Good

This option takes a little longer to apply than Draft quality, but applies the blur more evenly with less noise. Use this to preview the Amount of the blur.

Best

Apply the filter in this mode only after determining the Blur Center and the Amount using Draft and Good quality settings.

Smart Blur

This filter is excellent for removing low-intensity noise from an image, such as film grain. It blurs while preserving edge detail. Smart Blur works by identifying areas of the image where substantially different colors meet. The filter protects these areas, while blurring areas of similar color. This filter works well for removing film grain, since the grain typically differs in color slightly from the surrounding areas. The grain can be blurred away, and detail is left unharmed since it substantially differs in color from the surrounding area.

The Smart Blur Dialog

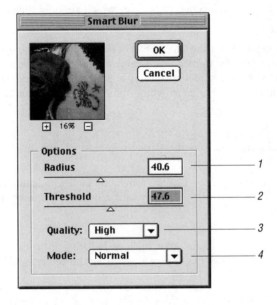

1. Radius (0.1 to 100 pixels)

   This value sets the distance from the center of each pixel that colors are blurred together. The higher the setting, the greater the amount of blurring.

2. Threshold (0.1 to 100)

   This setting determines the amount of difference between colors that the filter will define as an edge. Edge pixels are not blurred. At low settings, only pixels with very similar colors are blurred. At higher settings, substantially different colors are blurred together.

3. Quality (Low, Medium or High)

   Reducing quality speeds processing time, but produces less satisfactory results. Use lower quality settings when using the filter for artistic purposes, but use the High setting for production.

4. Mode

   Mode provides different methods for applying the Smart Blur filter:

   Normal
   Normal applies blurring to the image without altering it further.

   Edge Only
   Instead of blurring the image, this option traces the center of areas the filter defines as edges with white, non-anti-aliased, single pixel lines, and fills the remaining image with black.

   Overlay Edge
   Instead of blurring the image, this option traces areas the filter defines as edges with white, non-anti-aliased, single pixel lines over the original image.

Filter: Brush Strokes

Brush Strokes function almost identically to the Artistic series of filters. They identify areas of similar colors. These areas are blurred, filled with the average of the colors within each area, or areas are altered in other ways. The Brush Strokes filters also add colors to the edges of the colored areas, or over the entire image.

Accented Edges

This filter traces the edges in the image, then darkens or lightens them. Low settings produce a slight glowing or an increase in shadows. At higher settings, the image appears massively darkened and grime-spattered, or glowing is if lit by a strange alien light. At highest settings, the image is distorted beyond recognition.

The Accented Edges Dialog

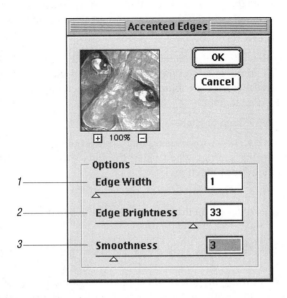

1. **Edge Width (1 to 14)**

   This setting controls the width of the edges that are brightened or darkened. A value of 1 produces a thin line over the edges. A value of 14 creates very thick lines covering most of the image.

2. **Edge Brightness (0 to 50)**

   This setting determines the amount edges are darkened or lightened. A value of 0 darkens edges to black. A value of 25, the neutral setting, retains the original lightness values of the image. A value of 50 makes edges almost white, eliminating most detail.

3. **Smoothness (1 to 15)**

   This setting determines the amount of blurring done to the image after edges are found. With a high smoothness, major edges are still present, but most detail information is lost.

Angled Strokes

This filter identifies areas of similar colors and blurs within those areas, preserving the edges between different colors. It adds streaks to the areas by lightening or darkening the existing colors in narrow strokes. Strokes are rendered at left or right diagonals. Within a single area of color, all streaks are made in the same direction.

The Angled Strokes Dialog

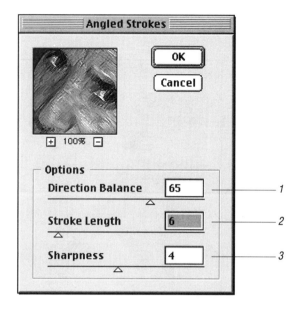

1. **Direction Balance** (0 to 100)

   This setting determines if all areas are stroked at a right diagonal or a left diagonal, or if some areas are stroked at a left diagonal and others at a right diagonal. At 0, the strokes are entirely at a left diagonal. At 100, the strokes are entirely at a right diagonal. Numbers in between mix the two angles.

2. **Stroke Length** (3 to 50)

   This setting determines the distance of the blurring and streaking. Lower settings preserve more of the image's original detail, while higher settings produce a more pronounced stroke.

3. **Sharpness** (0 to 10)

   This setting controls the amount of sharpening done to the image after blurring and streaking. Sharpness intensifies highlights and shadows, creating more of a 3-D appearance. Too much sharpening produces *artifacting,* or pixels with color obviously inconsistent with the rest of the image, and *haloing,* or areas of light pixels surrounding dark areas.

Crosshatch

This filter is very similar to the Angled Strokes filter. It identifies areas of similar colors and blurs within those areas, preserving the edges between different colors. It adds streaks to the areas by lightening or darkening the existing colors in narrow strokes. Strokes are rendered at left or right diagonals. Unlike Angled Strokes, Crosshatch overlaps the strokes.

The Crosshatch Dialog

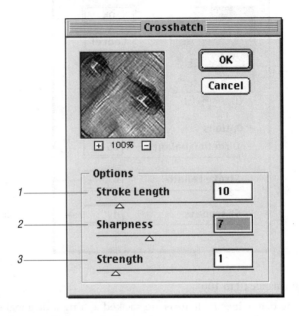

1. **Stroke Length (3 to 50)**

   This setting controls the amount the image is blurred and the length of the shadow and highlight streaking. Higher settings result in more obvious cross-hatching, but result in the loss of more detail information from the original image. A value of 0 does not change the image. A value of 50 retains only the largest colored areas.

2. **Sharpness (0 to 20)**

   This setting determines the amount of sharpening done to the image after blur-ring and streaking. Sharpness increases the highlight and shadow detail, creating more of a 3-D appearance. Too much sharpening produces artifacting, pixels with color obviously inconsistent with the rest of the image, and haloing, overly bright pixels surrounding dark areas.

3. **Strength (1 to 3)**

   Strength increases the differences between colors in the image. Settings of 2 or 3 can cause substantial artifacting when all color values are pushed to their maximum values of 0 or 255.

Dark Strokes

This filter identifies areas of similar colors and blurs within those areas, preserving the edges between different colored areas. It then adds dark strokes over the areas at left or right diagonals. The darker the area, the darker the stroke. The darkest image areas are filled with black.

The Dark Strokes Dialog

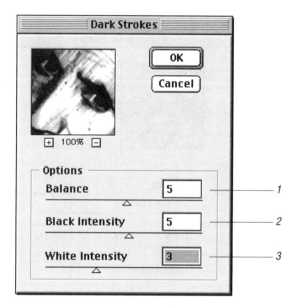

1. Balance (0 to 10)

   This setting controls the quantity of strokes made at left or right diagonals. At 0, all strokes are at a right diagonals. At 10, all strokes will be at a left diagonals. Between 0 and 10, the strokes are a mixture of the two angles.

2. Black Intensity (0 to 10)

   This setting determines the length and intensity of the dark strokes. At 0, the image is stroked lightly, with only the darkest areas of the image filled with black. At 10 all but the lightest pixels are filled with solid black. Settings above 5 cover most of the image with black strokes. A value of 1 or 2 substantially darkens the image while leaving recognizable detail from the original image.

3. White Intensity (0 to 10)

   This setting controls the amount an image is lightened before being stroked. A value of 0 performs no lightening. A value of 10 obliterates most color variation, leaving large areas of very bright color.

Ink Outlines

This filter identifies areas of similar color and blurs within those areas, preserving the edges between different colors. Edges are outlined with black, and color areas covered with a dark haze, as if a black ink wash had puddled on the image and dried roughly in the shadow areas. Finally, light areas are lightly streaked over with black at a right diagonal.

The Ink Outlines Dialog

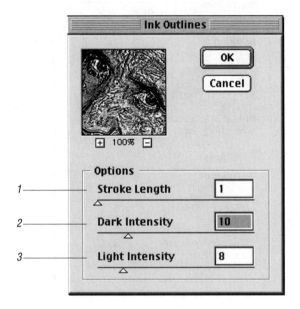

1. **Stroke Length (1 to 50)**

   This setting determines the amount of blurring and streaking applied to the image. A value of 1 blurs and strokes the image very slightly, but still produces substantial puddling. A value of 50 leaves a vague blur of the original image.

2. **Dark Intensity (0 to 50)**

   This setting controls the darkness of the strokes and puddles. A value of 0 produces pale, gray ink blotches over most of the image. A value of 50 darkens all but the lightest areas to black.

3. **Light Intensity (0 to 50)**

   This setting determines how much the image is lightened beneath the added darkness. At 0, no lightening occurs. At 50, colors are intensely bright.

Spatter

This filter reproduces the image as though it were created with a clogged airbrush, with the image appearing to be spattered onto the canvas. It differs from other Brush Strokes filters in that it doesn't find edges or blur the image. Rather, it groups pixels into randomly sized and shaped groups, then randomly moves the groups. Pixels retain their original color values.

The Spatter Dialog

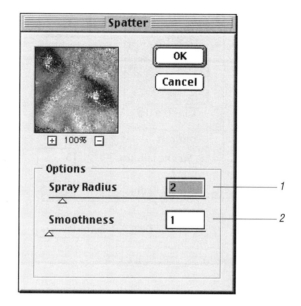

1. **Spray Radius (0 to 25)**

   This value sets the distance pixels are moved from their original locations. A value of 0 does not move pixels. A value of 25 with a low Smoothness value reduces the image to a haze of pixels.

2. **Smoothness (1 to 15)**

   This value sets the size limit of the grouped pixels. The larger the groups, the less the image is distorted. At 1, pixels are moved separately, with no grouping. At 50, the image is only slightly distorted, even when spray radius is at its highest setting.

Sprayed Strokes

This filter is almost identical to Spatter, but it moves pixels less randomly. Sprayed Strokes constrains pixels within specified distances. The resulting image appears tightly rippled.

The Sprayed Strokes Dialog

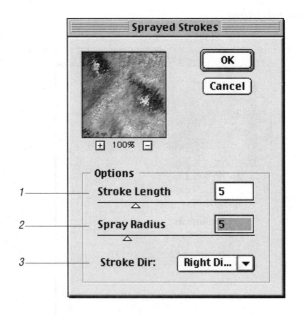

1. **Stroke Length (0 to 20)**

   This setting determines the distance pixels are moved in the direction specified by the Stroke Dir. setting. The higher the setting, the more apparent the stroke will be. At 0, the image is composed of very jittery ripples. At 20, the ripples are longer and more obvious.

2. **Spray Radius (0 to 25)**

   This setting determines the distance pixels are moved in any direction. When Stroke Length is low and a Spray Radius is high, pixels are moved very randomly. With a high stroke length and a high spray radius, pixels are moved very far along in the direction of the stroke.

3. **Stroke Dir**

   The crests and troughs of the ripples point in the direction specified in this pop-up.

Sumi-e

This filter identifies areas of similar colors and blurs within those areas, preserving the edges between different colors. It then adds dark strokes over the edges and shadow areas at right diagonals. It is almost identical to the Dark Strokes filter. The difference is in the shape of the strokes—Dark Strokes uses fine strokes, while Sumi-e uses larger, roughly rectangular, blotches.

The Sumi-e Dialog

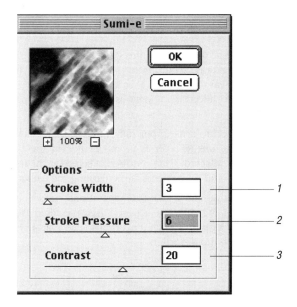

1. Stroke Width (3 to 15)

   This setting controls the quantity and intensity of the semi-rectangular strokes. A value of three produces a few light gray strokes. A value of 15 produces many solid black strokes. In spite of the name of the setting, the actual width of the stroke changes little regardless of the setting.

2. Stroke Pressure (0 to 15)

   This setting controls the darkness of the strokes. The higher the pressure, the darker the strokes. Stroke Width also increases and decreases the darkness of strokes.

3. Contrast (0 to 40)

   This setting controls the darkening and lightening of colors in the original image. A value of 0 does not change values. Higher settings eliminate all detail, reducing the image to solid areas of black or very bright colors.

Filter: Distort

With the exception of Diffuse Glow, the Distort filters change the position of existing pixels without changing their color values. Some Distort filters emulate real-world effects, such as the appearance of an image reflected in rippling water or textured glass. They can also move pixels to match patterns in another image.

Special Notes

- When the image layer is unselected, most Distort filters move pixels into transparent areas. They also move transparency into vacated areas. Pixels can't be moved outside of an active selection, however, but transparency can still be moved into the selected area.

- The result of filters that distort from the center, such as Twirl and Pinch, are dependent on the selection. When there is no selection, the filter applies from the center of the canvas. When there is an active selection, the filter applies from the center of the selection. Selections can be used to position the center of the twirl.

  To twirl an image layer from its upper right-hand corner, draw the selection so that the corner of the image layer is at the center of the selection, and the entire image layer is selected. This requires a selection marquee much larger than the target image, and may necessitate enlarging the canvas.

- Distort filters such as Spherize calculate distortions based on the height and width of the selection. When no selection exists, the filter uses the height and width of the canvas. As with Center distortions, use marquees larger than the image layer to position the distortion.

Diffuse Glow

This filter should be placed under the Artistic filters—it is not a Distort filter, since it does not move pixels, and has nothing in common with other Distort filters. Instead, it changes highlight areas to the background color. When a light color is selected as the background color, it creates a glowing effect. When a dark color is selected, it appears as a grime layer over the image.

The Diffuse Glow Dialog

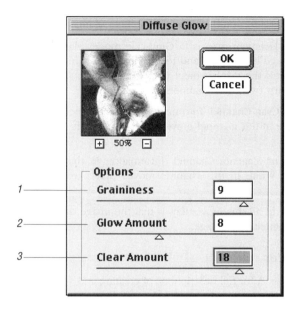

1. Graininess (0 to 10)

This setting determines whether the glow is a smooth haze or noise. A value of 0 produces a glow that is solid white over the highlight areas, and transitions smoothly to the non-highlighted areas. A value of 10 changes pixels randomly, adding monochrome noise over highlight areas.

2. Glow Amount (0 to 20)

This setting controls the range of colors identified as highlights and replaced with the background color. A value of 0 produces no effect when the Graininess is also set to 0. A value of 0 with a Graininess of 1 or higher produces a light haze of noise evenly over the entire image, ignoring highlight values. Settings above 1 define a wider range of colors as the foreground color. At 20 the image fills with solid foreground color.

3. Clear Amount (0 to 20)

This setting determines to what extent non-highlighted areas of the image are filled with background color. A value of 20 produces no clearing. A value of 0 completely fills the image with the background color.

Displace

This filter distorts an image using the lightness values of another image (called the displacement map). One of the most useful Photoshop filters, it is vital for compositing images convincingly over texture, such as adding a shadow over rippling desert sands, or reflecting an image onto turbulent water.

Any image can be a displacement map, provided that the image is in RGB, CMYK, or Grayscale color mode, and if the image is saved in the native Photoshop format. The brightness values and color mode of the displacement map determine the distance and direction that pixels in the filtered image are moved.

When the displacement map is in Grayscale mode, black always moves pixels in the filtered image both down and to the right, and white always moves pixels up and to the left. If the displacement map is an RGB or CMYK image, movement is based on the first two color channels:

- **The Red or Cyan Channel.** Information in this channel controls horizontal movement. White in this channel moves pixels to the left, and black moves pixels to the right.

- **The Green or Magenta Channel.** Information in this channel controls vertical movement. White in this channel moves pixels up, and black moves pixels down.

The end result of all this movement is that the image distorts to match the texture of the displacement map image.

Special Notes

See Appendix A for full descriptions of creating and applying a displacement map.

The Displace Dialog

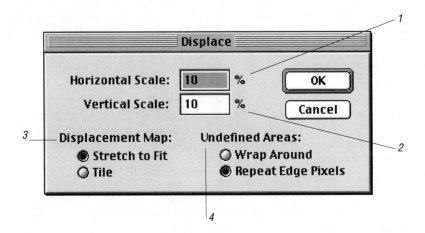

1. Horizontal Scale (-999% to 999%)

   This setting controls the amount pixels move along the horizontal axis. At 100%, pixels move one pixel width for every level of brightness above or below neutral gray. At a 100% setting, pure white moves pixels to the right 127 pixel widths (128 subtracted from 255). The higher the setting, the further pixels move. At 0, pixels do not move along this axis. Negative values move pixels in the opposite directions. Black moves pixels up and to the left instead of down and to the right and vice versa.

2. **Vertical Scale (-999% to 999%)**

   This setting controls vertical movement using math identical to Horizontal Scale.

3. **Displacement Map**

   When the pixel dimensions of the displacement map and the image differ, you must choose one of the following methods:

   Stretch to Fit
   This option resizes the displacement map while it is being applied to the proportions of the image.

   Tile
   This option repeats the displacement map to cover the entire image.

4. **Undefined Areas**

   This option is only relevant when the filter is applied to a background layer. Pixel data must be generated to fill areas that can't be filled with transparency. The Undefined Areas options determine how this information is generated.

   Wrap Around
   This option fills in the empty areas with the pixels that were moved off the opposite edge of the displaced image.

   Repeat Edge Pixels
   This option duplicates pixels on the very edge of the image to fill in the empty areas. If the edge pixels are not one solid color, obvious streaking occurs as the filter repeats each pixel in a straight line out to the edge of the selection or canvas.

Glass

This filter distorts the image as though it were being viewed through textured glass. Similar to the Displace filter, it uses information from a second image to move pixels in the target image. The second image can be any of the four displacement maps built into the filter, or any file saved in the native Photoshop format. Unlike the Displace filter, there is far less control over how far the pixels are moved and in what direction. The Glass filter finds the edges of the displacement map, then duplicates pixels in the target image and moves them to match the edges of the displacement map.

Special Notes

- The Glass filter does not automatically anti-alias displaced pixels. Anti-aliasing is done by the displacement map. If pixels in the displacement map are anti-aliased, the pixels it displaces will also be anti-aliased.

- Unlike other Distort filters, the Glass filter does not wrap, repeat, or fill with transparency areas left empty at the edge of the filtered area when pixels are displaced inwards. Instead, it fills the empty areas with the background color. Areas filled with the background color are not anti-aliased.

The Glass Dialog

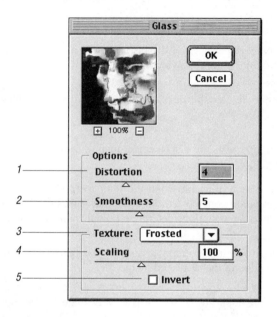

1. **Distortion (0 to 20)**

   Distortion is the distance the filter offsets duplicated pixels from their original location. A value of 0 produces very little change. A value of 20 distorts the image heavily.

2. **Smoothness (1 to 15)**

   Smoothness blurs the displacement map before applying the distortion. This produces distortions occurring gradually and over a wider area. Low settings produce extreme distortions. High settings produce more even distortions.

3. **Texture**

   Textures are used as displacement maps to distort the image. The Glass filter comes with four built-in textures. Any image saved in the native Photoshop format can be selected as a displacement map by choosing Load Texture. An Open dialog appears. Choose the Photoshop file and click OK.

4. **Scaling (50% to 200%)**

   This setting controls the amount the displacement map is enlarged or reduced before displacing the target image. This creates a larger or smaller grain in the image.

5. Invert

Check the Invert box to invert the displacement map before distorting the image.

Ocean Ripple

This filter distorts an image according to the filter's built-in mathematics in order to create the impression that the image is under rippling water.

Special Notes

There is little to recommend about Ocean Ripple. It provides no control over the shape of the ripples, and it does a poor job of anti-aliasing the distorted image. To attain a quality ocean ripple effect, scan in a photograph of real ocean ripples, then use it as a displacement map for Distort: **Displace**, or use Distort: **Wave** or **Ripple**.

The Ocean Ripple Dialog

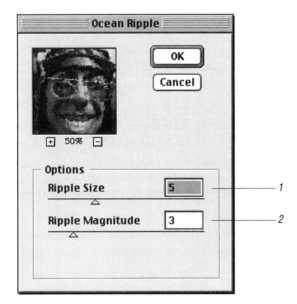

1. **Ripple Size (1 to 15)**

   This controls the frequency of the ripples. The higher the number, the more ripples there are and the smaller they will be.

2. **Ripple Magnitude (0 to 20)**

   This controls the amplitude of the ripples. The higher the amount, the greater the distortion.

Pinch

This filter shrinks or enlarges an image within a radius from the center of the filtered area. The size change diminishes the further from the center. At the edge of the affected area, there is no change at all. The effect makes the image appear to be sucking inwards or swelling outwards.

The Pinch Dialog

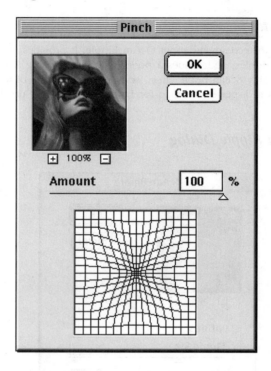

Amount (–100% to 100%)

This setting controls the amount the image pinches or swells. Settings below 0 bloat the image. Above 0, the image is pinched.

Polar Coordinates

This filter changes two-dimensional representations of three-dimensional spherical objects that distribute information according to the coordinates of the poles of the sphere. It is a very specific function: converting Mercator projections to azimuthal equidistant projections, and vice versa. These projections are different methods of translating information of a 3 dimensional sphere into 2 dimensions.

The Polar Coordinates Dialog

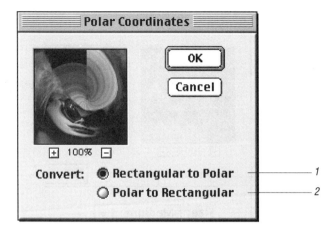

1. Rectangular to Polar

   If the image is a Mercator projection, this option changes the image to an azimuthal equidistant projection. If the image is not a Mercator projection, the filter distorts the image. It takes the top of the image and compresses it to a single point in the middle of the selection, while stretching the bottom of the image in a circle until the left and right hand corners of the image meet. Then it redistributes all pixels proportionally.

2. Polar to Rectangular

   If the image is an azimuthal equidistant projection, this option changes it to a Mercator projection. If the image is not a Mercator projection, the filter distorts the image. It takes the center pixel of the image and stretches it along the top of the rectangle. It pulls the left and right sides of the image down to form the bottom side, splits the center top-half of the image in two, and stretches the center out to form the new left and right hand sides of the image. Remaining pixels are distributed proportionally.

Ripple

This filter distorts an image to create the impression that the image is under rippling water.

Special Notes

This filter is virtually identical to Ocean Ripple, but there are three important differences:

- Ripples produced by this filter slant left, while Ocean Ripples are random.
- Ripple provides better anti-aliasing than the Ocean Ripple filter.
- The Ripple filter moves pixels into transparent areas and vice versa.

The Ripple Dialog

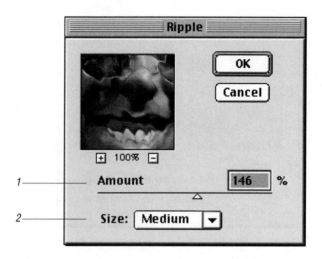

1. **Amount (-999% to 999%)**

   This setting controls the amplitude of the ripples. A value of 0 produces no distortion. The further a number is from 0, the larger the ripples. With positive values, the ripples go up and down, while with negative values, the ripples go down and up. The difference is a slight shift in the position of the ripples.

2. **Size (Small, Medium, or Large)**

   This setting controls the wavelength and frequency of ripples. The smaller the ripples, the more ripples there are.

Shear

This filter distorts an image by pushing rows of pixels to the left or to the right along the horizontal axis.

Special Notes

Unlike most Distort filters, transparency won't be moved into an active selection by the Shear filter.

The Shear Dialog

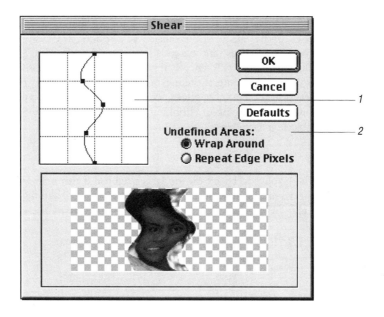

1. Distortion Grid

    A grid with a line running vertically down the middle determines how the image is distorted. The line represents the center of the image. Distortion is controlled by dragging control points on the line. The line has control points on its top and bottom. Additional control points are added by clicking anywhere on the line. Drag the control points to the left or right to move the pixels at that relative height in that direction.

2. Undefined Areas

    These options determine how empty areas left by displaced pixels are dealt with when transparency can't be moved into them. This happens inside active selections, and when pixels are moved at the edge of a background layer.

    Wrap Around

    This option puts the image information moved off the canvas on one side of the image or selection to the opposite side.

    Repeat Edge Pixels

    For an unselected image layer, this cuts off any pixels moved off the canvas, but still allows transparency to be moved into the image. For a background layer or selected image, this removes pixels moved off the canvas or outside the selection, then fills the spaces with the sampled color of the edge pixels in a straight line to the edge.

Spherize

This filter makes a convex or concave distortion to the image, as though the image were reflected on the inside or the outside of a sphere. The distortion starts at the center of the selected area, and extends to its height and width. Spherize is very similar to Pinch. The only difference is that Pinch fades the amount of distortion as it gets to the edge, so the shrinking or enlarging blends with the image. Spherize increases distortion at the edges, creating a hemispheric appearance. Pinch is better suited for enlarging or shrinking parts of objects, while Spherize is best for turning objects into spheres.

Special Notes

Spherize creates hemispheres, based on the largest ellipse it can make within the selection. To avoid having unaffected areas within a selection, make the selection with an elliptical marquee.

The Spherize Dialog

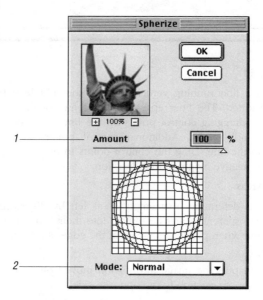

1. Amount (–100% to 100%)

   This setting determines the amount of distortion. Negative values produce a concave sphere. Positive values produce a convex sphere. –100% and 100% settings produce distortion equivalent to one hemisphere.

2. Mode

Normal distorts the image into the largest elliptical shape that can be fit within the selected area. Horizontal Only and Vertical Only distort the selected area along the horizontal or vertical axis, as if wrapping the image around a cylinder.

Twirl

This filter rotates the center of the selection while leaving the edges in place. The center of the image rotates the full amount specified by the Angle setting. The amount of rotation diminishes proportionally until it reaches the edge of the image.

The Twirl Dialog

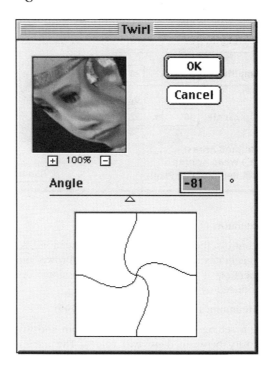

Angle

This setting ranges from –999 to 999°. This controls the number of degrees that the center rotates, and the direction of rotation. Negative values rotate the center counter-clockwise, while positive values rotate it clockwise. The center is rotated by the degree entered. A value of 999° rotates the center clockwise 2.775 times.

Wave

Similar to Ocean Ripple and Ripple, this filter distorts an image by rippling it as if it were beneath water. Wave provides much more control over the amount of variation between waves than Ocean Ripple or Ripple.

The Wave Dialog

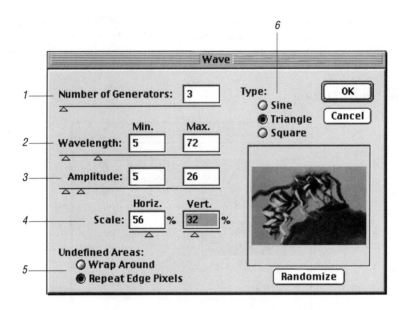

1. **Number of Generators (1 to 999)**

   This setting controls the quantity of wave generators. A wave generator is anything that generates a wave, such as a rock thrown into the water. One or two wave generators is enough to produce substantial distortion. 999 creates waves as if produced by ultra-sonic noise.

2. **Wavelength (Minimum: 1 to 999, Maximum: 1 to 999)**

   The Wavelength setting has two values: minimum and maximum. The length of the waves vary between these two values. The minimum setting controls how narrow the narrowest wavelengths will be. The maximum setting controls how wide the widest wavelengths will be. The wavelengths vary randomly between these two settings.

3. **Amplitude (Minimum: 1 to 999, Maximum: 1 to 999)**

   Amplitude is the height of the waves. Like Wavelength, the amplitude setting has two values: minimum and maximum. The minimum setting controls how short the shortest wavelengths will be, and the maximum setting controls how tall the tallest wavelengths will be. The amplitudes vary randomly between these two settings

4. **Scale (Horizontal: 0%; Vertical: 100%)**

   This setting reduces the total amount of distortion. At 100% the filter runs at the full settings. Lower percentages reduce the amount of distortion until at 0% the filter makes no change to the image.

5. **Undefined Areas**

   These options determine how empty areas left when pixels are moved are dealt with when transparency can't be moved into them. This happens when pixels are moved at the edge of the canvas on a background layer.

   Wrap Around
   This option places the pixels moved off the canvas on one side to the opposite side of the image or selection.

   Repeat Edge Pixels
   For an unselected image layer, this cuts off any pixels moved off the canvas, but still allows transparency to be moved into the image. For a background layer or selected image, this removes pixels moved off the canvas or outside the selection, then fills the spaces with the sampled color of the edge pixels in a straight line to the edge.

6. **Type**

   These options determine the shape of the waves:

   Sine
   This option produces the familiar sine wave, or bell-curve shape.

   Triangle
   This option produces jagged waves that move in straight diagonals.

   Square
   This option does not produce a wave form at all. The Square setting breaks the image into randomly sized rectangles. When Square is selected, the Amplitude setting controls the distance rectangles are moved from their original position. Unlike the Sine and Triangle setting, Square does not stretch pixels. It just moves them. Pixels maintain the same relative positions within the individual scales.

ZigZag

This filter ripples the image in concentric rings from the center, as if the image were underwater and a pebble were thrown into its center.

The ZigZag Dialog

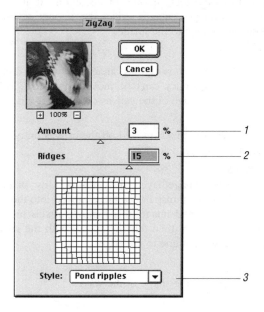

1. Amount (-100% to 100%)

   This setting determines the amount of distortion the ripples create. The higher or lower the setting, the greater the distortion. 0 causes no distortion. Negative values produce crests where positive values produce troughs, and vice versa.

2. Ridges (1% to 20%)

   This setting controls the quantity of ripples. The higher the percentage, the more ripples there are.

3. Style

   These options produce ripple patterns of differing complexity.

   Around center
   This option creates the simplest ripple pattern, producing ripples similar to those created by throwing a single pebble into still water, with a light source directly overhead, so that rings are perfectly concentric.

   Pond ripples
   This option creates a slightly more complex pattern of ripple than Around center, as if the light source were moved off to the side, adding jagged distortions within the concentric circles.

   Out from center
   This option creates ripples as if two pebbles were thrown into the pond very close together. Ripples emanate from a common center, but the concentric circles overlap each other in places, producing additional patterns of interference. This adds more jagged distortions to the image than Pond ripples.

Filter: Noise

Noise is considered to be single stray pixels or small groups of pixels whose colors deviate noticeably from the colors of nearby pixels. The Noise filters are intended to create or eliminate this effect.

Add Noise

This filter randomly increases or decreases the color values of single pixels, adding noise to the image. At its lowest settings, it is useful for adding film grain to an image, or to prevent banding when using a large gradient in print.

The Add Noise Dialog

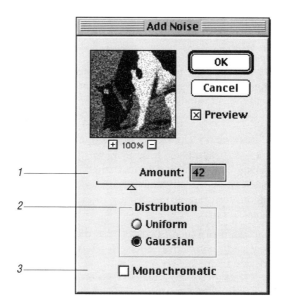

1. **Amount (1 to 999)**

   This setting controls the range the amount pixel colors are varied from their original color. At 255, the total amount of noise reaches a maximum. Pixels can possess any of the 16.7 million color values possible. However, enough pixels will remain similar to the original image to see a vague outline. Above 255 the quantity of noise can't increase, but the variation between the colors becomes more extreme. The higher the value, the more pixels will possess pure black, white, and the primary colors of whatever color mode the image is in. The lower the value below 255, the less noise there will be, and the more the original image is visible.

2. **Distribution**

These options determine how the noise is distributed over the image.

Uniform
This option spreads the noise randomly, but at the same density throughout the image, producing even randomness.

Gaussian
This option spreads the noise more randomly (using a Gaussian distribution, a mathematical theory that describes the "true" randomness occurring in nature). The Gaussian setting can produce single pixels of noise, clumps of noise, and areas of no noise.

3. **Monochromatic**

Check this box to produce noise that lightens or darkens existing pixels without changing their hue. At the highest setting, nearly all pixels will be black or white.

Despeckle

This filter reduces random light pixels, such as those resulting from grainy film, or dust on the scanner. It locates stray light pixels and very small groups of pixels, then fills them with the surrounding color.

Special Notes

- Despeckle is a destructive filter. It destroys image data, resulting in a blurred, less detailed image and a narrowed tonal range. It provides no preview. It has no controllable settings, but arbitrarily decides what a "speckle" is. It should be used with caution, for example, applying it to individual channels instead of to all color channels at once.

- To remove film grain or other "speckles" use the Smart Blur filter. It provides both a preview and control over effected pixels, and is much less damaging than the Despeckle filter.

Dust & Scratches

This filter removes dust and scratches by blurring information over small or narrow areas of lighter or darker pixels. Unfortunately, the Dust & Scratches filter blurs the entire image as well, resulting in a less detailed, fuzzy image. This is only acceptable in situations where getting the job done quickly is more important than image quality. It is not a substitute for removing dust and scratches using the clone tool.

Special Notes

Pay close attention to the image preview while using this filter. The goal is to have the lowest Radius setting and the highest Threshold setting that still removes the dust and scratches you wish to remove. This produces the desired effect while retaining as much image information as possible.

The Dust and Scratches Dialog

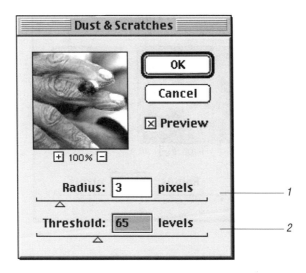

1. Radius (1 to 16)

   This setting determines the size of the area considered to be dust or a scratch. A value of 1 will only affect single rows of pixels or solitary pixels. A value of 16 includes all areas of similar colors 16 pixels wide or less, that are different from the colors around them. The higher the setting, the blurrier the image will be overall.

2. Threshold (1 to 255)

   This setting controls how much the color of the dust and scratches needs to vary from surrounding colors in order to be considered dust and scratches, and therefore become blurred. A value of 1 recognizes everything as a scratch, blurring the entire image. A value of 255 tolerates all color differences, producing no change.

Median

This filter eliminates noise by averaging pixel color values together. Unfortunately, this action is not restricted to noise. Even at its lowest setting, Median also eliminates detail information.

Special Note

Median has little value in production. As an artistic tool, it can produce interesting blurring effects different from Blur: **Gaussian Blur** since it's flatter and less detailed. The effect is more reminiscent of pastels than the Artistic: **Rough Pastels** filter.

The Median Dialog

Radius (1 to 16)

This setting determines the number of pixels the filter will include when it averages pixels. With a Radius of 1, the filter only averages adjacent pixels. A value of 16 averages pixels within sixteen pixels of each other.

Filter: Pixelate

The Pixelate filters all work by breaking the image into shapes of solid color. The Pixelate filters are for artistic purposes only. They are designed to thoroughly destroy detail information, generating heavily altered color information.

Color Halftone

This filter mimics the color halftone printing process. Halftone printing uses dots of CMYK ink. The dots vary in size to create tone, using smaller dots to create lighter colors and larger dots to create darker colors. Color Halftone recreates the image using dots of 100% values for each color channel. The dots are absurdly large. Real halftone dots can only be seen with the naked eye when you look very closely. The Color Halftone filter creates dots intentionally visible to the naked eye.

Special Note

The Color Halftone filter works in RGB, Lab, and CMYK mode. However, a true color halftone emulation can only be created when the image is in CMYK mode, since color halftoning is a CMYK printing process.

The Color Halftone Dialog

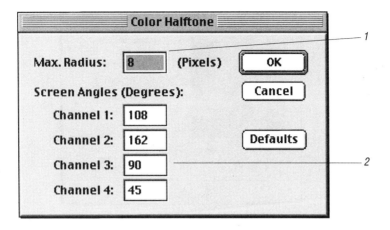

1. Max. Radius (4 to 127)

    This setting determines the size, in pixels, of the largest halftone dot. A value of 4 produces dots visible to the naked eye. Settings above 20 look more like polka dots.

2. Screen Angles (0 to 360)

    In half-tone printing, screen angles are varied in order to avoid moiré patterns. In the Color Halftone filter, they are for strictly stylistic purposes. Color dots are placed in separate grid pattern for each color. A separate setting exists to control the angle of each color channel. When the image is in RGB or Lab color mode, the setting for the fourth channel is ignored.

Crystallize

This filter converts the image into randomly shaped polygons of roughly the same size. The filter first defines the polygonal areas over the image. It then averages the color values of pixels within those areas together and fills them solidly with the averaged color.

The Crystallize Dialog

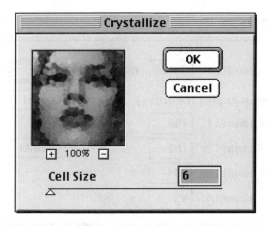

Cell Size (3 to 300)

This setting controls polygon size. At settings under 10, the image is generally recognizable as the original image. Above 10, only a vague outline of the image remains. Above 20, the image consists solely of large, geometric shapes.

Facet

This one-step filter removes anti-aliasing from an image, as well as much image detail. It examines the image to find large colored areas. Then it replaces the anti-aliasing pixels between those colors, producing jagged, pixelated edges. This makes an image appear as though it were created using a primitive paint program such as Paintbrush or MacPaint, which were incapable of anti-aliasing.

Fragment

This one-step filter duplicates the image multiple times, reducing the opacity and offsetting the duplicated images in different directions. The resulting image appears to be vibrating.

Special Notes

To create a controllable fragmenting effect, duplicate the image layer multiple times using Layer: **Duplicate Layer**. Reduce the opacity of each layer using the **Layers Palette**, and offset them individually using the **Move Tool**.

Mezzotint

Mezzotint is an artistic process producing images with engraved metal plates. This filter bears little resemblance to this process, breaking the image into small groups of non-anti-aliased pixels over a white background. All color values are pushed to

---

their absolute values. In an RGB image, blues are all converted to 255 in the blue channel, and 0 in the red and green channels. Reds are converted to 255 in the red channel, and so on.

The Mezzotint Dialog

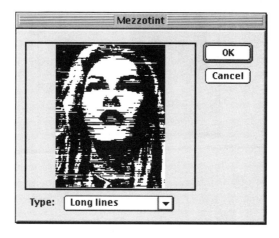

Type

The Type options control the shape and length of the colors that make the mezzotint pattern:

Fine, Medium, Grainy, or Course dots.

Here, dots redraw the image in randomly sized and shaped groups of pixels.

Short, Medium, or Long lines.

Here, lines are narrow, horizontal rows of pixels. The lines are of random length.

Short, Medium, or Long strokes.

Here, strokes run horizontally, and are slightly wider than lines. Strokes are of random length.

Mosaic

Like images created with mosaic tiles, this filter recreates the image using nothing but squares of color. The filter places a grid over the image. It averages the colors within each square of the grid, then fills each square solidly with that color. The Mosaic filter is useful for obscuring parts of the image in a way that lets the viewer know that the area is deliberately hidden.

The Mosaic Dialog

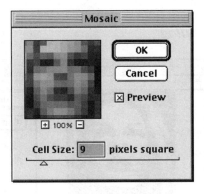

Cell Size

The Cell Size is the size, in pixels, of each square of the grid, and varies from 2 to 64. The higher the setting, the less recognizable the image will be.

Pointillize

Pointillism is an artistic technique popularized by such French impressionist painters as Georges Seurat. The technique creates images using points of pure color. Up close, the image appears to be nothing but points of color. From a distance, the points blend together and the image becomes apparent. This filter selects the image using many circles. The filter samples the color of the center pixel of each circle and fills the circle with that color. Each circle is offset slightly in a random direction. Areas around circles are filled with the background color.

The Pointillize Dialog

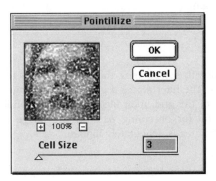

Cell Size (3 to 300)

This setting controls the diameter of the circles of color. This is roughly the pixel size of the points, though points vary slightly from each other. Higher settings require that the viewer be further from the image in order for it to be recognizable. Settings higher than 50 generally produce images consisting of large, overlapping circles, with no discernible image. Settings from 3 to 6 create the most convincing recreations of the Pointillist technique.

Filter: Render

The Render filters add new information to the image based on the mathematics of the filter, rather than using data from the image itself. This data can be new detail placed over the existing image, such as the Clouds or Flare filters, or information altering the existing image, such as the Lighting Effects filter.

Clouds

This one-step filter fills the selected area with clouds using the filter's own mathematics and the foreground and background colors. Data in the image does not influence the way the clouds are created, and the clouds completely replace the selected image.

Special Notes

This filter and Difference Clouds are the only filters that can create new image information in an empty image layer.

Difference Clouds

This filter generates clouds using its own mathematics and the foreground and background colors, just like the Clouds filter. Instead of replacing the selected image, however, Difference Clouds combines the clouds with the image using a Difference calculation (see "Blend Modes" in Chapter 20 for more information).

Special Notes

Instead of using the Difference Clouds filter, apply the Clouds filter to an empty image layer. Then change the blend mode for the layer to Difference. This produces an effect identical to Difference clouds, but provides a level of control.

Lens Flare

Professional photographers take great pains to avoid lens flare, an accident in flash photography when too much light enters the lens and reflects off the various elements inside the lens. Using this filter, you can recreate these accidents.

Of all Photoshop filters, the Lens Flare does the best job of emulating the traditional effect it is supposed to reproduce. Lens flare is useful for creating starbursts and sunrises, and it can add a touch of realism to 3-D renderings by making the image appear to have been photographed rather than created on the computer.

Special Notes

For the best results, apply a lens flare to a layer filled with the neutral color of a blend mode. (See Layer: New: **Layer** for more information.)

The Lens Flare Dialog

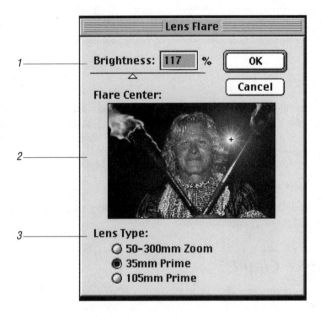

1. **Brightness (10% to 300%)**

   This setting controls how bright the flare is, from a small flash at 10% to a blinding light that obliterates most of the image at 300%.

2. **Flare Center**

   Use this option to position the center of the flare. Flare Center consists of a thumbnail of the selected image, a crosshair, and a preview of the flare. Position the crosshair to place the center of the flare on the image.

3. **Lens Type**

   The difference between these options are primarily in refracted circles of light:

50–300mm Zoom
This option produces a greater number of smaller refractions.

35mm Prime
This option produces larger, darker refraction rings.

105mm Prime
This option produces a large, white flare with few refraction rings.

Lighting Effects

This filter takes the lighting controls typically found in a 3-D modeling program and brings them into Photoshop. The Lighting Effects filter adds highlights, shadows, and shifts colors in the image as if there were light sources projecting onto the image. Up to sixteen light sources can be added to the image.

Each light source can be one of three different styles of light and possess one of 16.7 million colors. There are ten additional settings that modify how each light source affects the image.

Lighting possibilities are virtually infinite, with effects ranging from subtle corrections to radical distortions. The filter can even use the lightness values of any color channel or mask channels to apply embossing effects.

Special Notes

- The Lighting Effects filter only works on RGB images.

- For the best results, apply this filter to a layer filled with the neutral color of a blend mode. (See Layer: New: **Layer** for more information.)

- Shift-drag any control point to resize the light while preserving the current direction. (Command) [Control]-drag to change the direction while preserving the size.

- Duplicate a light by (Option) [Alt]-dragging it to a new location in the preview.

- Choosing a lighting style from the style submenu irretrievably eliminates any custom lights you have created unless they have been saved using the Save option located in the Style options.

The Lighting Effects Dialog

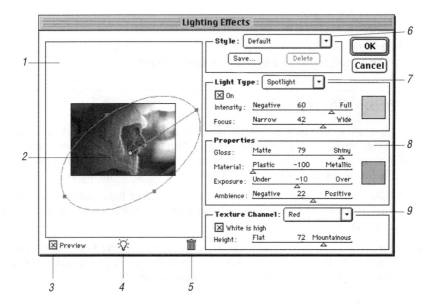

1. **The Stage**

   The Stage previews the image, showing how the lighting will effect the image before the filter is applied. Lights are added, removed, and positioned on the stage.

   Preview Image

   The preview image shows the entire area of the image affected by the Lighting Effects filter. The image updates automatically every time lights or properties are changed, previewing how the image will look when the filter is applied.

   Off Canvas

   Lights can be placed off-canvas, represented by the white area surrounding the preview image. Lights placed off-canvas will be more diffused than those directly on the image.

2. **Lights**

   Control the position of the light, as well the size and shape of the area effected by the light, by clicking on the light's control points on the stage. Lights are represented by open circles filled with the color of the individual light. To make changes to the light, it must be made active by clicking on it. When the light is active, its control points are shown. There are three different styles of control points, corresponding to the type of light specified in the Light Type submenu.

Directional

This type of light consists of a single control point with a line connecting it to the light. The distance between the control point and the light controls the intensity of the Directional light. The position of the light does not matter when there is no texture selected in the Texture Channel submenu. When no texture is selected, Directional lights light the image evenly. When a texture is selected, the direction the line makes from the control point to the light determines the direction of the highlights and shadows in the image.

Omni

When an Omni light is selected, there are four control points connected by a perfect circle around the light. Dragging any of these control points increases or decreases the radius of the omni light. Omni lights are always circular, so their directions can't be changed.

Spot

The four spot light control points are arranged in an ellipse, with a line from one control point to the light point. This line represents the direction of the spot light. The control point at the end of the line represents the outside edge of the light. Change the direction and distance by dragging this point. Drag the adjacent control points to increase the width of the beam of light.

3. **Preview**

Click this button off to stop the lights from previewing. The unaltered image preview still appears, as do the light points, but changes are not previewed. This can speed up working with the filter on slower computers.

4. **New Light**

Click and drag from the light bulb at the bottom center of the stage to add additional lights. New lights are always small, white spotlights. After adding the light, change to a different type of light using the Light Type settings.

5. **Delete Light**

Drag any light to the trash can to permanently remove it.

6. **Style**

This section stores settings so that they can be reloaded. It includes a set of pre-saved lighting styles.

Style

This pop-up contains all lighting styles that came pre-saved with the program, and any additional styles you add. Choose any style to load it, replacing any lights and their setting with the saved lights and settings.

Save

Save allows you to save the placement and settings of all lights on the stage as a Style. Reload saved settings using the Style submenu.

Delete

Choosing the Delete option permanently removes the currently selected style from the Style submenu.

7. **Light Type**

These options control the individual lights on the Stage. Set the brightness, color, and shape of the light here. Settings only apply to the currently selected light. There are four settings:

Light Type

This option determines the nature of the light.

— Directional provides an even light to the entire image, as if from the sun or another distant, bright light source.

— Omni creates a circular, omni-directional light, as if from a bare light bulb held close to the image.

— Spot emulates a spot light, a projected beam of light that can be focused intensely on a single spot or widened into a broad beam.

Color

Clicking on the color square opens the default color picker. Here you can specify the color of the light.

On

Turn lights on or off individually using the On check box. This lets you eliminate the effects of a light without permanently removing it.

Intensity (–100 to 100)

This option controls how bright the light is. Unlike real-world lights, Lighting Effect lights can also absorb light. At 0, the light produces no light. If there are no other lights and ambiance is set to 0, the image will be black. Negative values darken the image. The lower the setting, the more the light absorbs other light. Positive values produce light. The higher the setting, the brighter the light.

Focus (Narrow: –100 to Wide: 100)

This option only appears when Spot light is selected. The area a Spot light potentially effects is defined by its control points. The Focus setting determines how much of that area is actually changed by the light. A Narrow setting produces a small circle of light. A Wide setting effects all pixels within the control points.

8. **Properties**

These options control the way the image reflects light. They have a greater impact on the appearance of the filtered image when a texture is selected in the Texture Channel submenu. Properties apply to the entire image, not to individually selected lights.

Gloss (Matte: –100 to Gloss: 100)

This option sets reflectivity of the surface. Matte is still reflective, but produces less overall lightening than Gloss. Matte preserves more detail information than Gloss. Gloss produces the most lightening, but can also eliminate much of the detail of the image.

Material (Plastic: –100 to Metallic: 100)

This option affects the highlight areas, darkening or lightening the brightest areas of the image. Plastic produces the brightest highlights.

Exposure (Under: −100 to Over: 100)

This option is virtually identical to Intensity, but it affects all lights simultaneously, not just the active light. A value of -100 produces a solid black image. A value of 100 makes all lights intensely bright.

Ambiance (Negative: −100 to Positive: 100)

This option lightens or darkens all pixels in the image with an even, non-directional light that produces no shadows. Pixels are lightened or darkened regardless of whether they are directly lit by lights.

Color

Clicking on the color square opens the default color picker. Here you can specify the color of the ambient light.

9. **Texture Channel**

Using texture channel, you can add texture and embossing to the image. Texture is based on the information in a color channel or mask channel within the image. The filter uses the channel's lightness values to add highlights and shadows to the image.

Texture Channel

This submenu lists each color channel, the layer transparency, and all mask channels in the image. Select the channel to use as the texture channel from this menu. Choose "None" to prevent adding texture to the image.

White is high

When this option is selected, highlights are added where the texture channel is lightest, and shadows are added where the channel is darkest. When unselected, the opposite occurs.

Height (0 to 100)

This setting determines the amount of shading and highlighting added to the image by the texture channel. A value of 0 adds no extra highlighting or shading. A value of 100 creates a highly three-dimensional image.

Texture Fill

This filter is designed to complement the Lighting Effects filter. In order to be used as a Texture Channel in the Lighting Effects Filter, textures must exist as channels in the image. Use Texture Fill to import a grayscale image into a mask channel. Use this filter before running the Lighting Effects filter.

Filter: Sharpen

Sharpening is the opposite of blurring. Where the Blur filters make the colors of adjacent pixels more similar, the Sharpen filters increase the differences. This creates the impression that the image is more in-focus and detailed.

The Sharpen filters can compensate for the loss of detail occurring when images are resized, rotated, or adjusted. They can also improve images that were scanned on a non-production level scanner, or were scanned from out-of-focus photographs.

Special Notes

Sharpen filters only create the illusion of restored detail. Once detail information has been lost through resizing or other adjusting of the image, it can't be restored. The Sharpen filters can restore the overall range of colors, but not the precise detail information.

Sharpen

This filter slightly increases the differences between the colors of adjacent pixels. This can be useful for removing the slight haze commonly associated with images scanned on low-end flatbed scanners.

Special Notes

Sharpen should only be used when the slightest amount of sharpening is required. Since there is no preview and no way to control the amount of sharpening, this filter is of limited use in a production environment.

Sharpen Edges

This filter identifies the larger areas of similar colors of pixels in an image and isolates the edges between these colored areas. It then increases the color differences between the edges.

Special Notes

Sharpen should only be used when the slightest amount of sharpening is required. Since there is no preview and no way to control the amount of sharpening, this filter is of limited use in a production environment.

Sharpen More

This filter sharpens the image approximately three times more than the Sharpen filter.

Special Notes

Unlike the Sharpen and Sharpen Edges filters, Sharpen More sharpens enough to produce a substantial difference in the image. There is no preview and no way to control the amount of sharpening. Additionally, the filter produces harsh and unrealistic sharpening. Use Sharpen: **Unsharp Mask** whenever more than a minute amount of sharpening is called for.

Unsharp Mask

This filter helps compensate for lack of detail, or blurriness, in an image by increasing the color differences between pixels. Unlike other Sharpen filters, Unsharp Mask allows you to precisely adjust the amount of sharpening. The effects can be restrained to edges, or applied evenly to the entire image. The effects can also be restrained to within a range of color differences.

The Unsharp Mask filter duplicates the image and applies a Gaussian Blur to it. This second image is never visible, but is used as a mask that protects and exposes certain areas of the image.

The filter compares the original and the blurred image. The differences between the two images determine the amount of sharpening applied to each pixel in the image. The greatest amount of sharpening occurs where the two images are most different. Little sharpening occurs in areas which are most similar.

Special Notes

- Unsharp Mask provides a full-image preview which dynamically shows the exact effects of the Unsharp Mask filter on the image before applying any changes. In order to take full advantage of this, image should be viewed at 100%, or Actual Pixels.

  This is the most accurate representation of the image on screen. Other view proportions can blur the preview image and lead to over-sharpening.

- A potential adverse effect of the Unsharp Mask filter is *artifacting*, which occurs when the Amount value is set too high, resulting in pixels that stand out as obviously different from surrounding areas. When this happens, decrease the Amount value.

- Another adverse effect is *haloing*, which appears when the Radius value is set too low, resulting in a ring of noticeably light pixels around dark areas. Sharpening happens so intensely around the edges that they don't blend with the rest of the image. Increasing the Radius spreads the sharpening further into the image, allowing it to blend with the unsharpened areas of the image.

The Unsharp Mask Dialog

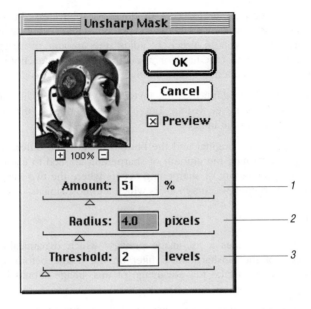

1. **Amount (1% to 500%)**

   This setting determines the amount pixels are lightened or darkened. No pixel in an image will be sharpened by that precise amount, however. The exact amount of sharpening varies from pixel to pixel, and is affected by the Radius and Threshold settings.

   The total amount of sharpening an image needs depends on the size and the content of the image. An image with a higher resolution may require a higher Amount setting than the same image at a lower resolution, because the effects of the filter are spread out over a wider range of pixels. Images with crisp details will require little or no sharpening.

2. **Radius (0.1 to 250 pixels)**

   This setting controls the amount of blurring applied to the mask image. Low settings produce an image which is substantially different from the original image only along the edges. This sharpens edges the most, while areas in the original image where colors are similar are sharpened little. At high settings, the entire mask image differs from the original image, and sharpening occurs more evenly throughout the image.

3. **Threshold (0 to 255 levels)**

   This setting constrains sharpening to pixels differing from each other above a certain level. Only pixels differing in color value from adjacent pixels by the Threshold amount or higher are sharpened. A value of 0 sharpens everything. A value of 255 prevents all sharpening.

Raising the threshold level is useful to protect tones you don't want sharpened. Film grain, for example, consists of small patches of pixels which differ slightly from surrounding pixels. Sharpening film grain with a low threshold setting turn the subtle grain into unwanted texture.

Similarly, sharpening areas of subtle tonal change, such as flesh tones, can destroy the subtle changes and create banding. Increasing the Threshold level protects such areas.

Filter: Sketch

The Sketch filters primarily emulate sketching techniques, creating rough outlines of the image using little detail and few colors. Most Sketch filters reduce all colors in an image to shades of the foreground and background colors.

While they work with any colors as the foreground and background colors, the filters produce the most realistic results when the foreground and background colors are set to the default black and white. Since the Sketch filters use such a limited range of specifiable colors, they are more controllable and predictable than the Artistic or Brush Strokes filters.

Special Notes

Set the foreground or the background to a neutral blend mode color, and apply a Sketch filter to an image layer. When the layer is set to the blend mode, the neutral color becomes transparent, leaving just the lines of the other color over underlying images. (See Layer: New: **Layer** for more information.)

Bas Relief

Bas Relief is a technique sculpting figures nearly flat to the surface they are created from. This filter attempts to recreate the three-dimensional bas relief feel by reducing the image to shades of the foreground and background colors, then adding highlight and shadow detail to create a three-dimensional feel. It identifies areas of similar colored pixels, then performs an action similar to the Image: Adjust: **Threshold** command. Areas change to the foreground or the background color, depending on their lightness values and the Light Direction setting.

The Bas Relief Dialog

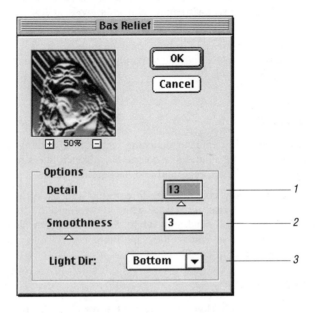

1. Detail (1 to 15)

   Detail sets the amount of pixels need to differ from each other to be considered an area. At low settings, pixels must differ from each other substantially in order to be considered separate colored areas. This produces an image consisting of a few large areas of foreground and background colors, with very little detail. Higher settings identify more areas, producing a more detailed and more recognizable image.

2. Smoothness (1 to 15)

   Smoothness controls the amount of blurring done to the image after it is converted to the foreground and background colors. A value of 1 produces no blurring. At this setting all pixels in the image consist of the foreground or background color, except for anti-aliased pixels. At higher settings, the foreground and background colors blur together, eliminating detail information.

3. Light Dir

   This option determines whether areas are assigned the foreground color or the background color. The filter assumes that the foreground color is lighter than the background color. Colors are assigned so that the image appears to be lit from the specified Light Direction.

Chalk & Charcoal

This filter reproduces the image as though it were created using chalk and charcoal on gray construction paper. The filter uses the foreground color as Charcoal and the background color as Chalk. All chalk strokes travel at a right diagonal, while all charcoal strokes are made at a left diagonal. The textures of the strokes differ, emulating the media they represent. Chalk marks appear thick and powdery. Charcoal marks are rough and flat. Highlight areas are stroked with Chalk. Shadow areas are stroked with Charcoal. Mid-tone areas become neutral gray.

The Chalk and Charcoal Dialog

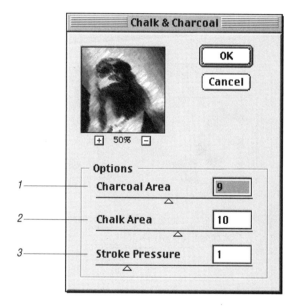

1. **Charcoal Area (0 to 20)**

   This setting controls the range of color values considered to be shadow areas and stroked with Charcoal. The higher the number, the wider the range. At 0, only the darkest colors in the original image receive charcoal strokes. At 20, all pixels darker than 50% are given a charcoal stroke.

2. **Chalk Area (0 to 20)**

   This setting controls the range of pixel colors considered highlight areas. The higher the number, the wider the range of colors. At 0, only the lightest colors in the original image receive chalk strokes. At 20, all pixels lighter than 50% are given a chalk stroke. When Charcoal Area and Chalk Area are both set to 20, there is no neutral gray in the image.

3. **Stroke Pressure (0 to 5)**

This setting controls the intensity of the color of the chalk and charcoal strokes. Settings of 0 and 1 produce rough, textured strokes, creating the most realistic chalk and charcoal feel. Settings higher than 1 produce solid strokes with no texture.

Charcoal

This filter reproduces the image as though it were rendered with charcoal on paper. It uses the foreground color as the charcoal color and the background color as the paper color. Shadow information in the image receives charcoal strokes. Strokes are rough, irregularly sized, and always at a right diagonal. Midtone and highlight information is filled with the background color.

The Charcoal Dialog

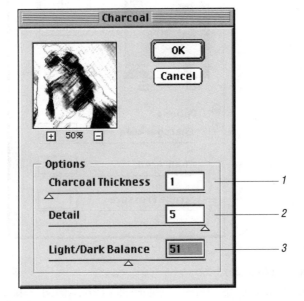

1. **Charcoal Thickness (1 to 7)**

This setting controls the stroke thickness: a value of 1 produces narrow strokes; a value of 7 produces wide strokes.

2. **Detail (0 to 5)**

Detail sets the range of colors defined as shadows and stroked with charcoal. A value of 1 defines only the darkest pixels as shadows. A value of 5 increases the range a little, but not substantially. Since highlight and midtone information converts to solid background color, it is generally best to leave the Detail setting at 5, so that there is enough information left to make the image recognizable.

3. Light/Dark Balance (0 to 100)

This setting controls the ratio of foreground to background color. At 0, the charcoal strokes very muted, blended with the background color throughout the image. At 100, the most strokes consist of pure foreground color. A value of 50 produces a pleasing balance of dark and light charcoal strokes.

Chrome

This filter recreates the image as though it were stamped into highly reflective metal. It does this by thoroughly distorting the image, blurring it, sharpening it, reducing the range of colors, and converting it to grayscale, until it appears to be made of bulging, shiny, silver metal.

The Chrome Dialog

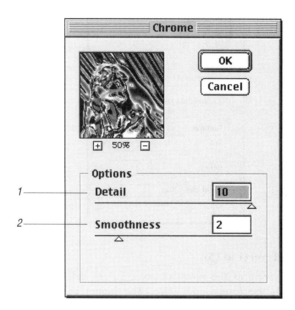

1. Detail (0 to 10)

Detail is the number of reflective surfaces the filter creates. The higher the number, the greater the amount of highlight and shadow areas.

2. Smoothness (0 to 10)

Smoothness controls the amount of midtone information between the shadows and highlights. At 0, the image consists of highlights and shadows with little midtone information to provide a transition between the two. At 10 there is much midtone information, and highlights and shadows are reduced, producing a much more fluid image.

Conté Crayon

Conté crayons are hard, waxy, black or white sticks of color. This filter defines areas of similar colors and blurs within the areas, preserving the edge detail. Then it converts shadows to the foreground color, highlights to the background color, and the midtones to neutral gray. The result is a soft-focused image with hard edges, much like conté crayons produce. It can also add texture to the image to create the impression that the image was created on textured paper.

The Conté Crayon Dialog

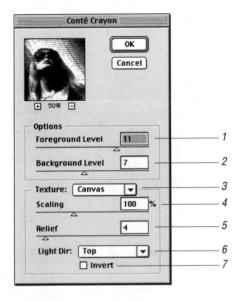

1. **Foreground Level (1 to 15)**

   This setting controls the range of color values defined as shadow areas and stroked with the foreground color. The higher the number, the wider the range. At 1, only the darkest colors in the original image are stroked. At 15, all pixels darker than 50% in the original receive a conté crayon stroke.

2. **Background Level (1 to 15)**

   This setting controls the range of color values defined as highlight areas and stroked with the background color. The higher the number, the wider the range. At 1, only the lightest colors in the original are stroked. At 15, all pixels lighter than 50% are stroked. When both Foreground Level and Background Level are set to 15, there is no neutral gray in the image

3. **Texture**

   The lightness values of the texture are used for adding highlight and detail information. When "Load Selection" is selected, Photoshop prompts you to select a Photoshop file to use as a texture. The texture is tiled if it is smaller than the image, or cropped if it is larger than the image.

4. **Scaling (50% to 200%)**

   This setting alters the size of the texture before it is applied to the image, from half its size to twice its size.

5. **Relief (0 to 50)**

   This setting controls the amount of highlight and shadow the texture adds to the image. Highlight and shadow detail is based on highlights and shadows in the texture. A value of 0 adds no texture at all. A value of 50 makes most pixels solid black or white, destroying all tonal information and producing harsh, jagged, non-anti-aliased lines. Settings from 3 to 7 produce the most realistic appearing texture.

6. **Light Dir**

   The Light direction setting increases the shadows and highlights along the direction of the light, creating the appearance that the image is being lit from that direction.

7. **Invert**

   Check the Invert box to invert the color values of the texture.

Graphic Pen

This filter mimics images drawn with Rapidograph-style pen. It only makes lines in one direction per image. All lines are single-pixel wide, non-anti-aliased lines. All lines are of roughly the same length as well.

The Graphic Pen uses the foreground color as the ink color, the background color as the paper color. It strokes where shadow detail is in the original image. Midtones and highlights are filled with solid background color.

Filter Menu

The Graphic Pen Dialog

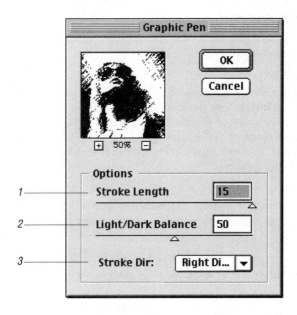

1. Stroke Length (1 to 15)

This setting determines the length of the pen stroke. A value of 1 produces single-pixel dots. A value of 15 produces short lines.

2. Light/Dark Balance (0 to 100)

This setting controls the range of colors defined as shadow and stroked. At 0, no shadows are defined, filling the image with solid background color. At 100, the entire range of colors are recognized as shadows, producing an image completely filled with the foreground color.

3. Stroke Dir

This setting determines the direction of the stroke marks.

Halftone Pattern

This filter emulates the appearance of an image printed using halftone screens. The filter uses the foreground color as the ink color, and the background color as the paper color. It converts the image to two colors, using the foreground color to represent shadow and midtone information and the background color for high-light information.

The Halftone Pattern Dialog

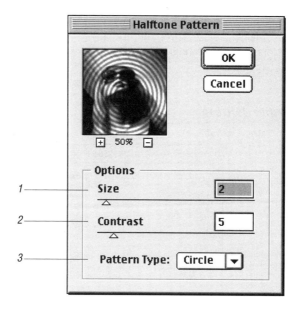

1. Size (1 to 12)

    This option sets the size of the halftone pattern. A value of 0 applies fine lines or small dots. A value of 12 produces a large pattern that nearly obliterates the image.

2. Contrast (0 to 50)

    This setting controls the amount of midtone information in the image. The higher the setting, the greater the amount of pixels of pure foreground or background colors. At 0, the image emulates a tonal range similar to the original image. At 50, the image will be 100% foreground and background colors, with no midtone values.

3. Type

    This setting determines the shape of the simulated screen:

    Circle

    This option produces a pattern of concentric circles starting at the center of the selected area.

    Dot

    This option produces a pattern similar to the traditional halftone screen.

    Line

    This option reproduces the image as a horizontal line pattern.

Note Paper

This filter attempts to create the look and feel of an image printed on a piece of paper. Similar to Image: Adjust: **Threshold**, it converts all colors to foreground or background colors based on brightness values. It applies paper texture and embosses the image to create the impression that the image has been stamped into paper.

The Note Paper Dialog

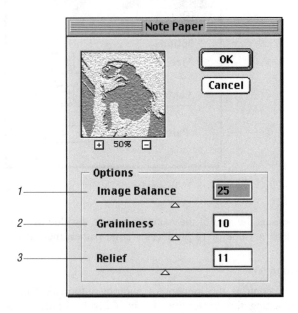

1. Image Balance (0 to 50)

   This setting determines the point at which pixels change into foreground or background color. At 0, the entire image fills with the background color. At 50 the entire image fills with the foreground color. At 25, pixels with lightness values higher than 50% are filled with foreground color, and lower than 50% with background color.

2. Graininess (0 to 20)

   This setting controls the amount of simulated paper texture added to the image. A value of 0 adds no paper texture. A value of 20 adds rough texture over the entire image.

3. Relief (0 to 25)

   This setting determines the amount of black lines added to edges where foreground and background colors meet, and how much Graininess is darkened. A value of 0 adds no black lines. A value of 25 adds thick black lines.

Photocopy

This filter makes the image appear photocopied. The foreground color is used as the toner color, and the background color is the paper color. The filter converts shadow and midtone information to the foreground color, and uses the background color for the highlights. Like a true photocopier, it also eliminates most detail.

The Photocopy Dialog

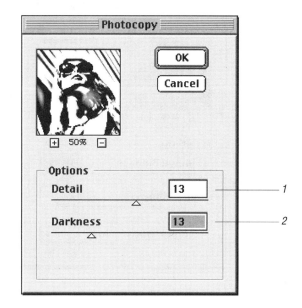

1. Detail (1 to 24)

   This setting determines the amount of detail information the filter retains from the original image. The higher the setting, the more detail. At 24, the image retains much shadow and midtone detail, but changes highlights to solid background color. At 0, only thin edge outlines remain of the darkest areas of the image.

2. Darkness (1 to 50)

   This setting emulates a photocopier's darkness setting. It controls how much toner (foreground color) is put down where the detail information is. A value of 1 produces a very light image. At 50 all lines are solid foreground color.

Plaster

If wet plaster spilled on the ground and miraculously puddled in the shape of an image, it might look something like the results of this filter. It finds the major edges in the image, eliminating all detail information except for the shadows, which it fills with the foreground color. The remainder of the image is filled with the background color. It adds highlight and shadows around the edges, creating a loosely three-dimensional liquid impression. Finally, it runs a gradient across the background-colored areas. The gradient starts with the background color and ends with the foreground color.

The Plaster Dialog

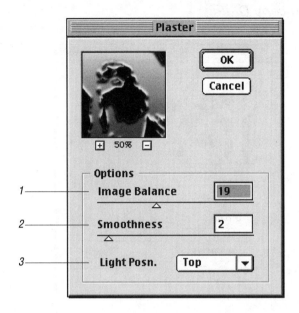

1. **Image Balance (0 to 50)**

   This setting determines what is defined as shadow and filled with foreground color. At 50, the image fills solidly with the foreground color. At 0, the image is filled with the gradient. Recognizable images fall between the two values.

2. **Smoothness (1 to 15)**

   This setting determines how closely the filter follows the edges of the image. The filter degrades the image so much, however, that a value of 1 differs little from a value of 15.

3. **Light Posn.**

   Highlights and shadows are added to the image to create the appearance that it is lit from the direction specified by Light Position. Also, the gradient is drawn starting with the background color from the direction of the light position.

Reticulation

Artistic reticulation represents images using web-like crisscrossing often seen in traditional Celtic art. This filter has nothing in common with reticulation, however. It makes the image appear as if it were printed with India ink on crepe paper:

very distorted, textured, with little detail information from the original image. It converts shadows to the foreground color, highlights and midtones to the background color, and applies texture according to mathematics built into the filter.

The Reticulation Dialog

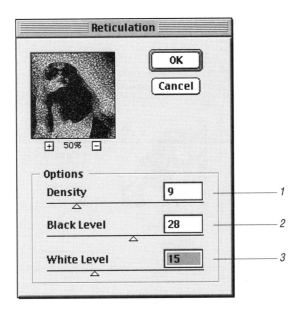

1. **Density (0 to 50)**

   This setting controls the amount of texture added to the image. At 0, the image is created primarily with shades of the foreground color, and there is no texture. At 50, highlight areas are filled solidly with background color, and there is no texture. At settings between 0 and 50, the image is highly textured over all areas. The lower the setting, the greater the amount of foreground color appears in the texture.

2. **Black Level (0 to 50)**

   This setting determines the amount the foreground color blends with the background color. At lower settings, there is more background color texture in areas that are primarily foreground colors.

3. **White Level (0 to 50)**

   This setting determines the amount the background color blends with the foreground color. At lower settings, there is more foreground color texture in areas that are primarily background colors.

Stamp

This filter produces a fairly accurate reproduction of an image created with a rubber stamp. Stamp uses the foreground color as the ink color and the background color as the paper color. The filter finds edges and strokes them with the foreground color. Dark colors convert to the ink color, and light colors to the background color, with no tonal variation in between.

The Stamp Dialog

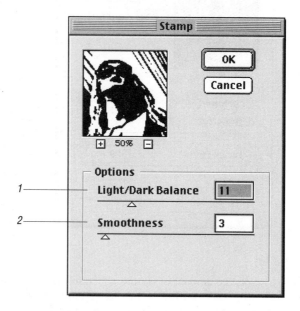

1. **Light/Dark Balance (0 to 50)**

   This setting determines the threshold where dark colors become the foreground color and light colors become the background color. At 0, the entire image fills with solid background color. At 50, the entire image fills with solid foreground color. At 25, pixels darker than 50% change to the foreground color, while pixels lighter than 50% become the background color.

2. **Smoothness (1 to 50)**

   Smoothness is the amount of blurring done to the image before colors are changed. The higher the smoothness, the simpler the final image. A value of 1 typically produces the most realistic rubber stamp emulation.

Torn Edges

This filter is similar to the Cutout filter, in that it recreates the image as though it were made from torn paper—however, it uses a single paper color. Colors are converted to the foreground or background color, then texture is applied to the edges to create a torn paper appearance.

The Torn Edges Dialog

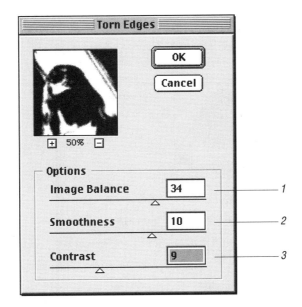

1. **Image Balance (0 to 50)**

   This setting determines the threshold at which colors are changed to the foreground or background color, based on their lightness value. At 0, the image fills with background color. At 50, the image fills with foreground color. At 25, pixels darker than 50% become foreground color, while pixels lighter than 50% become background color.

2. **Smoothness (1 to 15)**

   This setting controls the amount of texture applied to the edges. A value of 1 is the maximum amount of texture, reducing narrower lines to patches of rough texture over the background color. At 15, no roughening occurs, producing solid, non anti-aliased areas of foreground or background color.

3. **Contrast (1 to 25)**

   This setting determines the amount of difference between colors in the final image. At 25, all pixels are pure foreground or background color. At 1, blending occurs between the two colors.

Water Paper

Traditional water paper technique involves soaking paper in water before painting on it with water color paints. Colors bleed together, and puddle into the grain of the paper because the paper itself can't absorb the paint. This filter produces a fairly convincing water paper emulation. It blurs the image in the direction of the paper grain, as if the colors ran along the paper grain before they dried. Brightness and contrast of the image can also be adjusted through the filter.

The Water Paper Dialog

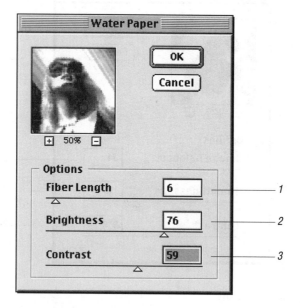

1. **Fiber Length (3 to 50)**

   This setting controls the amount of blurring in the direction of the paper grain. A value of 3 produces slight mottling, while a value of 50 produces a very cross-hatched image, as if paint were applied to a window screen instead of to textured paper. Values between 5 and 10 produce the most realistic water paper emulation.

2. **Brightness (0 to 100)**

   This setting controls the amount pixels are brightened or darkened. A value of 0 darkens the entire image to black. A value of 100 brightens most pixels to white. Values between 50 and 60 come close to the brightness of the original image.

3. **Contrast (0 to 100)**

   This setting increases or decreases the differences between colors in the image. At 0, colors are very close to the average of all colors in the image. At 100, color variations are extreme, anti-aliasing is totally eliminated, and many colors become totally black or white.

Filter: Stylize

With the exception of Solarize and Emboss, the Stylize filters do not attempt to emulate traditional artistic methods or styles. They create a very computer-generated feel.

Diffuse

Diffuse randomly duplicates and offsets single pixels without changing their color values. The result is noise based only on colors that already exist in the image.

The Diffuse Dialog

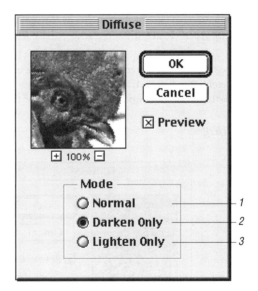

1. Normal

   Normal duplicates and offsets pixels randomly.

2. Darken Only

   Darken duplicates and offsets pixels randomly, but only pixels lighter than the offset pixels are replaced.

3. Lighten Only

   Lighten Only duplicates and offsets pixels randomly, but only pixels darker than the offset pixels are replaced.

Emboss

This filter is a pre-filter used to prepare images for simulating the effect of pressing a three-dimensional shape into a flat surface. Embossed images are created in two ways:

- **Displacement Maps.** Emboss creates displacement maps to be used by Filter: Distort: **Displace.** That filter uses the neutral gray, black, white, red and green colors into which Emboss converts an image to move pixels in specific directions. When used as a displacement map by the Displace filter, pixels are moved such that the final image appears to have the embossed image pressed into it.

- **Image Layers.** When the blend mode of an embossed image layer is set to Overlay, Hard Light, or Soft Light, it becomes transparent except for highlight and shadow detail. This creates the appearance that the image has been embossed into underlying layers.

Special Notes

- After applying Emboss to an image layer, choose Image: Adjust: **Desaturate** to remove the red and green details the filter adds strictly for use in the Displace filter.

- Occasionally, Emboss is used as a stand alone filter. It can emulate bas relief better than Filter: Sketch: **Bas Relief.** Use Image: Adjust: **Desaturate** after applying the filter to remove the red and green details generated for the Displace filter.

The Emboss Dialog

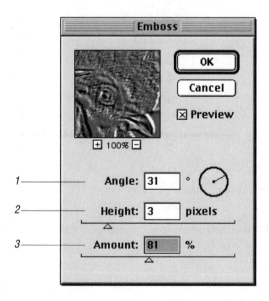

1. **Angle (–180˚ to 180˚)**

   Angle controls the direction of the highlights and shadows. Highlights are added around edges from the direction light is coming from. Shadows are added to the opposite edges.

2. **Height (1 to 10)**

   This setting emulates the amount of force that the image is embossed with. The higher the setting, the greater the amount of shadows and highlight detail.

3. **Amount (1% to 500%)**

   This setting controls the number of edges the filter finds. A value of 1% finds no edges in the image, and converts it to neutral gray. Higher settings define smaller and smaller colored areas as being different. The most realistic embossing effects happen between 100% and 200%.

Extrude

This filter makes an image appear to be created using blocks or pyramids. The cubes or pyramids appear to project outward from the image, like an aerial view of a city.

When blocks are extruded image is defined as a grid, then squares are offset in different directions. Lines are drawn from the corners of the squares to their original location, to define the sides of the cubes. The sides are then filled with color. The surface of the cube can be the offset image, or an average of the colors inside each square.

When extruding pyramids, the filter again defines a grid over the image, then creates a pyramid shape within each grid, using the averaged colors of the pixels in the original image.

Special Notes

Extrude is not available if an image layer is active and an active selection is present. It will function within an active selection on the background layer, and it will also function on an active image layer if there is no active selection.

The Extrude Dialog

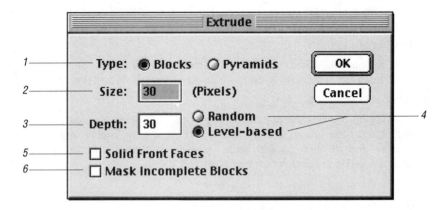

1. **Type**

   This option determines whether the image will be extruded as blocks or as pyramids.

2. **Size (2 to 255)**

   This option specifies in pixels the width of the face of each block, or of the base of each pyramid.

3. **Depth (1 to 255 pixels)**

   This option sets the outer limit for how far a block face is moved from its original location, or how long the longest pyramid edges are. The actual distances they are moved vary based on the extrusion method.

4. **Extrusion Method**

   These options determine how the distance of the extrusion is calculated:

   Random

   This option randomly varies the distance the faces are moved or the height of the pyramids.

   Level-based

   This option varies the distance based on the average lightness values of the pixels within each face or pyramid.

5. **Solid Front Faces**

   Check this box to fill each face with the average color value for all pixels within that square, instead of using the image. This option is only available when Blocks are selected as the Type. When Pyramids is selected, the side of each pyramid is filled automatically with the average color value.

6. **Mask Incomplete Blocks**

   When this option is checked, blocks or pyramids that would be extruded past the edges of the target area are not extruded. Pixel data in such areas is unchanged by the filter.

Find Edges

This one-step filter outlines the edges between areas of similar-colored pixels with lines that are the saturated color values of those pixels. Outlines are thick and solid when colors differ substantially, and are thin and light when there is little difference. Areas without edges are filled with white. The result is a highly stylized image that looks as though it has been outlined using colored pencils.

Special Notes

Find Edges is purely a special effect. You cannot control the number of edges it finds nor the thickness of the lines it traces. Glowing Edges performs functions identical to Find Edges, and has adjustable settings. That filter inverts the color values after tracing the edges, so if you choose Image: Adjust: **Invert** after applying it, you can simulate an adjustable Find Edges filter.

Glowing Edges

This filter outlines the edges between areas of similar-colored pixels using lines of the saturated color values of those pixels. Outlines are thick and solid when colors differ substantially, and are thin and light when there is little difference. Areas without edges are filled with white. It then inverts the entire image. The resulting image looks like it was created using colored neon lights.

The Glowing Edges Dialog

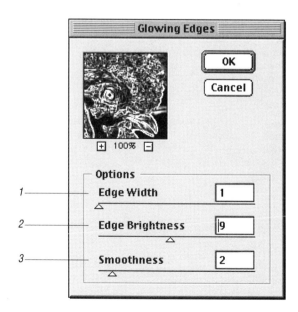

1. **Edge Width (1 to 14)**

   This setting controls the width of the lines edges are traced with. The widest lines are roughly double the pixel width of the setting.

2. **Edge Brightness (0 to 20)**

   This controls how bright the lines are. At 0, all edges are completely black, producing a solid black image. At 20, edges are glow brightly.

3. **Smoothness (1 to 15)**

   Smoothness controls the number of edges the filter finds. A value of 1 finds the most edges, producing many edge lines. A value of 15 only traces the edges where colors vary the most, leaving the essential outlines of the image.

Solarize

This filter is an homage to the Solarization technique popularized by Man Ray, who composited positive and negative film to achieve special effects. The Solarize filter inverts all color values above 128, or 50%.

Shadows and midtones below 50% are unchanged by the filter. Highlights become shadows, lighter midtones above 50% become darker midtones. Light colors become their opposites as well. Light magenta becomes dark green. Light blue becomes dark red. Dark colors are unchanged.

Special Notes

Man Ray seldom solarized an entire image. Instead, he would solarize a background, or part of the subject. For a most convincing solarizing effect, duplicate the image into another image layer. Solarize the duplicate, then composite the two by adding a layer mask and hiding portions of the solarized image. (See Layer: **Add Layer Mask** for more information.)

Tiles

This filter breaks the image into squares, then randomly offsets them within a specified distance. It offers several options for filling the area of the image left empty when pixels are moved.

The Tiles Dialog

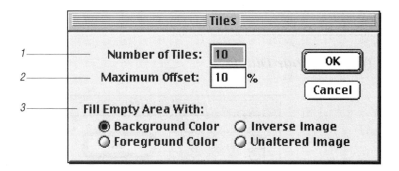

1. **Number of Tiles (1 to 99)**

   This setting determines the number of full tiles per row. There can be any number of tiles per column. A partial tile may be added to allow the row to fill the entire width of the image.

2. **Maximum Offset (1% to 99%)**

   This setting limits the maximum amount pixels can move from their original location. At 99%, any tile could be moved from 1% of its width to 99% of its width.

3. **Fill Empty Area With**

   These options determine how areas of the image left empty when pixels are moved are dealt with.

   Background Color
   This option fills empty areas with the background color.

   Foreground Color
   This option fills empty areas with the foreground color.

   Inverse Image
   This option fills empty areas with the original image, inverted.

   Unaltered Image
   This option fills empty areas with the original image.

Trace Contour

This filter finds edges between specific lightness values. For example, when a value of 150 is entered, the filter places a black (0 or 100% K) pixel between every point in the image where pixels darker than 150 are next to pixels lighter than 150. It does this for each color channel separately, then fills the image with white wherever no pixels are added. Since pixels are added in individual channels, the result is an image defined in pure cyan, magenta and yellow. In CMYK images, black is used. The result is an image defined by single color, single pixel-width, non anti-aliased lines over a white background.

Special Notes

The effects of Trace Contour are very different when the image is in Lab mode. Because lightness values occupy a separate channel, Trace Contour produces black lines over the image's color information.

The Trace Contour Dialog

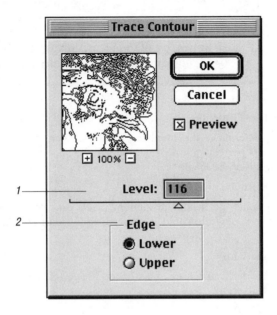

1. **Level (0 to 255)**

   This value sets the lightness value that the filter finds edges around.

2. **Edge (Lower or Upper)**

   This option specifies the side of the pixel edge to trace. Lower traces the darker side of the edge, Upper traces the lighter side.

Wind

This filter randomly shifts entire rows of pixels to either the left or right.

The Wind Dialog

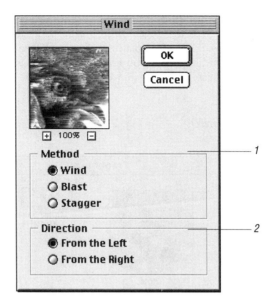

1. **Method**

   The Method options determine how far pixels are shifted.

   Wind
   This option shifts the pixels slightly.

   Blast
   This option shifts the pixels approximately twice as far as Wind.

   Stagger
   This option shifts the pixels approximately twice as far as Blast.

2. **Direction**

   This setting determines the direction of the wind. From the Left moves pixels as if wind were blowing from the left of the image. From the Right moves pixels as if wind were blowing from the right of the image.

Filter: Texture

The Texture filters create the appearance of three-dimensional texture. They do this by generating a texture over the image based on mathematics built into the filter, or by altering existing color information. Texture filters are typically applied as the final step in an image creation to give the impression that it has been created on a textured surface.

Craquelure

This filter is intended to make the image appear to be a very old, cracked, and decayed oil painting. It finds the edges of the image, blurs the contents slightly, and sharpens the edges. Then it emulates three-dimensional cracks by adding highlight and shadow details. Inside the cracks, the image is darkened and the contrast reduced to emulate the appearance of pigment left in the canvas after paint cracks off.

The Craquelure Dialog

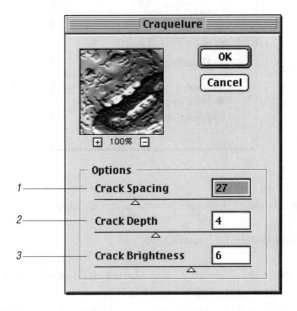

1. **Crack Spacing (2 to 100)**

   This setting determines the quantity of cracks. Lower settings produce more cracks. At 2 all paint cracks off, leaving a dark, low contrast image. Settings between 50 and 100 produce the most believable effects. A value of 100 still produces significant cracking.

2. **Crack Depth (0 to 10)**

   This setting controls the amount of highlight and shadow detail added to the edges of the cracks. Detail is added as if a light source were shining on the image from the top. Shadows are added along the top edges of the cracks, and highlights along the bottom, to create the illusion of depth. A value of 0 produces no depth. A value of 10 produces unrealistic solid black and white highlights. Settings between 2 and 5 produce the most realistic feelings of depth.

3. Crack Brightness (0 to 10)

This setting determines the amount areas inside cracks darken. At 0, the contents of the cracks are unrealistically dark. At 10, the contents are darkened very little from the original image. Middle settings produce the most convincing cracks.

Grain

This filter provides a variety of ways to add noise to an image, or to turn an image into noise. Noise is single pixels or small groups of pixels whose colors deviate substantially from adjacent pixels. Its effects range from subtle, such as adding a slight film grain to an image, to extreme, such as covering the image with a layer of black grime. Grain can also alter contrast before adding noise.

The Grain Dialog

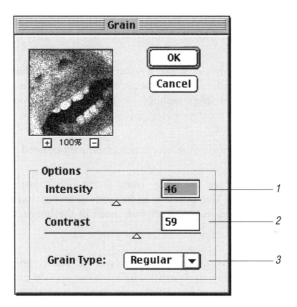

1. Intensity (0 to 100)

This setting controls how much grain is added to the image. The higher the intensity, the greater the effects of the filter. The exact effects of this setting depend on the selected Grain Type.

2. Contrast (0 to 100)

This setting reduces or exaggerates the difference between colors in the image. Settings below 50 bring all colors closer to neutral gray. Above 50, lights become lighter, darks become darker, and midtones are eliminated. At 50, there are no changes in contrast.

3. **Grain Type**

   These options determine the style of grain added to the image.

   Regular

   This option is similar to Filter: Noise: **Add Noise**, set to uniform distribution. While Add Noise converts pixels to noise, Grain blends noise with existing pixels, producing a recognizable image even at the highest settings. At lower settings, Regular adds a light grain to the image very much like film grain. At higher settings, all pixels in the image are blended with noise.

   Soft

   This option is identical to Regular, except that it adds noise at half the opacity, so that more detail information from the image remains. This produces a much more subtle effect than Regular or the Add Noise filter.

   Sprinkles

   This option adds randomly placed pixels using the background color.

   Clumped

   This option adds noise at the Regular setting, then blurs the entire image. At low settings, it produces a mottled and blurred image. At high settings, it produces an image with many blurred patches of primary colors.

   Contrast

   This option adds noise at the Regular settings, then blurs the image and boosts the contrast. At low settings, the filter produces a high-contrast, blurred image. At high settings, it produces a high-contrast, mottled, textured image.

   Enlarged

   This option adds noise in small clumps of primary-colored pixels.

   Stippled

   This option recreates the image using single pixels, just as stippling uses single dots of ink. This option uses the current foreground color. Contrast is created by using more pixels in dark areas of the image, and fewer pixels in light areas.

   Horizontal

   This option covers the image with layer of black, grimy noise that is streaked horizontally, as though India ink were applied to the image with a tooth brush.

   Vertical

   This option covers the image with a layer of black, grimy noise that is streaked vertically, as though India ink were applied to the image with a tooth brush.

   Speckle

   This option boosts the contrast of the image, then puts black specks over the shadows.

Mosaic Tiles

This filter is almost identical to Craquelure, only it adds cracks in a regular pattern instead of randomly.

The Mosaic Tiles Dialog

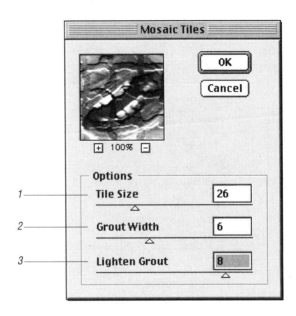

1. **Tile Size (2 to 100)**

   This setting controls the width of the areas between cracks. Lower settings produce smaller areas, and more overall cracking. At 2, the entire image will be one big crack. At 100, tiles are so big that the image looks more like a weird quilt than a cracked painting. The most realistic looking cracking happens between 10 and 20.

2. **Grout Width (1 to 15)**

   This setting controls the width of the cracks. A value of 1 produces hairline cracking. A value of 15 looks as though paint has been gouged off with a linoleum cutter. The size that works best for this setting is dependent on the Tile Size. Larger tiles look best with wide grout, smaller tiles with small grout.

3. **Lighten Grout (0 to 10)**

   This setting controls how much the cracks are darkened. A value of 10 darkens the contents of the cracks slightly. A value of 0 turns the contents into dark gray.

Patchwork

This filter produces nothing resembling patchwork, but creates more convincing mosaic tiles than Mosaic or Mosaic Tiles. Like Mosaic, it breaks the image into a grid, then averages the colors of the pixels within each square of the grid individually, and fills the square with that color. It then adds shadows and highlights to each square to give a three-dimensional beveled-edge appearance to each tile.

The Patchwork Dialog

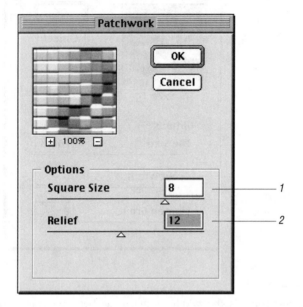

1. Square Size (0 to 10)

   This setting determines the size of the squares. A value of 10 produces small squares. A value of 0 produces extremely small squares.

2. Relief (0 to 25)

   This setting controls the appearance of the beveled edges of the image. Bevels are shaded as though a light were shining on the image from the top. A value of 0 adds very slight shadows to the edges. A value of 25 unrealistically blackens or whitens the sides. The most realistic shading occurs between 5 and 10.

Stained Glass

This filter defines the image with randomly-shaped hexagons. It samples the color of the pixel at the center of each hexagon and fills the hexagon with that color. Then it borders each hexagon with the foreground color. Additionally, pixels can be lightened in a gradient from the center of the image, as if the sun were shining from behind.

The Stained Glass Dialog

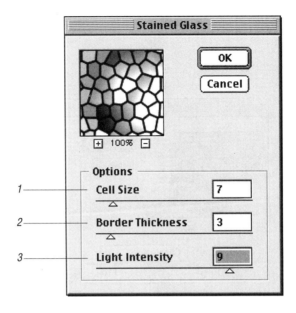

1. Cell Size (2 to 50)

   This setting controls the relative size of each hexagon. Settings above 2 typically reduce the image to vague outlines of the original image. A value of 50
   diagonally divides the image into two colors.

2. Border Thickness (1 to 20)

   This setting determines the thickness of the line of foreground color hexagons
   are outlined with. A value of 1 produces a thin line. A value of 20 produces a
   line so thick that it will be larger than any hexagon under a 20 cell size.

3. Light Intensity (0 to 10)

   This setting defines the intensity of the light shining from the center of the
   image. A value of 0 produces no lightening. A value of 20 produces a very
   beatific light.

Texturizer

This filter creates the impression that an image has been created on a surface that
has three-dimensional texture. It does this by adding highlight and shadow detail
based on the lightness values of a second image. Shadows in the second image
become shadows in the target image, and highlights become highlights. The
texture image can be selected from textures built into the filter, or from any image
saved in the native Photoshop format.

Special Notes

Texturizer should be the last filter run on the image. If anything is added to the image after texture is applied, it will not be textured, thus destroying the illusion the filter.

The Texturizer Dialog

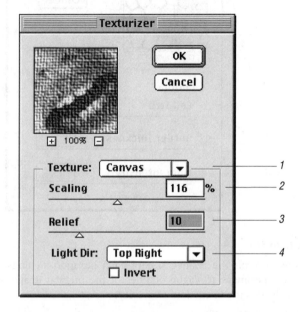

1. Texture

   Textures resemble the substance they are named after. Select your own texture by choosing Load Texture. When you select Load Texture, an Open dialog appears. Select the Photoshop file you wish to use as a texture and click OK.

2. Scaling (50% to 200%)

   This setting controls the size of the selected texture as it is applied to the image, from half its size to twice its size.

3. Relief (0 to 50)

   This setting determines the extent to which areas of the image are lightened or darkened according to the lightness values of the texture image. A value of 0 produces no change. A value of 50 reduces the image to solid black and white pixels. Realistic texture occurs with settings from 2 to 6.

4. Light Dir

   The filter adds shadows and highlights as though light were shining from a certain direction.

Filter: Video

The Video filters are created exclusively for images captured from video or destined to be written out to videotape. They are not useful for any other purpose.

De-Interlace

Video is created by interlaced scan lines, or beams of light that alternate rows every time the screen is redrawn. This happens so quickly and the lines are so narrow that we perceive it as a constant image. When the video image is captured as a computer graphic, these scan lines can be out of synch, producing an image that is blurry or noisy. De-interlace can help compensate for this.

Special Notes

De-Interlace only works occasionally. The only way to find out if it works is to run it on the image. If the filter does not produce satisfactory results, you may need to recapture the video frame.

The De-Interlace Dialog

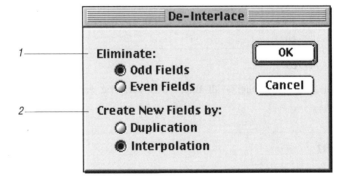

1. **Eliminate**

   These options determine fields removed by the filter:

   Odd Fields
   This option eliminates every other row starting from the top row.

   Even Fields
   This option eliminates every other row starting from the second row from the top.

2. **Create New Fields by**

These options determine how new fields are added by the filter:

Duplication
This option fills the empty rows by duplicating the immediately previous row.

Interpolation
This option averages the pixel values of the rows before and after the empty row to create the data for the empty row. Typically, Interpolation produces the best results.

NTSC Colors

This one-step filter changes the colors of images to broadcastable colors. Just as with printing inks, television monitors use a different set of colors than a computer monitor. Not every color displayed on a computer monitor will display properly on a television monitor. NTSC Colors examines the values of every pixel in the image and changes it to the nearest displayable color.

Special Notes

NTSC Colors should be the very last step before saving an image to video tape. While it eliminates non-displayable colors, it will not prevent new ones from being created if you do additional editing after applying the filter.

Filter: Other

The Other submenu collects all filters that can't be easily classified into other categories.

Custom

This filter is the least intuitive part of Photoshop, and also one of the least useful, since it alters the image in ways that can be done more efficiently using other filters. It does provide interesting insight into the mathematics that filters use to calculate pixel changes.

Using the Custom filter successfully requires a certain amount of skill and luck. Literally millions of effects can be generated using the Custom filter. Fortunately, the filter previews the change to the image with every value entered. The best way to learn the filter is to open the filter and start entering values into the Matrix.

Follow these guidelines when entering values into the Custom filter:

- Enter values starting from the center field.

- If you like the general effect, but feel it is applied too strongly, increase the Scale value, since the total effect of the Matrix values is divided by the Scale value.

- If you like the effects of the Matrix and Scale values, but feel the image is too dark, enter positive values into the Offset field. If it is too light, enter negative values.

The Custom Dialog

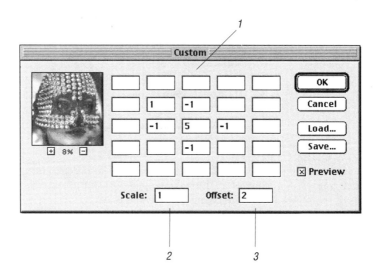

1. **Matrix**

   The main part of the Custom filter is the Matrix, a grid of 25 fields. When the filter is applied to an image, it examines every pixel in the image. It multiplies the brightness value of the pixel by the value entered in the center field. Then it multiplies adjacent pixels by the numbers in the fields surrounding the center field.

2. **Scale**

   The filter totals the products of pixels multiplied by the Matrix, then divides them by the value entered in the Scale field.

3. **Offset**

   The value entered in the Offset field is added to the quotient of the Matrix divided by the Scale.

High Pass

This filter changes areas of an image to neutral gray, based on the amount of difference between the colors of adjacent pixels. This is a valuable tool for finding edges between areas of different colors, since it allows you to eliminate all information in an image other than the highest contrasting areas. It is an excellent pre-filter for creating line art using Image: Adjust: **Threshold**, because it allows you to eliminate unwanted shading and detail.

The High Pass Dialog

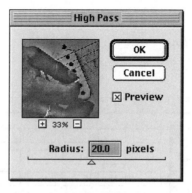

Radius (0.1 to 250)

This value determines how similar colors need to be in order to be changed to neutral gray. With a value of 25, for example, all adjacent pixels differing by 25 levels of brightness or less are changed to neutral gray.

Maximum

This filter spreads areas of light pixels over areas of dark pixels. It was created before the Select: Modify: **Expand** command was added to the program, and the Expand function needed to be created using mask channels. Maximum increases the selection area of a mask channel, just as Expand does for an active selection. Maximum can be applied to color channels for artistic effect.

The Maximum Dialog

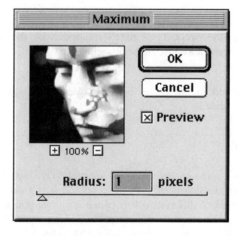

Radius (1 to 10)
> This is the distance that light pixels are copied over dark pixels. This expands all light areas in the image.

Minimum

This filter spreads areas of dark pixels over areas of light pixels. It was created before the Select: Modify: **Contract** command was added to the program, and the Contract function needs to be created using mask channels. Minimum decreases the selection area of a mask channel, just as Contract does to an active selection. Minimum can be applied to color channels for artistic effect.

The Minimum Dialog

Radius (1 to 10)
> This is the distance that dark pixels are copied over light pixels. This expands all dark areas in the image.

Offset

This filter moves selected pixels in the specified direction. It is commonly used to create seamlessly tiling patterns. Depending on where this filter is applied, it has the following effects:

- **Offsetting a layer.** Here, its function is identical to the Move tool: it moves the layer a specified number of pixels.

- **Offsetting an active selection.** Here it moves only the contents of the selection. Offset is one of the only filters that can move pixel information into an active selection from outside the selection. When an area is offset, the area scrolls pixel data into the image from outside the selection to fill in areas left empty.

The Offset Dialog

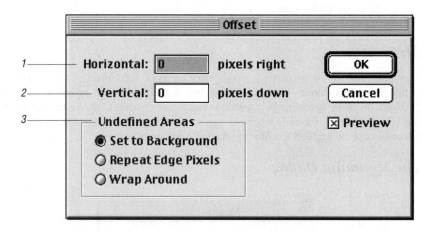

1. Horizontal (–30,000 pixels to 30,000 pixels)

   This setting controls the amount the of horizontal offset. Negative values move the image to the left; positive values to the right.

2. Vertical (–30,000 pixels to 30,000 pixels)

   This setting controls the amount the of vertical offset. Negative values move the image down; positive values up.

3. Undefined Areas

   When there is no image data to move into the image—for example, when the entire background layer is offset—it leaves empty spaces. These options determine how to deal with these areas:

   Set to Transparent
   This option leaves the empty areas transparent.

   Repeat Edge Pixels
   This option fills the area by repeating the pixels on the very edge of the empty area. This produces obvious streaking when edge pixels are not one solid color.

   Wrap Around
   This option moves any part of the image moved outside the selected area or off the canvas to the opposite side.

Filter: Digimarc

The Digimarc filters are owned by the Digimarc Corporation, but are installed automatically with Photoshop. They are not fully functional unless an additional fee is paid to the Digimarc Corporation. They embed information into an image as background noise. Embedded information is only visible to the trained eye, but it can be interpreted as data by the Read Watermark filter. Embedded information provides a means to contact the original creator of the image, and theoretically hinders illegal usage of images. Once the information is embedded in the image, it stays with that image through printing, re-scanning, and other manipulations. As of this writing, there have been no legal cases involving digital watermarks, so the effect of the Digimarc filters as a hindrance to copyright violation is purely theoretical.

Embed Watermark

This filter embeds specific information into the image: the Digimarc Locator Service ID Number, a content rating to specify adult content, and a URL for the Digimarc Locator Service.

The Digimarc Locator Service ID Number is a number which is embedded into the image. Anyone desiring to contact the creator of the image can scan in the image and obtain the Digimarc Locator Service ID Number using the Read Watermark filter. Then they can contact the Digimarc Corporation via phone or Internet to obtain creator contact information. In order for people to contact you, you must register with the Digimarc Corporation and pay a monthly fee.

Special Notes

You can register with Digimarc by selecting Embed Watermark, clicking Personalize, then clicking Register. This will launch your web browser and connect you directly to Digimarc's registration site. A toll-free number is provided if you do not have an Internet connection.

Read Watermark

This filter decodes the embedded information from a watermarked image. Scan or download the image and open it in Photoshop. If the creator of the image used the Embed Watermark filter on the image, a copyright symbol (©) appears before their name in the title bar of the image window. When this symbol appears, use the Read Watermark filter to obtain the creator ID. With the ID, you can call Digimarc's toll-free 800 number (listed in the filter dialog) or click the Web Lookup button to connect to Digimarc's database of artists and contact information. If the creator has paid his or her monthly dues to the Digimarc Corporation, creator and contact information are provided to you.

Special Notes

Use of the Embed Watermark filter is not yet widespread. It is likely that your time will be better spent contacting the publisher of the publication the image appears in, rather than taking the time to scan and run the Read Watermark filter on an image which may or may not have an embedded creator ID.

CHAPTER 14

The View Menu

When Photoshop creates or opens a file, the information is displayed in an *image window*. The commands in the View Menu affect how this window displays an image on-screen.

The image window itself contains another set of commands.

Magnification Box

Located in the lower left corner of the window, this box displays the current zoom percentage. If desired, you can enter a value by double-clicking on the box, typing a number between 1 and 1600, and pressing the Enter key. There is no need to add the percent symbol—Photoshop automatically interprets the number as a percentage.

Previous versions of Photoshop did not use percentages. Instead, they used a ratio that compared the size of the image pixels to the size of the monitor pixels. For optimal viewing, the relative size of each pixel had to be the same, or exist at a ratio of 1:1. Since images and monitors rarely share the same resolution, the results could be confusing. Images range from 72 ppi for on-screen graphics, to 300 ppi for high-resolution images, to 1200 ppi for line art scans. On the other hand, monitors rarely exceed 72–80 ppi. In order to make the pixels of a high-resolution image appear to be the same size as the monitor pixels, the magnification had to be significantly increased. At a 1:1 ratio, a 2 × 2–inch, 300-ppi image would appear to be 10 inches wide.

That same phenomenon exists, but now Photoshop calls the 1:1 ratio "100%." This style is different from page layout and illustration software, which refer to the actual print size as 100%. When Photoshop displays a high-resolution image at actual print size, it cannot display every pixel. Instead, it averages the on-screen pixel values. This obscures detail, making fine edits difficult at best. At 100%, every pixel is fully visible, giving you the best view of the image contents.

Image Data

The Image Data is located to the right of the Magnification Box. It displays information about the active image and the current status of Photoshop. It cannot be edited directly—you must select one of four available options from the adjoining pop-up menu:

Document Sizes

This is Photoshop's default. When this option is selected, the data field displays two numbers separated by a slash. The number on the left is the base file size, or the size of the image with no additional channels or layers.

Photoshop uses a simple formula to determine file size. Measuring in pixels, it multiplies an image's width and height. It multiplies that number by the depth of one pixel, or the number of bytes it uses to display color. A Bitmap pixel uses 1 bit, or .125 bytes. A Grayscale pixel uses 8 bits, or 1 byte. An RGB pixel uses 24 bits, or 3 bytes. A CMYK pixel uses 32 bits, or four bytes. Therefore, a 500×500–pixel RGB image contains 750,000 bits ($500 \times 500 = 750{,}000$). Since one byte contains 1,024 bits, the image size is 733K. This figure does not account for any compression that occurs after saving and closing the image.

The number on the right is the current file size, including any additional layers and channels.

Scratch Sizes

The first number represents the amount of RAM occupied by the active image. When an image is first opened, it uses a little more than 3 times its own size in RAM. As you apply commands and create layers, Photoshop is forced to access more RAM , which increases this value.

The second number is the total amount of RAM available to Photoshop. This number does not change unless you reset Photoshop's RAM allocation.

If the first number is greater than the second, it means Photoshop is using virtual memory, or space from your hard drive, as additional RAM. See File: Preferences: **Plug-ins & Scratch Disk** for more info.

Efficiency

When this value reads 100%, Photoshop has more than enough RAM to process the active image. Lower values mean the program has begun using virtual memory. This makes Photoshop run more slowly, because instead of executing your commands in RAM, it must use space from your hard drive. The easiest solution to this problem is to allocate more RAM to Photoshop. If you've allocated all you can and the Efficiency percentage routinely dips below 80%, consider purchasing more RAM.

Timing

This value displays the amount of time Photoshop took to process the last-applied command.

Image Data Shortcuts

- **Image dimensions**. Hold down the (Option) [Alt] key and click the field to display the current width, height, mode, and resolution.

- **Page position.** Hold down the (Command) [Control] key and click the field to see where the image will appear on the page when you print directly from Photoshop. If you've chosen any options in the File: **Page Setup** dialog such as crop marks or color bars, they appear in the preview as well.

- **Tile info.** Hold down the (Command) [Control] key and click the field to display the size and number of image tiles. Photoshop breaks an image into a series of tiles to facilitate display and redraw. The only time you see these tiles is when you zoom in or out and the image refreshes, or if you apply a command to a large image and Photoshop applies the results one block at a time.

Scroll Bars

Like any other window, a Photoshop image contains scroll bars. These, however, are the least efficient method of scrolling. The most common technique is using the **Hand Tool**, which you can access at any time by pressing the spacebar.

Scrolling Shortcuts

- **Up one entire screen.** Press the Page Up key or choose Control-K.

- **Down one entire screen.** Press the Page Down key or choose Control-L.

- **Up 10 pixels.** Hold down the Shift key and press Page Up, or choose Control-Shift-K.

- **Down 10 pixels.** Hold down the Shift key and press Page Down, or choose Control-Shift-L.

- **To upper-left corner.** Press the Home key or choose Control-A.

- **To bottom right corner.** Press End or choose Control-D.

View: New View

This command opens a new window that displays exactly the same data as the active image. The second view allows you to create a *reference window.* Both images can scroll and magnify independently, so the reference window reflects all the current edits, regardless of the other window's settings.

Common Uses

Refer to Appendix A for full descriptions of the following:

- Creating a reference window
- Creating a CMYK Preview window

Special Notes

Do not confuse View: **New View** with Image: **Duplicate**, which creates a separate copy. To illustrate how both images read from the same source, make a change in one window; the edit automatically appears in the other.

See Also

Appendix A (View: **New View**)
Image: **Duplicate**
View: **CMYK Preview**

View: CMYK Preview
(Command) [Control]-Y

When preparing full-color images for a print-oriented project, you ultimately have to convert them to CMYK mode. CMYK has a much smaller gamut than RGB or Lab Color, so many colors do not translate perfectly to the new mode (See the Image Mode Overview for more info).

When editing an RGB or Lab image, there are three ways to predict how current colors will appear after converting to CMYK:

- **Set the Second Color Readout in the Info Palette to CMYK.** This displays the CMYK equivalents of the targeted RGB or Lab values. Out-of-gamut percentages are tagged with an exclamation point. Unless you're well-versed in CMYK theory, the percentages give you little information about the converted values.

- **Convert the image to CMYK.** This gives the most accurate results, but as a preview, it has two drawbacks. First, images can take a long time to convert to CMYK, and it takes just as long to reverse the command. Second, unless you immediately undo the command, you cannot switch back to the earlier mode and regain the previous color values.

- **Choose View: CMYK Preview.** This changes the on-screen appearance of the colors to their CMYK equivalent without changing the current mode. No pixel values are changed, and you can select the command again to remove the preview at any time.

Special Notes

- This command uses the values in the File: Color Settings: **Monitor Setup** and **Printing Inks Setup** dialogs. Ordinarily, Photoshop uses this information to display the colors of an image already in CMYK mode.

- You can continue editing an image with the Preview turned on. In theory, this allows you to see the final color results as you work. In practice, it can be confusing, since RGB or Lab adjustments will not have the same effect you have come to expect.

View: Gamut Warning
(Command-Shift) [Control-Shift]-Y

This command highlights all current color values falling outside the CMYK gamut. This creates a sort of mask, which conceals all out-of-gamut colors.

View Menu

The effect is more obvious than View: **CMYK Preview**, but it also makes this command less useful. You receive no indication of how the colors will appear in CMYK mode. Also, if enough pixels are concealed, continued editing is difficult at best.

Special Notes

The concealing color defaults to gray. Choose another color or lower its opacity in the File: Preferences: **Transparency & Gamut** dialog. If you lower the opacity, the masking color combines with the underlying tones, creating new colors that simply do not exist in the image.

View: Zoom In
(Command) [Control] - +

This command has the same effect as clicking on an image with the **Zoom Tool**. The on-screen pixels enlarge, creating the impression of zooming in closer to the image. This allows you to edit an image in much finer detail.

Unlike the Zoom Tool, you cannot specify the center of a zoom by clicking. Selecting View: **Zoom In** uses the center point of the current window.

Special Notes

Double-click on the Zoom Tool to reset the magnification to 100%.

View: Zoom Out
(Command) [Control] --

This command has the same effect as holding down the (Option) [Alt] key and clicking with the **Zoom Tool**. The on-screen pixels condense, creating the impression of moving away from the image. This allows you to see a larger image in its entirety.

Special Notes

Both View: **Zoom In** and **Zoom Out** resize the image window in an attempt to accommodate the larger on-screen image. This effect is the same as checking the Resize Windows to Fit box in the Zoom Tool Options Palette. Override this option by holding down the (Option) [Alt] key when you select the command or shortcut.

View: Fit on Screen
(Command) [Control]-Zero

This command expands the edges of the window to the perimeter of the screen, displaying the entire image at the largest possible size.

View: Actual Pixels

This command automatically sets the magnification to 100%. When an image is set to this view, the pixels are enlarged on-screen to match the size of the monitor pixels. See "Magnification Box" earlier in this chapter for more info.

View: Print Size

This command automatically resizes the window to display the image at its actual measured size, regardless of its resolution. Choose View: **Print Size** to evaluate the status of the image at the size it will ultimately print.

Special Notes

Since most web and multimedia graphics share the same resolution as your monitor, this command will have no effect on them.

View: Hide/Show Edges
(Command) [Control]-H

This command only affects the visible outline of an active selection. Choose View: **Hide Edges** to hide it from view without deactivating the selection. Choose the same command to display the outline again.

Special Notes

Once you become familiar with creating and working with selections, the outline quickly becomes intrusive. By hiding it, you can continue editing without having part of the image obscured.

View: Hide/Show Path
(Command-Shift) [Control-Shift]-H

Similar to View: **Hide Edges**, this command hides a path created with the **Pen Tool** from view. The effect is the same as choosing Turn Off Path from the **Paths Palette** submenu.

Special Notes

- Because the path has been turned off, it does not appear on-screen when you select the path in the future. You must select the path and choose View: **Show Path**.

- If you have chosen Turn Off Path from the Paths Palette submenu, you must use this command to make the path visible again. There is no Turn On Path command.

View Menu

View: Hide/Show Rulers
(Command) [Control]-R

This command reveals and hides the horizontal and vertical rulers. The rulers are closely related to measurement values in the Info Palette.

The rulers measure in Pixels, Inches, Centimeters, Points, or Picas. Establish these units in the File: Preferences: **Units & Rulers** dialog. You can open the dialog by double-clicking the ruler, or you can change the values on the fly from the pop-up menu in the lower left of the Info Palette.

Common Uses

- **Positioning items across the width or height of an image.** In Photoshop, the position of an item is based on the coordinates of its upper left corner. When moving an element across an image, this appears as the ?X and ?Y values in the upper right panel of the Info Palette.

- **Repositioning the Zero Origin.** Click and drag from the criss-cross icon in the upper left of the image, where the two rulers meet. Two crosshairs representing the X axis and Y axis converge on the cursor. Using the rulers or image contents as a guide, release the crosshairs at the desired position. The rulers reflect the change.

- **Creating accurate selections.** Use the rulers to target the starting point of a selection. This value appears as the XY anchor in the upper right panel of the Info Palette.

- **Creating guides.** Non-printing guide lines can be dragged from the rulers onto an image.

Special Notes

- Constrain the crosshairs to the ruler tickmarks by holding down the Shift key while dragging.

- Regardless of the specified unit, the rulers always measure from the *zero origin*, or the point where the horizontal plane (X) crosses the vertical plane (Y). Once you reposition the zero origin, Photoshop displays its measurement values slightly differently. If you remember your high school algebra, you'll recall the *Cartesian plane*, which measures the position of a point based on X and Y coordinates. By moving the zero origin and exposing the two axes, you divide the plane into four quadrants. Photoshop mixes positive and negative values to display precise X and Y measurements:

  - **Lower-right quadrant:** positive X and Y values.

  - **Lower-left quadrant:** negative X and positive Y values.

  - **Upper-left quadrant:** negative X and Y values.

  - **Upper-right quadrant:** positive X and negative Y values.

- You do not encounter negative measurement values until you move the zero origin. Since it defaults to the upper left corner, the image exists entirely in the lower right quadrant, which displays only positive X and Y values.

View: Hide/Show Guides
(Command) [Control]-;

This command hides and reveals all existing guides. It does not remove them from the image. A guide is a non-printing horizontal or vertical line, similar to a blue-line drawn in a conventional page design. This feature is identical to guides found in page layout and illustration software.

The rulers must be visible in order to place a guide. Create a horizontal guide by clicking and dragging from the horizontal ruler; create a vertical guide by clicking and dragging from the vertical ruler. Constrain the guides to the ruler tickmarks by holding down the Shift key while dragging.

Special Notes

- After placing a guide, you can move it again by dragging with the **Move Tool**. If you're using another tool, hold down the (Command) [Control] key and drag.
- Set the guide color and line type in the File: Preferences: **Guides & Grid** dialog. If desired, open the preference by double-clicking one of the guides.

View: Snap To Guides
(Command-Shift) [Control-Shift]-;

Turn this command on to create a snapping guide. Whenever the cursor or an item is dragged close enough to a guide, they automatically align to it. This allows for the precise alignment of an element, selection, or paint command. Turn this command off to disable the alignment.

Special Notes

- The snapping distance is equivalent to eight monitor pixels, or approximately eight points.
- To center-align the contents of a layer to a guide, turn on View: **Snap to Guides**, hold down the (Command) [Control] key, and drag the layer toward the guide.

View: Lock Guides
(Option-Command-Shift) [Alt-Control-Shift]-; (semi-colon)

This command disables the ability to reposition a guide. You can still place new guides, but they are locked as soon as you release the mouse button. Choose the same command to unlock the guides.

View: Clear Guides

Choose this command to remove all existing guides. This is the only command in the View Menu that can be reversed by selecting Edit: Undo.

View: Hide/Show Grid
(Command) [Control]-" (close quotation mark)

The grid is a criss-crossing series of guides. Use the grid to create a rigid and highly structured work environment.

Special Notes

The increments, line type, and color are set in the File: Preferences: **Guides & Grid** dialog.

View: Snap To Grid
(Command-Shift) [Control-Shift]-" (close quotation mark)

Turn this command on to create a snapping grid. Whenever the cursor or an item is dragged close enough to a gridline, it automatically aligns to it. This allows for the precise alignment of multiple elements, selections, and paint commands. Turn this command off to disable the alignment.

Special Notes

Like ruler guides, the snapping distance is equivalent to eight monitor pixels, or approximately eight points.

PART III

Palettes

This section covers Photoshop's palettes, in the order they appear under the Window Menu. The only exceptions are the following:

- The Toolbar. We cover the contents of the Toolbar in the seven chapters of Part I.

- The Options Palette. The contents of this palette depend on the currently selected tool. Therefore, we've included these items in each of the first seven Tool chapters.

Palette Shortcuts

At any time, you can hide or display a palette by choosing its name from the Windows menu. Or, you can use the following shortcuts:

- Hide all palettes. Press the Tab key to hide all open palettes, including Toolbar. Press the Tab key again to reveal the palettes.

- Hide all palettes except the Toolbar. Hold down the Shift key and press the Tab key. Press Shift-Tab again to reveal the palettes, or press Tab to hide the Toolbar.

Palette Grouping

Palettes can be grouped together or left separate. To group two palettes, drag the title-tab of one palette directly onto another. Release the mouse button when the second palette highlights. To remove a palette from a group, drag its title-tab away from the current grouping and release.

For the best results, evaluate your work methods, determine which palettes you use most frequently, and make the appropriate groupings. For example, we prefer having the Info Palette visible at all times, so we keep it separate and leave in the upper-left corner of our monitor.

Palette Sizes

Since palettes can easily consume a lot of on-screen space, you can shrink their size by double-clicking the empty space next to the title-tab. Double-click again to expand the palette.

CHAPTER 15

The Navigator Palette

The Navigator Palette provides easy access to different portions of an image.

Depending on the images you work with, however, it may not be necessary to use the Navigator Palette. Photoshop redraws on-screen images faster than ever—especially on PowerPC and Pentium workstations—and it may be more intuitive to use traditional keyboard shortcuts for panning and zooming.

Common Uses

- Navigating when your workstation has a small monitor (12–15 inches) that cannot display the entire image at a useful size.
- Navigating when you work with exceptionally large high-resolution files, such as poster-sized images for large-format output.

Special Notes

Use the following shortcuts at any time to pan and zoom without the Navigator Palette:

- **Pan.** Hold down the space bar to access the **Hand Tool.**
- **Zoom in.** Hold down the (Command) [Control] key with the space bar to access the Zoom Tool.
- **Zoom out.** Hold down the (Option) [Alt] and (Command) [Control] keys with the space bar.

Image Thumbnail

The Image Thumbnail is a low-resolution preview of the entire image. Although it defaults to 1 × 1.25 inches, its overall size depends on the size of the Navigator Palette. Resize the palette by dragging the Resize Window button in the lower right corner. Click the Original Size button in the upper right to return to the default size.

View Box

The shape of the View box mimics the current dimensions of the active image window. If the window is altered, the View box immediately changes to match it. The contents are proportional as well; the information inside the View box equals the contents of the image window.

Common Uses

- **Panning.** Drag the View box across the thumbnail to pan the image. The image dynamically redraws in the window, as if you were manipulating the two scroll bars simultaneously. If your computer is fast enough—or if the image size is small enough—the image pans in real-time.

- **Zooming.** Hold down the (Command) [Control] key and drag to create a new box in the thumbnail. When you release the mouse button, the selected area fills the image window.

Special Notes

The color of the View box is of little consequence, unless an image contains an abundance of the same color. Change the box's color by choosing Palette Options from the palette submenu. This provides three different methods of setting a new color: choose a color from the pop-up menu, click on the color swatch to access the Color Picker, or click on any color in the open image.

Zoom Percentage

Enter a new zoom percentage in the lower left corner of the palette. This feature is identical to the box in the lower left of the image window—double-click the value to highlight it, type in a new number, and press the Enter key to apply the zoom. The maximum value is 1600%, but the smallest value depends on the width, height, and resolution of the open image. Usually, it falls between 0.01 and 0.3%.

Special Notes

If you hold down the Shift key while applying a new percentage, the number remains highlighted. This way, you can enter a series of zoom percentages in quick succession by typing new values and pressing Enter.

Zoom In/Zoom Out

Zoom incrementally by clicking the Zoom Out and Zoom In buttons, on the left and right of the Zoom Slider. This method zooms at the same percentages as the standard Zoom Tool and its keyboard shortcuts (Command) [Control]-plus to zoom in, (Command) [Control]-minus to zoom out. These buttons never resize the image window, as the Zoom Tool does when the Resize Windows to Fit box is checked in the Zoom Options palette. The keyboard shortcuts always resize the image window.

Zoom Slider

The least precise tool in the palette, the Zoom slider is used to dynamically zoom in or out. Photoshop centers the zoom on the point in the middle of the View box. Drag to the right, toward the Zoom In button, to zoom in. Drag to the left, toward the Zoom Out button, to zoom out.

Special Notes

Double-click on the Zoom Tool icon to automatically zoom to 100%.

Navigator Palette

CHAPTER 16

The Info Palette

Use the Info Palette to evaluate the contents of an image. It displays two essential values: the color of the image pixels beneath your cursor and information on the currently selected tool.

Common Uses

- **Reading color values.** The Info Palette displays color values in two different ways. When it shows the values of the current color mode, it can display the relative values of any other color mode. For example, while you edit an RGB image, you can also read the colors as CMYK percentages. This way, you know what the values will be before you convert to another mode.

- **Plotting cursor coordinates.** Regardless of the tool currently in use, the Info Palette always displays the X and Y coordinates of the cursor. These values are based on the zero-points of the horizontal and vertical rulers (see View: **Show Rulers**).

- **Gauging the effect of tools in use.** As certain tools are utilized, the Info Palette displays their status, including any appropriate sizes, angles, and distances.

- **Predicting image adjustments.** When the dialog for any Image: **Adjust** command is open, the Info Palette displays two different color values. The first is the original color value, and the second shows the change that will take place when the command is applied. This way, you can monitor the range of each adjustment before making any final decisions.

- **Tracking transformations.** When transformations such as scaling or rotation are manually applied, the degree of change is reflected in the Info Palette. This allows for very precise adjustments without having to make the changes using numerical dialogs.

Special Notes

- Although this information appears on an easily-hidden palette, it should always be displayed on-screen. If your work involves any color adjusting, complex selections, precise measurements, or transformations, the Info Palette proves an invaluable tool.

- The Info Palette is the only place in Photoshop where you can read the converted color values in an image before you changing from one mode to another.

- The Info Palette is divided into four panels. Each one displays a particular form of information.

Panel One: Primary Color Info

The upper left panel always displays color values. There are two methods of determining the type of values it displays: select Palette Options from the Info Palette submenu, or click on the small eyedropper icon in the first panel to access its pop-up menu.

Special Notes

- For the most accurate readings, leave this section set to Actual Color. Set Section Two to the target color mode, which indicates how the colors convert when you change color modes.

- Whenever one particular color channel is chosen—regardless of the color mode—the Actual Color setting switches to Grayscale percentages.

- Since HSB is based on the traditional color theory taught for years in art classes, this model is often more intuitive for those trained in traditional painting and other artistic techniques.

- If the Info Palette is set to CMYK values while editing an RGB or Lab Color image, the Info Palette displays colors that fall out of CMYK gamut. When this occurs, Photoshop replaces the percent symbols with exclamation points (!). The remaining numerical values represent the closest color in the CMYK gamut.

Info Palette

The Info Options Palette

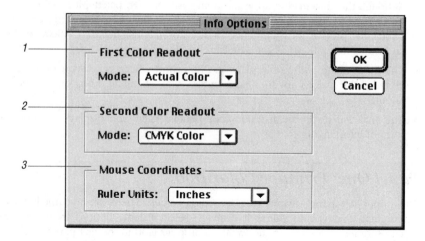

1. **First Color Readout**

   Actual Color
   This is the default setting. Its color values are based on the current color mode of the image.

   Grayscale
   This value is labeled with a K, which stands for the amount of black ink required to print the image as a halftone. If the current image is in color, it displays the values that result when the image is converted to Grayscale. Tones are displayed as output values, which range from 0% (white) to 100% (black).

   RGB Color
   This displays color as brightness values, or the 256 tones of the Grayscale spectrum. When the open image is RGB, it displays the tonal values of the red, green, and blue channels for each pixel. If the image is Grayscale, the three values are always equal. If the image is in Lab Color, then these values display what the exact colors will be when the image is converted to RGB. If the image is CMYK, however, these values are of little use— the converted values are affected by the File: Color Settings: **Printing Inks Setup** and **Separation Setup** dialogs.

   HSB Color
   This option displays color values in terms of Hue, Saturation, and Brightness. Hue values, or a pixel's particular color, range from 0 to 360 . This number represents the location of the color on the RGB/CMY color wheel. Saturation values, or color intensity, ranges from 0% (gray) to 100% (full color intensity). Not to be confused with RGB's brightness values, Brightness here is a measure of how light or dark a color is. Values range from 0% (black) to 100% (full brightness). (See the Image: **Mode Overview** for more information.)

CMYK Color

These values are based on the four individual Grayscale channels of a CMYK image that control the cyan, magenta, yellow, and black ink densities. Since CMYK images are always destined for printing, the colors display as output percentages.

Lab Color

These display the values found in the three Lab channels. The L value is the Lightness value, similar to HSB's Brightness, and ranges from 0 (black) to 100 (full lightness). The values of the a and b channels are positions in Lab Color space, and range from -128 to 127. The a value represents a color's location between magenta and green, and the b value represents its location between yellow and blue.

Total Ink

This displays the total ink density of a particular color, or its combined CMYK percentages. If this option is selected for a non-CMYK image, the value represents the ink density that would result if it was converted to CMYK.

The Total Ink Limit, or the maximum amount of CMYK percentages, is determined under File: Color Settings: **Separation Setup**. This amount is applied when an image is converted from RGB or Lab Color to CMYK. Once in CMYK mode, it's possible to increase the Total Ink value beyond the specified limit, so this option provides a way to keep track of your darkest colors.

Opacity

This gives the combined opacity levels of all layers in particular area. If the background layer is visible, it will always read 100%. Hide the background layer to get an accurate reading.

2. **Second Color Readout**

This pop-up contains the same items as First Color Readout. Choosing an option here determines the color values that display in Panel Two.

3. **Mouse Coordinates**

From this pop-up, select your preferred unit of measurement. Choosing an option here determines the values that display in Panel Three.

See Also

File: Color Settings: **Printing Inks Setup**
File: Color Settings: **Separation Setup**
Image: Mode: **Grayscale**
Image: Mode: **RGB**
Image: Mode: **CMYK**
Image: Mode: **Lab Color**

Info Palette

Panel Two: Secondary Info

The upper right panel displays two types of information. If no tool or Layer: **Transform** command is being used, it displays color values. As with Panel One, options are selected in two ways: select Palette Options from the Info Palette submenu, or click on the small eyedropper icon in the second panel to access its pop-up menu. When a tool or transformation is in progress, it displays a variety of other data.

Common Uses

- **Marquee tool status.** The second panel displays the X and Y coordinates of the origin, or anchor point, of the selection. When you drag an active selection, the values change to the distance moved along the horizontal and vertical axes (?X and ?Y), the angle of its direction (A), and the distance from its original location (D).

- **Crop tool status.** When drawing a crop marquee, the Info Palette displays the XY coordinates of its origin point. When the mouse button is released, the Info Palette displays the marquee's angle of rotation.

- **Move tool status.** Dragging the contents of a layer is similar to dragging a selection: the values change to the distance moved along the horizontal and vertical axes (?X and ?Y), the angle of its direction (A), and the distance from its original location (D).

- **Pen tool status.** The values of this panel only change when you manipulate a curve handle or reposition a point with the Arrow Tool. The Info Palette displays the change in XY coordinates (?X and ?Y), the angle (A), and the distance (D) of the handle from the point.

- **Line tool status.** When drawing a line, this panel displays the distance moved along the horizontal and vertical axes (?X and ?Y), the angle of its direction (A), and the distance from its original location (D).

- **Gradient tool status.** While a gradient is being drawn, this panel displays the distance moved along the horizontal and vertical axes (?X and ?Y), the angle of its direction (A), and the distance from its original location (D). The distance value also tells the width of the active gradient.

- **Zoom tool status.** When dragging with the Zoom Tool to zoom in on an image, this panel displays the XY coordinates of the anchor point.

- **Layer: Transform status.** This panel displays percentage change in width (W) and height (H), the angle of rotation (A), and the angle of horizontal or vertical skew (H or V).

Special Notes

You can use the **Line Tool** to measure the width, height, or angle of specific image areas. Under Line Tool Options, set the pixel width to 0. By drawing a line and holding the mouse button, you can use the values in the second panel to measure distance (D) and angle (A).

See Also

The Line Tool
Layer: **Transform**

Panel Three: Cursor Coordinates

The lower left panel displays the XY coordinates of whatever pixel the cursor is over. The units of measurement for these values are in pixels, inches, centimeters, points, or picas. Specify a new unit in three places: under File: Preferences: **Units and Rulers**, by selecting Palette Options from the Info Palette submenu, or by clicking the axis icon in the third panel to access its pop-up menu. Whatever method is used changes the default unit of measurement throughout the entire program.

Panel Four: Selection Dimensions

The fourth section of the Info Palette only displays information when there is an active selection or crop marquee. If the selection is a rectangular selection, it displays the width (W) and height (H). For irregular selections, it displays the height and width of the selection at its tallest and widest points.

Info Palette

CHAPTER 17

The Color Palette

The Color Palette contains options similar to the Color Picker. Rather than define colors using an extensive dialog, you can enter specific numerical values or manipulate sliders on the fly. While this palette lacks the Picker's precision, it offers a certain degree of speed and efficiency—and can still be used to access the Picker, if necessary. On the whole, it offers no new capabilities; indeed, on small monitors its usefulness may be outweighed by the amount of on-screen space it occupies.

The Color Palette is often used in conjunction with the Swatches Palette (see Chapter 18, *The Swatches Palette*), which is used to contain custom color values. Once you've taken the time to define a specific color, add it to the Swatches Palette to save your work.

Foreground/Background Color

The overlapping squares in the upper left of the palette represent foreground and background color. These are identical to the same swatches found in the Toolbar—in fact, changes made in one tool are automatically reflected in the other.

Special Notes

A double border indicates the active color, or which one receives the changes when a new color is defined in the palette. Click once on the inactive swatch to make it the active color. Click once on the active color to open the Color Picker.

See Also

Color Controls: **Foreground Color**
Color Controls: **Background Color**
Color Controls: **Color Picker**

Slider Bar

Using the sliders, you can define new colors in two ways:

- **Move the sliders back and forth.** This is useful for on-screen colors only.

- **Enter specific values in the numerical fields.** This is useful when you know the exact values of the colors you require.

The color sliders default to the current mode of the active image. In addition to Grayscale values, they can be changed to represent any of Photoshop's supported color models.

Special Notes

- Although you can define colors using different color models, the actual colors are still restricted to the available gamut. So even though you can define RGB colors at any time, they cannot be applied as such in a CMYK image.

- Using the Color Picker to define values in a Grayscale image can be a frustrating process. Since there is no place to enter black percentages, the closest substitute is the K value under CMYK. This value is affected by the Dot Gain setting under File: Color Setting: **Printing Inks Setup**, so the color you define does not match the color you apply. This is Photoshop's attempt to compensate for on-press darkening. Using the Color Palette to define black percentages overrides that setting and gives you the precise values.

- Beneath each color slider is a colored band. If nothing else, these bands illustrate the cause-and-effect relationship that exists between the different sliders. As one is moved, the other bands change to reflect the available colors.

Gamut Warning

When defining colors using the RGB, HSB, or Lab Sliders, you are warned when you select a color outside the range of printable CMYK colors. If such a color is chosen, two things appear in the lower left of the palette:

- **An exclamation point,** Photoshop's standard out-of-gamut symbol.

- **A small color swatch.** This contains the CMYK value that exists closest to the currently selected color.

Special Notes

If you click on either of these symbols, the current color is replaced with the in-gamut variation. Ignore this warning when creating on-screen images.

See Also

Color Controls: **Color Picker**
Image: **Mode Overview**
View: **Gamut Warning**

Color Bar

The Color Bar is found at the bottom of the palette. If desired, define foreground or background colors by clicking anywhere on the bar—but this technique is wildly inaccurate, given the tiny size of the color range.

Special Notes

• Four possible ranges are available: RGB, CMYK, Grayscale, and Current Colors. The last option creates a gradient between the current foreground and background colors. The bar displays CMYK by default, but any range can be selected independently of the color sliders.

• There are two ways to select a new color range:

   – Select Color Bar from the Color Palette submenu and choose a new option from the pop-up menu.

   – (Command) [Control]-click the bar to cycle through the Color Bar options.

The Color Palette Submenu

Grayscale Slider

This offers one slider, ranging from 0% to 100% black. The values are misleading, however. If a black percentage is applied to a CMYK image, the resulting gray depends on the Black Generation setting under File: Color Settings: **Separation Setup**.

RGB Sliders

This option offers three sliders, one each for the red, green, and blue content. Enter RGB brightness values in the fields to define specific colors.

CMYK Sliders

This option offers four sliders, one each for the cyan, magenta, yellow, and black components. Enter output percentages in the fields to define specific colors.

HSB Sliders

This option offers three sliders, one each for the Hue, Saturation, and Brightness levels. The H slider, ranging from 0° to 360°, sets the innate color. The S slider, ranging from 0 to 100%, controls color intensity. The B slider, also ranging from 0 to 100%, controls the amount of brightness.

Lab Sliders

This option offers three sliders, one each for Lightness, Lab's a channel, and Lab's b channel. The L slider, ranging from 0 to 100, controls the amount of Lightness. The a slider repositions a color in the spectrum between green and magenta. The b slider repositions a color in the spectrum between blue and yellow.

See Also

File: Color Settings: **Separation Setup**
Image: Mode: **Grayscale**
Image: Mode: **RGB**
Image: Mode: **CMYK**
Image: Mode: **Lab Color**

CHAPTER 18

The Swatches Palette

The Swatches Palette displays a set of *swatches*, or blocks of pre-defined color. These are used to redefine the foreground or background color at the click of a button. By creating a swatch, you save yourself the repetitive task of defining colors manually. By saving a series of swatches, you can easily use a large range of preset values in the future.

Common Uses

Refer to Appendix A for full descriptions of the following:

- Organizing swatches
- Loading an indexed color palette
- Loading the browser-Safe web palette
- Loading custom ink colors
- Loading swatches from Adobe Illustrator 7 graphics

Special Notes

The Swatches Palette is closely related to the Color Palette (see Chapter 17, *The Color Palette*). Although the two palettes are grouped together by default, separating them provides quicker access to both sets of commands.

Using the Swatches Palette

Colors are not created in the Swatches Palette—they are first defined in either the Color Picker or the Color Palette. Only then are they added, replaced, or used as a reference for the foreground and background color.

The palette itself consists only of swatches. All actions are performed by clicking with a series of keys held down.

Adding Swatches

After properly defining the foreground color, there are three different ways to bring new colors into the Swatches Palette:

- **Add a new swatch.** Move the cursor to the white space at the bottom of the palette. Click to add a new swatch at the very end of the list.

- **Replace a swatch.** Move the cursor over an existing swatch, hold down the Shift key, and click.

- **Insert a swatch.** Move the cursor over a swatch, hold down the (Option-Shift) [Alt-Shift] keys, and click. The remaining swatches move to make space for the new color.

Specifying Color with Swatches

When you simply move the cursor over the swatches, it becomes an eyedropper. Clicking on any swatch applies that color to the foreground or background color.

The Swatches Palette pays close attention to the foreground and background swatches of the Color Palette. If the foreground swatch is selected, then clicking on a swatch automatically sets the foreground color. If the background swatch is selected, then clicking on a swatch automatically sets the background color. To override whichever color is selected in the Color Palette, hold down the (Option) [Alt] key while clicking a swatch.

Removing Swatches

Hold down the (Command) [Control] key and click on a swatch. It is removed from the palette.

The Swatches Palette Submenu

The following commands affect the entire range of available swatches.

Reset Swatches

This command offers two options: clicking OK replaces the current palette with Photoshop's default swatches. Clicking Append adds the default list to the existing palette.

Load Swatches

This command allows you to load a previously saved list of swatches. Typically, these come from two sources:

• Any swatches saved from the Swatches Palette.

• Any color table saved from the Image: Mode: **Color Table** dialog.

Whenever this command is used, the new swatches are appended, or added to the current list.

Replace Swatches

This command is the same as Load Swatches, except the current list of swatches is replaced by the new list.

Save Swatches

This command saves the current list of swatches into an external file. These files are used on two occasions:

• To save the list of colors used in a specific project. Typically, these colors are chosen from libraries such as Trumatch or Pantone Process.

• To load the swatches as an Indexed palette in the Image: Mode: **Color Table** dialog.

CHAPTER 19

The Brushes Palette

The Brushes Palette contains the different brush shapes used by Photoshop's eleven Paint Tools (see Chapter 2, *The Paint Tools*). Although the ultimate behavior of each brush depends on the tool, their essential characteristics are defined here.

The active brush is highlighted by a thick black border. To select a new brush, click on any other icon in the Brushes Palette. A brush is always active whenever a Paint Tool is selected, even if that tool has never before been used. Paint Tools also retain their last-used brush. For example, if you choose a small brush for the Airbrush Tool then a large brush for the Smudge Tool, the Airbrush Tool remembers the small brush until a new one is selected.

Common Uses

- **Selecting brushes.** Choose a new brush shape by clicking one of the small icons in the palette.

- **Define custom brush shapes.** Photoshop allows you to create your own brushes of nearly any size and shape.

- **Loading a series of predefined brushes.** Similar to the Swatches Palette, you can save brush sets for future use, rather than clutter the palette with too many options. Also, Photoshop supplies a folder of predefined sets, as do many third-party developers.

Special Notes

- The Brushes Palette is closely related to the Options Palette, which further defines how a tool uses a particular brush. Photoshop separates these two palettes by default, but they are used much more efficiently if they are combined.

- When using a pressure-sensitive tablet, only standard brushes vary in size depending on the pressure you apply to the tablet. The size of custom brushes remains constant, regardless of the pressure applied.

- Photoshop defaults to Standard paint cursors under File: Preferences: **Display & Cursors**, which does not show the size of a selected brush on-screen. By setting the preference to Brush Size (or to Precise and pressing the Caps Lock key), the cursor changes to an outline that matches the brush size. While this does allow for more accurate use of the brush, only parts of the brush with an opacity of 50% or more are outlined. The outlines of very soft brushes appear smaller than the area they affect.

- If desired, use the following keyboard shortcuts in the Brushes Palette:
  - **Select the brush before the current selection.** Press the open-bracket key ([).
  - **Select the brush after the current selection.** Press the close-bracket key (]).
  - **Select the first brush in the palette.** Press Shift-[.
  - **Select the last brush in the palette.** Press Shift-].

See Also

Chapter 2, *The Paint Tools*
File: Preferences: **Display & Cursors**

Brushes Palette Submenu

The commands of the Brushes Palette submenu allow you to create, modify, and delete brush shapes. You can also save and load series of brushes.

New Brush

This command only creates the standard, elliptical brushes. Clicking on any blank space in the palette is the same as selecting New Brush. After closing the dialog, the new brush shape appears in the Brushes Palette at the end of the current list of brushes.

Common Uses

- **Creating standard brushes.** These brushes imitate the behavior of actual paint brushes. If you use a drawing tablet, these brushes can emulate natural, non-digital media. Their shape is always elliptical. Unless an image is in Bitmap mode (or the Pencil Tool is being used), they are always anti-aliased, and can even be softened to create a diffuse, feathered effect. All of Photoshop's default brushes are standard.

- **Creating custom brushes.** These are user-defined brushes, and can be based on any shape or image created in Photoshop. Even though they may be made from colored pixels, custom brushes are based on brightness values. Black areas result in totally opaque applications of color, while lighter gray areas apply color semi-transparently. All custom brushes have the appearance of Grayscale images in the Brushes Palette.

Special Notes

- When Spacing is set very low (under 20%), there may be a delay between the time it takes to apply the brush stroke and the time it takes for the effect to appear on-screen. The lower the spacing, the more times Photoshop has to draw the brush shape in a given space. Increasing the value increases the speed of the stroke. The trick is finding a balance between smoothness and speed, instead of using one universal low Spacing value.

- Set Angle and Roundness manually using the Brush Outline in the lower left of the dialog. Click-drag the two points to reset the Roundness. Click-drag anywhere else to reset the Angle. The preview in the lower right displays the changes on the fly.

The New Brush Dialog

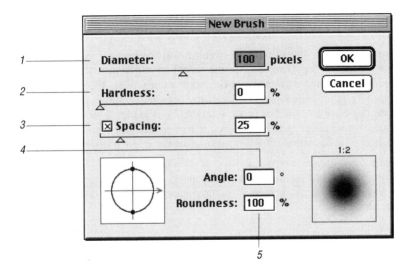

1. Diameter

The Diameter is the width of the widest part of the brush. This value can range from 1 to 999 pixels. Since the value is measured in pixels, the same brush has different relative sizes in low- and high-resolution images. Set the Diameter by dragging the slider to the proper width. If desired, enter a value in the Diameter field.

Brushes under 74 pixels in diameter appear in the lower-right preview at their actual size. Larger brushes appear as large as possible, but are reduced in scale to preview the entire brush.

The Brushes Palette itself only displays brushes up to 27 pixels in diameter. Standard brushes over 27 pixels wide display as scaled-down representations with their pixel size listed beneath.

2. Hardness

Lowering the Hardness value softens the outer edge of a brush. A Hardness value of 100% results in a totally opaque brush, except for a thin anti-aliased edge. By entering a lower value, the center point of the brush fades to transparency. The lower the value, the softer the edge.

This effect is an attempt to emulate specific real-world brush types. Harder brush edges are like stiff-bristled paint brushes, which produce crisp and even strokes. Softer brush edges mimic soft-bristled paint brushes, which apply heavier densities of paint at the center of a brushstroke.

As the Hardness value lowers, the effective size of the brush increases beyond its defined value.

3. Spacing

When you paint with one of Photoshop's brushes, you're actually applying a repeating series of brush marks. When these shapes are spaced close enough together, they create the appearance of a solid line. If they're spaced far enough apart, the individual shapes become visible.

Spacing controls the distance between brush marks. This value is based on a percentage of the Diameter, or the width of the brush. Values under 100% produce overlapping brush marks, and values over 100% produce evenly spaced but separate brush marks. If the Spacing option is turned off, spacing then depends on how fast or slow the stroke is made. Slow strokes make solid lines, while faster movements begin to separate the brush marks. Spacing should only be turned off when such an artistic effect is desired.

For most purposes, a spacing value of 25% produces brush strokes that appear solid. Large brushes, usually with Diameters higher than 75 pixels, often need a lower Spacing percentage. If bumps appear along the brush stroke, reduce the value.

4. Angle

The Angle determines the slant of an elliptical brush. This is similar to the angle of a flat paintbrush or calligrapher's pen. Round brushes are unaffected by this value.

Set the brush angle by entering a value in the Angle field, or use the Angle and Roundness box in the lower right hand corner of the New Brushes dialog. Click anywhere on the circle to change the angle to that degree.

5. Roundness

This value determines the overall shape of a standard brush. A Roundness of 100% produces a perfectly circular brush, while lower values result in thinner shapes. All elliptical brushes are a combination of Roundness and Angle settings.

Set the brush roundness by entering a value in the Roundness field, or use the Angle and Roundness box in the lower-righthand corner of the New Brushes dialog. Click and drag on either black dot on the edge of the circle to set the roundness.

Delete Brushes

Permanently remove a brush by selecting the brush in the Brushes palette, then choosing Delete Brush from the Brushes palette flyout menu. Or, bypass this step by holding down the (Command) [Control] key and clicking on the desired brush.

Brush Options

This command lets you redefine the settings of an existing brush. The Brush Options dialog that appears depends on the type of brush you wish to edit.

For standard brushes, the Brush Options dialog is identical to the New Brush dialog, described above. The only difference is that clicking OK applies the changes to an existing brush, instead of creating a new brush.

The Brush Options Dialog (Custom Brushes)

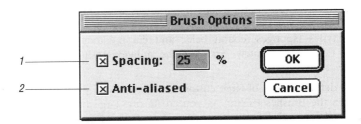

1. **Spacing**

    Spacing can be turned on or off, and the spacing percentage can be set. Similar to the Spacing value in the New Brush dialog, it controls the distance between the brush marks that the Paint Tools apply.

    Spacing is increased to over 100% more often for custom brushes than for standard brushes. Custom brushes are defined using image information. Often, custom brushes are created as an easy way to repeatedly apply an image. To do this without the images overlapping, Spacing must be set to over 100%.

    Spacing can be turned off altogether. This, too, can be more useful when working with custom brushes than with standard brushes. For example, if you have a custom brush shaped like a snowflake, you can apply it much more randomly with spacing turned off.

2. **Anti-aliased**

    This option is available on brushes 32 × 32 pixels or less. It blends the colors of the edge pixels of the brush with the colors of adjacent pixels, producing a more visually pleasing brush stroke.

Define Brush

Use Define Brush to create custom brush shapes. The contents of any active selection can be made into a brush. Color information, however, does not translate into the brush—remember, this information is used as a basis to *apply* new color, not to reproduce it. This command uses brightness values of as the basis of the new brush.

The gray values of the brush determine its opacity: 100% black equals 100% opacity; 75% black equals 75% opacity; 50% black equals 50% opacity; 25% black equals 25% opacity. If the initial selection contains any white information, it translates to fully transparent pixels.

Special Notes

- Custom brushes are based on active selections between 1 and 999 pixels wide. If the brush is larger than 27 × 27 pixels, only the upper left of the brush is displayed in the palette.

- Custom brushes are useful to traditional artists who find the elliptical standard brushes too constraining. Many users scan in a series of different real-world brush types (sponges, cotton balls, and cut potatoes are good examples), adjust them appropriately, and use the individual shapes to create custom brushes.

- If you define a series of large custom brushes, you may not be able to identify them in the Brushes Palette. As you create one large brush, quickly scale the sample down and define a second version of the same shape. This way, each brush is followed by a small, easily identifiable preview.

Reset Brushes

This command restores Photoshop's default set of brushes. When you select Reset Brushes from the submenu, an alert appears, offering two options. Click OK to delete the entire set of current brushes before restoring the defaults. Click Append to add the defaults to the existing set of brushes.

Special Notes

If you have added custom shapes to the Brushes Palette or have any standard brushes with special settings, save the palette before restoring the default brushes. The Reset Brushes command cannot be reversed with Edit: **Undo**.

Load Brushes

This command allows you to access pre-saved brush shapes. The set you choose is added to the existing set of brushes.

Special Notes

Photoshop's Goodies folder contains three sets of custom brushes, ranging from whimsical to useful.

Replace Brushes

This command is similar to Load Brushes, except that it deletes all existing brushes and replaces them with the selected set. If necessary, save the current set of brushes before choosing this command.

Save Brushes

Use this command to save all current brushes and their settings into a separate file. Name each file descriptively and save them into Photoshop's Goodies folder. Saved brushes are loaded using Load Brushes or Replace Brushes.

CHAPTER 20

The Layers Palette

In the Layers Palette, all layers are listed in hierarchical order. Layers at the top of the list appear in front of layers at the bottom.

There are three types of layers: background layers, image layers, and adjustment layers. Although each of them are used for different purposes, they are treated identically by the tools of the Layers Palette.

Common Uses

Refer to Appendix A for full descriptions of the following:

- Loading layer-based selections
- Adding a layer mask
- Switching between a layer and layer mask
- Linking a layer and mask
- Viewing and hiding a layer mask
- Viewing a layer mask overlay
- Deleting a layer mask
- Creating a clipping group
- Ungrouping a clipping group
- Copying a layer to another image
- Creating a soft drop-shadow
- Neutral color effects

Special Notes

See Chapter 11, *The Layer Menu*, for more information on background layers, image layers, and adjustment layers.

Blend Modes

Multiple layers allow many pixels to share the same XY coordinates in the image window. For display and print purposes, however, only one pixel can appear at each coordinate. The Layers Palette contains a pop-up menu of different brush modes, which affect how the contents of one layer combine with the color values of the underlying pixels.

Do not confuse blend modes with the *brush modes* found in the Options Palette of each **Paint Tool**. Although the options of both lists are largely the same, the techniques required to apply them are different. Blend modes affect the contents of an entire layer. Using the Paint Tools, brush modes can affect a smaller portion of a layer.

When you apply a blend mode, every non-transparent pixel in the active layer is recalculated and changed to a new value. Therefore, layering involves three values:

Base Colors
> The base colors are the values contained in the underlying layers.

Blend Colors
> The blend colors are the values contained in the layer receiving the change in blend modes.

Result Colors
> The result colors are the values ultimately determined by a blend mode, or the colors that result from combining the blend colors and base colors. These values change every time you select a new blend mode, but they become permanent when the layer is merged or the image is flattened.

Special Notes

- Each blend mode has a neutral color, or a value that results in no visible effect on the underlying information. Many filters, such as Filter: Render: **Lens Flare** or **Lighting Effects**, cannot be applied to the transparent pixels of an empty image layer. By choosing a blend mode and filling a layer with its neutral color, you apply the effect of these filters without permanently altering any underlying color values. Neutral colors are set in the Layer: New Layer dialog. There are three neutral colors:

  - **Black.** The neutral color for Screen, Color Dodge, Lighten, Difference, and Exclusion.
  - **White.** The neutral color for Multiply, Color Burn, and Darken.
  - **50% Gray.** The neutral color for Overlay, Soft Light and Hard Light.

- The Normal, Dissolve, Hue, Saturation, Color, and Luminosity blend modes have no neutral colors.

Normal

This mode displays the full values of the blend colors (if the opacity is set to 100%). All non-transparent pixels conceal any underlying pixels.

Dissolve

The effect of this mode is most visible when a layer's opacity is less than 100%. Here, the layer contents do not blend with the underlying pixels. Rather, certain pixels are made transparent while the rest remain at 100% opacity, resulting in a scattered, diffuse effect.

The amount of scattered pixels is determined by the transparency value of the layer. If its opacity slider is set to 60%, then 60% of the pixels in the layer remain fully opaque, and 40% of the pixels become fully transparent.

If a layer's opacity is 100%, this mode still affects semi-transparent pixels such as soft-edged brushstrokes or anti-aliased shapes.

Behind

This mode is only available when a floating selection exists above the active image layer. (See Chapter 1, *Selection Tools*, for more information.)

When this blend mode is selected, filling or painting the contents of the floating selection only affects pixels less than 100% opaque.

Clear

This mode is only available when a floating selection exists above the active image layer. (See Chapter 1, *Selection Tools*, for more information.)

Once this mode is chosen, the contents of the floating selection become fully transparent. If you reposition the floating selection, you reposition this transparent "hole" without altering the previously affected pixels.

When the layer is 100% opaque, the floating selection is completely transparent. Settings below 100% set the transparency to the inverse value of the setting of the opacity slider. For example, an opacity setting of 80% results in a 20% opaque floating selection.

Multiply

This mode multiplies the brightness values of the base colors and blend colors to create darker tones.

To multiply color values, Photoshop regards the 256 brightness values as a range that extends from 0 to 1. Zero is black, or a brightness value of 0. One is white, or a brightness value of 255. The remaining values are treated as fractions.

For example, a brightness value of 100 is regarded as 100/255. A value of 200 is regarded as 200/255. If you apply one value to the other using Multiply, the resulting color value is the product of the two fractions, or 78 (78/255). Treating the values as fractions guarantees that all subsequent values fall between 0 and

255. Since multiplying two fractions always results in a smaller fraction (or lower brightness value), the result color is always darker.

Special Notes

Another method of calculating the result color is to multiply the brightness values of the base and blend color, and divide that number by 255.

Screen

This mode produces the opposite effect of Multiply, resulting in lighter colors.

To create Screen values, Photoshop multiplies the inverted values of the base colors and blend colors. It then inverts the new brightness values, creating lighter tones.

For example, if you apply a value of 100 to a value of 200 (similar to the example described under Multiply), Photoshop inverts the values and multiplies 155/255 and 55/255. The product is 33, which is inverted to create the resulting value of 222.

Where the blend color is black, the base colors are not affected. Where the blend color is white, the result color is always white. Shades of gray lighten underlying pixels without changing their hue.

Special Notes

To invert a tone, subtract its brightness value from 255. For example, inverting a value of 50 results in 205. (See Image: Adjust: **Invert** for more information.)

Overlay

The effect of this mode is the same as either Multiply or Screen, depending on the values of the base colors. The hues of the base colors shift toward the blend colors, and the general contrast is increased.

In the underlying layers, brightness values lower than 128 are multiplied by the blend colors. Brightness values higher than 128 are screened by the blend colors.

Where either the blend color or the base color is middle gray, this mode has no effect.

Soft Light

The effect of this mode is similar to Overlay, only less intense.

Hard Light

The effect of this mode is similar to Overlay, only more intense.

Color Dodge

This mode lightens the base colors. The resulting hues are shifted toward the blend colors. Lighter blend colors cause more intense changes, while darker colors cause a more subtle effect.

Where the blend color is black, this mode has no effect.

Color Burn

This mode lightens the base colors. The resulting hues are shifted toward the blend colors. Lighter blend colors cause more intense changes, while darker colors cause a more subtle effect.

Where the blend color is white, this mode has no effect.

Darken

This mode compares the component brightness values of the base colors and blend colors. The result colors are formed by the darkest brightness values of each channel.

For example, if a blend color is R: 160, G: 70, B: 220 and a base color is R: 80, G: 120, B: 155, the result color is R: 80, G: 70, B: 155.

Lighten

This mode compares the component brightness values of the base colors and blend colors. The result colors are formed by the lightest brightness values of each channel.

For example, if a blend color is R: 160, G: 70, B: 220 and a base color is R: 80, G: 120, B: 155, the result color is R: 160, G: 120, B: 220.

Difference

This mode compares the component brightness values of the base colors and blend colors. The result colors are formed by subtracting the smaller values from the larger values.

For example, if a blend color is R: 160, G: 70, B: 220 and a base color is R: 80, G: 120, B: 155, the result color is R: 80, G: 50, B: 65.

Where a blend color is white, the base color inverts. Where a blend color is black, this mode has no effect.

Exclusion

The effect of this mode is similar to Difference, but the result colors are more inclined to contain neutral grays.

Where a blend color is white, the base colors invert. Where a blend color is black, this mode has no effect. Where a blend color is middle gray, it replaces the base colors completely.

Hue

This mode replaces the hue values of the base colors with the values of the blend colors. The saturation and lightness levels of the base colors are not affected. (See "The HSB Model" under "Image: Mode Overview" in Chapter 10, *The Image Menu* for more information.)

Saturation

This mode replaces the saturation values of the base colors with the values of the blend colors. The hue and lightness levels of the base colors are not affected. (See "The HSB Model" under "Image: Mode Overview" in Chapter 10 for more information.)

Color

This mode replaces the hue and saturation values of the base colors with the values of the blend colors. The lightness levels of the base colors are not affected. (See "The HSB Model" under "Image: Mode Overview" in Chapter 10 for more information.)

Luminosity

This mode replaces the lightness values of the base colors with the values of the blend colors. The hue and saturation levels of the base colors are not affected. (See "The HSB Model" under "Image: Mode Overview" in Chapter 10 for more information.)

Opacity Slider

This slider allows you to change the opacity setting of the active image or adjustment layer. Depending on the type of layer selected, manipulating the opacity slider produces different effects:

- **Image layers.** Reducing the opacity of an image layer creates the appearance of semi-transparency. Actually, Photoshop combines the color values of the active layer with the values of the underlying image information. For example, if the opacity is reduced to 70%, 30% of the visible color values are based on the underlying colors.

- **Adjustment layers.** Reducing the opacity of an adjustment layer lessens the effect of its adjustment command. For example, if an adjustment layer darkens the underlying pixels by 20%, lowering its opacity to 50% reduces the impact of the command by half—the underlying pixels are only darkened by 10%.

- **Background layers.** The opacity slider is not available when the background layer is selected in the Layers Palette.

Special Notes

- If desired, enter opacity values by typing numbers on the keyboard. Opacity values for single numbers register in multiples of 10—type 1 for a value of 10%, 8 for a value of 80%, and so on. Type 0 to set the opacity to 100%. To enter a precise two-digit value, enter the numbers in rapid succession.

- See Chapter 11, *The Layer Menu* for more information on opacity and transparency.

Preserve Transparency
(type "/")

When this box is unchecked, you can add color to the transparent areas of an image layer. When this box is checked, the transparent areas are protected, allowing you to edit only the pixels containing color values. Semi-transparent pixels retain their level of transparency, regardless of the commands you apply.

Special Notes

Preserve Transparency does not restrict the effect of the Layer: **Transform** commands.

View Box

Click this box to hide or reveal the contents of a layer. When a layer is visible, an eyeball icon appears in the box.

Common Uses

- **Hiding a layer.** Hide a layer by clicking the eyeball in its view box. This allows you to preview an image without the contents of that layer.

- **Revealing a layer.** Reveal a layer by clicking its empty view box.

- **Hiding or revealing multiple layers.** Click and drag over multiple view boxes to affect several at a time.

- **Hiding all other layers.** Hold down the (Option) [Alt] key and click the view box to hide every other layer. (Option) [Alt]-click the box again to reveal all layers.

Special Notes

Hidden layers have the following characteristics:

- They do not affect the appearance of an image. When you hide an adjustment layer or an image layer set to a blend mode other than Normal, the impact on underlying layers is turned off.

- You can create an active selection when a hidden layer is active in the Layers Palette, but you cannot edit the pixels in any way.

- If a hidden layer contains no active selections, you can reposition its contents with the **Move Tool**.

- They cannot be printed.

Status Box

The status box contains one of four icons:

Paintbrush
> This indicates that the layer is active, and any edits will affect its contents.

Dotted Circle
> This applies to adjustment layers and the mask thumbnail of a layer mask. It indicates that a mask item is selected, and any edits will affect this temporary channel.

Three-link Chain
> This indicates that a layer is linked to the active layer. This is the only status icon which appears when a layer is not selected.

Empty Square
> This indicates that the layer is not selected and it is not linked to the selected layer (although it might be linked to an unselected layer).

Activating Layers

Before you can edit any layer, you must select it in the Layers Palette. Only one layer can be active at a time. To activate a layer, click once on its name or its image thumbnail.

To activate a layer mask, you must click its individual thumbnail. The layer highlights and the thumbnail's border thickens, but the border and the mask are often the same color (black), making it difficult to see if the mask is selected. If you wish to edit the layer mask, make sure the dotted circle icon appears in the status box.

Moving the Contents of a Layer

Once a layer is made active, you can reposition its contents using the **Move Tool**. Unlike previous versions of Photoshop, elements in an image layer are not deleted if they are moved off the canvas. At any time, you can reveal the hidden contents by dragging with the Move Tool again.

Special Notes

If the contents of a layer are contained in an active selection outline, the rule changes. As long as the selection remains active, you can move it off the canvas and back again. If you move part of it off the canvas and deactivate the selection, the hidden contents are clipped.

Reordering Layers

Move a layer by clicking its name and dragging it to a new position. When the item is between two other layers, the line between them highlights, representing the layer's new position when the mouse button is released.

Changing the order of an image layer directly affects the on-screen appearance of the image—the contents are layered in a different order.

If any Blend Mode other than Normal has been applied to an image layer, it affects a new series of underlying layers. If you move an adjustment layer, its built-in commands only apply to the new series of underlying layers.

Special Notes

Use the following shortcuts to reorder items in the Layers Palette:

- **Move the active layer up one level.** Hold down (Command) [Control] and press the close-bracket key (]).

- **Move the active layer down one level.** Hold down (Command) [Control] and press the open-bracket key ([).

- **Move the active layer to the top.** Hold down (Command-Shift) [Control-Shift] and press the close-bracket key.

- **Move the active layer to the bottom.** Hold down (Command-Shift) [Control-Shift] and press the open-bracket key. If the image contains a background layer, the active layer is placed directly in front of it.

Linking Layers

Typically, you can only edit layers one at a time. By linking two or more layers, you create a connection that results in the following:

- When multiple layers are linked, you can reposition their contents simultaneously with the **Move Tool.**

- The Layer: **Transform** commands affect all layers linked to the active layer.

To create a link between two layers, activate one layer and click the empty status box of another. The three-link chain icon appears. To link additional layers, click the appropriate status boxes. Unlink a layer by clicking its three-link chain.

Special Notes

By default, new layer masks are linked to their image layer. When linked, the contents of the layer mask move and transform with the image layer. Unlink a layer mask the three-link chain between the two thumbnails. You can then move or transform the image or its layer independently by clicking on the appropriate thumbnail and applying the desired command. Restore the link by clicking the empty space between the two thumbnails.

Grouping Layers

A *clipping group* is another masking technique performed in the Layers Palette. Instead of using a temporary mask channel (like a layer mask does), a clipping group uses the contents of one layer to mask the contents of another. Photoshop uses the transparent pixels of the lower layer as the basis for masking the upper layer. When the layers are grouped, the information of the upper layer only appears wherever non-transparent exist in the base layer.

Although you can use the Layer: **Group with Previous** and Layer: **Group Linked** commands to create a clipping group, you can do it much more efficiently using the Layers Palette. After making sure your layers are properly ordered in the Layers Palette, hold down the (Option) [Alt] key and click the dotted line dividing the two layers.

Special Notes

To add multiple layers to the group, make sure it's positioned above the group and (Option) [Alt]-click the dotted dividing line.

See Also

Layer: **Group with Previous**
Layer: **Group Linked**

Control Buttons

The Control buttons are found at the bottom of the Layers Palette. They provide easy access to the most frequently used commands of the palette submenu.

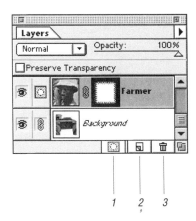

1. **Add Layer Mask**

   Click this button to add a layer mask to the active layer. If a selection is active, it forms the basis of the layer mask. If no selection is active, the layer mask is white, and has no immediate affect on the active layer—you must manually edit the mask. (See Layer: **Add Layer Mask** for more information.)

2. **Create New Layer**

   Click this button to create a new layer. This button can be used in four ways:

   Creating an empty image layer. Simply click this button to create a new, empty image layer. The layer is fully transparent, and based on the default settings of the New Layer dialog. Hold down the (Option) [Alt] key while clicking to access the New Layer dialog before the new layer appears. (See Layer: **New Layer** for more information.)

   Creating a new layer from a floating selection. If a floating selection is active, click this button to place its contents on a new image layer. The selection outline disappears. (See "Floating Selections" in the **Selection Tools Overview** for more information.)

   Creating a new adjustment layer. Hold down the (Command) [Control] key and click this button to create a new adjustment layer. The New Adjustment Layer dialog automatically appears.

   Duplicating a layer. Drag an existing layer onto this button to create a duplicate. The new layer is placed directly above the original in the Layers Palette.

3. **Delete Layer Button**

   Click this button to permanently remove the active layer from the Layers Palette. An alert appears, giving you the option of canceling the command. To avoid the alert, hold down the (Option) [Alt] key while clicking.

See Also

Layer: **New Layer**
Layer: **Add Layer Mask**
Layer: **Delete Layer**

Layers Palette Submenu

With the exception of Palette Options, all commands in the Layers Palette submenu appear under the Layer Menu. They are available here only for your convenience—their function is exactly the same.

New Layer

Choose this command to open the New Layer dialog. Hold down the (Option) [Alt] key to bypass the dialog and create a new layer based on Photoshop's default settings. (See Layer: **New** for more information.)

New Adjustment Layer

Choose this command opens the New Adjustment Layer dialog. (See Layer: **Adjustment Layer Overview** for more information.)

Duplicate Layer

Choose this command to create a duplicate of the currently active layer. (See Layer: **Duplicate Layer** for more information.)

Delete Layer

Choose this command to permanently remove the active layer from the Layers Palette. (See Layer: **Delete Layer** for more information.)

Layer Options

Choose this command to open the Layer Options dialog. (See Layer: **Layer Options** for more information.)

Merge Down/Grouped/Linked

Choose this command to merge the contents of the active layer with one or more of the remaining items in the Layers Palette. The command that appears in the submenu depends on whether or not the active layer is part of a clipping group or linked to other layers. (See Layer: **Merge Down/Grouped/Linked** for more information.)

Merge Visible

Choose this command to merge the contents of all visible layers into one item in the Layers Palette. (See Layer: **Merge Visible** for more information.)

Flatten Image

Choose this command to reduce the contents of all visible layers into a non-transparent background layer. (See Layer: **Flatten Image** for more information.)

Palette Options

Choose this command to open the Palette options dialog. Here, you can change the size of the item thumbnails in the Layers Palette.

CHAPTER 21

The Channels Palette

Channels are one of the fundamental components of any Photoshop image. Although they're used for different things, they exist in exactly the same form: an 8-bit, 256-level Grayscale image. There are five types:

- **Color channels.** Every color image contains multiple channels. Each channel represents the values of one specific color. To facilitate editing, Photoshop offers a composite channel that combines the different values on-screen to present a full-color image.

- **Mask channels.** When you save an active selection using Select: **Save Selection**, the shape of the selection is saved as an additional 8-bit channel, or *mask*. This information can be edited and reloaded as a selection later on. It also can be combined with other saved selections or brought into different images.

- **Quick Mask channels.** When you access the Quick Mask Mode using the Toolbox, a special, temporary channel is created. You can view, activate, delete, duplicate and change the channel options of this channel just as you can with any other mask channel. As soon as Quick Mask Mode is deactivated, however, the Quick Mask channel disappears.

- **Layer mask channels.** If an image layer with a layer mask is active in the **Layers Palette**, it appears as a channel in the Channels Palette. Here the layer mask can be viewed, activated, deleted, duplicated and its channel options changed, just as you can with any other mask channel. This channel does not appear when the image layer is not selected in the Layers Palette.

- **Alpha channels.** You can define an additional channel to achieve a specific effect in separate software packages:

  Alpha channels allow web browsers like Netscape Navigator and Microsoft Internet Explorer to utilize transparent pixels.

PICT files containing an alpha channel can be masked in multimedia software like Adobe After Effects, and can form the basis for an additionally imported masking image in Macromedia Director.

PlateMaker, a Photoshop plug-in by In Software, uses channels to define spot colors in an image, in addition to CMYK inks.

Alpha channels are used by video editing software for *chroma-key*, or blue-screen editing.

Special Notes

- You can create up to 24 additional masking channels, but only files saved in the Raw, TIFF and native Photoshop formats can retain this many. Other file formats allow you to save one additional channel: GIF89a, PICT, PICT Resource, PNG, Pixar, and Targa. The remaining file formats either discard additional channels automatically, or are simply not available in the Save As dialog if the image contains additional channels.

- The only way to read the color values of an image is through the **Info Palette**. This palette should be visible on-screen at all times.

See Also

Quick Mask Tools
File: **Supported File Formats**
File: Export: **GIF89a Export**
Image: Mode: **Grayscale**
Image: Mode: **RGB**
Image: Mode: **CMYK**
Image: Mode: **Lab Color**
Layer: **Add Layer Mask**
Select: **Save Selection**
Select: **Load Selection**
The Info Palette

Using the Channels Palette

In order to work with channels most flexibly, you must use the tools of the Channels Palette.

Common Uses

Refer to Appendix A for full descriptions of the following:

- Combining channels using the Load Channel button
- Creating complex masks
- Defining spot colors in Photoshop
- Rearranging the color channels of an image
- Creating a vignette

- Fading from one image to another
- Partial filtering
- Drop shadows on full color backgrounds

Activating Channels

By default, all color channels are active. To select a specific channel, perform one of the following:

- Click the appropriate item in the Channels Palette.
- Hold down the (Command) [Control] key and type the number of the channel. Use this technique to select the first nine channels. (Command) [Control]-~ (tilde) displays Photoshop's composite view.
- Click the top item of the Channels Palette to activate all color channels.

Special Notes

Shift-click to activate multiple channels.

Arranging Channels

Generally, only mask channels can be rearranged in the Channels Palette. Do so by dragging the appropriate item. A thick black line appears between channels, indicating the new position of the channel when you release the mouse button.

Special Notes

- In Grayscale, CMYK, RGB, or Lab Color images, a color channel can't be replaced with a mask channel, and the order of the color channels can't be rearranged by dragging. Doing so would alter output/brightness settings by substituting the color values in one channel for the values of another.

- Rearranging mask channels does not alter the appearance or function of the image or its mask channels. The only time the order of these channels matters is when you save into a file format capable of containing only one additional channel. Saving into such a format discards all mask channels but the first. Move the channel you wish to keep into the alpha position (channel #2 for a Grayscale image, #4 for an RGB or Lab image, and #5 for a CMYK image) before saving into these formats.

Viewing Channels

Use the following commands to view the contents of a channel:

- **Displaying a channel.** Click its View box to make the eyeball icon appear.
- **Activating and viewing a channel.** Click on the name of the channel in the Channels Palette. All other channels will be hidden and deactivated.

- **Hiding a channel.** Click on the eyeball icon in its View box.

- **Editing a single color channel.** It is often useful to view the color composite while editing a single color channel, such as when you wish to edit a single color channel while seeing the effects to the overall image. To do this, activate a channel, then click on the color composite View box.

- **Simultaneously viewing color and mask channels.** Activate the mask channel and click its View box. The mask channel appears as a 50% transparent red overlaying the color composite.

Special Notes

Viewing individual channels is a vital part of high-end image editing. Due to deficiencies in scanning hardware, different color channels can be scanned with varying quality. Fuzziness in an image can be attributable to fuzziness in a single channel. While other channels need no adjustment, the appearance of whole image can be affected by the imperfections of a single channel. Before editing the entire image, view each channel individually by clicking on it in the Channels Palette.

Channels Palette

The Channels Palette Buttons

The four buttons at the bottom of the Channels Palette are shortcuts for Channels Palette menu and Selection palette commands, but they function slightly differently from their Menu counterparts.

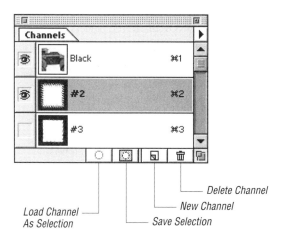

Load Channel as Selection

Clicking the Load Channel button creates a selection based on the active channel. (See Select: **Load Selection** for more information.)

Special Notes

Use the following shortcuts when loading selections from the Channels Palette:

- **Load channel as selection.** (Command) [Control]-click the item in the Channels Palette. Or, hold down (Option-Command) [Alt-Control] and press the number of the channel you want made into a selection.

- **Add channel to active selection.** (Command-Shift) [Control-Shift]-click the item in the Channels Palette to add to an active selection

- **Subtract channel from active selection.** (Option-Command-Shift) [Alt-Control-Shift]-click the channel in the Channels Palette to subtract from an active selection.

- **Intersect channel with active selection.** (Option-Command-Shift) [Alt-Control-Shift]-click the item in the Channels Palette to subtract any selected area that is not included in both the active selection and the mask channel.

See Also

Select: **Load Selection**

Save Selection

Clicking the Save Selection button saves an active selection as the next available channel, using the default settings (Name: Channel number; Color indicates: Masked Areas; Color: 100% Red; Opacity: 50%).

Special Notes

(Option) [Alt]-click the button to bring up the Select: Save Selection dialog.

See Also

Select: **Save Selection**

New Channel

Click this button to create a new channel, similar to choosing New Channel from the palette submenu. The new channel is positioned as the next available channel, regardless of which channel is active.

Special Notes

- The new channel will be a total mask—solid black or solid white, depending on the most recent setting in the Channel Options dialog. You must edit it further to achieve a visible effect.

- To bring up the Channel Options dialog, (Option) [Alt]-click the Create New Channel button.

Delete Channel

Click this button to permanently remove the active channel. This technique results in an alert, asking if you really want to delete the channel. Click OK to eliminate the channel.

If the active channel in the Channels Palette is a layer mask, an alert appears, asking if you wish to apply the mask before discarding. Click Apply to make the effects of the channel permanent to its associated image layer before discarding the layer mask. Click discard to eliminate the channel without changing the image layer. This Alert can't be bypassed by (Option) [Alt]-clicking the Delete Channel button.

Special Notes

- Deleting a color channel from an image will automatically convert the image to Multichannel mode.

- (Option) [Alt]-click the Delete button to bypass the alert and remove the channel.

The Channels Palette Submenu

You can further control and edit image channels by using the commands in the Channels Palette submenu.

New Channel

This command creates a new mask channel, placing it after all existing channels. You cannot use this command to create new color channels.

Special Notes

- Give a new channel a name descriptive of its function, such as "hair mask" or "select foot". This is because channels are not automatically renamed if another channel is deleted. If you delete channel #4, channel #5 becomes the fourth channel, but it's still named #5. If you create a new channel without naming it, it will also be named #5, giving you two channels with the same name.

- In order to keep the same areas masked or selected, changing from one Color Indicates option to the other inverts the channel.

- Hold down the (Option) [Alt] key while selecting New Channel to bypass the Channel Options dialog.

The Channel Options Dialog

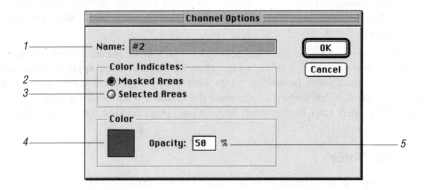

1. Name

Enter a name for the channel in this field. Always name channels if you're planning to use more than one additional channel. If you choose not to name a channel, Photoshop applies the next available number in the sequence of channels. For instance, the first channel added to an RGB file is named "#4" by default. If you add another channel, it's named "#5".

2. Masked Areas

When this is chosen, black areas in the mask channel or color in the Quick Mask indicate the parts of an image that are *masked*, or protected. White indicates unmasked, unprotected areas. This is the default setting when you create a new channel via Select: **Save Selection**.

3. Selected Areas

The opposite of Masked Areas. When this is chosen, white areas in the mask channel or the fully transparent parts of the Quick Mask indicate parts of the image that are protected or unselected. Black indicates *unmasked*, or unprotected areas.

4. Color

Change the color of the Quick Mask by clicking this box. The standard color picker appears.

5. Opacity

This determines the opacity of the mask when it's viewed in the Quick Mask mode. This only affects the way it appears, not the way it functions. Vary the opacity to make the Quick Mask easier to discern from other channels.

Duplicate Channel

This command duplicates the active channel. This applies to color channels as well as mask channels.

Common Uses

- **Reducing file size.** Multiple channels can significantly increase file size and slow the performance of Photoshop. This problem may be solved by duplicating channels into new files, then deleting them from the source image. If necessary, the duplicated channels can be reloaded from the new files.

- **Creating new masks based on old masks.** This way, you can combine the masks of two individual channels into one.

- **Creating Grayscale images from color images.** Since each color channel is actually a Grayscale image, you can sometimes use them to create separate, usable halftone images.

- **Making mask channels out of image channels.** Creating masks by duplicating and modifying color channels is often an effective way to create complex masks.

Common Errors

Drag-copying a channel between images of different dimensions. If any of the channel falls off the canvas when you release the mouse button, it's automatically cropped.

Special Notes

Hold down the (Option) [Alt] key while selecting this command to bypass the Duplicate Channel dialog. This duplicates the active channel as the next available channel in the active image, based on the last-applied settings of the Channel Options dialog.

The Duplicate Channel Dialog

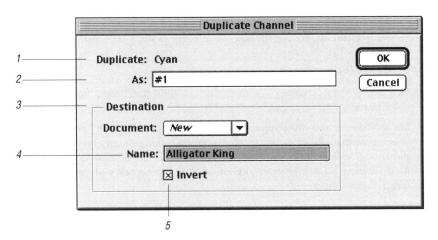

1. **Duplicate**

   This field displays the name of the active channel.

2. **As**

   Name the duplicate channel in this field. If the selected channel has no name, then Photoshop names the duplicate channel numerically.

3. **Destination Document**

   Using this pull-down menu, choose the destination of the new channel:

   Same Document
   This is the default setting. If you wish to duplicate the active channel as a new channel in the same document, do not change this option.

   Different Document
   Channels can be duplicated from one Photoshop image into another, but two requirements must be met: both images must have identical pixel dimensions, and both images must be open. They do not have to be in the same color mode. Select the appropriate image title.

   New
   This option uses the duplicate channel as the basis for a new Grayscale document.

4. **Name**

   The Name field is grayed out unless New is selected in the Destination Document field. If it's available, you can title the new image. It still must be saved.

5. **Invert**

   Check this box to invert the color values of the duplicate channel.

Delete Channel

This command permanently removes a channel or layer mask. Use it to discard unnecessary channels, reduce file size, or improve system performance.

Special Notes

- Deleting a color channel automatically converts the image from its original color mode to Multichannel.

- Mask channels and image channels are discarded without any alert or prompt. When deleting a layer mask, an alert appears, asking "Apply layer mask before discarding?" Click Apply to retain the effects of the layer mask before the mask itself is deleted. Click Discard to eliminate the layer mask without changing the image layer.

Split Channels

This command separates all color and mask channels into individual Grayscale images. The file name of each new image is the name of the original file and its channel name, separated with a dot (such as "House.Red" or "House.Green").

Special Notes

Splitting an image into channels was popular when the only form of removable storage media was the 44 Mb SyQuest drive. To transport a color image larger than 44 Mb to the service bureau, you had to split the image into separate files, copy the files onto separate SyQuest cartridges, copy the files from the SyQuest cartridges onto the service bureau's hard drive, and merge the channels into one image again.

Merge Channels

This command was originally created to reverse the effects of the Split Channels command. However, it can combine any open images to create a single image, proved they meet the following requirements:

- **They have identical pixel dimensions.** If the width, height, or resolution of the images are different by even one pixel, they can't be merged.

- **They are Grayscale.** Images in any other mode can't be merged.

- **They possess no image layers.** Images with layers other than the background layer can't be merged.

- **They have only one channel.** Images possessing channels other than the Black image channel can't be merged.

Special Notes

- If the images possess channel tags, such as the ".red", ".green," and ".blue" that the Split Channels command gives them by default, they appear in their proper order by default in their respective Specify Channels pull-down menus.

- At any time, you can click the Mode button to go back to the Merge Channels dialog and select a different number of channels, or change from Multichannel to CMYK, Lab Colors, or RGB.

- The Merge command will not allow you to merge additional channels as mask channels when you merge images into RGB, Lab, or CMYK images. To accomplish this, merge the channels into a Multichannel image, making sure the first three or four channels are merged in their proper color channel order. Then use Image: **Mode** to convert the image into your desired color mode. The first three or four channels are converted into their respective color channels, and the remaining channels become mask channels.

The Merge Channels Dialog

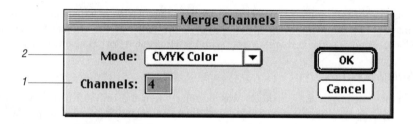

1. **Channels**

   Enter the number of channels you intend to merge. Selecting any number other than 3 or 4 when merging as an RGB, Lab Color, or CMYK file changes the mode to Multichannel.

2. **Mode**

   Here, you select the mode the merged images will take:

   Multichannel
   Two or more images can become Multichannel images, regardless of whether they began as mask channels or not.

   RGB & Lab
   Three channels are required for RGB and Lab Color mode. Mask channels can't be added when merging an RGB or Lab image.

   CMYK
   Four channels are required for a CMYK image. Mask channels can't be added when merging an RGB or Lab Color image.

Palette Options

The only option available here is whether or not to change the size of the little thumbnails that appear next to each item in the Channels Palette. Select a different size by clicking on the radio button beside the desired choice.

Thumbnails enable you to identify different channels more efficiently than if the channels were listed by name alone, since the eye recognizes graphic shapes more quickly than it does text. Larger graphics allow you to identify individual channels more quickly. Unfortunately, larger thumbnails use up more of your monitor's real estate. Choose the largest thumbnail which still allows you to work efficiently.

CHAPTER 22

The Paths Palette

If you've worked with Bézier curves in a program like Adobe Illustrator, Macromedia FreeHand, or CorelDRAW, then Photoshop's paths are a familiar technology. (See "Pen Tool" in Chapter 3, *Special Tools* for more information.)

Once you create a path, the Paths Palette contains the path management commands required to save, manipulate, and utilize paths. In the previous version of Photoshop, the Pen Tool and its associated toolset also resided in the Paths Palette. They've since been moved to the Toolbar.

Common Uses

Refer to Appendix A for full descriptions of the following:

- Combining two paths into one
- Filling a path
- Stroking a path
- Creating a clipping path

Special Notes

Each path has its own designation in the Paths Palette, similar to a layer or a channel. Since so many programs use the term "path," Photoshop's system seems misleading at first. The following terms are used:

- **Subpath.** Other programs refer to an individual object-oriented shape as a path. Photoshop refers to them as *subpaths*, since each item in the Paths Palette can contain multiple shapes.

- **Path.** Each item in the Paths Palette is referred to as a *path*, even if it contains a grouping of subpaths.

425

Creating and Adding Paths

The following techniques automatically place a new item in the Paths Palette:

- **Using the Pen Tool.** Here, you manually draw a subpath point-by-point.

- **Converting an active selection to a path.** When told to do so, Photoshop traces a selection outline with a new path.

- **Dragging and dropping a path from another image.** Drag a path from the Paths Palette of one image onto any other open image. When the second image highlights, release the mouse button to add the path.

- **Applying Edit: Copy and Paste.** To copy and paste a new path, you must deactivate all current paths. If you copy a subpath, deactivate all current paths, and choose Edit: **Paste**, you add a new path to the palette.

- **Applying Edit: Copy and Paste from Adobe Illustrator.** When you paste any shapes that you copied from an Illustrator graphic, you're given a choice: Paste as Pixels or Paste as Paths. Choose Paste as Paths to convert the shapes into a Photoshop path. (See "Pasting Shapes from Adobe Illustrator" under Edit: **Paste** for more information.)

Work Paths

When you add a path to the Paths Palette, it initially appears as a *work path*, or a temporary, unsaved item.

In earlier versions of Photoshop, you could not deactivate an unsaved path. The path would simply disappear, and you'd have to start over from scratch. Now, you can hide, re-activate, and save work paths along with the image. You can even convert them to selections and export them to an Illustrator file. Despite their seeming flexibility, work paths are still of limited use—above all else, they're unstable: if you create a new path when a work path is deactivated, it is discarded.

Special Notes

- Duplicating a saved path is the only technique that doesn't result in a work path—here, the new item appears as a saved path.

- Avoid the work path altogether by choosing New Path from the palette submenu before creating any subpaths.

- There is no tangible reason to leave a path as a work path. Lower the risk of losing your work by saving a path soon after its creation. Use one of the following techniques:

  - Activate the work path and choose Save Path from the palette submenu.

  - Double-click the work path item in the Paths Palette to access the Save Path dialog.

  - Drag the work path item onto the New Path control button.

Viewing a Path

Use the following techniques to control how a path displays in an image:

- **Activate a path.** Click a path in the Paths Palette to activate it and display its subpaths on-screen.

- **Deactivate a path.** Click the blank space at the bottom of the Paths Palette to deactivate it and hide its subpaths.

- **Hide a path.** When you hide a path, it remains hidden from view, even when you activate it and apply path-based editing commands. Activate a path and choose View: **Hide Path**. To show the path again, activate it and choose View: **Show Path**.

Special Notes

You can only display the contents of one path at a time. Therefore, the only way to simultaneously view two subpaths is when they're part of the same path. To combine the contents of two paths, you must cut from one and paste into the other.

Reordering Paths

When an image contains multiple paths, you can reorder them in the Paths Palette by clicking and dragging an item. When the item is between two other Paths, the line between them highlights, representing the path's new position when the mouse button is released. Changing the order of the paths only affects the appearance of the palette. It does not alter their function in any way.

Renaming Paths

Double-click an item in the Paths Palette to rename a path. When the Rename Path dialog appears, enter a new name and click OK.

Control Buttons

The Control Buttons at the bottom of the palette provide easy access to the most frequently used commands of the palette submenu.

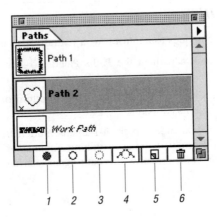

1. **Fill Path**

   Click this button to fill the active path with the most recent settings in the Fill Path dialog. If you desire different fill specs, (Option) [Alt]-click the button or choose Fill Path from the palette submenu.

2. **Stroke Path**

   Click this button to stroke the active path with the most recent settings in the Stroke Path dialog. If you desire different stroke specs, (Option) [Alt]-click the button or choose Stroke Path from the palette submenu.

3. **Make Selection**

   Click this button to convert the active path to a selection outline, based on the most recent settings in the Make Selection dialog. If you desire different selection specs, (Option) [Alt]-click the button or choose Make Selection from the palette submenu.

4. **Make Work Path**

   Click this button to convert an active selection to a path, based on the most recent setting in the Make Work Path dialog. If you desire a different path tolerance, (Option) [Alt]-click the button or choose Make Work Path from the palette submenu.

5. **New Path**

   Click this button to add a new, pre-saved path in the Paths Palette. You can also duplicate an existing path by dragging it onto this button.

6. **Delete Path**

   Click this button to permanently remove the active path. Or, delete a path by dragging it onto this button.

Paths Palette Submenu

The palette submenu contains the majority of the path management commands. Certain listings in the submenu depend on whether or not a specific subpath is selected. For example, if you activate a path in the Paths Palette, the fill command appears as Fill Path. If you select a subpath with the Arrow Tool, the same command appears as Fill Subpath.

New Path/Save Path

When no paths are active, this command creates a new, pre-saved path. Choosing it from the submenu opens the New Path dialog, allowing you to name the path. This is recommended, but not necessary—if you don't enter a name, Photoshop automatically enters Path 1, Path 2, Path 3, and so on.

Special Notes

When a work path is active, this command appears as Save Path in the submenu. The Save Path dialog appears, allowing you to name the path.

Duplicate Path

This command creates a copy of the currently active path. Choosing it from the submenu opens the Duplicate Path dialog, allowing you to rename the path. This is recommended, but not necessary—if you don't enter a name, Photoshop automatically enters the name of the original path with "copy" tagged at the end.

Turn Off Path

This command deactivates the currently active path. Usually, clicking the blank space below the items in the Paths Palette is the most efficient way to do this. If you're working with a large number of paths, however, there is simply no room in the palette to click. In this case, choose Turn Off Path to avoid unintentionally activating another path.

Make Work Path

This command converts an active selection to an object-oriented path.

Special Notes

Unless it consists only of straight lines, this command never matches a selection perfectly. Low-tolerance paths are jagged and distorted. High-tolerance paths are loose and unruly. To create your desired path, you have two options: use the Pen Tool to create the path manually, or edit the automatically generated path. Often, properly editing the automatic path takes longer than creating a path by hand.

Paths Palette

The Make Work Path Dialog

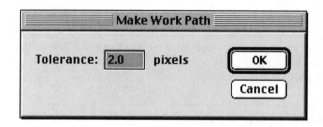

Tolerance

The Tolerance value determines how closely the new path adheres to the selection outline. Possible values range from 0.5 to 10. Lower values create a path that follows the selection more tightly, but result in a greater number of points. Higher values create a smoother path that follows the selection more loosely

---

Make Selection

This command converts the currently active path into a selection.

Special Notes

Use the following keyboard shortcuts to apply the Operation options, bypassing the Make Selection dialog:

* **New Selection.** Activate a path and press the Enter key. Or, (Command) [Control]-click the desired item in the Paths Palette.

* **Add to Selection.** Activate a path, hold down the Shift key, and press Enter. Or, (Command-Shift) [Control-Shift]-click the desired item.

* **Subtract from Selection.** Activate a path, hold down the (Option) [Alt] key, and press Enter. Or, (Option-Command) [Alt-Control]-click the desired item.

* **Intersect with Selection.** Activate a path, hold down the (Option-Shift) [Alt-Shift] keys, and press Enter. Or, (Option-Command-Shift) [Alt-Control-Shift]-click the desired item.

The Make Selection Dialog

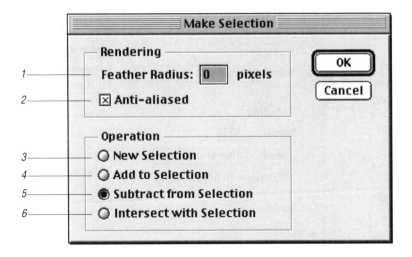

1. **Feather Radius**

   This value applies a feathered edge to the new selection. (See Select: **Feather** for more information.)

2. **Anti-aliased**

   Check this box to anti-alias the edge of the next selection, or apply a one-pixel transition into the surrounding image information. Unless you have a reason for doing so, leave this box checked.

3. **New Selection**

   This replaces the current selection with the new selection.

4. **Add to Selection**

   This adds the new selection to the current selection.

5. **Subtract from Selection**

   This subtracts the new selection from the current selection.

6. **Intersect with Selection**

   This removes the intersecting areas of the two outlines from the current selection.

Fill Path/Fill Subpath

This command fills the contents of a path or subpath. The path itself is not filled—rather, it is used as a guide for applying a colored fill to the currently active layer.

The Fill Subpath Dialog

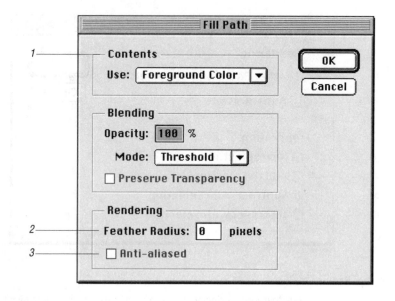

1. **Contents and Blending**

   These options are identical to Photoshop's standard Fill dialog.

2. **Feather Radius**

   This value applies a feathered edge to the new selection.

3. **Anti-aliased**

   Check this box to anti-alias the edge of the next selection, or apply a one-pixel transition into the surrounding image information. Unless you have a reason for doing so, leave this box checked.

See Also

Edit: **Fill**
Select: **Feather**

Stroke Path/Fill Subpath

This command allows you to trace a path using any of the **Paint Tools**. This way, you can apply specific, detailed brushstrokes without attempting to apply them by hand. This is helpful if you use a mouse—which quickly appears clunky and primitive when you begin painting—instead of a drawing tablet and stylus.

The Stroke Path Dialog

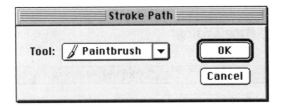

Tools

Select one of the 11 Paint Tools from this pop-up. When you click OK, Photoshop traces the path using the current brush shape and Options Palette settings of the selected tool. However, you must adjust your desired tool settings before opening the Stroke Path dialog. If you stroke with the Rubber Stamp Tool, you must (Option) [Alt]-click to define a starting point.

Clipping Path

The only way to successfully layer an imported Photoshop image is to use a *clipping path*, or an object-oriented mask. After tracing an image with the Pen Tool, you can create an output command that tells other programs and printing devices to ignore the pixels falling outside the mask.

Photoshop images are always rectangular. When you import a print-oriented image into a page layout or illustration program, it retains that shape—even if you've created a silhouette by surrounding part of an image with white pixels. In other programs, you cannot place one silhouette on top of another image or color. If you try, one of two things happens:

- **The image is surrounded by a white field.** This occurs in Pagemaker, Illustrator, and FreeHand. This happens because the programs recognize 0% ink coverage as an actual color: white.

- **"Garbage mask."** When you import a silhouette into QuarkXPress, you have the misleading ability to set the background color of the picture box to None. On-screen, it appears that the white pixels have been removed, allowing you to safely place the image on top of other page elements. In reality, Quark mishandles the anti-aliasing of the silhouette, resulting in a prominently jagged image edge. Unfortunately, this may not be apparent until you output the document.

Special Notes

- When importing silhouettes and halftones into QuarkXPress, always set the background color of the picture box to White.

- You must create and save a path before choosing this command.

- After a path is designated as the clipping path, its name displays in outlined text. This allows you to identify the clipping path when an image contains multiple paths.

The Clipping Path Dialog

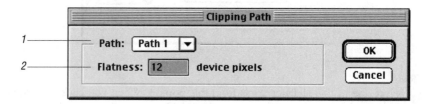

1. **Path**

   Choose the name of the path you want to use as the clipping path from this pop-up.

2. **Flatness**

   This value allows you to print the curves of the clipping path as a tiny series of straight lines. It is not necessary to enter a value here—the only reason to do so is to shorten output times. Values range from 0.2 to 100, which represent the length of the tiny lines in terms of printer dots. For example, if a Flatness value of 33 is output to a 2400 dpi imagesetter, each line segment is 1/72 of an inch, or one point long. Use a value of 5 or below to avoid visible lines.

Palette Options

This dialog allows you to change the size of the item thumbnails in the Paths Palette.

CHAPTER 23

The Actions Palette

A great many production-oriented tasks are based on repetitive commands. Whether adjusting common color flaws, creating drop shadows, or converting a series of images to a different color mode, a large percentage of your work can be condensed to a routine sequence of steps.

Photoshop's Actions automate the commands you apply to an image. Now, you can record a series of commands to play back with a single mouse click or keystroke. When used properly, it is one of Photoshop's most powerful and time-saving features.

Common Uses

- **Creating and running scripts.** A *script* is a prerecorded series of commands and mouse-clicks, similar to a macro created with a program like CE Software's *QuicKeys*. Actions are scripts, and they can be simple or complex. Simple Actions only apply one command, such as filling with semi-opaque white or rotating a selection by a specific value. Complex Actions can involve multiple layer, channel, and filter-based adjustments.

- **Batch processing.** When you batch process, you automatically edit an entire series of images. Instead, opening the images and working on them one by one, you can tell Photoshop to affect all the images in a particular folder with the same commands.

- **Creating new keyboard shortcuts.** Actions are controlled by their own keyboard shortcuts, which facilitate your most commonly applied commands. If desired, you can assign function keys to any command lacking its own keystroke.

- **Maintaining consistency.** When preparing multiple images for a catalogue, multimedia presentation, or web site, consistent editing technique is critical. Actions allow you to record the settings of every command to play back on subsequent images, making it easier to maintain the look and feel of a project.

435

• **Saving new techniques.** Every so often, you discover a new and useful technique you know you'll want to use again. In the past, you had to write it down or commit it to memory. Now, you can record the technique as an Action and save it for future reference.

Using the Actions Palette

The face of the palette contains the controls for recording, duplicating, arranging, and running your Actions.

Common Uses

Refer to Appendix A for full descriptions of the following:

• Recording an Action

• Adding to a Preexiting Action

• Using Record Again

• Using Record "Command Title" Again

• Using Insert Menu Item

• Using Insert Stop

• Preparing a Batch Process

• Running a Batch Process

• Recreating the Commands Palette

Special Notes

• The Actions Palette defaults to a series of prerecorded scripts, but it's not necessary to keep these Actions. Since they were not tailored to your specific work, they're probably of little use. They do illustrate the basic functions of the Actions Palette, however, so consider hanging on to them while you become more familiar with the palette. Then delete them to make room for your own Actions.

• Only scripts contained in the palette can be executed—although you can record an unlimited number of Actions, only 30 can be loaded in the palette at one time.

Selecting Actions and Commands

Before an Action or any of its commands can be edited or played, you must make a selection from the Actions Palette. To target an entire Action, click the name of the Action in the palette. To target a command within an Action, click the Show arrow to view the commands, then click the appropriate command.

Organizing Actions and Commands

Actions and commands can be reorganized, similar to repositioning Layers or Channels in their respective palettes.

Move an Action by clicking on its name and dragging it to a new position. When the item is between two other Actions, the line between them is highlighted. This represents the Action's new position when the mouse button is released. Changing the order of the Actions only affects the appearance of the palette. It does not alter their function in any way.

Move a command by clicking on its name and dragging it to a new position, similar to moving an Action. Here, however, moving a command changes the order of its appearance in the Action, which poses problems if you aren't careful.

Special Notes

- A command can be dragged out of one Action and placed into another. It's no longer applied by the original Action, but it maintains the same settings when run by the new one.

- Hold down the (Option) [Alt] key while moving an Action or command to place a duplicate in the new position. The original item is left in its original position.

Actions Control Buttons

The Control Buttons are found at the bottom of the Actions Palette, when the palette is in List view. The first three are labeled with the same symbols for Stop, Record, and Play found on most tape recorders and VCRs. In fact, their function is almost identical.

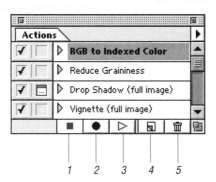

1. Stop

    This button is only available when an Action is recording or playing. Click it to stop the current function. The Stop button has the same effect as choosing

Stop Recording or Stop Playing from the palette submenu. Key equivalents include pressing the Escape key or (Command) [Control]-Period.

2. **Record**

Click this button to record additional commands into an existing Action. New commands are inserted after the currently selected item. If the Action itself is selected, new additions are placed at the end of the current list of commands. The Record button has the same effect as choosing Start Recording from the palette submenu.

3. **Play**

The effect of this button depends on the selected item.

If an Action is selected, click this button to execute its sequence of commands. This is the same as choosing Play "Action Title" from the palette submenu.

If a single command is selected from within an Action, click this button to execute the sequence from that point onward. This is the same as choosing Play From "Command Title" from the palette submenu.

To play only the selected command, hold down the (Command) [Control] key while clicking this button. This is the same as choosing Play Only "Command Title" from the palette submenu.

4. **New Action**

Click this button to access the New Action dialog, similar to choosing New Action from the palette submenu. See New Action, later this chapter, for more info.

5. **Delete**

Click this button to permanently remove the currently selected item. An alert appears, asking if you want to delete the Action or command. Click OK to continue. To bypass the alert, hold down the (Option) [Alt] key while clicking Delete, or drag the item and drop it on the button.

Checkboxes

When the Actions Palette is in List Mode, each Action (and its component commands) are preceded by either one or two checkboxes.

Enable/Disable

When a checkmark is visible in the first box, it indicates that an Action is enabled, and can be played at any time. If there is no check mark, the Action is disabled—selecting it and clicking the Play button has no effect. By default, this box is checked when an Action is created.

To disable an individual command within the Action, click the Open triangle next to the Action's title and click the appropriate checkbox. The next time you play the Action, Photoshop skips any disabled commands. The primary checkmark for the entire Action appears red when any of its commands are disabled. Clicking this checkmark again enables all disabled commands.

Open Dialog

The second check box is only available to commands controlled by a dialog. Commands without a dialog, such as Image: Mode: **Invert**, display a blank space instead.

This box determines whether or not the dialog appears while the Action is running. By default, Photoshop retains the settings that you applied while recording an Action. With Open Dialog off, the Action simply uses all the recorded settings without opening the dialog. With Open Dialog on, the command's dialog is opened the next time you play the Action. This way, you can enter different settings for a command without the need to record a new Action. Click OK to close the dialog and continue the sequence.

When one command within an Action has Open Dialog turned on, a red mark appears in the box next to the Action's title. Clicking this mark once turns on all the Open Dialog marks; clicking it again turns them all off.

Actions Palette Submenu

The commands in the palette submenu are used primarily for editing, saving, and loading Actions. It contains the same commands as the control buttons, but accessing them from this menu is somewhat less efficient.

Certain listings in the submenu are based on the title of the currently selected Action or command. For example, if an Action titled "Convert to Grayscale" is selected, the submenu commands appear as Play "Convert to Grayscale," Delete "Convert to Grayscale," and so on.

New Action

This command is the equivalent of the New Action control button. Two things happen when you choose this command. It opens the New Action dialog, where you name the Action and assign a keystroke. After you close the dialog, it immediately starts recording an Action.

Special Notes

F-key assignments are only visible when the Actions Palette is in Button mode. To see the keyboard shortcut while in List mode, include the name of the F-key in the title of the Action.

The New Action Dialog

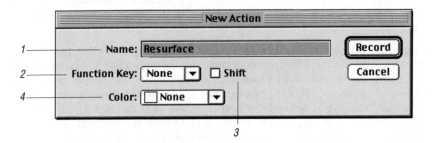

1. Name

   Name the new Action in this field. Be as descriptive as possible, so the Action is quickly identifiable. The name can be up to 32 characters long.

2. Function Key

   The only key equivalent you can assign to an Action is one of the 15 Function keys of your keyboard. The pop-up menu lists all currently available keys, or the ones that have not been assigned to an Action. Even though Photoshop defaults to its own set of F-key shortcuts, they are overridden by an Action using the same key. In the future, pressing the assigned F-key executes the Action, similar to selecting an Action from the palette and pressing the Play button.

3. Shift

   After checking this box, you must hold down the Shift key when pressing the assigned F-key. This increases the possible number of key equivalents to 30.

4. Color

   This option colors the Action when the Actions Palette is in Button view.

Duplicate "Action Title," Duplicate "Command Title"

This command makes an exact copy of the current selection, similar to holding down the (Option) [Alt] key and dragging.

Delete "Action Title," Delete "Command Title"

This command permanently removes the current selection from the Actions Palette, similar to pressing the Delete button.

Special Notes

The Delete command cannot be reversed by choosing Edit: **Undo**. Once an Action or command is removed, it can only be restored if it was saved using Save Actions.

Play "Action Title,"
Play from "Command Title"

When an Action is selected, this command runs its sequence of commands. When a single command within an Action is selected, it runs the Action from that command onward. This command is the equivalent of pressing the Play button.

Play Only "Command Title"

This item plays the currently selected command at its recorded settings, similar to holding down the (Command) [Control] key while pressing the Play button.

Special Notes

• This command can be applied in two additional ways: hold down the (Command) [Control] key and press Play, or hold down the (Command) [Control] key while double-clicking the command.

• Double-clicking on a command in the Actions Palette opens its dialog. You can enter new settings and click OK to apply the command, but watch out— the new settings are recorded in the Action, and the old settings are discarded.

Actions Palette

Start Recording

This allows you to add commands to an existing Action, similar to pressing the Record button. If the Action's title is selected, the new commands are placed at the bottom of the list. If a specific command is selected, the new commands are inserted immediately after it.

Special Notes

Edit: **Undo** cannot be recorded as part of an Action. Not only does it reverse the last command, it erases it from the recording. This allows you to undo erroneous commands and continue recording an Action without stopping.

Record "Action Title" Again

This item replaces all the commands of an Action, while leaving its name, F-key, and color untouched.

Record "Command Title" Again

This command allows you to replace a single, selected command within an Action.

Insert Menu Item

Certain menu items may not be remembered when an Action is recorded. This command allows you to insert them after the Action is defined.

When you insert a menu item that uses an editable dialog, it will always appear when the Action is run. Since no Open Dialog checkbox is available for inserted commands, you cannot turn this feature off. Once you enter the desired settings in the dialog and click OK, the Action executes the remaining commands. Click the dialog's Cancel button to stop the Action at its next command.

Insert Stop

Although this command claims to insert a *stop*, it does not stop an Action from running. Rather, it pauses the Action in progress and displays a dialog containing a user-defined message.

Common Uses

- **Manually executing commands.** Certain commands cannot be included in an Action, such as painting or manipulating a transformation box. By inserting a stop, you pause the Action long enough to perform the necessary work by hand. When you press the Play button again, the Action resumes.

- **Sending a message to the user.** If desired, you can set your own message to appear when the Action reaches a Stop. For example, a Stop dialog inserted at the beginning of an Action could thoroughly describe the Action and any special preparations it requires. Messages inserted in the middle of an Action usually contain special instructions.

Special Notes

Like other commands, the dialog of an inserted Stop is controlled by the Open Dialog checkbox in the Actions Palette. To have the dialog appear, check the box. To ignore the dialog and only pause the Action, uncheck the box. Disable the Stop completely by unchecking the Enable box.

The Record Stop Dialog

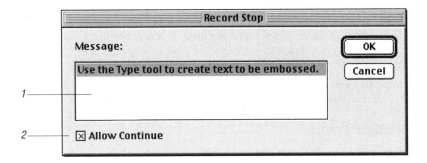

1. Message Box

Here, you can enter a message up to 200 characters long. It should clearly communicate the purpose for stopping. For example, a Stop dialog at the beginning of an Action could say, "This Action creates embossed text—create text using Type Mask Tool before continuing." A Stop inserted in the middle might say, "Action stopped because original image window must be made active before continuing."

2. Allow Continue

Checking this box allows the user to choose between continuing or stopping an Action from the Stop dialog. If this button is left unchecked, the only available option is stopping.

Action Options

This command allows you to change the name, F-key, and color of the selected Action. The Action Options dialog is identical to the New Action dialog, but it simply changes the appearance of an existing Action.

Batch

When you *batch process,* you automatically edit multiple images, instead of just one. Here, it refers to having Photoshop apply the same Action to a series of images. The images do not even have to be opened—they only need to be stored in the same folder. Batch processing is a valuable time-saver whenever you have a series of images that need to share the same characteristics.

Common Uses

- **Making color mode conversions.** For example, when converting a series of RGB scans to Grayscale. If desired, you could also have the Action set the endpoints and apply a simple adjustment for contrast.

- **Making color and tonal adjustments.** For example, you can apply a group of Adjustment Layers to a series of color images. Each image may need some fine tuning, but the tedious task of defining the Adjustment Layers would be automated.

- **Setting custom crops and resolution values.** When preparing a series of graphics for the Web, you could automatically crop to a specific size while reducing their resolution to 72 ppi.

- **Importing and editing images from a remote device.** This includes scanners, digital cameras, and any device that supports Photoshop's technology.

Common Errors

- **Failing to prepare the images of a batch process.** See "Preparing and Running a Batch process" in Appendix A for more information.

- **Failing to properly flatten batch images.** If you are batch processing a series of images containing multiple layers, be sure to include a Layer: **Flatten Image** in the Action. Otherwise, the Action is only applied to the layer selected when the image was last open.

Special Notes

The Action you wish to perform may require a specific image to be open—for example, if the Action loads a selection based on a channel in another image. To avoid conflicts, open that image first, then run the Batch command with the Override Action "Open" Commands box checked.

The Batch Dialog

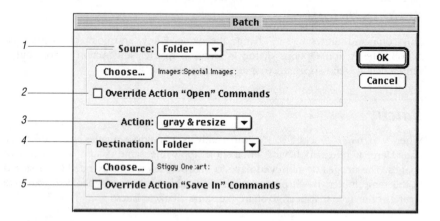

1. Source

   From this pop-up, select the location of the images to be included in the batch:

Folder

If your images have been placed in a Source Folder as described above, choose this option from the Source pop-up. When the source is a folder, the Choose button appears. Click this button to target the folder containing your images. In the navigation dialog, find the right folder, select it, and click the Select Folder button. The name of the folder is listed next to the Choose button.

Import

To import a series of images from a digital camera or similar source, choose this option from the Source pop-up. The From pop-up appears, listing the same options as the File: **Import** submenu. See File: **Import** for more information.

2. **Override Action "Open" Commands**

If the Action you wish to apply contains the File: **Open** command, check this box. Since batch processing repeats the same Action every time, leaving this option unchecked tells Photoshop to open the same image over and over. An alert appears claiming that "This document is already open," interrupting the batch process.

3. **Action**

This pop-up lists all the Actions present in the Actions Palette. Choose the Action you wish to perform in the batch process.

4. **Destination**

From this pop-up, select the destination of the processed images.

None

This option leaves the images open without saving any changes. Select None if you want to continue editing the images before saving them.

Save and Close

This option saves the images back into the Source Folder, overwriting the originals. This option is not available when importing a series of images.

Folder

This option allows you to target a Destination Folder. When you select Folder from the pop-up, the Choose button appears. Click this button to target the folder receiving the processed images. In the navigation dialog, find the right folder, select it, and click the Select Folder button. The name of the folder is listed next to the Choose button.

5. **Override Action "Save In" Commands**

If the Action you wish to apply contains File: **Save**, File: **Save As**, or File: **Save a Copy** commands, check this box. This tells the Batch command to save the images into the Destination Folder, instead of the location defined in the Action.

Checking this box does not override the File Format setting in the Save command, allowing you to specify format changes while batch processing.

See Also

Appendix A (The Actions Palette)
File: **Open**
File: **Save**
File: **Save As**
File: **Save a Copy**
File: **Import**
Layer: **Flatten Image**

Clear Actions

This permanently removes all current Actions from the Actions Palette. You cannot Undo this command—once the Actions are cleared, there is no way to bring them back. The only Actions you can recover are the Photoshop defaults and any you have already saved.

Reset Actions

This replaces all current Actions with the Photoshop defaults. If you have custom-tailored some of those defaults or do not want to replace your current Actions, click Append in the alert. The defaults are added to the end of the Palette.

Load Actions

Use this command to add a set of saved Actions to the end of the current list.

Replace Actions

Use this command to remove the current list of Actions and replace them with a saved set.

Save Actions

Use this command to save the current list of Actions.

Common Uses

- Creating Actions files specific to different types of work.
- Accessing more than 30 Actions.
- Copying Actions to other workstations.

Button Mode

Although only Button Mode is listed at the bottom of the palette submenu, repeatedly selecting it toggles between the two views of the Actions Palette:

List View

This option is indicated by the lack of a check mark next to Button Mode in the submenu. Here, the Actions are arranged vertically. Each one has a Show arrow. Turn the arrow to display an Action's commands; turn the arrow next to a command to display its settings and values.

Actions and commands can only be recorded, rearranged, and edited in List view. It also provides a status report while the Action is running—when the commands are shown, each one highlights while it is being applied. If the list is too long to display completely in the Actions Palette, it automatically scrolls.

The List view displays the control buttons at the bottom of the Actions Palette, giving you quick access to the New, Record, Stop, Play, and Delete commands.

Button View

This view strips the Actions Palette to its barest essentials, making it easier to use. Actions are reduced to single buttons labeled only with the name of the Action and its assigned F-key. Simply click a button to run an Action.

Actions can only be played in this view—they cannot be created or edited. You must change back to List view to edit Actions. All control buttons are hidden.

Since Button Mode does not show commands, provides no feedback, and prohibits editing, its usefulness is extremely limited. Button view is most useful for emulating the Commands Palette, an ancestor of the Actions Palette found in earlier versions of Photoshop.

Actions Palette Strategies

The following sections offer advice on how to efficiently use the tools of the Actions Palette, as well as how to avoid some of the most commonly encountered pitfalls.

Strategic Recording Tips

Recording an Action is a straightforward process. Recording a complex Action that performs correctly the first time may take some practice.

Several commands and techniques are not recognized when you record an Action. While this may be confusing at first, there are workarounds and solutions for most problem areas. The following items are not included in a recorded Action.

Tools

You cannot record any edit made with one of Photoshop's tools. This includes painting, drawing selections, and changing the values in a tool's Options Palette. The only exceptions are changes to the foreground or background color.

As a solution, insert a stop in the Action at the point you wish to use a tool. This way, you can run an Action, have it pause while you make manual edits, then continue the Action. See Insert Stop under the Actions Palette Submenu.

Non-Image-Altering Commands

Mostly, these are commands from the View Menu and Window Menu—zooming in and out, opening the image in a new window, and so forth. They also include panning and activating other images.

As a solution, most of these can be added using Insert Menu Item from the Actions Palette menu. If they cannot, you must insert a stop and apply the command manually. See Insert Menu Item under the Actions Palette Submenu.

Layer: Transform Commands

These include any command that uses a transform box: scaling, skewing, rotating, distorting, adding perspective, and applying a free transform. The problem is that the box needs to be adjusted manually. An Action containing a Transform command brings up a transform box, but it does not apply any changes. It tries to run the remaining commands without removing the box, which brings up an alert stating, "The selected command is not available."

As a solution, insert these commands into an Action by choosing Insert Menu Item from the palette submenu. After inserting a Transform command, insert a stop immediately afterward. Otherwise, the Action attempts to run the remaining commands while the Transform box is still active.

Incremental Movement

You cannot record any movements made with either the Move tool or the arrow keys.

As a solution, apply Layer: Transform: **Numeric Transform** to perform the movement while recording the Action.

Avoiding Image-Specific Commands

You may not be able to apply an Action to other images, depending on the methods used to record its commands. This defeats the purpose of Actions altogether. Following are some of the most common problems and some recommended solutions:

Selecting Layers

If a specific layer is selected while recording, the Action looks for that layer whenever it's run on another image. Problems arise when the Action cannot find a layer of the same name. When this happens, either part or none of the Action is performed.

As a solution, use menu commands or keyboard shortcuts whenever possible. For example, instead of manually selecting the bottom layer in the Layers Palette, type (Option-Shift) [Alt-Shift]-[(the keyboard shortcut for selecting the bottom layer). This way, the shortcut is recorded instead of the manipulation of a particular layer.

Resetting Image Dimensions

By entering measurements in the Image: **Image Size** and **Canvas Size** dialogs, the results are absolute. This means the exact same values are applied to every image, regardless of their original dimensions. This can result in unintended image cropping, or images that are too large or small to perform the Action.

As a solution, use percentages when resizing whenever necessary. This keeps the changes proportional.

Avoiding Undesirable Save Commands

When you record a File: **Save As** or File: **Save a Copy** command, do not enter a new file name. If you do, that act is recorded, and every image that Action is applied to is saved under that name. If it's applied to a batch process, you could reduce hundreds of images to one single file—the last one processed.

As a solution, leave the file name alone when recording a Save command. Simply save the file under its current name. All images affected by the Action will retain their original names as well.

Actions Palette

PART IV

Appendixes

Each Appendix in this section further expands information covered in the main text.

Appendix A: Common Techniques

The techniques in this section are referenced by the Common Uses items in the main text. We've selected these techniques for two reasons:

- They best illustrate the proper use of a particular tool or command.
- They represent the dominant techniques and issues required by an advanced Photoshop user.

To make finding a technique easier, the appendix uses the same structure as the chapters in the book: first the tools are listed, then the menu commands, then the palettes.

Appendix B: Photoshop Shortcuts

This section lists nearly 300 keyboard shortcuts. These items also follow the organization of the book. Each section contains the shortcuts used by a particular toolset, menu, or palette, and appear in the same order as the chapters of the book. Within each section, shortcuts for each tool and command follow the same order as the items discussed in each chapter.

Appendix C: Resolution Types

The main text contains several references to different types of "resolution", whether referring to an image, a scanner, or an output device. This appendix briefly defines the six types of resolution, and how they impact your work.

Appendix D: Image Credits

With the exception of Photoshop's dialogs and a few graphics from our own archives, the images used in this book are from the John Foxx Images collection. They appear primarily in the Filters chapter and Appendix A. This section lists the title and CD volume of each image.

APPENDIX A

Common Techniques

Chapter 1: The Selection Tools

Marquee Tool

The following techniques involve the rectangular and elliptical Marquee Tools.

Selecting a Constrained Circle or Square

Hold down the Shift key while creating the marquee.

Radiating a Marquee from a Center Point

Hold down the (Option) [Alt] key while creating the marquee.

Radiating a Constrained Marquee

Hold down the (Option-Shift) [Alt-Shift] keys while creating the marquee.

Adding a Constrained Marquee to an Existing Selection

After creating an initial selection, follow these steps:

1. Hold down the Shift key.
2. Drag a preview marquee. Do not release the mouse button.
3. Release the Shift key.
4. Press the Shift key again and continue dragging. The preview marquee snaps to a constrained shape.

Subtracting a Constrained Marquee from an Existing Selection

After creating an initial selection, follow these steps:

1. Hold down the (Option) [Alt] key.

2. Drag a preview marquee. Do not release the mouse button.

3. Without releasing the (Option) [Alt] key, hold down the Shift key and continue dragging. The preview marquee snaps to a constrained shape.

Adding a Radiating Marquee to an Existing Selection

After creating an initial selection, follow these steps:

1. Hold down the Shift key.

2. Drag a preview marquee. Do not release the mouse button.

3. Release the Shift key and hold down the (Option) [Alt] key. As you continue dragging, the preview snaps to a radiating marquee.

Adding a Constrained Radiating Marquee to an Existing Selection

After creating an initial selection, follow these steps:

1. Hold down the Shift key.

2. Drag a preview marquee. Do not release the mouse button.

3. Hold down the (Option) [Alt] key in addition to the Shift key. As you continue dragging, the preview snaps to a constrained radiating marquee.

Subtracting a Radiating Marquee from an Existing Selection

After creating an initial selection, follow these steps:

1. Hold down the (Option) [Alt] key.

2. Drag a preview marquee. Do not release the mouse button.

3. Release the (Option) [Alt] key.

4. Hold down the (Option) [Alt] key again and continue dragging. The preview snaps to a radiating marquee.

Subtracting a Constrained Radiating Marquee from an Existing Selection

After creating an initial selection, follow these steps:

1. Hold down the (Option) [Alt] key.

2. Drag a preview marquee. Do not release the mouse button.

3. Release the (Option) [Alt] key.

4. Hold down the (Option) [Alt] key again. The preview snaps to a radiating marquee.

5. Hold down the Shift key and continue dragging. The preview snaps to a constrained marquee.

Creating Geometric Shapes

After creating a new image layer, follow these steps:

1. Use the elliptical or rectangular Marquee Tool to draw a geometric selection.
2. Define your desired color value as the foreground color.
3. Use Edit: **Fill** to fill the selection outline with the foreground color.
4. Position the shape appropriately with the **Move Tool**.

Cropping Tool

Fixed Target Size Variations

You don't have to set all the values to use the Fixed Target Size feature. You can achieve additional effects by leaving one or more of the fields blank:

- **Blank Width.** The crop marquee is not constrained. The cropped image is resized to accommodate the Height value, regardless of the marquee's width.
- **Blank Height.** The crop marquee is not constrained. The cropped image is resized to accommodate the Width value, regardless of the marquee's height.
- **Blank Resolution.** The crop marquee constrains to the Width and Height ratio. The cropped image is appropriately resized, but the pixels are not interpolated to maintain a specific resolution: if the final size is smaller than the actual crop marquee, the resolution increases; if the final size is larger, the resolution decreases. This effect is similar to changing the width and height in the Image: **Image Size** dialog without resampling the image.
- **Blank Width and Height.** The crop marquee is not constrained. The cropped image is reduced or enlarged to match the specified resolution without resampling the pixels.
- **All three values blank.** The Cropping Tool performs as if the Fixed Target Size box is unchecked.

Move Tool

A series of key combinations allow you to make more precise movements:

Constraining Motion

Hold down the Shift key while dragging to constrain the motion to 45 angles.

1-pixel Increments

Nudge a selection outline by pressing the arrow keys. If the Move Tool is selected or the (Command) [Control] key is held down, the selection contents are repositioned.

10-pixel Increments

Hold down the Shift key while pressing the arrow keys. This shortcut also works while holding down the (Command) [Control] key to access the Move Tool.

Lasso Tool

Including Edge Pixels in a Selection

To select pixels at the edge of the image window, move the cursor beyond the edge while dragging. The selection outline traces the edge pixels until you move the cursor back onto the image.

Add Straight Segments to a Selection

1. Begin drawing a free-form outline with the Lasso Tool.

2. When you get to the point where the straight line begins, hold down the (Option) [Alt] key.

3. Release the mouse button. As you continue moving the cursor, you do not add to the selection. Rather, a straight line extends from the point at which you released the mouse button to the cursor.

4. Position the cursor at the point the straight line ends.

5. Click to add the straight line to the outline.

6. At this point, you can move the cursor and click again to add more straight segments, or hold the mouse button down and release the (Option) [Alt] key to continue drawing free-form shapes.

Polygon Lasso Tool

Including Edge Pixels in a Polygon Selection

To include edge pixels, you must be able to click along portions of the window just outside the image. If you click along the image itself, you may neglect the edgemost pixels. If you click outside the window, you activate a background application. There are two ways to accomplish this:

- Choose View: **Show Rulers**. This way, you can click along the rulers and scroll bars to extend the selection beyond the edges.

- If your image is small enough, resize the image window so it's larger than the image. Click the gray area surrounding the image to extend the selection beyond the edges, thereby selecting the edge pixels.

Including Free-Form Outlines in a Selection

1. Begin creating a polygon selection.

2. When you need to draw a free-form line, hold down the mouse button.

3. Hold down the (Option) [Alt] key.

4. Draw the outline as you would with the Lasso Tool.

5. To return to clicking straight lines, release the mouse button and (`Option`) [`Alt`] key.

6. Complete the selection.

Chapter 2: The Paint Tools

The following technique applies to all Paint Tools:

Painting Perfectly Straight Brushstrokes

1. Establish the proper settings of your brush.

2. Hold down the Shift key.

3. Click once at the start of the line.

4. Without dragging, click again at the end of the line. The space between the two points is automatically filled with a brushstroke.

5. If desired, continue clicking to create a series of lines.

Constraining to a Horizontal or Vertical Plane

Hold down the Shift key before applying the brush stroke. Release the Shift key at any time to continue painting in any direction. Hold down the Shift key again to constrain the stroke to the original plane.

Chapter 3: Special Tools

Pen Tool

The only way to become truly proficient with the Pen Tool is through experience. The following techniques will prove helpful:

Drawing a Basic Path

The easiest path to create is made entirely of straight lines: just click a series of corner points. Most paths, however, require a little curving. Although the sequence of point types and editing techniques are unique for each path, follow these basic steps:

1. When placing your first point, click-drag to add curve to your first segment. The forward handle (the one guided by Pen Tool) curves the segment, which appears when you place the next point.

2. While placing each point, try to position each segment exactly as desired. As you become accustomed to the curve handles, this may take several moments for each segment.

3. If you've determined that you need a closed path, remember to end on the same point you first placed.

4. Use the remaining path tools to fine-tune the path.

5. Refer to the commands of the **Paths Palette** to save and further utilize the new path.

Deleting an Entire Path

If any single portion of a path is selected, press the Delete key to remove that one point or segment. Press the key again to remove the remainder of the path.

Continuing an Existing Path

A path in progress may become unselected. Usually, this happens as a result of accessing the Arrow Tool while using the Pen Tool. If you try to continue an unselected path, you create an entirely separate path instead. To continue adding points to an open path, follow these steps:

1. Select the path and activate the endpoint by clicking or dragging either end of a path with the Pen Tool.

2. Continue placing new points.

Creating Multiple Open Paths

To create multiple open paths, you must deselect one completed path before starting the next. Otherwise, a segment connects the two paths. To create separate subpaths, follow these steps:

1. Create the first path.

2. Hold down the (Command) [Control] key to access the Arrow Tool.

3. Deselect the path by clicking elsewhere on the image.

4. Create the next path.

Joining Two Open Paths

To turn two separate paths into one, follow these steps:

1. Click or drag either end of one open path with the Pen Tool. This selects the path and activates the endpoint.

2. Click or drag either end of the other open path.

Transforming a Path

Unlike other vector-based programs, Photoshop has no tools to scale, rotate, or otherwise transform a path.

This is not a problem if you own Adobe Illustrator. Since you can freely copy and paste between Photoshop and Illustrator, you can easily transform a path:

1. Create an initial path in Photoshop.

2. Select the entire path and choose Edit: **Copy**.

3. In Illustrator, choose Edit: **Paste**.

4. Use Illustrator's tools to apply the desired transformation.

5. Select the entire path and choose Edit: **Copy**.

6. In Photoshop, choose Edit: **Paste**.

If you don't own Illustrator, your options are limited. The only way to transform a path is to apply a command to the entire image (see instructions later in this section).

Scaling a Path in Photoshop

1. Choose Image: **Duplicate** to make a copy of the image.

2. Activate the duplicate image and open the Image: **Image Size** dialog.

3. In the Pixel Dimensions section, choose Percent from the pop-up menus.

4. Enter your desired scale percentage and click OK.

5. Activate the desired path in the Paths Palette.

6. Use the Arrow Tool to select the entire path.

7. Choose Edit: **Copy**.

8. Close the duplicate image without saving it.

9. In the original image, choose Edit: **Paste**.

Rotating a Path in Photoshop

1. Choose Image: **Duplicate** to make a copy of the image.

2. Activate the duplicate image and choose an option from Image: **Rotate Canvas**.

3. After applying the rotation value, activate the desired path in the Paths Palette.

4. Use the Arrow Tool to select the entire path.

5. Choose Edit: **Copy**.

6. Close the duplicate image without saving it.

7. In the original image, choose Edit: **Paste**.

Type Tool

Literally hundreds of possible type effects can be achieved using Photoshop's commands. Nearly all of those effects are based on the following techniques:

Transforming Type

To scale, rotate, or otherwise transform type, follow these steps:

1. Use the standard Type Tool to create a series of type.

2. Making sure the appropriate layer is active, choose any of the Layer: **Transform** commands.

Creating Semi-transparent Type

1. Define the desired foreground color. To achieve a ghosting effect, set it to white.

2. Add type to the image using the standard Type Tool.

3. After the type appears on-screen, select the new layer.

4. Manipulate the Opacity slider in the **Layers Palette** (see Figure A-1).

Figure A-1: Black and white type, set to 60% opacity

Creating a Character Mask

A *character mask* refers to type filled with an image, as opposed to a solid color. There are three ways to achieve this effect.

First, you can use a series of selection techniques:

1. Open the image you wish to mask.

2. Create type using the Type Outline Tool. The type appears as an active selection.

3. Position the type appropriately.

4. Copy the information into a new image, either by choosing Edit: **Copy** and creating a new document, or by holding down the (Command) [Control] key and dragging the selection to another open image.

Second, you can create a layer mask, which does not clip the original image information:

1. Open the image you wish to mask. It must reside in its own image layer—background layer images cannot be converted into layer masks.

2. Create type using the Type Outline Tool. The type appears as an active selection.

3. Position the type appropriately.

4. Making sure the appropriate image layer is active, choose Layer: Add Layer Mask: **Reveal Selection**.

Third, you can create a clipping group:

1. Open the image you wish to mask. It must reside in its own image layer—background layer images cannot be converted into clipping groups.

2. Create type using the Type Tool. The type appears in a new layer, which you should position directly underneath the image to be clipped.

3. In the **Layers Palette**, hold down the (Option) [Alt] key and click the dotted line separating the two layers.

4. To add multiple image layers to the group, drag their palette items between two grouped layers.

Creating a Type Channel

By using selection-based type to create a mask channel, you can graphically edit the shape of the outlines before reloading them as a new selection. Follow these steps:

1. Create type using the Type Outline Tool. The type appears as an active selection.

2. Position the type appropriately.

3. Choose Select: **Save Selection**. This creates a mask channel based on the active selection.

Transforming Selection-Based Type

Applying the Layer: **Transform** commands to selection-based type affects only the contents of the selection. To transform the actual selection outlines, follow these steps:

1. Use the standard Type Tool to create a series of type. The color of the type does not matter.

2. Use the Layer: Transform commands to manipulate the type as desired.

3. Hold down the (Command) [Control] key and click the type layer. This creates a selection based on the contents of the layer.

4. Delete the type layer. The selection remains active, ready for the next command.

Creating Custom Path Shapes

By converting selection-based type to paths, you can further edit its shape using the **Pen Tool** and **Paths Palette**. Follow these steps:

1. Use the Type Outline Tool to create a series of type.

2. Choose Make Work Path from the Paths Palette submenu. For best results, enter a Tolerance value between 1.5 and 3 (see Figure A-2).

3. Save the new path by double-clicking its item in the Paths Palette.

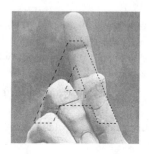

Figure A-2: Choose Make Work Path to convert outline type to paths

---

NOTE

Photoshop is never able to precisely convert a selection outline to a path—some line distortion will always occur. If possible, create type-shaped paths by setting type in Adobe Illustrator, converting it to paths, and pasting them as paths into Photoshop. (See Edit: **Paste** for more information.)

Line Tool

The following techniques offer more flexibility when creating lines in Photoshop. Not all of them involve the Line Tool.

Create an Editable Line

By default, the Line Tool adds information to the currently active layer. To create a line you can edit separately, follow these steps:

1. Before creating a line, click the New Layer button in the **Layers Palette**.

2. Leaving that layer active, draw with the Line Tool.

Creating a Dashed Line

Photoshop has no option to automatically create a dashed line. Instead, follow these steps:

1. Draw a line on a new layer, as described above.

2. Choose the **Eraser Tool** and manually remove segments of the line. For best results, choose Paintbrush from the Erasing Mode pop-up in the Eraser Tool Options Palette. Select an anti-aliased brush from the Brushes Palette (see Figure A-3).

Figure A-3: Use the Eraser Tool to create a dashed line

Creating a Curved Line

1. Draw a path with the **Pen Tool**.
2. Edit the shape of the path appropriately.
3. Choose Stroke Path from the Paths Palette submenu. If desired, create a curved dotted line by clicking the New Layer button before stroking the path, and using the Eraser Tool as described above (see Figure A-4).

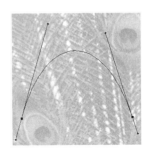 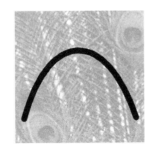

Figure A-4: Stroke a path to create a curved line

Adding an Arrowhead to an Existing Line

1. Specify the desired arrowhead settings in the Line Tool Options Palette. Check the End box for the best results.
2. Set the foreground color as desired.
3. Use the Zoom Tool to enlarge the end of the line on-screen.
4. Starting from the tip of the existing line, draw a new line the precise length of the arrowhead. Use the preview outline as a guide (see Figure A-5).

Figure A-5: Adding an arrowhead to a curved line

Use a Line as a Measuring Tool

To mimic the measuring tools found in most illustration programs, follow these steps:

1. Choose Show Info Palette from the Windows menu.

2. In the Line Tool Options Palette, enter 0 in the Line Width field.

3. Draw a line that spans the distance you wish to measure. The D value in Panel Two of the Info Palette displays the length of the line, giving you a precise measurement. Since the width is 0, no line is accidentally created.

Chapter 6: Quick Mask Tools

When you feel comfortable painting a Quick Mask selection, try the following techniques:

Using an Active Selection in Quick Mask Mode

If a selection is active when you switch to Quick Mask mode, it changes into a colored overlay. Once you've switched, however, the Selection Tools continue to function normally. As long as you remain in Quick Mask mode, the Selection Tools only affect the overlay (or more specifically, the contents of the Quick Mask channel).

You can also create a selection by (Command) [Control]-clicking an existing image layer or mask channel.

Cloning Part of the Overlay

There are two ways to clone a selected portion of the Quick Mask overlay:

• Choose the Move Tool, hold down the (Option) [Alt] key, and drag the selection.

• Choose Edit: **Copy** and **Paste**.

Both of these methods result in a floating selection. Choose Select: **None** after positioning the clone as desired.

> **NOTE**
>
> Ordinarily, the act of pasting a selection results in a new image layer. It is impossible to create a new layer based on a selection made in Quick Mask mode.

Transforming a Quick Mask Selection

You can apply all Layer: **Transform** commands to the Quick Mask overlay. If no selection exists, the transform box is placed around the entire Quick Mask channel. If a selection is active, you can scale, rotate, distort, and skew just that portion of the overlay.

Using Quick Mask in an Individual Channel

To paint a selection based on the contents of one particular color channel, you must choose that channel in the **Channels Palette** before switching to Quick Mask mode. If you're already in Quick Mask mode, hide all channels except the Quick Mask and the one you wish to see by turning off their view boxes (the eyeball icons) in the Channels Palette.

Creating a Mask Channel from a Quick Mask Selection

You may decide to save your temporary Quick Mask selection as a permanent mask channel. There are two ways to do this:

- Immediately after clicking the Make Selection Tool, choose Select: **Save Selection**.

- In the **Channels Palette**, drag the temporary Quick Mask channel onto the New Channel button. Although this creates a new mask channel, the temporary channel remains in the palette until you exit Quick Mask mode.

Viewing a Standard Mask like a Quick Mask

It's possible to edit a mask channel just like a Quick Mask selection:

1. Save a selection to create a mask channel.

2. If the selection is still active, choose Select: **None**.

3. In the **Channels Palette**, click the view button next to the mask channel. The black areas of the channel appear as the overlay color.

4. Activate the mask channel in the Channels Palette. If you don't, your painting will affect the actual image.

5. Edit the channel using the same techniques described above.

6. Hold down the (Command) [Control] key and click the mask channel to convert it to a selection.

7. Click the view button to hide the mask channel and continue editing.

Chapter 8: The File Menu

Supported File Formats: PICT Resource

Creating a Macintosh Startup Screen

1. In Photoshop, create an image that matches your monitor's screen resolution (13 to 15-inch monitors: 640 × 480 pixels; 16- and 17-inch: 832 × 624 pixels; 19- and 20-inch: 1024 × 768 pixels; 21-inch: up to 1600 × 1200 pixels).

2. Make sure the resolution is set to 72 ppi.

3. Make sure the image is in RGB mode (those of you still using slower computer models can convert to Image: Mode: **Indexed Color** for quicker display).

4. In the Save As dialog, name the image "startupscreen" (written as one word).

5. Also in the Save As dialog, choose PICT Resource from the File Format pop-up.

6. Ignore the PICT Resource Options dialog—don't change the ID, don't worry about the name, and don't select any compression. Applying JPEG compression makes the file unreadable by the operating system.

7. Save the image into the root directory of the System Folder—that is, drop the image right into the System Folder, storing it on the same level as the System and Finder files.

8. Restart your computer. The image should appear on-screen while the Extensions and Control Panels load.

File: Import: TWAIN Acquire

Accessing the TWAIN Interface

1. Before you can get to the interface, Photoshop must know where the information is located on the hard drive. Choose File: Import: **TWAIN Select** and select the device you're using from the dialog. This step only needs to be performed prior to the very first time you use the TWAIN module. However, if more than one TWAIN device is installed in your system and you want to switch from one to another, use the Select Source command to choose the new device.

2. Under File: **Import**, Mac users should choose **TWAIN Acquire** and Windows users the appropriate TWAIN command to access the interface.

File: Export: GIF89a

There are two techniques to create a transparent GIF, as described in the following sections.

Exporting an Indexed Color Image

1. Choose File: Export: **GIF89a**. The two primary elements of the dialog are an image preview and the color palette. There are 256 tiny squares in the palette,

one for each possible color. It's here that you determine which color or colors are rendered transparent.

2. Click on each color intended to be transparent. Do this by clicking on an area in the preview or by selecting a swatch in the color palette. If it's a solid background, select just the one color. If more than one color is set to transparency, continue to click appropriately. (Command) [Control]-click to deselect a color, rendering it opaque again. Whenever a color is selected, it turns gray in the image preview. This is the information Photoshop uses to create the additional masking channel.

3. If the image already contains light-gray pixels, remap the Transparency Index Color. This helps avoid confusion with the pixels you want to remain opaque. After selecting at least one color, click on the box labeled Transparency Index Color. From the color picker, choose a vivid color not found in the image, like neon green or orange. After clicking OK, all the transparent pixels are represented by the new color.

4. Choose whether or not to interlace the GIF.

5. Click OK, name the file, and save.

Exporting an RGB Image

1. To form the basis of the transparent GIF, isolate the important image information on its own layer. Often, choosing Layer: New: **Layer Via Cut** after making a selection is sufficient.

2. Hide all other layers, regardless of their type. All visible layers are included in the exported GIF.

3. Choose File: Export: **GIF89a Export**.

4. Choose an option from the Palette submenu. To use a custom palette you have already saved—like the 216-color Web palette, for example—click the Load button.

5. Click Preview to see how the image will appear in a Web browser. If dissatisfied with the results, hold down the (Option) [Alt] key, press Reset, and begin again.

6. When satisfied with the colors, click OK and name the file.

NOTE

If desired, you can use a feathered selection to create the basis for your image layer. For the best results, keep as many colors in the indexed file as possible. GIF89a's can only use one color for transparency, and must therefore create a black-and-white dither in the alpha channel in an attempt to duplicate the soft edge. If there are too few colors, the transitions are poor.

File: Export: Paths to Illustrator

Exporting Paths to Illustrator

1. Create a path in Photoshop, either using the Pen Tool or converting an active selection into a path. Saving the path is advised, but not necessary.

2. Choose File: Export: **Paths to Illustrator**.

3. In the Paths to Illustrator dialog, choose the path to be exported (Mac users only).

4. Click Save to write the Illustrator file.

5. Open the file in Illustrator or FreeHand and edit the path like any other object-oriented shape.

Positioning Customized Type

1. In Photoshop, draw a path exactly where the type will flow.

2. Export the path to an Illustrator file.

3. Add type to the path in a vector-based program, adjusting the tracking, kerning, and coloring.

4. Select the type and convert it to outlines. In Illustrator, apply Type: **Create Outlines**. In FreeHand, apply Type: **Convert to Paths**. Because Photoshop sometimes has difficulty reading font information, converting the type to outlines ensures that the information rasterizes correctly.

5. Import the file into the original Photoshop image using File: **Place**. The type appears to flow along the line of the original path (see Figure A-6).

Figure A-6: Create the initial path in Photoshop (l). After exporting the path, use Illustrator or FreeHand to set the type (c). Import the type back into the original image (r).

Editing a Manually Traced Photoshop Image

Occasionally, you'll need to translate a Photoshop image into object-oriented shapes. This is done to create an effect that's only possible using that program's tools, or because you want the graphic to have the flexible scaling and crisp output of vector-based artwork. Usually, the image is a scan, like a company logo or clip art comprised of bold, clearly defined shapes—very rarely will it be a continuous-tone graphic.

There are three ways to trace an image, and the first two take place outside of Photoshop:

* Use an automatic tracing program like Adobe Streamline. It does a quick and passable job on basic shapes, but the results usually require further editing in Illustrator. Its tools aren't sensitive enough to re-create fine details like type or intricate line art.

* Import the graphic into Illustrator or FreeHand, lock it, and manually trace it using that program's Pen Tool. Again, it works well for more basic shapes, but the limited amount of detail in an imported image prevents you from capturing finer details.

* When capturing detail is most important, trace the image in Photoshop using the Pen Tool, then export the paths to an Illustrator file. When tracing in Photoshop, you're able to zoom in incredibly close to the image and create your paths with precision. (See **The Pen Tool** for more information.)

File: Page Setup

Editing a Transfer Curve

To create a tone curve that applies during output, follow these steps:

1. Open the original corrected image.

2. Select File: **Page Setup** and click the Transfer button.

3. Edit the curve. In this example, we lighten the midtones from 50% to 40%.

4. The bottom left of the curve represents 0%, or the point at which on-screen colors and printed areas are totally white. The upper right of the line represents 100%, or the point at which on-screen colors and printed areas are totally black. The dotted lines represent values in 10% increments. To lighten image tones, click on the line and drag it down; dragging up will darken the tones instead. In this case, click on the very center of the curve (50%) and drag straight down to the next dotted line (40%). This means that all pixels with a 50% value will output at 40%. Since the line is curve-shaped, the tones are lightened most in the midtones, but are applied less gradually throughout the rest of the image.

5. Save the image as a Photoshop EPS file.

6. In the EPS Options dialog, check Include Transfer Functions.

File: Preferences: Plug-ins & Scratch Disk

Specifying a New Plug-ins Folder

1. Create a folder called Central Plug-ins. Place it someplace visible but safe, like the folder containing your different applications.
2. Drag the plug-ins from all applications into the folder. It doesn't matter if they are contained in multiple folders, so just relocate all plug-ins folders.
3. Rename the individual folders according the program they came from.
4. Tell each application to recognize the new Plug-ins folder. In Photoshop, click the Choose button, find the new folder, highlight it, and click the Select button at the bottom of the dialog.

File: Color Settings: Printing Inks Setup

Defining a Non-Standard Ink

Occasionally, printers use non-standard inks. We recently worked with a newspaper who had replaced their magenta with a brighter red spot ink. The red worked great when used in headlines, boxes and rules, but wrought havoc when reproducing CMYK images. Since it was economical for them to continue using it, the best we could do is make Photoshop aware of the different ink's properties by changing its brightness values in the Printing Inks Setup dialog.

When you print with a non-standard ink, such as substituting a Pantone spot ink for one of the four process inks, follow these steps:

1. Print some test bars of the ink in question.
2. Measure the bars with a colorimeter.
3. Choose Custom from the Ink Colors pop-up.
4. Enter the Yxy values for the substituted ink received from the colorimeter.

If the substitute ink is from the Pantone system, you can avoid using the colorimeter:

1. Open the color picker in Photoshop.
2. Click Custom and enter the Pantone color number.
3. Click the Picker button to return to the color picker window.
4. Write down the three Lab Color values.
5. Return to the Printing Inks Setup dialog.
6. Choose Custom from the Ink Colors pop-up.
7. Click on the swatch next to the substituted color.
8. Enter the three Lab Color values in the Lab fields.
9. Save the setting to avoid repeating these steps in the future.

File: Color Settings: Separation Setup

Typical Conversion Scenarios

If there is any uncertainty about your RGB to CMYK conversion information, your print shop will hopefully be able to assist. If not, the following list of typical printing types is a strong starting point.

Coated Stock

Ink Colors:
  SWOP (Coated)

Dot Gain:
  12–25%

Separation Type:
  GCR

Black Generation:
  Light

Black Limit:
  90–100%

Total Ink:
  290–340%: less for web press, more for sheetfed

UCA:
  0–10%: typically 0%

Uncoated Stock

Ink Colors:
  SWOP (Uncoated)

Dot Gain:
  18–29%

Separation Type:
  GCR

Black Generation:
  Light

Black Limit:
  90–100%

Total Ink:
  270–300%: less for web press, more for sheetfed

UCA:
  0–10%: typically 0%

Newsprint (GCR)

Ink Colors:
  SWOP (Newsprint)

Dot Gain:
30–35%

Separation Type:
GCR

Black Generation:
Medium

Black Limit:
90–100%

Total Ink:
250–280%: less for web press, more for sheetfed

UCA:
0–10%: typically 0%

Newsprint (UCR)

Ink Colors:
SWOP (Newsprint)

Dot Gain:
30–35%

Separation Type:
UCR

Black Limit:
70–80%

Total Ink:
250–280%: less for web press, more for sheetfed

Chapter 9: The Edit Menu

Edit: Paste

Pasting Pixels to the Same Image

The most common occurrence of pasting involves selected pixels. When you paste a selection, it automatically appears in a new layer:

- If you choose Select: **None** before pasting, then the new layer is slightly offset from its original position.

- If you leave the selection active while choosing Edit: **Paste**, the new layer retains its original position.

The only time a pasted selection is not placed into a new layer is when you paste into an individual channel:

- If you paste into an existing color channel (like the Red channel in an RGB image), you replace the brightness values that Photoshop uses to display color. The result appears as color changes in the composite channel.

- If you paste into a "mask" channel, you affect the information that Photoshop reads when a saved selection is made active.

Pasting Shapes from Adobe Illustrator

This is another, more dynamic method of importing information from an Adobe Illustrator file (this technique requires Illustrator—it will not work with other vector-based graphics programs). Here, you copy information from an open Illustrator file to paste directly into a Photoshop image. Follow these steps:

1. Open the target Photoshop image.

2. Open the Illustrator graphic to be copied.

3. Select the shapes you want to paste into Photoshop. Make sure every path is completely selected; partially selected paths will not paste correctly into Photoshop.

4. Use Illustrator's Edit: **Copy** command to copy the selected shapes to the Clipboard.

5. Switch to the Photoshop image. You'll briefly see a message reading "Converting Clipboard to EPS (AICB) Format." This refers to Adobe's Adobe Illustrator ClipBoard format, used to transfer vector-based information between applications.

6. Select Photoshop's Edit: **Paste** command. A dialog appears with two options: Paste as Pixels and Paste as Paths. Choosing Paste as Pixels rasterizes the Illustrator shapes, just as if you'd selected File: **Open** or File: **Import**. Checking Anti-Alias ensures the edges of the shapes are rendered smoothly. Choosing Paste as Paths translates the Illustrator paths into Photoshop paths, fully editable using the Pen Tool.

7. If you Paste as Pixels, the image appears as a new layer. If you Paste as Paths, the new path appears as an item in the Paths Palette (see Figure A-7).

Figure A-7: When pasting Illustrator shapes, you can paste as pixels (l) or paths (r)

Pasting from Other Pixel-Based Applications

Photoshop accepts information copied from any other pixel-based editing program. Successfully handling this information depends on two things:

- **The color depth of the other program.** If it only works in 8-bit color or uses a limited color palette, pasting into a 24-bit Photoshop image does not automatically increase the range of colors. You can add them as you edit the image further, but if certain colors are dithered in another program, they paste that way in Photoshop.

- **Whether the image will be pasted back into the first program.** If the original program cannot handle the color depth of a Photoshop image, much of the color information may be lost or inaccurately displayed.

Pasting Text

You can paste any text-based information into the text fields in Photoshop's dialogs. You can also paste text copied from another program, such as Quark-XPress or Microsoft Word. The only time you'd do this is when you want to paste into one of Photoshop's larger text fields, such as the Caption field under File: File Info: **Caption** or the field in the Text Tool dialog.

Edit: Fill

Filling with Saved

By choosing Saved from the Contents pop-up, you fill a selection with the last saved version of a file. (If the entire image is selected, it's exactly the same as choosing File: **Revert**). Using the selection tools, you can revert very specific areas of the image. This is particularly useful when you need to access part of the original.

Filling with Saved only works with matching layers. This means you can't fill the contents of Layer 1 if the last saved version of the image only has a background layer. If the last saved image had more than one layer, then you can fill only with the saved contents from the same layer.

Photoshop depends on the Layer names to make these distinctions. To copy the saved contents of one layer into a new layer, follow these steps:

1. Create a new layer.

2. Name the new layer the same as the originally saved layer (layers can share the same name).

3. Make sure the new layer is active.

4. Apply Edit: **Fill**, choosing Saved from the Contents pop-up.

To apply this technique to the background layer, follow these steps:

1. Duplicate the current background layer. This way, you can still refer back to the contents of this layer, if you need to.

2. Select the original background layer.

3. Apply Edit: **Fill**, choosing Saved from the Contents pop-up.

If you've changed the resolution, canvas size, or color mode of an image, you can't Fill with Saved. The best you can do is change the saved version to match the new image specs, and *then* apply the Fill command. Follow these steps (this only works on flattened images):

1. (Option) (Alt)-click on the lower-left corner of the image window to display the current image specs. Write them down.

2. Select the entire image by choosing Select: **All**.

3. Copy the entire image to the Clipboard by choosing Edit: **Copy**.

4. Revert to the originally saved image by choosing File: **Revert**.

5. Make the appropriate file changes, based on the information written down earlier.

6. Save the image (or save a copy of the image, just in case).

7. Paste the most recent edits by choosing Edit: **Paste**. Now, when Photoshop refers to the saved information, it will match the current specs.

Filling with Snapshot

Filling with a Snapshot is similar to Filling with Saved, but with two important differences:

- You don't need to save the image in order to take a snapshot. This means you can take a snapshot and fill with it at any stage of the editing process.

- You can fill a selection on any layer, regardless of which layer the snapshot originally came from.

NOTE

Like Filling with Saved, you can't Fill with a Snapshot if you've changed the resolution, canvas size, or color mode. This shouldn't be a problem, however—immediately after making one of these changes, just choose Edit: **Take Snapshot** again.

Ghosting

The Fill command is commonly used to create a *ghost*, or a portion of an image filled with semi-opaque white. A common technique is placing a ghost on a large grayscale or full-color image and laying text over it. The lighter area still appears to be part of the image (since you can still see image pixels beneath the text), but it's not so dark that the text is obscured.

Ghosts are measured by the amount of information that remains—for example, if you fill with White set to 75% opacity, it's a 25% ghost. Depending on the type of image, ghosts usually range from 10% to 30%. Darker images require lower value ghosts (closer to 10%), while lighter images lose too much information if the opacity is set too high (set them closer to 30%) (see Figure A-8).

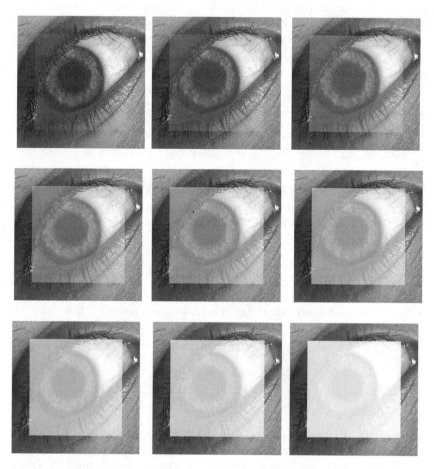

Figure A-8: Top row (l to r): 90%, 80%, and 70% ghosts. Middle row (l to r): 60%, 50%, and 40% ghosts. Bottom row (l to r): 30%, 20%, and 10% ghosts.

Although you can fill with semi-opaque white using the Edit: **Fill** dialog, we prefer to create a ghost following these steps:

1. Create a new layer.

2. Draw the area you wish to ghost with the rectangular Marquee Tool. The dimensions for this area are usually determined before you create the ghost, so display the Rulers and use the width and height values in the Info Palette. If you are ghosting the entire image, do not make a selection.

3. Fill the selection with the Contents set to White and the Opacity set to 100%. The selection fills with solid white.

4. In the **Layers Palette**, use the slider to lower the opacity to the desired setting.

---

5. Examine the ghost, making sure the pixels showing through are not too dark or too light. If necessary, move the cursor to different points on the image and read the values in the **Info Palette**.

6. Increase or decrease the opacity as needed.

7. Flatten and save.

Creating a Resizable Ghost

Few things are more frustrating than importing a ghosted image into a page layout program, only to realize the position of the ghost needs to change. Unfortunately, once you apply Layer: **Flatten Image** to a ghosted image, the only way you can change its position is to create it again from scratch.

By following this technique, you can easily reposition a ghost from within the page layout program:

1. In Photoshop, open the image receiving the ghost.

2. Duplicate the image by selecting Image: **Duplicate**.

3. In the duplicate, apply a ghost to the entire image by following the steps listed above.

4. Save the ghost, making sure the original image is not overwritten (add the word "ghost" to the file name).

5. In your page layout program, import and position the original image.

6. Import the ghosted duplicate, positioning it *precisely* on top of the original. In QuarkXPress, apply Step and Repeat with no horizontal or vertical offset and import the ghosted image into the new picture box. In Adobe PageMaker, use the ruler guides and Control Palette to position both graphics.

7. Crop the ghosted image to the desired dimensions.

8. Resize and reposition the ghost by moving the crop edges. Never move the actual image.

NOTE

When this technique is used, both the original *and* the ghosted image must be present during output. Otherwise, one image or the other outputs at 72 dpi.

Edit: Stroke

Framing an Entire Image

If it's imperative that your image remains exactly the same size, follow these steps:

1. Select the image by choosing Select: **All**.
2. Choose Edit: **Stroke** and enter the desired Width, Opacity, and Mode.
3. In Location, choose Inside—choosing Center will cut your stroke in half, and choosing Outside will result in no change.
4. Click OK.

If it's imperative that no existing image pixels are obscured by the frame, follow these steps:

1. Set the Background Color to the desired color for the frame.
2. Choose Image: **Canvas Size**.
3. In the Canvas Size dialog, set the Width and Height pop-ups to "pixels".
4. Add twice the desired stroke width to the Width and Height values. For example, if you want a five-pixel frame, increase the width and height by 10 pixels. When you enlarge the canvas, the current image remains centered, creating a frame of half the increased value.
5. Click OK.

Creating Outlined and Stroked Type

Photoshop's Type Tool outlines poorly. You can't control the thickness of the stroke, nor can you select a blend mode or set an opacity value. Ordinarily, you would use a program like Illustrator to set and stroke your type before importing it into Photoshop. If this isn't possible (or if the type is simple enough to create in Photoshop), use Edit: **Stroke** to create a better outline (see Figure A-9).

Figure A-9: Type outlined with the Type Tool dialog (l), type stroked with a 5 pixel line (c), and type stroked with a 12 pixel line (r)

To create transparent type with a colored outline, follow these steps:

1. Select the Type Mask tool and click on the open image receiving the type.

2. Enter the appropriate type specifications; do not check the Outline box.

3. Click OK.

4. Position the type selection. Leave it active for the remaining steps.

5. Set the Foreground Color to the desired outline color.

6. Choose Edit: **Stroke** and enter the desired values.

7. Click OK.

To create colored type with a different color outline, follow these steps:

1. Set the Foreground Color to the desired type color.

2. Select the standard Type tool and click on the open image.

3. Enter the appropriate type specifications and click OK.

4. Position the type. Leave it active for the remaining steps.

5. Set the Foreground Color to the desired stroke color.

6. Choose Edit: **Stroke** and enter the desired values.

7. Click OK.

NOTE

Strokes often appear blocky around corners or curved shapes, especially when you apply thicker widths around a hand-drawn selection. If this happens, choose Edit: **Undo** and try smoothing the selection. Choose Select: Modify: **Smooth**, enter a pixel value to round off the more pronounced selection edges, and click OK. If the blockiness persists, choose Undo and smooth the selection with a higher value.

Edit: Create Publisher

The Edit: **Create Publisher** command creates a new file called an *edition*, which forms the link between Photoshop and another application:

1. Open the image to be published and choose Edit: **Create Publisher**.

2. Enter a name for the edition and specify its location. Don't use the same name as the original file.

3. Choose PICT, TIFF, or Photoshop EPS, depending on the format required by the subscribing application.

4. Click Publish.

5. Open the document that will receive the Photoshop image and subscribe to the edition. Each program has slightly different Publish and Subscribe

commands, so refer to your application's documentation for more information on using the Subscribe feature.

Now, each time you edit and save the published Photoshop image, it's automatically updated in any applications subscribing to it. If you don't want the published image to be updated automatically, you can change to manual updating in the Edit: **Publisher Options** dialog.

Edit: Define Pattern

Loading Predefined Patterns

Photoshop ships with 33 predefined tiles you can turn into patterns.

Twelve of them are really displacement maps, found in Photoshop's Plug-ins folder. Ordinarily, you'd access these images using Filter: Distort: **Displace**. Not all of them form seamless patterns.

The remaining 21 are Illustrator files. Mac users will find them in the Brushes and Patterns folder, located inside the Goodies folder. Windows users will find them in the Patterns directory, located inside the Photoshop directory. Unlike the displacement maps, these files were intended to be made into repeating patterns, so they're seamless. These files must be rasterized in order to open them in Photoshop, which gives you the advantage of setting them to any size. The same applies to any pattern you create yourself in a vector-based program.

To define a pattern based on one of these images:

1. Open the pattern file in Photoshop.
2. Choose Select: **All**.
3. Choose Edit: **Define Pattern**.
4. Apply the pattern in your desired image.

Defining a Pattern with Non-Adjacent Edges

These patterns consist of an image surrounded by a solid color. Since no different colors touch the edge of the tile, there is no risk of an obvious seam appearing when the pattern is applied somewhere. These patterns are often used to fill an entire layer, or to create a background for yet another image.

1. Isolate the image you want to tile. This may involve some selecting and filling.
2. Fill the surrounding pixels with your desired color.
3. Using the rectangular Marquee Tool, draw a selection around the image. Keep in mind that the amount of space left between the image and the selection edge determines the space between the tiled images: if the selection edge is close to the image, it tiles closer together; if the edge is farther away, it tiles farther apart (see Figure A-10)
4. Choose Edit: **Define Pattern**.
5. Apply the pattern as desired.

Figure A-10: Selecting the tile with Marquee Tool (l), and applying the pattern

Defining a Staggered Pattern with Non-Adjacent Edges

These patterns are similar to the one described above, but the result is staggered, instead of linear. This technique only works on a perfectly square image.

1. Isolate the image you want to tile.

2. Using the rectangular Marquee Tool, drag a selection closely around the image.

3. Choose Edit: **Copy**.

4. Choose Select: **None**.

5. Choose Filter: Other: **Offset**. Click the Wrap Around button and enter half the width and height of the image. Since this filter only measures in pixels, you must determine the precise measurements. Open the Image: **Image Size** dialog, read the first two values, and choose Cancel. When you offset by half the width and height, the image appears in the four corners of the window.

6. Choose Edit: **Paste**. The copied image appears in the center.

7. Choose Layer: **Merge Down** to combine the two layers.

8. Choose Select: **All**.

9. Choose Edit: **Define Pattern**.

10. Apply the pattern as desired (see Figure A-11).

Defining a Noncontinuous Pattern

These patterns are perhaps the simplest to create—just draw a rectangular selection in an image and choose Edit: **Define Pattern**. Once the pattern is applied, you see distinct edges between the tiles (see Figure A-12).

Defining a Simple Seamless Texture

For these patterns, it's common to use a series of filters on a blank image.

1. Choose File: **New** and create a square document. Since this image will be used as a repeating tile, it doesn't need to be very large.

2. Create a texture using a series of filters or paint tools.

Common
Techniques

Figure A-11: Offsetting the image (l), pasting the copied image in the center (c), and applying the staggered pattern

Figure A-12: Select the tile with Marquee Tool (l), and apply the noncontinuous pattern (r)

3. Choose Filter: Other: **Offset** to examine the tile's edges. For best results, click the Wrap Around button, and enter half the width and height of the image.

4. If the edges are visible, use the **Rubber Stamp Tool** to conceal the seam. Depending on the pattern, you could use the Smudge Tool or copy/paste selections with a feathered edge.

5. Apply Filter: Other: **Offset** again to make sure no new seams were accidentally created.

6. Select the entire image and choose Edit: **Define Pattern**.

7. Apply the pattern as desired (see Figure A-13).

NOTE

If you use a 128 by 128-pixel image as a template, you may not have to perform any additional editing to make a seamless pattern. This becomes apparent when you apply Filter: Other: **Offset**—if there are no visible seams, you're free to define the pattern. This is true for at least two commonly used patterns: a cloud pattern using Filter: Render: **Clouds**, and a raised, grainy texture using Filter: Noise: **Add Noise**, then Filter: Stylize: **Emboss**.

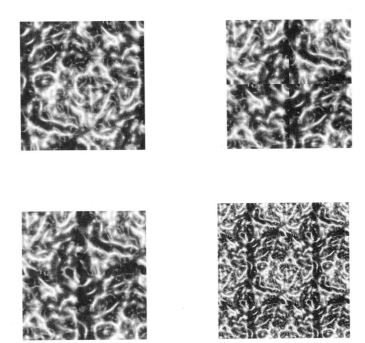

Figure A-13: Create the texture (upper l), then offset the contents of the image (upper r). After retouching the seams (lower l), define and apply the pattern

Defining a Seamless Image Pattern

Creating a seamless pattern from a scanned or Photo CD image is more complex than creating a simple texture. The information is more varied, and sloppy retouching is more pronounced when you apply the pattern. Therefore, the technique described above probably isn't enough. Try the following steps:

1. Draw a rectangular selection around the desired portion of an image. This method works best if you define a fixed-size square selection in the Marquee options dialog. In this example, the selection is 100 by 100 pixels.

2. Choose Edit: **Define Pattern**.

3. Choose File: **New** to create a new image window. Set the width and height to three times the size of the original selection (in this case, 300 × 300 pixels). Make sure the color mode and resolution are the same in as the original image.

4. Choose Edit: **Fill** and fill the entire image with the pattern (see Figure A-14).

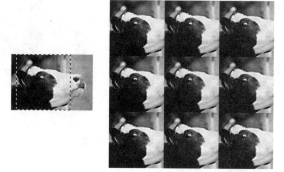

Figure A-14: Fill the new image with the initial pattern tile

5. Reposition the original image so you can see the first selected area.
6. In the current image, select the **Rubber Stamp Tool**. In the Rubber Stamp Options palette, choose Clone (Aligned) from the Options pop-up.
7. (Option) [Alt]-click in the original image to define the point you want to begin cloning from.
8. Focus on one seam, cloning pixels from the original image to fill in the spaces (see Figure A-15).

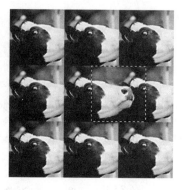

Figure A-15: Create the first continuous seam

9. After forming one continuous seam, place another fixed-size marquee straddling the new seam.
10. Choose Edit: **Define Pattern**, then apply the new pattern to the entire image (see Figure A-16).

Figure A-16: Fill the image with the current pattern tile

11. If necessary, repeat steps 6–10 for the remaining seams.

12. After the last seam is edited, place a final fixed-size marquee anywhere on the image and choose Edit: **Define Pattern**.

13. Either apply the pattern as desired, or paste a copy of it into a new file (sized exactly the same as one tile—in this case, 100 by 100 pixels) and save it for future use (see Figure A-17).

Figure A-17: Apply the completed seamless pattern

NOTE

To protect certain areas of your pattern from being cloned over, select them with the Lasso Tool or Pen Tool and choose Select: **Inverse** before cloning.

Defining a Seamless Pattern Using Third-Party Software

Some seamless patterns are too difficult to create using Photoshop alone. Products from two companies stand out in their ability to create extraordinarily complex patterns:

- **Terrazzo, from Xaos Tools.** This Photoshop Plug-in allows you to use 17 different "mathematical symmetries" to create seamless patterns from any source image. The resulting patterns are kaleidoscopic, fully editable, and very useful when creating Web graphics or texture maps for 3-D software.

- **Kai's Power Tools, from MetaCreations.** Two Plug-ins from this set are especially useful when creating patterns. KPT Seamless Welder allows you to create a seamless tile from any rectangular selection, avoiding the steps described above ("Simple Textures"). KPT Texture Explorer allows you to create expansive, non-repeating textures based on a wide selection of models and commands. These are not patterns per se, but are often used for the same purpose.

Defining a Pattern Containing Transparent Pixels

If more than one image layer is visible when you define a pattern, then all the visible information is included. To make a pattern that includes transparent or semi-transparent pixels, follow these steps:

1. Create a new image layer. This will not work on a background layer.

2. Create the pattern. In the example, we created a small, floating cartoon head.

3. Hide any other layers from view.

4. Draw a rectangular selection. Just like patterns with non-adjacent edges (described above), the amount of space left between the image and the selection edge determines the space between the tiled images.

5. Choose Edit: **Define Pattern.**

6. If necessary, delete the image used to make the pattern.

7. Apply the pattern as desired (see Figure A-18).

Figure A-18: Selecting the tile with the Marquee Tool (l), and applying the partially transparent pattern (r)

Chapter 10: The Image Menu

Image: Mode: Duotone

Using Duotone Presets

The easiest way to make a quality duotone is to use the presets that ship with Photoshop. Access these values by clicking the Load button in the Duotone Options dialog. They are located in the Photoshop application folder, inside the Goodies folder, inside the Duotone Presets folder. There are three folders, one each for duotones, tritones, and quadtones.

The presets for each type are split into three categories:

Gray/Black
   These presets are combinations of black and one or more gray Pantone inks. These combinations reproduce the greatest range of grays without adding any colored bias to the halftone.

Pantone
   These presets are combinations of different Pantone inks. Every one uses black as Ink 1, but not every Pantone ink appears as an option. Instead, colors representing a wide and uniform range of the Pantone spectrum are listed.

Process
   These presets are combinations of CMYK inks. Again, each one uses black as Ink 1.

NOTE

Each duotone and tritone preset has four variations. They range from warm, or higher color bias (#1), to neutral, or lower color bias (#4). The quadtone presets cover the same range, but offer fewer options.

When you create a duotone using a Pantone ink, don't be alarmed if your desired color isn't listed. Instead, follow these steps:

1. Refer to your Pantone swatchbook and find the preset color that most closely matches the color you want.

2. Load the preset containing that color into the Duotone Options dialog.

3. Click on that color's swatch to enter the Custom Color picker.

4. Select your Pantone color.

5. Click OK.

Creating a PMS Duotone

For this example, the inks are black and Pantone 287.

1. Open or acquire the Grayscale image you wish to convert to a duotone.
2. Adjust the image for contrast and sharpness, and perform any required retouching.
3. Choose Image: Mode: **Duotone**. The Duotone Options dialog appears.
4. Click Load and navigate to the Pantone Duotones folder.
5. Select the preset containing the color closest to the one you want. In this case, it's "blue 286 bl". Click Open.
6. Click on the blue Pantone 286 CV swatch.
7. In the Custom Color picker, select Pantone 287. Click OK.
8. Click OK to exit the Duotone Options dialog. If unsatisfied with the blend of inks, select Image: Mode: **Duotone** again and choose another preset.
9. Save the image as an EPS file, checking the Include Halftone Screens box.

Editing Duotones

Once a duotone is created, it's more difficult to adjust its tonal range. This is mainly due to two causes:

- **The colors you defined do not appear in the Info Palette.** Instead, you must select Actual Color from the Palette Options submenu. Then, the different inks appear as they were numbered in the Duotone Options palette: Ink 1, Ink 2, Ink 3, and Ink 4.

- **Regardless of how many inks you defined, the image has only one channel.** You cannot use Image: Adjust: **Curves** to edit the color content. Only one curve exists for the entire image, and that controls the overall brightness values. To adjust individual colors, you must edit their curves in the Duotones dialog, or load a new preset.

Inspecting Duotone Data

Since duotones only have one channel, the only way you can read the different ink densities is to check the Actual Color values in the **Info Palette**. If you have a question about how the inks are affecting specific parts of the image, however, you can perform the following:

1. Choose Image: Mode: **Multichannel**. This creates a file containing one channel for each ink.
2. Inspect the ink percentages by choosing individual channels in the **Channels Palette**, moving the cursor over the image, and reading the Info Palette. It is imperative that you *do not* make any edits to the Multichannel image.
3. Choose Edit: **Undo** to switch the image back to Duotone mode.

Creating a Frame of Reference for Duotone Editing

If your goal is to expand the tonal range of an image without adding any visible color shift, use this technique:

1. After creating your initial Duotone, create a new Grayscale image. Make it the same width as the Duotone, but only a quarter-inch high.

2. Using the **Gradient Tool**, create a horizontal black-to-white gradient the exact width of the new file.

3. Apply Image: Adjust: **Posterize**, set to 20 levels. This results in a gray ramp of roughly 5% increments.

4. In your Duotone, use Image: **Canvas Size** to add a half-inch to the bottom of the image.

5. Copy the gray ramp to the Duotone, placing it in the new space.

6. Keep both images open and visible. As you edit the Duotone, compare the values of the two gray ramps. The values should remain similar as you work.

7. When editing is complete, use the Cropping Tool to discard any unnecessary information.

Image: Mode: Color Table

Changing a Value in the Color Table

1. Determine the RGB value of the color you want to change. Do this by setting the First Color Readout in the Info Palette to RGB, and placing the cursor over a colored image pixel.

2. Locate the same color among the Color Table swatches. In tables with few colors, this is easy. In tables containing many colors, the only way to find the right one is to click a similar color and check the values until you find the right one.

3. Once you find the right color, enter the new RGB values in the color picker and click OK.

4. Click OK to close the Color Table dialog. If unsatisfied with the results, re-open the dialog and enter new values for the offending color.

Creating a Color Table Gradient

To create a gradient in the Color Table (similar to the Black Body and Spectrum options), follow these steps:

1. Drag the cursor from one color swatch to the another, rather than clicking on one in particular. The Color Picker appears.

2. Define the first color in the gradient.

3. Click OK. The Color Picker appears again.

4. Define the last color in the gradient.

5. Click OK. Photoshop fills in the necessary steps to complete the blend.

Image: Adjust: Levels

Although many publications suggest otherwise, the Levels command is best suited for evaluating rather than adjusting images. Although we describe two basic image-editing techniques using this command, both are better accomplished using Image: Adjust: **Curves**.

Evaluating the Tonal Range

After scanning an image, open the Levels dialog and examine the histogram. A typical continuous tone image should have a reasonably even distribution of tones. Of course, some images contain more light or dark tones than others. Be on the alert, however, for continuous tone scans containing gaps or spikes in the histogram. This is often an indication of a faulty scan or a light source on its last legs. When necessary, rescan the image and check again.

NOTE

When evaluating a color scan, however, you'll get the best results by using Image: **Histogram**, then returning to the Levels dialog to continue editing. That histogram provides a more accurate graph of the composite channel.

Identifying Endpoints

Endpoints are simply the lightest and darkest values in an image. You can identify them as the first and last vertical bars in the histogram. Nearly all scanners—particularly flatbeds—are incapable of capturing all the tones of the original artwork. When this happens, the histogram is seen to peter out before it reaches one or both ends of the spectrum.

Before you can properly reset the endpoints, you must locate the lightest and darkest pixels. Use the following method:

1. Make sure Video LUT Animation is turned on under File: Preferences: **Display & Cursors**.

2. Hold down the (Option) [Alt] key and grab the white slider. The image appears to turn black.

3. Move the slider to the left. As soon as the you reach the point in the histogram containing the lightest tones, those image pixels appear to turn white. They represent the lightest image pixels, or the current highlight endpoint.

4. Return the white cursor to its original position.

5. Hold down the (Option) [Alt] key and grab the black slider. The image appears to turn white.

6. Move the slider to the right. As soon as you reach the point in the histogram containing the darkest tones, those image pixels appear to turn white. They represent the darkest image pixels, or the current shadow endpoint.

Armed with this information, you'll know where to go when manually resetting the endpoints.

Expanding the Tonal Range

A slight variation on the above technique often compensates for the smaller tonal range captured in a scan. In a color or Grayscale image, perform the same steps described above to locate the highlight and shadow endpoints—only this time, leave the sliders at the beginning and end of the existing tonal range. Click OK to expand the range to encompass the values from black to white, creating the effect of a larger number of image tones.

This technique results in a more appealing on-screen image. If your image is being prepared for print, the endpoints must still be adjusted for press limitations (see Figure A-19).

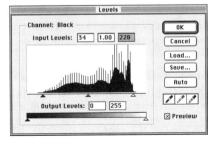

Figure A-19: Repositioning the sliders to expand the tonal range

---

NOTE

Do not expand the range of predominantly dark or light images. They were never intended to encompass the entire tonal range, and will appear incorrectly balanced and washed out due to the small number of tones being stretched so far.

Setting and Applying Endpoints for Print

Every printing press has a reproducible range smaller than the number of tones generated in Photoshop. When editing a Grayscale image on-screen, you work with dot sizes between 1% and 99% (0% and 100%, white and black, are not made of halftone dots). The average press can print dot sizes between 8% and 90%. Values lower than 8% break down to white, while values higher than 90% fill in to black. For the unadjusted image, this results in poor highlight and shadow detail.

Each press has its own reproducible range. If you're unsure, ask your printer. If they're unsure, ask them to run a test strip, or one black film plate that you can create in a page layout program:

1. In one percent increments, create a series of half-inch squares ranging from 1% to 30% and 70% to 99%.

2. Output this file to film on a well-calibrated imagesetter. If you will be using a digital press, process it using the actual press.

3. Run this chart on-press and evaluate the printed tones with a loupe. The first values that don't break down or fill in are the endpoints for that press.

Determining the precise range of a press is not always practical. When scanning and adjusting halftones, many professionals use the average values of 8% and 90% black until a specific project demands more exact values. CMYK images, which are a little more forgiving than one-color halftones, use the following endpoint values:

• **Highlight:** 5% cyan, 3% magenta, 3% yellow, 0% black.

• **Shadow:** Photoshop automatically enters the current default black, based on the File: Color Settings: **Separation Setup** dialog. (See Color Controls: **Default Colors** for more information.)

The standard highlight and shadow dot values differ for Grayscale halftones and CMYK images. You must reset these values by double-clicking on the appropriate eyedroppers when you switch from editing one color mode to another.

To set the highlight and shadow dot values, perform the following:

1. Open the Levels or Curves dialog.

2. To set the shadow dot, double-click the black eyedropper and enter the appropriate value.

3. To set the highlight dot, double-click the white eyedropper and enter the appropriate value.

Once these values are entered, they remain until they are manually changed. Apply them to an image in one of three ways:

• Select Image: Adjust: **Auto Levels.**

• Click the Auto button in the Image: Adjust: **Levels** or **Curves** dialog.

- Apply the endpoints manually:

  a. To set the shadow dot, select the black eyedropper.

  b. Using the **Info Palette** as a guide, move the cursor over the actual image until you find the darkest value.

  c. Click the darkest pixel.

  d. To set the highlight dot, select the white eyedropper

  e. Using the Info Palette as a guide, move the cursor over the image until you find the lightest value.

  f. Click the lightest pixel (see Figure A-20).

Figure A-20: A halftone before (l) and after (r) setting endpoints for press (note the highlight and shadow values)

NOTE

After setting the endpoints, you may notice an occasional pixel falling outside the established limits. Unless it occurs in a wide area, this will not hurt the final print quality.

After its endpoints are set for print, the image appears to flatten considerably. You still have to adjust the image for contrast.

Simple Image Enhancing

Although not as powerful or precise as the Curves dialog, it's possible to create rough-and-ready tonal adjustments using the Levels controls:

1. Open the Levels dialog.

2. Expand the tonal range by (Option) [Alt]-dragging the highlight and shadow sliders to the beginning and end of the histogram. This distributes the tones over the widest possible range, compensating for the limited sensitivity of your scanner.

3. Click OK and re-open the dialog. This way, you continue editing with a more accurate histogram.

4. If necessary, adjust the endpoints for print (see above techniques). Images destined for multimedia or the Web do not require this step.

5. Move the gray slider left or right to lighten or darken the midtones. Usually, dragging toward the apparent gravitational center of the histogram provides the best results (see Figure A-21).

6. Click OK to apply the changes.

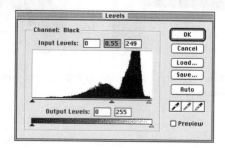

Figure A-21: Adjusting image midtones using the Levels dialog

Image: Adjust: Curves

The following represent some of the most commonly used curve-editing techniques. Unless otherwise noted, these examples use output percentages to measure color.

Adjusting a Halftone for Contrast

There are two stages of the imaging process that reduce the overall contrast of an image: scanning, and repositioning endpoints for print.

To compensate for this loss of information, you must use the Curves dialog to add contrast. Essentially, you create contrast by making the light tones lighter and the dark tones darker—but ultimately, your adjustments will depend on the image information at hand. In this and the following technique, we illustrate the "classic" contrast curve.

1. Open the Curves dialog. Make sure the Input/Output values read as percentages. Click the tone gradient if they do not.

2. Move the cursor to the three-quarter tones and add a point at 75% (click when both Input/Output values read 75%).

3. Drag this point straight up until the Output value reads 80%. The Input value should still read 75% (see Figure A-19).

4. Move the cursor to the quarter tones and add a point at 25% (click when both Input/Output values read 25%).

5. Drag this point straight down until the Output value reads 20%. The Input value should still read 25% (see Figure A-22).

6. Click OK and save.

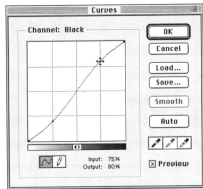

Figure A-22: This simple curve lightens the quarter tones and darkens the three-quarter tones, leaving the midtones untouched

Adjusting an On-Screen Image for Contrast

Adding contrast using brightness values is similar to adding contrast to a halftone, but you must work in the opposite direction:

1. Open the Curves dialog. Make sure the Input/Output values read as brightness levels. Click the tone gradient if they do not.

2. Move the cursor to the three-quarter tones and click to add a point at 191 (click when both Input/Output values read 191).

3. Drag this point straight down until the Output value reads 205.

4. Move the cursor to the quarter tones and click to add a point at 64 (click when both Input/Output values read 64).

5. Drag this point straight up until the Output value reads 50. The Input value should still read 64 (see Figure A-23).

6. Click OK and save.

Since you do not apply print endpoints to on-screen images, you may not need to apply as steep a curve adjustment to create satisfactory contrast.

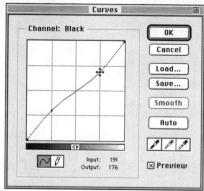

Figure A-23: This simple curve lightens the quarter tones and darkens the three-quarter tones, leaving the midtones untouched

Adjusting a Halftone for Dot Gain

When you convert an RGB image to CMYK, Photoshop automatically compensates for dot gain (see File: Color Settings: **Printing Inks Setup**). When editing halftones, however, you must account for dot gain manually. In this example, we lighten the midtones to accommodate an expected 20% dot gain:

1. Open a Grayscale image you've already adjusted for contrast.

2. Open the Curves dialog.

3. Move the cursor to the midtones and click to add a point at 50%.

4. Drag this point straight down until the Output value reads 40% (see Figure A-24).

5. Click OK and save.

When you make this type of adjustment, a lot of image data is irreversibly thrown away. Therefore, it's wiser to save a copy of the image instead of overwriting the original file. That way, the original can still be used in the future.

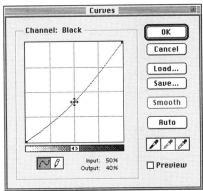

Figure A-24: This simple curve lightens the image midtones, leaving the endpoints untouched

---

NOTE

You may consider building a transfer function into your file, or a curve that reduces the midtones during output (see File: Page Setup: **Transfer**). Their advantage is that the original image data is not affected. Their disadvantage is that the file must be saved as an EPS, which means larger file sizes and images that cannot be recolored or otherwise adjusted in another program.

Identifying and Adjusting a Color Cast

A full-color image may contain a color bias, or a pronounced cyan, magenta, or yellow cast. Always evaluate color by examining the values in the Info Palette.

Here, the diffuse highlight has a value of 5% cyan, 5% magenta, and 3% yellow, or a slight magenta cast. As a result, the lightest values appear somewhat warm and pinkish. The deeper image tones are unaffected, so you can correct the bias with a small curve adjustment:

1. Open the Curves dialog.

2. Select Magenta from the Channel pop-up.

3. Anchor the curve by clicking on the 50% and 75% points. Do not move these points—they prevent the adjustment from affecting the entire image.

4. Move the cursor to the highlights. Click to add a point at 5%.

5. Drag this point straight down until the Output value reads 3% (see Figure A-25).

6. Click OK. Check the results by repeatedly choosing Edit: **Undo**.

This is the most basic color correcting strategy: identify a problem, make a very slight change to correct it, review the result, and proceed if necessary.

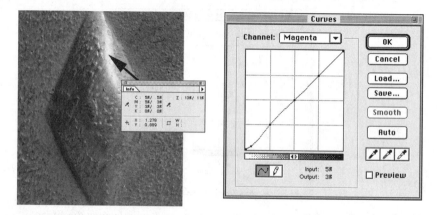

Figure A-25: Lightening the magenta highlight by 2%

Identifying Neutral Tones

Another cause of color bias is incorrect *gray balance*, or the CMYK combinations that form neutral gray tones. The most common example of neutral grays are the standard diffuse highlight or shadow values, although a neutral can exist at any tone. If the neutrals are unbalanced, the image has a cast. However, if you know the percentages that equal neutral gray, you can use them as a basis for removing it.

As you inspect the neutral areas, let the cyan value be your guide. Due to ink impurities, the cyan content in a neutral gray is a little higher than the magenta and yellow, which are equal. The resulting gray value is roughly equal to the cyan percentage. For example, a highlight value of 5% cyan, 3% magenta, 3% yellow forms the equivalent of 5% black.

Refer to the following neutral values as you evaluate an image:

Cyan	Magenta	Yellow	Neutral Gray (K)
5%	3%	3%	5%
10	6	6	10
25	16	16	25
30	21	21	30
40	29	29	40
50	37	37	50
60	46	46	60
75	64	64	75
80	71	71	80
90	82	82	90
95	87	87	95

Adjusting Neutral Tones

Depending on the extent of the color cast, there are two different ways to bring the neutrals back in line: you can make a focused curve adjustment, as described in the previous technique, or you can reapply neutral endpoints, which shifts the entire color range.

In the next example, the same image has two problems. First, the diffuse highlight is 4% cyan, 1% magenta, and 2% yellow, which is too low and non-neutral. Second, the shadows have a yellowish cast. These problems can both be addressed by applying neutral endpoints:

1. Open the Curves dialog.

2. Double-click the shadow eyedropper to open the color picker.

3. In the CMYK fields, make sure the appropriate CMYK default black appears. If you have recently adjusted a series of one-color halftones, this field may still contain only a single black value. Click OK when finished.

4. Double-click the highlight eyedropper to open the color picker.

5. In the CMYK fields, enter 5% cyan, 3% magenta, 3% yellow, and 0% black. Click OK when finished.

6. Select the shadow eyedropper.

7. Using the **Info Palette** as a guide, find the darkest tone in the image and click on it.

8. Select the highlight eyedropper.

9. Find the lightest tone in the image and click on it (see Figure A-26).

By resetting the endpoints to neutral grays, you remove the two color casts. At the same time, you ensure that the lightest and darkest values fit within the range of a standard printing press. After applying such an adjustment, you must double-check the midtone values for any new color bias. If the midtones require additional correction, use a more focused curve adjustment.

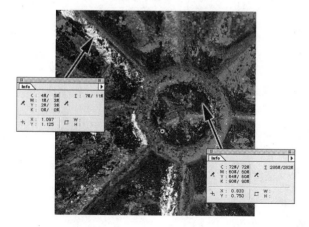

Figure A-26: A CMYK image before (l) and after setting neutral endpoints (note the highlight and shadow values)

NOTE

Bear in mind that neutrality is a proportional relationship. It's possible to make every gray level a neutral tone, but that would take unnecessary time and could create an unnatural balance of colors. The neutral chart is a guide, and doesn't necessarily outweigh the colors of the original artwork.

Half Cast Removals

Sometimes, attempting to remove a cast by neutralizing gray moves the overall color content too far from the original artwork. In this case, you can strike a compromise by applying a *half cast removal*, or removing only half the value required to make a gray tone neutral.

For example, if removing 6% yellow from the shadows would fully neutralize the color, a half cast removal would subtract 3%. This method helps remove unpleasant casts without dramatically shifting the overall color.

Image: Adjust: Equalize

Mapping Your Scanner Bed

As a rule, flatbed scanners are inexpensive, low-end devices. Although their overall quality is certainly rising, their basic architecture leaves them prone to certain problems. One in particular is the inability to read color information

---

uniformly throughout the scanner bed. By equalizing an empty scan, you can pinpoint the less-effective points of your scanner:

1. Place a large sheet of highly reflective white paper in the bed (RC paper works best).

2. Scan the entire preview window as a 72 ppi RGB image. Leave the remaining scanner settings at their defaults.

3. Open the image in Photoshop.

4. Exaggerate any existing tones by selecting Image: Adjust: **Equalize**. Here, any areas that did not scan as fully white appear as dark splotches—typically, these begin appearing around the edges. Avoid placing artwork on these parts of the scanner bed.

5. If desired, print out the Equalized result. Cut out the cleaner areas to create a mask for your scanner bed.

Image: Adjust: Threshold

Preparing Detailed Line Art

Many flatbed scanners do a poor to fair job of capturing fine details when scanning line art. The details are either filled in with black (threshold too high) or blown out to white (threshold too low). Once a line art scan is opened in Photoshop, nothing can be done to recapture this information. Consider the following technique instead:

1. Scan your line art as a Grayscale image, making sure the resolution meets line art requirements (600–1200 ppi).

2. Open Image: Adjust: **Threshold**.

3. Move the slider to the right or left, paying close attention to the problem details.

4. When the image appears satisfactory, click OK (see Figure A-27).

5. Choose Image: Mode: **Bitmap** to convert the image to 1-bit line art.

NOTE

If you use this technique to create line art, you must still convert the image to Bitmap mode. Failure to do so results in a file that does not print properly. If the image is left in Grayscale, the edges and details are obscured by a halftone screen; if it's left in RGB, it may not print at all.

Common Techniques

Figure A-27: Line art scanned as a Grayscale image (l), with a Threshold of 80 (c), and a Threshold of 150.

Creating Black Masks

If you apply a threshold level of 255 to an image layer or selection, all the pixels turn 100% black. The shape of the original object, however, is fully retained. This is useful when you need a black duplicate of a given object for techniques such as drop-shadows (see Chapter 20, *The Layers Palette*, for more information).

Image: Calculations

Combining Masking Channels

The only time the Calculate commands stand out is when they're used to combine masking channels. Since you can't edit individual channels using the **Layers Palette**, there are only two ways to combine the values of two saved selections:

- **Do it manually.** Choose one masking channel from the Channels palette, load another as a selection, and fill it with either black or white. Or, load both channels using the Operation controls in the Select: **Load Selection** dialog and choose Select: **Save Selection** to create a third channel based on the combined selection.

- **Use Image: Calculations.** This way, you can automatically create a new masking channel, and you have more blending options at your disposal than if you created the channel by hand.

In this example, we create a third channel based on two saved selections in the same image:

1. Open the image in Photoshop. Since there's only one, you don't have to worry about its dimensions.

2. Under Source 1, set up the first channel. Since we just want to combine masks, choose Merged from the Layers pop-up so the information is not restricted to the contents of one layer. Choose the appropriate channel number from the Channels pop-up.

3. Under Source 2, set up the second channel. Again, choose Merged from the Layers pop-up and the appropriate channel number from the Channels pop-up.

4. Select the blend mode that gives you the best result. In this case, choosing Normal simply displays the Source 1 image. We chose Screen to combine the two selection areas.

5. Under Result, make sure the same file name as Source 1 and Source 2 appears. This way, the new channel is written into the same file.

6. Under Channel, choose New (see Figure A-28) .

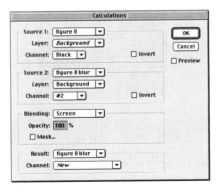

Figure A-28: Using Calculations, combine two mask channels (upper images) into one

---

NOTE

When using Image: **Calculations**, always have the Preview box checked. When it's used to combine masking channels, it displays the possible results regardless of which layer or channel was active when you first selected the command.

Image: Image Size

Reducing Moiré in a Scanned Prescreened Image

The process of downsampling a high-resolution image can often compensate for the moiré pattern that results from scanning a prescreened image. Follow these steps:

1. Scan the image at twice the normal resolution. For example, if you are scanning a halftone at 300 ppi, scan it at 600 ppi.

2. Select Image: **Image Size**.

3. Check the Constrain Proportions and Resample Images boxes. This allows you to change the resolution without affecting the width and height. Also, make sure the Interpolation is set to Bicubic.

4. Enter 300 in the Resolution field.

5. Click OK. By cutting the resolution in half, you remove three-quarters of the image pixels. Often, this removes most of the pattern as well (see Figure A-29).

6. Continue editing the image.

Figure A-29: A scan containing moiré, acquired at double resolution (l), and after reducing the resolution with Image Size (r)

Repurposing Print Graphics for the Web

This command is the tool of choice for making print-oriented graphics suitable for multimedia and the World Wide Web. Since high-resolution print graphics don't translate well to these low-res arenas, use Image: **Image Size** to downsample them appropriately:

1. Open the high-res image in Photoshop.

2. Select Image: Image Size.

3. Check the Constrain Proportions and Resample Images boxes. This allows you to change the resolution without affecting the width and height.

4. Enter 72 in the Resolution field.

5. Click OK.

6. Convert the image to the appropriate color mode.

7. Save the image in the appropriate file format.

Chapter 11: The Layer Menu

Layer: Add Layer Mask

Using the Paint Tools to Create Feathered Image Transitions

There are two ways to apply this technique. You can use the brushstrokes to hide or reveal an image.

To hide an image, follow these steps:

1. In the **Layers Palette**, choose the image layer you wish to partially hide.

2. If the layer contains no transparent pixels, choose Select: **All**. If the layer contains transparent pixels, (Command) [Control]-click its item in the Layers Palette.

3. Choose Layer: Add Layer Mask: **Reveal Selection**.

4. Click the layer mask thumbnail to select it.

5. Choose the **Paintbrush Tool**, selecting a soft-edged brush in the **Brushes Palette**.

6. Set the foreground color to black.

7. Paint the portions of the image you wish to hide. By adding black to the layer mask channel, you completely mask the image pixels. Since the soft-edged brush adds tones of gray to the channel, the resulting edges are feathered, or semi-transparent (see Figure A-30).

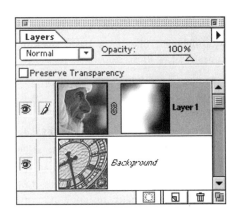

Figure A-30: Painting a layer mask to hide the layer's contents

To reveal an image, follow these steps:

1. In the **Layers Palette**, choose the image layer you wish to partially hide.

2. If the layer contains no transparent pixels, choose Select: **All**. If the layer contains transparent pixels, (Command) [Control]-click its item in the Layers Palette.

3. Choose Layer: Add Layer Mask: **Hide Selection**.

4. Click the layer mask thumbnail to select it.

5. Choose the **Paintbrush Tool**, selecting a soft-edged brush in the **Brushes Palette**.

6. Set the foreground color to white.

7. Paint the portions of the image you wish to reveal. By adding white to the layer mask channel, you expand the visible image area. Since the soft-edged brush adds tones of gray to the channel, the resulting edges are feathered, or semi-transparent (see Figure A-31).

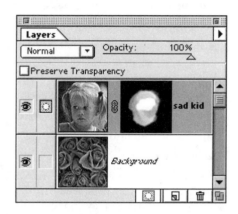

Figure A-31: Painting a layer mask to reveal the layer's contents

Creating Custom Image Frames

By applying a filter to a basic layer mask, you can create a variety of image frames. Follow these steps:

1. In the layer you wish to mask, make a selection smaller than the image window. For this example, we use the Marquee Tool to create a rectangular selection.

2. Choose Layer: Add Layer Mask: **Reveal Selection**.

3. Click the layer mask thumbnail to select it.

4. Apply a filter that visibly distorts the contents of the mask, such as Filter: Distort: **Ripple** or Filter: Pixelate: **Color Halftone**. The filter affects the mask instead of the image, resulting in an irregular image frame (see Figure A-32).

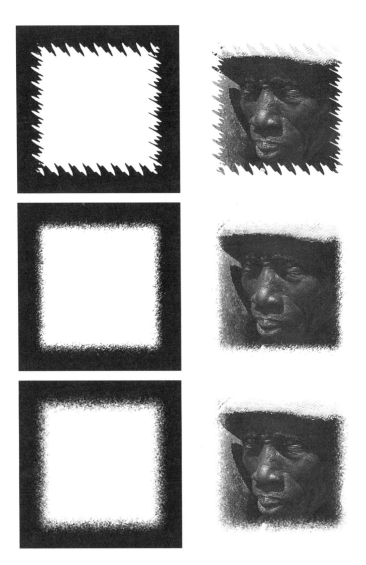

Figure A-32: Custom layer mask frames—Ripple: Large, 500% (top); Gaussian Blur: 6, Graphic Pen: 3, 90 (center); Gaussian Blue: 6, Splatter: 10, 5 (bottom)

NOTE

In general, blurring the layer mask before applying a filter results in interesting semi-transparent effects. Some filters, such as Filter: Sketch: **Graphic Pen**, have no effect on purely black and white information. Blurring the mask channel adds a radius of gray information to the frame, allowing such filters to generate a visible result.

Viewing the Contents of a Layer Mask

After creating a layer mask, perform the following:

1. In the Layers Palette, choose the item containing the layer mask.

2. In the Channels Palette, click the View box of the layer mask channel. The mask appears in the image as a semi-transparent overlay, similar to a selection in Quick Mask mode.

3. Click the View box of the composite channel to reveal only the mask channel.

NOTE

You can bypass the Channels Palette altogether by (Option) [Alt]-clicking the layer mask thumbnail to reveal only the mask channel.

Chapter 12: The Select Menu

Select: Inverse

Creating a Silhouette

Typically, this command is applied after a selection is drawn with a selection tool. Rather than use a selection to target a specific area, this command allows you to target everything *but* a specific area. This is useful when creating effects such as a silhouette, where a target image is removed from its background pixels:

1. Surround the image you want to silhouette with a selection path. The **Lasso Tool** allows you to draw a manual outline, but the **Pen Tool** allows you create a more flexible, re-useable path.

2. Once the image is selected, choose Select: **Inverse**. Now, all the pixels except the target image are selected.

3. Set the background color to white (0% black).

4. Hold down the (Command) [Control] key and press Delete. The pixels surrounding the target image fill with white.

5. Save the image in the proper file format. If it's destined for print, save it as a TIFF. If it's destined for the Web, convert it to Indexed Color and save it as a transparent GIF by choosing File: Export: **GIF89a Export**.

Select: Color Range

Removing Red-Eye

When a camera flash is set too close to the lens, its light reflects off the subject's retinas and back onto the film, giving the eyes a red glow. This is a result of a

---

lower-quality camera, and may occur over an entire series of images. The offending color is consistent from photo to photo, and is fairly unique from the surrounding image colors. These factors make it an ideal candidate for Select: **Color Range**. Follow these steps:

1. Open a scanned image with red-eye.

2. Choose Select: **Color Range**.

3. Move the Color Range dialog to the side so you can see both the dialog and the open image. If necessary, zoom in and scroll the image to make the eyes more clearly visible.

4. Choose Sampled Colors from the Select pop-up and None from the Selection Preview pop-up.

5. Click on the red of the eye with the Target Eyedropper.

6. Set the Selection Preview to Grayscale and examine the eye in the image window. Only the area of red-eye should appear white.

7. Switch between the None and Grayscale Selection Previews to compare the targeted area to the actual image. If additional colors are selected, decrease the Fuzziness. If the area of red-eye is not completely white, increase the Fuzziness.

8. Save the targeted range by clicking the Save button in the Color Range dialog. This way, similar images can use the same settings.

9. Click OK to apply the selection. Eliminate the red-eye using the Rubber Stamp Tool or the Paintbrush Tool. The selection protects the areas of the image which do not need to be fixed, enabling you to work more efficiently.

NOTE

When making a drastic color change, apply a feather value to the selection before editing. After clicking OK, choose Select: **Feather** and enter a value of 1. This conceals the jagged edges of the selection.

Select: Feather

Creating Glow

By feathering a selection, you form the basis for creating a glowing effect surrounding an image.

1. If the image does not exist on a separate layer, select it and choose Layer: New: **Layer Via Copy**.

2. Create a new layer and position it beneath the layer containing the object. Name this layer Glow.

3. After choosing the Glow layer, hold down the (Command) [Control] key and click the image's layer. This creates a selection on the Glow layer in the exact shape of the image.

4. Choose Select: **Feather**. Enter a Feather radius of 10 pixels.

5. Define a foreground color to use as the glow color.

6. Fill the selection by holding down the (Command) [Control] key and pressing Delete. Note how the feathered edges allow the underlying information to show through (see Figure A-33).

Figure A-33: An image element before (l) and after (r) adding glow

Select: Modify: Contract

Removing Edge Pixels

Two different situations result in visible edge pixels surrounding an image layer. Occasionally, when a layer is composited from another image, it has a visible fringe. This is a range of pixels lifted from the original image which don't match the pixels of the current background. Also, any layer created by selecting an image with Select: **Color Range** is surrounded with a jagged edge. Use Select: Modify: **Contract** to shave off the offending fringe:

1. Select the image layer from the Layers Palette.

2. Select its contents by hold down the (Command) [Control] key and clicking the same layer in the Layers Palette.

3. Choose Select: Modify: **Contract** and enter a value of 1 pixel.

4. Choose Select: **Inverse** to reverse the selection.

5. Press the Delete key to remove the edge pixels. The resulting anti-aliased edge ensures a smooth transition with the background image.

Select: Similar

Selecting One Color

Select: **Similar** is the most efficient method of selecting all pixels of one specific color. This is particularly useful when editing an image containing solid colors, such as a logo or an imported Illustrator graphic.

1. Set a low Tolerance in the **Magic Wand Tool** Options Palette (0 to 32).

2. Check Anti-aliasing in the same palette to generate an anti-aliased selection. Turn this option off only when selecting images with harsh transitions between colors, such as an Illustrator graphic that was rasterized without anti-aliasing.

3. Select a portion of color with the **Marquee Tool** or the Magic Wand Tool.

4. Choose Select: Similar.

5. After performing the next edit to the selected pixels, choose Select: **Hide Edges** to check the integrity of the selection.

NOTE

If you detect a slight fringe due to any pre-existing anti-aliasing, the Tolerance must be increased. Choose Edit: **Undo** to reverse the last edit and Select: **None** to remove the current selection. Raise the Tolerance in the Options Palette and repeat steps 2 through 5.

Selecting a Range of Color

Select: **Similar** can also be used to select a range of subtly varying color, similar to the Magic Wand Tool and Select: Color Range. Instead of selecting one color as the basis for the command, make a series of selections that contain the desired range.

1. Set a Tolerance in the Magic Wand Tool Options Palette. The final value depends on the level of contrast that exists between the targeted colors. Typically, a value between 16 and 32 is sufficient. Never use a value of 0.

2. Use the Marquee Tool to create a series of selections throughout the targeted color range. Make sure the selections only contain the colors you want included in the final selection.

3. Choose Select: **Similar**. Every occurrence of each selected color value is added to the selection.

4. If necessary, add to or remove from the selection using the Lasso Tool.

Chapter 13: The Filter Menu

Filter: Distort: Displace

Embossing with a Displacement Map

Although this technique works on any image, simpler images like large block type produce the most realistic embossing effect.

1. Set the foreground and background colors to the default setting.

2. Use the Type Tool to add type to the image. When it appears in a new layer, position it appropriately.

3. Create a new layer directly beneath the type layer. Since the Emboss filter does not affect transparent pixels, you must place the type on a white background.

4. Fill the new layer with white by holding down the (Command) [Control] keys and pressing Delete.

5. Click the type layer in the **Layers Palette** and choose Layer: **Merge Down**. This combines the type with the white layer, allowing the Emboss filter to work properly.

6. Apply Filter: Stylize: **Emboss** to the type layer.

7. Select Layer: **Duplicate Layer**. In the Duplicate Layer dialog, choose New Document and click OK.

8. When the new image appears, save it using the Photoshop file format and close it.

9. In the original image, hide or delete the embossed type layer.

10. Activate the layer you wish to displace.

11. Choose Filter: Distort: **Displace**. Select the embossed type file and click OK. The separate type file displaces the pixels, as though the embossed text were actually a three-dimensional object being pushed into the image (see Figure A-34).

Figure A-34: An image before displacing (upper l), the displacement map (upper r), and the final result

Filter: Render: Lens Flare

Creating Editable Flares

Lens flares are much more useful when they exist as separate layers, where they can be moved and adjusted without affecting the underlying image. Since this filter cannot be applied to a layer containing transparent pixels, you must use a blend mode's neutral color. Follow these steps:

1. Choose Layer: **New Layer**.

2. Under the Mode pop-up, choose Hard Light.

3. Check the Fill with Neutral Color box and click OK. The new layer appears to be filled with transparent pixels, but in fact, it's filled with 50% gray—a color that only appears transparent when the Hard Light blend mode is chosen.

4. Apply Filter: Render: **Lens Flare**. The flare appears the same as any other, but this one can be repositioned, edited and adjusted independently of other layers.

5. To soften the effect of the flare, set the blend mode to Overlay or Soft Light, which share the same neutral color. Or, reduce the layer's opacity.

NOTE

Lens Flare only affects visible pixels. If you apply a flare close to the image edge and then reposition it, a harsh transition appears. For best results, apply the flare to the center of the image, then move it to the proper location.

Filter: Stylize: Emboss

Embossing Using Blend Modes

While this technique does not displace pixels, it creates a very convincing embossing effect by adding highlights and shadows. This technique requires two image layers. One layer produces the emboss effect, the other receives it. The layer producing the effect must be positioned over the other in the **Layers Palette**.

1. Apply Filter: Stylize: **Emboss** to the appropriate layer.

2. If any red and green details result from the Emboss filter, remove them by applying Image: Adjust: **Desaturate**. These are intended for a displacement map, and will interfere with this technique.

3. In the Layers Palette, choose Overlay from the blend mode pop-up. For a softer effect, choose Soft Light. For a more severe effect, choose Hard Light (see Figure A-35).

4. Invert the embossed layer to reverse the direction of the emboss.

Figure A-35: Embossed text in Normal (upper l), Overlay (upper r), Soft Light (lower l), and Hard Light modes (lower r)

Chapter 14: The View Menu

View: New View

Creating a Reference Window

1. Open an image and choose View: **New View**.
2. Set the magnification of the new window to 100% and place it in the upper right corner of your monitor.
3. Position the original image so it overlaps the reference window as little as possible.
4. Edit the original image, clicking on the reference window when you want to review your work.
5. When you no longer need the additional view, discard one of them by clicking its Close box. It disappears without asking to be saved.

Creating a CMYK Preview Window

1. Open an RGB or Lab image.
2. Choose View: New View to create a reference window.
3. Set the reference window to CMYK Preview. Only the active window is affected by this command.
4. Continue editing the original image. Refer to the reference window to see how the changes will affect the final color.

View: Show Rulers

Repositioning the Zero Origin

1. Click and drag from the crisscross icon in the upper left of the image, where the two rulers meet. Two crosshairs representing the X axis and Y axis converge on the cursor.
2. Using the rulers or image contents as a guide, release the crosshairs at the desired position. The rulers reflect the change.
3. Perform your desired action. The measurements in the **Info Palette** are based on the new zero origin.
4. Reset the zero origin to its default by double-clicking the crisscross icon.

NOTE

You can constrain the crosshairs to the ruler tickmarks by holding down the Shift key while dragging.

Chapter 18: The Swatches Palette

Organizing Swatches

If you have defined your own colors (as opposed to importing one of Photoshop's preset palettes), it is difficult to read the color content of individual swatches. An unorganized palette quickly leads to confusion. If defining your own ranges of color is an essential part of your work, organizing your different swatch lists saves time and energy. In the following example, we create a series of swatches from scratch:

1. Move the cursor to the upper left swatch, hold down the (Command) [Control] key, and click. Continue clicking until all swatches are removed, leaving an empty, white palette.
2. Set the foreground color to black.

3. Click in the swatches palette to add a black swatch. Continue clicking until the palette is filled with 20 to 25 rows.

4. As you add new colors to the swatches palette, hold down the Shift key and click the black swatches.

5. When all the swatches are created, save the list into your Color Palettes folder. This way, black swatches can be used as dividing lines between colors, allowing you to organize them logically, intuitively, and usefully. In the examples below, we've created gray ramps, CMYK color combinations, and variations of corporate colors (see Figure A-36).

NOTE

Unfortunately, there's no easy command for deleting all swatches at once. Once you've manually deleted all the existing swatches, choose Save Swatches from the Swatches Palette submenu. Save the file into Photoshop's Color Palettes folder, in the Goodies folder. In the future, instead of deleting swatches by hand, choose Replace Swatches from the submenu and load this file. All swatches are instantly removed.

Creating Custom Swatches for the Web

When creating web graphics, there are two essential color issues. First, many images contain indexed palettes, or a limited number of colors. Second, only a limited number of RGB values can display consistently over the Web.

There are two strategies you can employ when working with Web graphics:

- When editing an Indexed Color image with a custom palette, you can create a list of swatches based on those specific color values. When editing future images, you then have easy access to the exact RGB values.

- Since the major browsers support the same 216-color Web Palette, you can create a list of swatches based on those specific values.

Loading an Indexed Palette

Whenever an image is converted to Indexed Color, the reduced number of colors is written into a color table. This table can be saved to your hard disk and loaded into the Swatches Palette:

1. Convert an RGB image to Indexed Color.

2. If necessary, edit the existing colors in the Image: Mode: **Color Table** dialog.

3. In the same dialog, click the Save button and save the color palette. Name it descriptively and save it into Photoshop's Color Palettes folder.

4. Click OK.

5. Under the Swatches Palette submenu, select Replace Swatches. Load the reduced color palette.

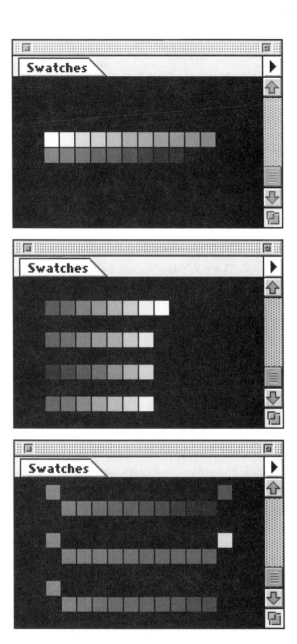

Figure A-36: The upper palette contains black values in 5% increments. The center palette contains a series of Trumatch presets that give the illusion of different tints. The bottom palette contains CMYK combinations (in this case, cyan to magenta, cyan to yellow, cyan to black)

NOTE

Although 256 colors are loaded into the Swatches Palette, the colors beyond the range defined in the Indexed Color dialog appear as black, or R: 0, G: 0, B: 0.

Loading the Browser-Safe Palette

Photoshop does not ship with the 216-color Web Palette in its Color Palettes folder, but you can easily create one:

1. Convert any RGB image to Indexed Color.

2. In the Indexed Color dialog, select Web from the Palette pop-up.

3. Click OK.

4. Select Image: Mode: **Color Table**. Although the Table pop-up lists Custom as the current option, the table itself contains the 216 browser-safe RGB values.

5. Click the Save button and save the color palette. Name it descriptively and save it into Photoshop's Color Palettes folder.

6. Load these colors into the Swatches Palette by choosing Replace Swatches from the Swatches Palette submenu.

Now, when you edit a GIF or JPEG image, you can ensure that any new colors you add are browser-safe. This reduces the amount of on-screen dithering that occurs when the image is viewed in a browser.

Loading Print-Oriented Libraries

Photoshop includes preset palettes for color matching systems like the Pantone and Trumatch libraries. These files are found in Photoshop's Color Palettes folder. To load a library into the Swatches Palette, follow these steps:

1. Choose Replace Swatches from the Swatches Palette submenu.

2. Load your desired color library.

3. To help find the appropriate color name, move the cursor over the different swatches. As you do so, the tab of the Swatches Palette displays the name of the color beneath the cursor.

Most color libraries are so large, however, that little efficiency is gained by loading them into the Swatches Palette. If you have already determined the specific colors you need, define them one by one in the Color Picker and load them into a custom swatch list, as described earlier in "Organizing Swatches."

When loading color libraries into the Swatches Palette, follow these guidelines:

- **Always work in CMYK mode when specifying process colors**. Pantone, Trumatch, and other print color matching systems are designed to work in CMYK mode, although their color swatches can be loaded regardless of the current

---

color mode. If a color is loaded and applied to an RGB image, the color values will change when the image is converted to CMYK.

- **Choose colors from a printed swatch book before selecting them from the Swatches palette.** Color libraries are based on swatch books that provide physical evidence of a color's printed appearance. Referring to these samples is the only accurate way to select preset CMYK values.

- **Avoid the Pantone spot color libraries.** They are only translated to CMYK values. Even if you attempt to use them as part of a duotone image—which allows you to define PMS colors—you have no control over the printed result.

Loading Swatches from Adobe Illustrator 7 Graphics

In theory, it's possible to drag and drop color swatches from the latest version of Illustrator into Photoshop. In practice, this technique skews the color values. There is, however, a technique you can use to generate a custom swatch list based on an Illustrator graphic:

1. Open an image in Illustrator 7 that contains the colors you want to use. If necessary, include some additional colored boxes to ensure all your desired colors are present.

2. Select File: **Export**.

3. Under the File Format pop-up, choose GIF89a.

4. Click OK.

5. Open the exported image in Photoshop.

6. Select Image: Mode: **Color Table**. The colors you defined in Illustrator are listed in the color table.

7. Click the Save button to save the color palette. Name it descriptively and place it into Photoshop's Color Palettes folder.

Chapter 20: The Layers Palette

Loading Layer-Based Selections

You can create an active selection based on the contents of the Layers Palette:

- **From an image layer.** Hold down the (Command) [Control] key and click the image layer thumbnail. The selection outline is based on the non-transparent contents. Semi-transparent pixels result in partial selections, based on the degree of their transparency.

- **From a layer mask.** Hold down the (Command) [Control] key and click the layer mask thumbnail. Unmasked areas—represented by white pixels—form the basis of the selection. Gray pixels result in partial selections.

- **From an adjustment layer.** Hold down the (Command) [Control] key and click the layer mask thumbnail. Similar to the layer mask option, unmasked areas form the basis of the selection, and gray pixels result in partial selections. If the adjustment layer mask has not been edited, the resulting selection includes the entire image window.

- **Add to an existing selection.** With a selection already active, hold down the (Command-Shift) [Control-Shift] keys and click a layer thumbnail.

- **Subtract from an existing selection.** With a selection already active, hold down the (Option-Command) [Alt-Control] keys and click a layer thumbnail.

- **Intersect with an existing selection.** With a selection already active, hold down the (Option-Command-Shift) [Alt-Control-Shift] keys and click a layer thumbnail.

NOTE

If the contents of an image layer contain an anti-aliased or feathered edge, the resulting selection contains a soft edge as well.

Grouping Layers (Creating a Clipping Group)

1. In the Layers Palette, position the clipping image at the bottom of the remaining layers of the group. The clipping layer must be an image layer.

2. Hold down the (Option) [Alt] key and click the dotted line separating the clipping layer and the layer directly above it.

3. To add multiple layers, drag a layer between two items of an existing group. Or, position a layer's item above an existing group and (Option) [Alt]-click the dotted line separating the new layer and the item below it.

Ungrouping Layers

- **Single layers.** (Option) [Alt]-click the dotted line between grouped layers.

- **Single layers by dragging.** In the Layers Palette, drag a member of a clipping group between two ungrouped layers.

- **All layers.** (Option) [Alt]-click the dotted line above the clipping layer.

Copying a Layer to Another Image

1. Open both images in Photoshop. Arrange them so both are visible.

2. Activate the image containing the layer to be copied.

3. Click-drag the layer from the Layers Palette.

4. Drop it directly into the window of the second image. When the image border highlights, release the mouse button.

> **NOTE**
>
> If the two images share the same width and height, the layer's contents maintain their original position. Otherwise, you must manually position the new layer.

Creating a Soft Drop-Shadow

1. Isolate the image that will project the shadow into its own image layer. Typically, drawing an anti-aliased selection and choosing Layer: New: **Layer Via Copy** is sufficient.

2. In the Layers Palette, duplicate the new layer by dragging its item onto the New Layer button. The copy appears over the original (see Figure A-37).

 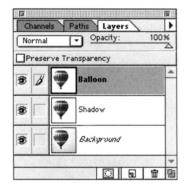

Figure A-37: Duplicating the isolated image layer

3. Hide the duplicate layer from view. This layer will cast the shadow.

4. Activate the visible layer. This layer will become the shadow.

5. Check the Preserve Transparency box.

6. Click the Default Colors icon in the toolbar, setting the foreground color to black and the background color to white.

7. Hold down the (Option) [Alt] key and press Delete to fill the non-transparent pixels with black.

8. Uncheck the Preserve Transparency box.

9. To soften the edges of the shadow, apply Filter: Blur: **Gaussian Blur**. Depending on the resolution of the image, a value between 4 and 12 is usually sufficient (see Figure A-38).

10. Click the View box of the hidden layer.

11. Leaving the shadow layer activated, position it using the Move Tool.

Figure A-38: Filling and blurring the shadow layer

12. If desired, lower the opacity of the shadow layer. This lightens the shadow, and allows any underlying colors to show through (see Figure A-39).

Link the two layers, or activate the top layer and choose Layer: Merge Down.

Figure A-39: Positioning the shadow and lowering its opacity

NOTE

If the shadow is going to be cast onto underlying colored pixels, choose Multiply from the blend mode pop-up before merging. This results in smoother color transitions, especially when the image is in CMYK mode.

Chapter 21: The Channels Palette

Combining Mask Channels

1. Open the Channel Options dialog for each button by double-clicking on them in the Channels Palette. Make sure both channels are set to Color Indicates Masked Areas.

2. Click the Default Colors icon in the toolbar, setting the foreground color to black and the background color to white.

3. In the Channels Palette, activate the channel you wish to combine with another channel.

4. Click the Load Channel as Selection button.

5. Activate the channel you wish to combine with your first channel.

6. To add the contents of the first channel, press (Option) [Alt]-Delete. This results in a channel that selects the same areas as both channels combined. To subtract the contents of the first channel, press Delete.

7. If desired, discard the first channel.

Creating complex masks

This technique works with complex images over simple backgrounds, such as flying hair or the nap of a sweater. The surrounding image information can ultimately determine your success—it's easier to mask the hair of a model who was photographed in front of a bluescreen, as opposed to a leafy tree.

1. Inspect each color channel individually. Choose the channel that offers the highest contrast between the object you wish to select and the background you are trying to separate it from. Leave that channel active (see Figure A-40).

Figure A-40: Inspecting the color channels

2. Duplicate the channel by dragging its Channels Palette item onto the New Channel button. The copy appears as a new mask channel. (For this example, the Channel Options dialog—accessed by double-clicking the channel—is set to Color Indicates: Masked Areas—see Figure A-41.)

Figure A-41: Duplicating the channel with highest contrast

3. Choose Filter: Sharpen: **Unsharp Mask**. Instead of adding crispness to the image, you can use this filter to accentuate the edges found in the channel. For best results, use a very high Amount setting, a Radius of 7 to 10, and a Threshold of roughly 50 (see Figure A-42).

Figure A-42: Accenting edges with a high Unsharp Mask value

4. Use **Image: Adjust: Levels** to reduce the levels of gray in the mask channel. The goal is to end up with as much black in the background and white in the image as possible. For best results, move both the shadow and highlight slider toward the center of the histogram. Pay attention to the edges of the image to make sure they stay consistent with the color composite. Click OK when finished (see Figure A-43).

5. Use the Lasso Tool to select large areas of unwanted information. When selecting part of the background, press (Option) [Alt]-Delete to fill with white. When selecting part of the mask area, press Delete to fill with white (see Figure A-44).

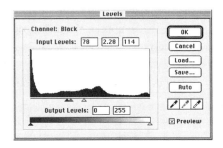

Figure A-43: Reducing the amount of gray with Levels

Figure A-44: Cleaning up the mask with the Lasso Tool

Figure A-45: Refining the mask with the Pencil Tool

6. For fine details, use the Pencil Tool to complete the mask. Paint any pixels outside the masked object black, and paint any pixels inside the object white.

If desired, click the View box of the composite channel to see the mask channel as a transparent overlay. This allows you to use the actual image information as a guide (see Figure A-45).

7. Activate the composite channel to view the entire image.

8. (Command) [Control]-click the mask channel to load it as a selection.

9. Choose Layer: New: **Layer Via Copy** to add the selection to a new image layer, or drag the selection into another open image (see Figure A-46).

Figure A-46: The masked element, copied to another image

Defining Spot Colors in Photoshop

Traditionally, spot colors are applied over Photoshop images after they are brought into page layout programs or vector-based drawing programs. Unfortunately, when you do this, you have none of Photoshop's abilities to edit the spot color. Using a Photoshop plug-in called PlateMaker (from In Software), you can use channels to define spot colors and save the Photoshop as a DCS file which can imported into Quark or other page layout program, and output on most imagesetters.

1. Select **New Channel** from the Channels Palette menu.

2. Name the new channel after the desired spot color. Use the same naming convention used by your page layout program. Do not attempt this technique without having a Pantone color swatch book on hand, since it is physically impossible to represent most spot colors on screen.

3. Click the color swatch to choose a new color. This will give you a rough preview of the spot color when you view the channel with the rest of the color channels. Try to choose a color close to the actual spot color.

4. Set the Opacity to 100% and click OK.

5. Click the View box for the color composite to view the image while you edit the channel. It's important to note that steps 2–5 have no affect on the function of the channel, only on how you preview it. These steps are optional, but they help to give you a better idea of what the printed image will look like.

6. Create the image in the mask channel to be used as the spot color. You can use one of the paint tools, paste information into the channel, or simply create a selection and fill.

7. If you do not wish for the spot color to overprint, you need to adjust your CMYK image appropriately. Activate the color composite. Load the spot color channel as a selection, and fill any area you do not wish to overprint with white.

8. Save the image, and export it using the PlateMaker plug-in.

Creating a Vignette

At the turn of the last century, a popular photographic technique was to make a portrait oval, fading to white at the edges. You can recreate this effect using channels:

1. Open a scanned portrait.

2. Select the head using the elliptical Marquee tool, leaving enough extra space around it to fade the image.

3. Save the selection by clicking on the Save Selection as Channel button.

4. Drop the active selection after it has been saved by choosing Select: **None**.

5. Activate the new channel by clicking it in the Channels Palette.

6. Choose Filter: **Gaussian Blur** and blur the oval mask. This has the same effect as feathering an active selection, but it provides an interactive preview of the amount of the feather. The higher the Radius, the softer the edge.

7. Choose Image: Adjust: **Invert** so the background is selected upon loading, instead of the portrait.

8. Activate the composite channel by clicking its item in the Channels Palette.

9. Load the selection by (Command) [Control]-clicking its item in the Channels Palette.

10. Fill the selection with white. The portrait is now in an oval, fading to white (see Figure A-47).

Creating a Fade from One Image to Another

Apply a gradient to a mask channel to create a fade from one image to another. Use this technique in lieu of creating a layer mask.

1. Open a source image and a target image. Make the source image the active image window.

2. Choose **New Channel** from the Channel Palette submenu. Name the channel Gradient, and choose Color Indicates: Masked Area.

3. Select the **Gradient Tool**. In the Gradient Options Palette, choose Gradient: Black, White, and Type: Linear.

Figure A-47: An image before (l) and after (r) creating a vignette

4. Drag a gradient across the channel. Make sure that the white end of the gradient is over the portion of the image you want opaque, and the black end of the gradient is over the portion of the image you want to fade out.

5. Activate the composite channel by clicking its item in the Channels Palette.

6. Load the Gradient channel as a selection by (Command) [Control]-clicking its item in the Channels Palette.

7. Choose Edit: **Copy**.

8. Activate the image window of the image you wish to paste into.

9. Choose Edit: **Paste**. The pasted image appears to fade into the target image.

Partial Filtering

By creating a stylized mask channel, you have great control over which image pixels receive the effects of a filter. In this example, we create the impression of an image fading into clouds.

1. Open an image. Choose New Channel from the Channels Palette submenu. In the Channel Options, select Color Indicates: Masked Area.

2. Select the Gradient tool. In the Gradient Tool Options Palette, set Gradient to Black, White and Type to Radial.

3. Draw a gradient in the channel, starting at the point you wish to preserve, and ending where you wish the image to fade completely.

4. Activate the composite channel by clicking its item in the Channels Palette.

5. Load the mask channel by (Command) [Control]-clicking its item in the Channels Palette.

6. After setting the desired foreground and background colors, apply Filter: Render: **Clouds**. The image at the center of the gradient is unaffected, but fades into the cloud effect toward the image edges (see Figure A-48).

7. Try this technique with other distorting or artistic filters.

Figure A-48: The mask channel (l) and the filtered effect

Drop Shadows on Full Color Backgrounds

When you import an image with a drop-shadow into a page layout program, it has certain limitations. Most obvious is that the shadow cannot be placed over other colored information. Compounding this problem is the fact that you cannot save a soft-edged shadow as part of a clipping path. In a print project, the only way to truly create a soft-edged drop shadow on a colored background is to combine both images in Photoshop. Some people don't like this idea. A background image may be too large to work with efficiently, and once the shadow is created, it's impossible to re-position. We offer this solution, based on an ancient method of creating drop-shadows:

1. Open the image that will cast the shadow. It should already be saved with a clipping path.

2. In the Paths Palette, activate the clipping path and click the Selection button to select the image.

3. Offset the selection by dragging the selection path.

4. Choose Select: **Inverse**. This selects everything but the image.

5. Click the Save Selection as Channel button in the Channels palette.

6. Activate the new channel and choose Select: **None**. You should see a sharp edged, solid-black version of the original image.

7. Soften the edges to taste by applying Filter: Blur: **Gaussian Blur**.

8. Choose Duplicate Channel from the Channels palette submenu. Choose New as a destination and name the file "Shadow".

9. In the original image file, delete the additional channel and close the file without saving.

10. Convert the new grayscale image to a bitmap, choosing Image: Mode: **Bitmap**. In the Bitmap dialog, choose Diffusion Dither under Method.

11. Save the image as a TIFF.

12. In your page layout program, position the original image and its shadow together. If possible, group the two images. Being a bitmap, the shadow will

automatically overprint the colored background, creating the illusion of a true drop-shadow.

Chapter 22: The Paths Palette

Combining Two Subpaths into One Path

There is no automatic command for combining the subpaths of two different paths. You can simply cut and paste, but Photoshop does not retain the exact location of the copied subpath. Follow these steps instead:

1. Activate the path you are going to cut.

2. Select the subpath to display the individual points.

3. Choose View: **Show Rulers**. Position a horizontal and vertical ruler guide so they intersect on one particular point.

4. Select the entire path by (Option) [Alt]-clicking it with the Arrow Tool.

5. Choose Edit: **Cut**.

6. Activate the path containing the remaining subpaths.

7. Choose Edit: **Paste**. The previous path appears in the center of the window.

8. Choose View: **Snap to Guides**. When you drag a path, only its points snap to the ruler guides.

9. Drag the path so its targeted point snaps to the crosshairs placed in Step 3.

Filling a Path

• **Filling an open subpath.** Photoshop automatically "closes" its endpoints with a straight line. If you do not want this effect, complete the path using the Pen Tool.

• **Filling a path within a selection.** If you fill a path that overlaps an active selection, only the area inside the selection is affected by the command.

• **Filling intersecting paths.** If two subpaths overlap each other, the intersecting area is ignored by the Fill Path command.

Stroking a Path

• **Stroke with multiple widths.** When you stroke a path, the specified tool only uses the path as a guide. Therefore, you can apply a series of brushes and colors to create a multicolored stroke. For best results, apply larger brushes before smaller brushes.

• **Paint only points.** When you use a brush with Spacing turned off, Photoshop does not trace the path. Rather, it applies one single brushstroke to every point comprising the subpaths.

Creating a Clipping Path

1. Trace the desired portion of an image using the Pen Tool.

2. Save and name the path.

3. Choose Clipping Path from the palette submenu. Choose the appropriate path name in the Path pop-up.

4. Save the image as an EPS file. In the EPS Options dialog, double-check the Clipping Path pop-up to make sure you selected the correct path name.

5. Import the image into another application.

As you create a clipping path, keep the following issues in mind:

- **Crop the image.** Crop the image as close to the clipping path as possible. If necessary, save a copy of the image before cropping, to preserve the original. Even though your output device only prints the information inside the clipping path, it still processes all of the "invisible" pixels.

- **Close the path.** Only use a closed path as a clipping path. If you define an open path, the two endpoints are automatically connected with a straight line, which may obscure part of the vital image area.

- **Keep the paths simple.** Paths containing a multitude of points take longer to output. Typically, a manually-drawn path contains fewer points—and causes fewer output-related problems—than a path automatically generated from an active selection.

- **Multiple Subpaths.** When a clipping path contains multiple subpaths, each one acts as a mask.

- **Intersecting Paths.** When a clipping path contains overlapping subpaths, the intersecting areas are left out of the mask. For example, if you draw a large path around a donut and a smaller path around its hole, only the information between the two paths displays and prints.

Chapter 23: The Actions Palette

Recording an Action

1. Choose New Action from the submenu, or press the New Action button.

2. Perform the commands you wish to record. For complex sequences, duplicate the image using **Image: Duplicate** and run a test before recording. Write down the dialog settings if necessary.

3. Click the Stop Recording button to complete the Action. If necessary, edit the Action using the remaining commands of the palette submenu.

Adding to a Preexiting Action

1. Select an Action or command.

2. Choose Start Recording from the palette submenu, or click the Record button.

3. Apply the commands you wish to record.

4. Click the Stop button. The new commands are added to the location you specified.

Using Record Again

1. Select the appropriate Action in the Actions Palette.

2. Choose Record Again from the palette submenu.

3. Perform the new series of commands you wish to record.

4. Click the Stop button. The former list of commands is replaced with the newly recorded sequence.

Using Record "Command Title" Again

This command replaces only a selected command within an Action:

1. Select the recorded command in the Actions Palette.

2. Choose Record "Command Title" Again.

3. Perform the command you wish to re-record.

4. Click Stop. The newly recorded command replaces the originally recorded command.

Using Insert Menu Item

1. Record an Action.

2. In the Actions Palette, click the Show arrow to view all the commands in the Action.

3. Select the command just above the desired position of the new item.

4. Choose Insert Menu Item from the palette submenu to open the Insert Menu dialog.

5. Set the desired item by choosing it from its menu, just as if you were applying the command. This does not affect the open image—its name is simply recorded in the Menu Item field.

6. Click OK to insert the new item into the Action.

NOTE

The Insert Menu command can be used while an Action is recording. When you reach a point in the recording where you wish to have a command open its dialog instead of applying recorded settings, select Insert Menu and choose the desired command. Click OK to add the command and resume recording.

Using Insert Stop

1. Record an Action.
2. In the Actions Palette, click the Show arrow to view all the commands in the Action.
3. Select the command just above the desired position of the Stop.
4. Select Insert Stop from the palette submenu.
5. In the Record Stop dialog, enter a message and click the Allow Continue box, if necessary.
6. Click OK to close the dialog.

Preparing a Batch Process

Before selecting this command to start a batch process, you must prepare your Actions and files:

1. Record the Action that the Batch command will apply to your images.
2. Add a File: **Save As** command at the end of the Action. This step is only required when you wish to change the file formats of the images. When you record this part of the Action, the only thing that matters is the option in the File Format pop-up. The file name and destination are overridden by the Batch command. If you do not need to set a new file format, ignore this step.
3. Create a Source Folder, or a single folder to contain all the images you wish to process. A batch only recognizes one folder at a time. If you place additional folders in the Source Folder, they will not be recognized.
4. Create a Destination Folder, or an empty folder to contain the new images after batch processing. You could use any existing folder, but with a new folder you can quickly compare the new and original files to make sure they were processed correctly. If the Source folder is used as the Destination folder, the original images will be overwritten.

Running a Batch Process

After recording the Action and collecting your files as described in the Actions Palette, follow these steps to batch process a series of images:

1. Choose Batch from the palette submenu.
2. From the Source pop-up, select Folder or Import. If you have a Source Folder, select Folder and click the choose button to point it out to the command. If you are importing images, select Import and choose a Plug-in from the From pop-up.
3. Choose the desired Action from the Action pop-up.
4. Choose Folder from the Destination pop-up. Click the choose button to target the right folder.
5. Check the Override Action "Save In" Commands box.

6. Click OK to run the batch. Keep an eye on the first image to make sure the Action runs properly.

Recreating the Commands Palette

Many long-time Photoshop users lament the passing of the Commands Palette. It was similar to the Actions Palette in Button view: it stored commands in an easy-to-use palette and let you assign F-keys to each one.

It had limited functionality, however. The effect of selecting from the Commands Palette was the same as choosing a command straight from the menu: only single commands were used, and you could not store any settings.

If the Command Palette offered everything you needed and you have no desire to create complex Actions, you can simulate it with the Actions Palette:

1. Choose Clear Actions from the palette submenu to remove all multi-command Actions.

2. Press the New Action button or choose New Action from the Actions Palette menu.

3. Name the Action after the menu command it will perform, assigning an F-key and color, if desired.

4. Click Record.

5. Immediately press the Stop button or choose Stop Recording from the Actions menu. Otherwise, you would record the command's settings.

6. With the new Action still selected in the Actions Palette, choose Insert Menu Item from the palette submenu.

7. Choose the desired Menu Item. Click OK. The command will now behave exactly as it would have in the Commands Palette.

8. Choose Button Mode under the palette submenu. This gives the palette a similar appearance to the Commands Palette and makes it show the Function key assignments. Switch back to List Mode if you wish to add more commands to the palette.

9. Apply a command by clicking it in the Actions Palette or typing its F-key.

APPENDIX B

Photoshop Shortcuts

Toolbar Shortcuts

Action	Macintosh Shortcuts	Windows Shortcuts
Marquee Tool	Type "M"	Type "M"
Crop Tool	Type "C'	Type "C'
Move Tool	Type "V"	Type "V"
Lasso Tool/ Polygonal Lasso Tool	Type "L"	Type "L"
Magic Wand Tool	Type "W"	Type "W"
Draw marquee from Enter	Option-drag	Alt-drag
Constrain marquee to square or circle	Shift-drag marquee	Shift-drag marquee
Move marquee while drawing	Press space bar while drawing	Press space bar while drawing
Draw straight selection outline	Option-click with Lasso Tool	Alt-click with Lasso Tool
Add to existing selection	Hold Shift key while making selection	Hold Shift key while making selection
Subtract from existing selection	Hold Option key while making selection	Hold Alt key while making selection
Intersect with existing selection	Hold Option-Shift while making selection	Hold Alt-Shift while making selection
Add text selection outlines to existing selection	Shift-click with Type Mask Tool	Shift-click with Type Mask Tool

Shortcuts

Action	Macintosh Shortcuts	Windows Shortcuts
Remove text selection outlines from existing selection	Option-click with Type Mask Tool	Alt-click with Type Mask Tool
Intersect text selection outlines with existing selection	Option-Shift-click with Type Mask Tool	Alt-Shift-click with Type Mask Tool
Move contents of selection or layer	Command-drag with any Tool, or drag with Move Tool	Control-drag with any Tool, or drag with Move Tool
Constrain movement vertically or horizontally	Press Shift while dragging	Press Shift while dragging
Move selection in 1 pixel increments	Command-arrow key	Control-arrow key
Move selection in 10 pixel increments	Command-Shift-arrow key	Control-Shift-arrow key
Duplicate selection	Option-Command-drag selection with any Tool, or Option-drag with Clone Tool	Alt-Control-drag selection with any Tool, or Alt-drag with Clone Tool
Duplicate selection and offset 1 pixel	Command-Option-arrow key	Control-Alt-arrow key
Duplicate selection and offset 10 pixels	Command-Option-Shift-arrow key	Control-Alt-Shift-arrow key
Duplicate selection into different image window	Command-Drag to different image window with selection Tool	Control-Drag to different image window with selection Tool
Move selection outline	Drag when selection tool is active	Drag when selection tool is active
Move selection outline in 1 pixel increments	Arrow key when selection tool is active	Arrow key when selection tool is active
Move selection outline in 10 pixel increments	Shift-arrow key when selection tool is active	Shift-arrow key when selection tool is active
Move selection outline to other image window	Drag selection outline to other image window with selection tool	Drag selection to other image window with selection tool
Float selection	Command-Option-up arrow	Control-Alt-up arrow
Defloat selection	Command-E	Control-E

Action	Macintosh Shortcuts	Windows Shortcuts
Set opacity of floating selection in multiples of 1%	Press 2 number keys in a row quickly while selection tool is active	Press 2 number keys in a row quickly while selection tool is active
Set opacity floating selection in multiples of 10%	Press 1 through 10 while selection tool is active	Press 1 through 10 while selection tool is active

Paint Tools

Action	Macintosh Shortcuts	Windows Shortcuts
Paint or edit in straight line	Click, then Shift-click	Click, then Shift-click
Display Crosshair cursor	Caps Lock	Caps Lock
Display Options palette	Return	Return
Set opacity, pressure, or exposure to multiples of 1%	Press 2 numbers in a row quickly while paint/edit tool is selected	Press 2 numbers in a row quickly while paint/edit tool is selected
Set opacity, pressure, or exposure to multiples of 10%	Press 1 through 10 while paint/edit tool is selected	Press 1 through 10 while paint/edit tool is selected
Airbrush Tool	Type "A"	Type "A"
Paintbrush Tool	Type "B"	Type "B"
Eraser Tool	Type "E"	Type "E"
Revert Image with magic eraser	Option-drag with eraser	Alt-drag with eraser
Cycle through eraser styles	Option-click on Eraser Tool, or press E key	Alt-click on Eraser Tool, or press E key
Pencil Tool	Type "Y"	Type "Y"
Rubber Stamp Tool	Type "S"	Type "S"
Specify an area to clone	Option-click with Rubber Stamp Tool	Alt-click with Rubber Stamp Tool
Cycle through rubber stamp Options	Option-click rubber stamp or press S key	Alt-click rubber stamp or press S key
Smudge Tool	Type "U"	Type "U"
Sample foreground color while smudging	Option-drag with Smudge Tool	Alt-drag with Smudge Tool

Focus Tools

Action	Macintosh Shortcuts	Windows Shortcut
Switch Blur/Sharpen Tool	Option-click Blur/Sharpen Tool, or type R key	Alt-click Blur/Sharpen Tool, or type R key
Sharpen Tool	Type "R"	Type "R"
Blur Tool	Type "R"	Type "R"

Tone Tools

Action	Macintosh Shortcuts	Windows Shortcuts
Dodge Tool	Type "O"	Type "O"
Burn Tool	Type "O"	Type "O"
Sponge Tool	Type "O"	Type "O"
Cycle through Toning Tools	Option-click Dodge/Burn/Sponge Tool or click "O"	Alt-click Dodge/Burn/Sponge Tool or click "O"
Darken with Dodge Tool	Option-drag with Dodge Tool	Alt-drag with Dodge Tool
Lighten with Burn Tool	Option-drag with Burn Tool	Alt-drag with Burn Tool

Special Tools

Action	Macintosh Shortcuts	Windows Shortcuts
Select Pen Tool	Type "P"	Type "P"
Move selected point	Drag point with Arrow Tool or Command-drag with Pen Tool	Drag point with Arrow Tool or Control-drag with Pen Tool
Select multiple points in path	Shift-click point with arrow or Command-Shift-click with Pen Tool	Shift-click point with arrow or Control-Shift-click with Pen Tool
Select entire path	Option-click on path with arrow, or Command-Option-click with Pen Tool	Alt-click on path with arrow, or Control-Alt-click with Pen Tool
Clone path	Option-Drag path with arrow, or Command-Option-drag with Pen Tool	Alt-Drag path with arrow, or Control-Alt-drag with Pen Tool
Convert corner to curve or curve to corner	Control-drag path with arrow, or Command-Option drag with Pen Tool	Control-drag path with arrow, or Control-Alt drag with Pen Tool
Convert corner to directional change	Control-drag handle with arrow, or Command-Control-drag with Pen Tool	Control-drag handle with arrow, or Control-drag with Pen Tool

Action	Macintosh Shortcuts	Windows Shortcuts
Insert point in path	Command-Option-click on segment with Arrow Tool or Control-click with Pen Tool	Control-Alt-click on segment with Arrow Tool or Control-click with Pen Tool
Remove point from path	Command-Option-click on point with arrow Tool, or Control-click with Pen Tool	Control-Alt-click on point with arrow Tool, or Control-click with Pen Tool
Convert Path to selection outline	Press Enter when the selection is active, or Command-click on path name in Paths Palette	Press Enter when the selection is active, or Control-click on path name in Paths Palette
Add Path to selection	Shift-Enter or Command-Shift-click path name in Paths Palette	Shift-Enter or Control-Shift-click path name in Paths Palette
Subtract path from selection	Option-Enter, or Command-Option-click path name in Paths Palette	Alt-Enter, or Control-Alt-click path name in Paths Palette
Intersect path with selection	Shift-Option-Enter, or Command-Option-Shift-click path name in Paths Palette	Shift-Alt-Enter, or Control-Alt-Shift-click path name in Paths Palette
Stroke around perimeter of path	Press Enter when Paint or Edit tool is active	Press Enter when Paint or Edit tool is active
Fill from Saved around perimeter of path	Option-Enter when Eraser Tool is active	Alt-Enter when Eraser Tool is active
Save path	Double-click Work Path in Paths Palette	Double-click Work Path in Paths Palette
Hide Path	Command-Shift-H	Control-Shift-H
Deactivate path	Click in empty portion of Paths Palette	Click in empty portion of Paths Palette
Type Tool	Type "T"	Type "T"
Line Tool	Type "N"	Type "N"
Gradient Tool	Type "G"	Type "G"
Paint Bucket Tool	Type "K"	Type "K"
Eye Dropper Tool	Type "I"	Type "I"
Sample foreground color from image	Option-click with paint tool or click with eyedropper	Alt-click with paint tool or click with eyedropper
Sample background color from image	Option-click with eye dropper	Alt-click with eye dropper

Shortcuts

View Tools

Action	Macintosh Shortcuts	Windows Shortcuts
Hand Tool	Type "H"	Type "H"
Convert any tool to Hand Tool	Space bar with any Tool	Space bar with any Tool
Scroll up one screen	Page Up	Page Up
Scroll Down one screen	Page Down	Page Down
Scroll up	Shift-Page Up	Shift-Page Up
Scroll-down	Shift-Page Down	Shift-Page Down
Scroll up one frame in FilmStrip file	Shift-Page Up	Shift-Page Up
Pan to upper left corner	Home	Home
Pan to lower right corner	End	End
Zoom Tool	Type "Z"	Type "Z"
Zoom Out	Option-click with Zoom Tool	Alt-click with Zoom Tool
Zoom In with any Tool	Command-Space bar with Tool	Control-Space bar with any Tool
Zoom Out with any Tool	Command-Option-Space bar with any Tool	Control-Alt-Space bar with any Tool

Color Controls

Action	Macintosh Shortcuts	Windows Shortcuts
Reset Foreground/ Background colors to Black and White	Type "D"	Type "D"
Switch Foreground and Background Colors	Type "X"	Type "X"
Quick Mask Tools		
Quick Mask Mode/Edit Mode	Type "Q"	Type "Q"
View just Quick Mask	Click color composite View box	Click color composite View box
View Options		

Action	Macintosh Shortcuts	Windows Shortcuts
Scroll through Standard Screen/ Full Screen with Menu Bar/Full Screen	Type "F"	Type "F"

The File Menu

Action	Macintosh Shortcuts	Windows Shortcuts
New	Command-N	Control-N
New, with default settings	Option-Command-N	Alt-Control-N
Open	Command-O	Control-O
Close	Command-W	Control-W
Save	Command-S	Control-S
Save As	Command-Shift-S	Control-Shift-S
Save a Copy	Option-Command-S	Alt-Control-S
Page Setup	Command-Shift-P	Control-Shift-P
Print	Command-P	Control-P
Preferences	Command-K	Control-K
Open last Preferences used	Command-Option-K	Control-Alt-K
Quit	Command-Q	Control-Q

The Edit Menu

Action	Macintosh Shortcuts	Windows Shortcuts
Undo/Redo last action	Command-Z	Control-Z
Cut	Command-X	Control-X
Copy	Command-C	Control-C
Copy Merged	Command-Shift-C	Control-Shift-C
Paste	Command-V	Control-V
Paste Into	Command-Shift-V	Control-Shift-V
Clear	Press Delete when image layer is active	Press Delete when image layer is active
Fill	Shift-Delete	Shift-Delete
Fill selection or layer with foreground color	Option-Delete	Alt-Delete

Shortcuts

Action	Macintosh Shortcuts	Windows Shortcuts
Fill selection on background layer with background color	Delete	Delete
Fill selection on any layer with background color	Command-Delete	Control-Delete
Fill layer with background color (preserve transparency)	Shift-Command-Delete	Shift-Control-Delete

The Image Menu

Action	Macintosh Shortcuts	Windows Shortcuts
Levels	Command-L	Control-L
Levels, with last settings	Option-Command-L	Alt-Control-L
Auto Levels	Command-Shift-L	Control-Shift-L
Curves	Command-M	Control-M
Curves, with last settings	Option-Command M	Alt-Control M
Color Balance	Command-B	Control-B
Color Balance w/last settings	Option-Command B	Alt-Control B
Hue/Saturation	Command-U	Control-U
Hue/Saturation w/last settings	Option-Command-U	Alt-Control-U
Desaturate	Command-Shift-U	Control-Shift-U
Invert	Command-I	Control-I
Delete item in Layers, Channels, Paths or Actions palette (no warning)	Option-click Delete button in the palette	Alt-click Delete button in the palette
Duplicate (no dialog)	Option-Image: Duplicate	Alt-Image: Duplicate
Display small Option names in Calculations dialog	Option-Image: Calculations	Alt-Image: Calculations
Cancel current operation	Command-. (period) or Esc	Control-. (period) or Esc

Action	Macintosh Shortcuts	Windows Shortcuts
Open Adjust Command dialog with last used settings	Option-choose Command from Image: Adjust submenu	Alt-choose Control from Image: Adjust submenu

The Layer Menu

Action	Macintosh Shortcuts	Windows Shortcuts
New Layer via Copy	Command-J	Control-J
New Layer via Cut	Command-Shift-J	Control-Shift-J
New Layer from floating selection	Command-Shift-J or click New Layer button	Control-Shift-J or click New Layer button
New Adjustment Layer	Command-click New Layer button in Layers Palette	Control-click New Layer button in Layers Palette
Activate layer above current layer	Option-]	Alt-]
Activate layer below current layer	Option-[	Alt-[
Activate top layer	Option-Shift-]	Alt-Shift-]
Activate bottom layer	Option-Shift-[	Alt-Shift-[
Move layer in 1 pixel increments	Command-arrow key	Control-arrow key
Move layer in 10 pixel increments	Command-Shift-arrow key	Control-Shift-arrow key
Group with previous	Command-G, or Option-click line between layers	Control-G, or Alt-click line between layers
Ungroup	Command-Shift-G, or Option click dotted line between layers	Control-Shift-G, or Alt-click dotted line between layers
Numeric Transformation	Command-Shift-T	Control-Shift-T
Free Transform	Command-T	Control-T
Distort contents of transform box	Command-drag corner Control handle	Control-drag corner Control handle
Symmetrically distort adjacent corners	Option-Command-drag Control handle	Alt-Control-drag Control handle
Bring to Front	Command-Shift-]	Control-Shift-]
Bring Forward	Command-]	Control-]

Shortcuts

Action	Macintosh Shortcuts	Windows Shortcuts
Send to Back	Command-Shift-[	Control-Shift-[
Send Backward	Command-[	Control-[
Defloat	Command-E	Control-E
Merge Layer w/ underlying layer	Command-E	Control-E
Merge Linked Layers	Command-E	Control-E
Merge Visible Layers	Command-Shift-E	Control-Shift-E
Copy Merged	Command-Shift-C	Control-Shift-C
Copy contents of layer to underlying layer	Command-Option-E	Control-Option-E
Copy merged contents of all linked layers into active layer	Option-Command-Shift-C	Alt-Control-Shift-C

The Select Menu

Action	Macintosh Shortcuts	Windows Shortcuts
Select All	Command-A	Control-A
Select None	Command-Shift-D	Control-Shift-D
Inverse	Command-Shift-I	Control-Shift-I
Feather	Command-D	Control-D

The Filter Menu

Action	Macintosh Shortcuts	Windows Shortcuts
Filter	Command-F	Control-F
Filter with Dialog	Command-Option-F	Control-Alt-F
Fade Filter	Command-Shift-F	Control-Shift-F
Zoom in on Dialog Preview	Command-click	Control-click
Zoom out of Dialog Preview	Option-click	Alt-click
Increase current setting by 1 or .1	Up arrow	Up arrow
Decrease current setting by 1 or .1	Down arrow	Down arrow
Increase current setting by 10 or 1	Shift-up arrow	Shift-up arrow

Action	Macintosh Shortcuts	Windows Shortcuts
Decrease current setting by 10 or 1	Shift-down arrow	Shift-down arrow
Adjust angle value in 15 increments	Shift-drag on angle wheel	Shift-drag on angle wheel
Reset filter settings	Option-click Cancel button, or Option-Esc	Alt-click Cancel button, or Alt-Esc
Specify Lens Flare location numerically	Option-click Flare Center	Alt-click Flare Center

The View Menu

Action	Macintosh Shortcuts	Windows Shortcuts
CMYK Preview	Command-Y	Control-Y
Gamut Warning	Command-Shift-Y	Control-Shift-Y
Zoom In (resize window)	Command-+ (plus)	Control-+ (plus)
Zoom In (don't resize window)	Command-Space bar-click or Option-Command-+ (plus)	Control-Space bar-click or Alt-Control-+ (plus)
Zoom to specified zoom ratio	Command-Space bar-Drag or Command-Drag in Navigator Palette	Control-Space bar-Drag or Control-Drag in Navigator Palette
Zoom Out (don't resize window)	Option-Space bar-click or Command-Spacebar–– (minus)	Alt-Space bar-click or Control-Spacebar–– (minus)
Fit on Screen	Command-0 (zero) or double-click on Hand Tool	Control-0 (zero) or double-click on Hand Tool
Actual Pixels	Option-Command-0, or Double-click Zoom Tool	Alt-Control-0, or Double-click Zoom Tool
Apply zoom value but keep magnification box active	Shift-Return	Shift-Return
Hide/Show Edges	Command-H	Control-H
Hide/Show Path	Command-Shift-H	Control-Shift-H
Show/Hide Rulers	Command-R	Control-R
Show/Hide Guides	Command-; (semicolon)	Control-; (semicolon)
Create Guide	Drag from ruler	Drag from ruler

Shortcuts

Action	Macintosh Shortcuts	Windows Shortcuts
Move Guide	Command-drag guide, or drag guide with Move Tool	Control-drag guide, or drag guide with Move Tool
Horizontal/ vertical guide toggle	Option-click guide	Alt-click guide
Snap guide to ruler marks	Shift-drag guide	Shift-drag guide
Snap to Guides on/off	Command-Shift-; (semi-colon)	Control-Shift-; (semicolon)
Lock/Unlock Guides	Command-Option-; (semi-colon)	Control-Alt-; (semicolon)
Show/Hide Grid	Command-" (quote)	Control-" (quote)
Snap to Grid on/off	Command-Shift-" (quote)	Control-Shift-" (quote)
Edit Guide Color/Grid increments	Command-double-click guide, or double-click guide with Move Tool	Control-double-click guide, or double-click guide with Move Tool

Palettes

Action	Macintosh Shortcuts	Windows Shortcuts
Show/Hide all palettes including Toolbox	Tab	Tab
Show/Hide all palettes except Toolbox	Shift-Tab	Shift-Tab
Un-nest palette	Drag palette tab	Drag palette tab
Snap palette to edge of screen	Shift-click palette title bar	Shift-click palette title bar
Delete item in Layers, Channels, Paths or Actions palette (no Alert)	Option-click Delete button in the palette	Alt-click Delete button in the palette
Snap palette to edge of screen	Shift-click palette title bar	Shift-click palette title bar
Fully collapse palette	Option-click collapse box, or double-click palette tab	Alt-click collapse box, or double-click palette tab

The Info Palette

Action	Macintosh Shortcuts	Windows Shortcuts
Show/Hide Info Palette	F8	F8
Change default unit of measurement	Click on X,Y in Info Palette, or double-click ruler	Click on X,Y in Info Palette, or double-click ruler

The Options Palette

Action	Macintosh Shortcuts	Windows Shortcuts
Show/Hide Options Palette	Return	Return
Set opacity, pressure, or exposure to multiples of 1%	Press 2 numbers in a row quickly while paint/edit tool is selected	Press 2 numbers in a row quickly while paint/edit tool is selected
Set opacity, pressure, or exposure to multiples of 10%	Press 1 through 10 while paint/edit tool is selected	Press 1 through 10 while paint/edit tool is selected

The Color Palette

Action	Macintosh Shortcuts	Windows Shortcuts
Show/Hide Color Palette	F6	F6
Cycle through color bars	Shift-click color bar	Shift-click color bar
Specify new color bar	Command-click color bar	Control-click color bar
Change foreground color to color from color bar (Color Palette)	Click color bar	Click color bar
Change background color to color from bar (Color Palette)	Option-click color bar	Alt-click color bar

Shortcuts

The Swatches Palette

Action	Macintosh Shortcuts	Windows Shortcuts
Sample foreground color from Swatches Palette	Click on swatch	Click on swatch
Sample background color from Swatches Palette	Option-click on swatch	Alt-click on swatch
Remove swatch from palette	Command-click on swatch	Control-click on swatch
Change swatch to foreground color	Shift-click on swatch	Shift-click on swatch

The Brushes Palette

Action	Macintosh Shortcuts	Windows Shortcuts
Show/Hide Brushes Palette	F5	F5
Cycle through Brushes Palette	[or] (left or right bracket)	[or] (left or right bracket)
Switch to first brush in Brushes Palette	Shift-]	Shift-]
Switch to first brush in Brushes Palette	Shift-[	Shift-[
Delete brush from Brushes Palette	Command-click brush	Control-click brush
New Brush	Click in empty area of palette	Click in empty area of palette
Edit Brush	Double-click brush in palette	Double-click brush in palette

The Layers Palette

Action	Macintosh Shortcuts	Windows Shortcuts
Show/Hide Layers Palette	F7	F7
Activate specific layer	Option-Command-Shift-click on image in that layer	Alt-Control-Shift-click on image in that layer

Action	Macintosh Shortcuts	Windows Shortcuts
Preserve Transparency on/off	/ (forward slash)	/ (forward slash)
New Adjustment Layer	Command-click New Layer button in Layers Palette	Control-click New Layer button in Layers Palette
Group with previous	Command-G, or Option-click line between layers	Control-G, or Alt-click line between layers
Ungroup	Command-Shift-G, or Option click dotted line between layers	Control-Shift-G, or Alt click dotted line between layers
Select non-transparent areas of image layer	Command-click image thumbnail in Layers Palette	Control-click image thumbnail in Layers Palette
Add non-transparent areas of image layer to existing selection	Command-Shift-click image thumbnail in Layers Palette	Control-Shift-click image thumbnail in Layers Palette
Subtract non-transparent areas of image layer from existing selection	Option-Command-click image thumbnail in Layers Palette	Alt-Control-click image thumbnail in Layers Palette
Intersect non-transparent areas of image layer with existing selection	Option-Command-Shift-click image thumbnail in Layers Palette	Alt-Control-Shift-click image thumbnail in Layers Palette
Link layer to active layer	Click Status box of layer	Click Status box of layer
Set opacity of layer in multiples of 1%	Press 2 number keys in a row quickly while selection tool is active	Press 2 number keys in a row quickly while selection tool is active
Set opacity of layer in multiples of 10%	Press 1 through 10 when no paint tool is selected	Press 1 through 10 when no paint tool is selected
Open Layer Options dialog	Double-click on layer in Layers Palette	Double-click on layer in Layers Palette
Set smooth transition in Layer Options dialog	Option-drag Blend slider triangles	Alt-drag Blend slider triangles
Create white layer mask	Click the New Layer Mask button in Layers Palette	Click the New Layer Mask button in Layers Palette
Create black layer mask	Option-click the New Layer Mask button in Layers Palette	Alt-click the New Layer Mask button in Layers Palette

Shortcuts

Action	Macintosh Shortcuts	Windows Shortcuts
Create layer mask from selection outline	Click New Layer Mask button while selection is active	Click New Layer Mask button while selection is active
Create layer mask which hides selection	Option-click New Layer Mask button while selection is active	Alt-click New Layer Mask button while selection is active
View layer mask	Option-click layer mask thumbnail in Layers Palette	Alt-click layer mask thumbnail in Layers Palette
View layer mask in QuickMask View	Option-Shift-click layer mask thumbnail in Layers Palette	Alt-Shift-click layer mask thumbnail in Layers Palette
Disable Layer mask	Shift-click layer mask thumbnail	Shift-click layer mask thumbnail
Edit layer mask	Command-\ (backslash)	Control-\ (backslash)
Edit image layer	Command-~(tilde)	Control-~(tilde)
Link/Unlink layer mask and image layer	Click between layer mask & image layer thumbnails	Click between layer mask & image layer thumbnails
Load layer mask as selection	Command-Option-\ or Command-click layer mask thumbnail	Control-Alt-\ or Control-click layer mask thumbnail
Add layer mask to existing selection	Command-Shift-click layer mask thumbnail	Control-Shift-click layer mask thumbnail
Subtract layer mask from existing selection	Command-Option-click layer mask thumbnail	Control-Alt-click layer mask thumbnail
Intersect layer mask with existing selection	Command-Shift-Option-click layer mask thumbnail	Control-Shift-Alt-click layer mask thumbnail

The Channels Palette

Action	Macintosh Shortcuts	Windows Shortcuts
Activate specific, single channel	Command-1 through Command-9	Control-1 through Control-9
Activate color composite	Command-~ (tilde)	Control-~ (tilde)
Activate/ Deactivate channel	Shift-click channel	Shift-click channel
Create mask channel from selection	Click Save Selection button	Click Save Selection button

Action	Macintosh Shortcuts	Windows Shortcuts
View Channel	Click View button for channel	Click View button for channel
Load channel as selection	Option-Command-1 through 9, or Command-click channel	Alt-Control-1 through 9, or Control-click channel
Add mask channel to existing selection	Command-Shift-click channel	Control-Shift-click channel
Subtract mask channel from existing selection	Option-Command-click channel	Alt-Control-click channel
Intersect mask channel with existing selection	Command-Shift-Option-click channel	Control-Shift-Alt-click channel

The Paths Palette

Action	Macintosh Shortcuts	Windows Shortcuts
Convert Path to selection outline	Press Enter when the selection is active, or Command-click on path name in Paths Palette	Press Enter when the selection is active, or Control-click on path name in Paths Palette
Add Path to selection	Shift-Enter; or Command-Shift-click path name in Paths Palette	Shift-Enter; or Control-Shift-click path name in Paths Palette
Subtract path from selection	Option-Enter, or Command-Option-click path name in Paths Palette	Alt-Enter, or Control-Alt-click path name in Paths Palette
Intersect path with selection	Shift-Option-Enter, or Command-Option-Shift-click path name in Paths Palette	Shift-Alt-Enter, or Control-Alt-Shift-click path name in Paths Palette
Save path	Double-click Work Path in Paths Palette	Double-click Work Path in Paths Palette
Deactivate path	Click in empty portion of Paths Palette	Click in empty portion of Paths Palette

APPENDIX C

Resolution Types

Resolution

Resolution is a measure of frequency, used to specify the size of pixels, printer dots, and halftone dots. Most often, resolution is referred to in terms of "dots per inch," which is not entirely correct. Understanding the proper terminology goes a long way toward achieving accurate communication with your service bureau, printer, or clients.

Monitor Pixels per Inch (ppi)

Your monitor uses a fixed grid of pixels to display information on-screen. These pixels are completely separate from the pixels of image—instead, the electron guns inside the monitor stimulate the phosphors in each tiny square, causing it to display a particular color.

Most monitors have 72-ppi grids (the very reason most web graphics exist at 72 ppi), although some models, including color laptop models, can approach 80–85 ppi.

Samples per Inch (spi)

Samples per inch refers to the number of times a scanner "looks" at an image during scanning. It is sometimes referred to as optical resolution, or native resolution.

Sampling is a true measure of the amount of information a scanner can read. Most scanners can *interpolate*, or further increase the resolution of an image after scanning, similar to upsampling with the Image: **Image Size** command.

The distinction between spi and ppi is an important one, because the two are not always the same. Scanner manufacturers often advertise scanner resolution in ppi, rather than spi. For example, a scanner might be advertised as capable of 1200 ppi, when it is really only sampling the image 400 times per inch. Therefore, the scan quality is probably not as high as a scanner with an optical resolution of 800 spi.

Image Pixels per Inch (ppi)

Once an image has been scanned (or created originally in Photoshop), it exists as a series of pixels. The more pixels that comprise an image, the more information it contains, and the larger its file size becomes.

Different types of graphics have different resolution requirements:

- Web graphics only need to exist at 72 ppi, the same resolution as the monitors used to display them.

- A print-oriented halftone must be scanned at a higher resolution. Since a line-screen will be applied to the continuous image tones during output (see "Lines per Inch (lpi)"), you must ensure that the image contains enough information to reproduce properly. After determining the linescreen value, double that number and scan halftones at that resolution.

- Print-oriented line art will not be halftoned. Rather, every single pixel will output as it exists in the file. To make sure the pixels are small enough to avoid being detected by the human eye, these images are scanned at very high resolutions—typically, 600–1200 ppi.

Dots per Inch (dpi)

The most often-used term, dpi actually refers to the tiny dots produced by an output device. These have nothing to do with image resolution—rather, they are a printer's smallest reproducible dot size.

With this in mind, it's easier to understand why higher-resolution printers produce more attractive results. A low-res printer—say, a 300-dpi laser printer—produces jagged lines, and cannot create very small halftone dots. A 2,400-dpi imagesetter, on the other hand, can produce halftone dots measured in microns, resulting in a smoother, almost continuous-tone appearance.

Lines per Inch (lpi)

To reproduce properly, continuous-tone images are converted to a series of half-tone dots of varying sizes. Linescreen determines how much space each dot can occupy. Low values result in large, visible dots. High values result in near-photo-graphic images.

Spots per Inch (spi)

A rarely used term, spots per inch refers to halftone dots that have been printed on-press, and exist as ink-on-paper.

APPENDIX D

Image Credits

With a few exceptions, all images in this book come from the John Foxx Images library. For full-size, full-color previews of these images, please visit their web site: *http://www.johnfoxx.com*, or contact them directly for a catalog:

John Foxx Images Europe & outside U.S.A.:
Amsterdam
tel. +31 20 644 8842
fax +31 20 642 1540

John Foxx Images U.S.A.
New York
tel. 212 644 9123
fax 212 644 9124

The following is a list of images used in the book. Images not credited here are from our personal archives.

Command	Image	Volume
File: Export: GIF89a	PP 1847	16
Filter: Artistic: all	HL 1805	1
Filter: Blur Gaussian Blur	BA 1844	2
Filter: Blur: Motion Blur	GD 0015	GD 01
Filter: Blur: Smart Blur	PE 1804	2
Filter: Brush Strokes: all	PE 1916	2
Filter: Distort: Diffuse Glow	MI 1838	11
Filter: Distort: Glass	PP 1992	16
Filter: Distort: Ocean Ripple	PP 1989	16
Filter: Distort: Pinch	PP 1843	16
Filter: Distort: Polar Coordinates	PP 1843	16

Command	Image	Volume
Filter: Distort: Shear	PE 1931	2
Filter: Distort: Spherize	TV 1849	5
Filter: Distort: Twirl	PP 1993	16
Filter: Distort: Wave	AN 2037	12
Filter: Distort: ZigZag	PP 1970	16
Filter: Noise: Add Noise	HL 1840	5
Filter: Noise: Dust & Scratches	ST 1837	5
Filter: Noise: Median	ST 1840	5
Filter: Pixelate: all	PP 1835	16
Filter: Render: Lens Flare	PE 1921	2
Filter: Render: Lighting Effects	PE 1924	2
Filter: Sharpen: Unsharp Mask	PP 1970	16
Filter: Sketch: all	PP 1843	16
Filter: Stylize: all	AN 2017	12
Filter: Texture: all	BA 1936	9
Filter: Other: Custom	PP 1980	16
Filter: Other: High Pass	MI 1838	11
Filter: Other: Maximum	PP 1992	16
Filter: Other: Minimum	AN 2037	12
Appendix A: Techniques:		
Semi-transparent Type	PE 1925	2
Custom Path Shapes	CC 1838	11
Creating a Dotted Line	HL 1803	5
Creating a Curved Line	AN 2029	12
Adding Arrowhead to Curve	EV 1839	11
Positioning Custom Type	HL 1828	5
Pasting from Illustrator	EV 1814	11
Ghosting	ST 1844	5
Outlined & Stroked Type	SP 1880	5
Non-Continuous Patterns	ST 1837	5
Seamles Image Patterns	HL 1828	5
Transparent Patterns	HL 1826, PE 1924	5, 2
Levels, Expanding Tonal Range	TV 1810	5
Levels, Setting EndPoints	TV 1806	5
Levels, Simple Image Enhancing	TV 1824	5
Curves, Adjusting Halftone	HO 1824	5
Curves, Adjusting On-Screen	HO 1824	5
Curves, Adjusting for Dot Gain	LS 1810	13
Curves, Adjusting Color Cast	OS 1830	13
Curves, Adjusting Neutral Tones	CB 1840	13

Command	Image	Volume
Feathered Transitions	PE 1924, EP 1813	2, 13
Feathered Transitions 2	BA 1844, RE 1814	2, 14
Layer Masks, Custom Frames	AG 1835	3
Creating Glow	SI 1819	9
Displace Embossing	FL 1853	12
Blend Mode Embossing	PEH1804	2
Soft Drop Shadow	SP 1880	5
Creating Complex Masks	GD 0039	GD01
Filtering Masks	ANH1849	3

Index

fading to background color, 20
filling with, 52, 147
swatch, 58
Fragment filter, 316
framing images, 478, 506
Free Transform (Layer Menu), 235
Frequency value
Halftone Screen method, 162
Halftone Screens dialog, 116
Fresco filter, 268
From Saved option (Rubber Stamp
Tool), 31
From Snapshot option (Rubber Stamp
Tool), 31
Front Image button (Cropping Tool
Options), 11
Full Screen views, 76
Full Size box (Preferences), 126
Fuzziness slider
Color Range dialog, 250
Replace Color dialog, 193

G
G radio button
Color Picker (Photoshop), 64
Hue/Saturation dialog, 191
gamma
adjusting, 182
for duotone ink distribution, 167
value for, Monitor Setup dialog, 134
gamut, 157
checking in Variations dialog, 203
defining out-of-gamut colors, 173
Gamut Alert Color Picker
(Photoshop), 65
out-of-gamut warnings, 129, 371, 389
preferences for, 128
selecting out-of-gamut colors, 250
Gamut Warning (View Menu), 371
Gaussian Blur filter, 282
GCR (Gray Component Replacement),
138
General Preferences dialog, 124–125
geometrically shaped selections
Marquee Tool for, 6, 455
Polygon Lasso Tool for, 14–15, 456
ghosting, 475–477
GIF file format, 89
exporting images to, 108–111

GIF87a vs. GIF89a, 108–111
GIF89a Export (File: Export), 108–111,
466
Glass filter, 299
Glowing Edges filter, 349
glowing effect, creating, 509
gradients, 46–50
color stops, 49
color table gradients, 489
Gradient Editor, 48–50
Gradient Tool, 46–48
status of, 386
tone, displayed in Curves dialog, 186
grain (see noise, filters for)
Grain filter, 355
Graphic Pen filter, 335
graphics formats (see file formats)
gray
editing in Selective Color dialog, 195
filling with, 146, 148
Gray Component Replacement
(GCR), 138
grayscale slider (Color Palette), 390
High Pass filter, 363
neutral, 226
adjusting appearance of, 137
brightness of, 182
in Quick Mask mode, 71
Gray Balance values (Printing Inks
Setup), 137
Gray radio button (Print), 123
grayscale images, 163–164
color table for, 177
colorizing, 191–192
converting to CMYK, 163
default colors for, 60
dot gain for, 137, 496
image mode of, 80
separate channels into, 423
Grayscale option (Color Range
Selection Preview), 251
green
selecting with Color Picker, 64
slider for (Color Palette), 390
Gridline Every value (Preferences), 130
grids
hiding/showing, 376
preferences on, 130
snapping to, 376
Group Linked (Layer Menu), 234

ink systems *(continued)*
  dot gain, 136
  duotone, 165
  halftones and, 114–117
  nonstandard, 66
  trapping, 217–219
Ink values (Halftone Screens), 116
Input Levels setting (Levels dialog), 182
Input value (Bitmap dialog), 161
Insert Menu Item (Actions Palette),
  442, 532
Insert Stop (Actions Palette), 442, 533
Inside option (Stroke dialog), 150
intensity, color (see saturation)
interlacing
  GIF89a images, 110
  PNG files, 97
interleaving, Raw file format and, 98
interpolation
  resampling images and, 211
  resolution and, 552
  types of, 125
Interpolation box (Page Setup), 121
Intersect with Channel option (Save
  Selection), 261
intersections of two selections, 4
Inverse (Select Menu), 247–248
Invert (Image: Adjust), 196
inverting
  images, 121, 196, 508
  selections, 247–248, 251, 258

J

JPEG compression (QuickTime), 95
JPEG file format, 92–93, 192

K

key number fields, 68
keyboard shortcuts, creating, 435
keywords for images, 113

L

L channel (Lab Color images), 174
Lab Color, 156–157, 174
  default colors for, 61
  image mode of, 80

out-of-gamut colors, 65
  slider for (Color Palette), 391
Labels box (Page Setup), 121
Lasso Tools, 13–15, 456
Last Filter (Filter Menu), 263
Layer Menu, 224–245
  shortcuts, 543
  techniques for, 505–508
Layer Options (Layer Menu), 230–232
Layer setting (Apply Image), 206
Layer Via Copy (Layer: New), 227
Layer Via Cut (Layer: New), 142, 228
layers
  activating, 409
  adding floating selections to, 5
  adjustment layers, 222–223
    creating new, 226–227, 413
  arranging order of, 240–242
  background, 220–221
  blend modes (see blend modes)
  changing order of, 410
  clipping groups, 234
  combining, 205–207
  composite, creating, 205–207
  copying images and, 204
  copying to other images, 520
  creating new, 224–228, 412
    by combining images, 207
  creating selections based on, 257–259
  cut/copy and, 142–144
  deleting, 230, 233, 412, 413
  duplicating, 228–229, 413
  editing, 230–232, 407
  filling, 46, 146, 226
  grouping (see clipping groups)
  hiding/showing, 408
  layer mask channels, 414
  layer masks, 232–234, 412
    creating, 259, 505
    creating mask channel from, 206
    saving selections as, 261
    viewing contents of, 508
  linked, 410
  Marquee Tool and, 7
  matting, 244–245
  merging, 102, 144, 222, 242–244, 413
  merging images to single, 413
  moving contents of, 409
  moving with Move Tool, 11

Split Channels (Channels Palette), 423
Sponge filter, 277
Sponge Tool, 34, 35
spot colors, 66, 526
spots-per-inch (spi) resolution, 553
Sprayed Strokes filter, 294
square selections, 8
staggered patterns, 481
Stained Glass filter, 358
Stamp filter, 342
Standard option (Other Cursors), 128
star targets, 121
start arrowhead, 45
Start Recording (Actions Palette), 441
Status box (Layers Palette), 409
Std Dev value (Histogram), 217
steps, tapering, 20
stochastic screens, 115
stopping Actions, 437, 442
streaking color, 275
Stroke (Edit Menu), 148–150
stroking, 478–479
  images, 148–150
  paths, 428, 432, 530
Style setting (Marquee Options), 8
style, type, 43
Stylize filters, 345–353
stylus pressure, 19
Subdivisions value (Preferences), 130
subpaths, 37
subpaths (see paths)
Subtract from Channel option (Save
    Selection), 261
Subtract from Selection (Load
    Selection), 258
subtractive primary color models, 155
Sumi-e filter, 295
swatches
  background color, 59
  in Color Picker (Photoshop), 65
  in Duotone Options dialog, 167
  foreground color, 58
  Hue/Saturation dialog, 191
  organizing, 515
  specifying color with, 393
  Swatches Palette, 392–394, 515–519
    shortcuts for, 548
  Switch Colors icon, 60
  system palette, 169
    color tables for, 177

exporting images as GIF files, 111
using as default, 127
Windows, error in, 168

T

Table setting (Color Table), 177
tables, separation, 140
Take Merged Snapshot (Edit Menu),
    152
Take Snapshot (Edit Menu), 152
tapering brushstrokes, 20
Targa file format, 100
Target field (Apply Image), 205
temperature, light, 135
text (see type)
Texture Fill filter, 325
Texture filters, 353–360
textures, seamless, 481
Texturizer filter, 359
thickness (see size)
This Layer slider (Layer Options), 231
3 by 3 Average Sample (Eyedropper
    Tool), 53
threshold
  bitmap conversion, 161
  bitmap images, 197–199
Threshold (Image: Adjust), 197–199,
    501–502
Threshold brush mode, 21
thumbnails, 379
  in Channels Palette, 424
  creating, 126
  in Open dialog, 82
  of Variations dialog, 200–202
TIFF file format, 100
tiles
  creating, 151–152
  information on, 370
  Mosaic Tiles filter, 357
  Offset filter, 365
  Patchwork filter, 358
  Tiles filter, 350
Timing value, 369
title (see name)
title, image, 121
tolerance
  filling, 51
  Magic Wand Tool, 16–17
Tonal Range option (Color Range), 250

About the Author

Donnie O'Quinn is a graphic arts consultant, on-site trainer, and author based in Portland, Maine. Classroom-based programs under his direction were described as "hands down, the best prepress training in the Northeast," by Printing Industries of New England. His past clients include Apple Computer, MetaCreations, and *MacUser* magazine, as well as service bureaus, designers, and printers from New York to Nova Scotia. When not working or writing, he readies his overpowered '74 Chevy for a top-down, high-speed pursuit of the American dream.

Matt LeClair has been involved in the computer graphics industry for the past decade as designer, artist, and educator. His clients have included Apple Computer, Microsoft, *Implosion Magazine*, and The Center for Creative Imaging. Most recently, he decided to turn the wealth of his experience to writing. You can find his work in *MacUser* magazine, and in *Digital Prepress Complete* (Hayden Books), which he co-authored with Donnie O'Quinn.

Colophon

Our look is the result of reader comments, our own experimentation, and feedback from distribution channels. Distinctive covers complement our distinctive approach to technical topics, breathing personality and life into potentially dry subjects.

The animal featured on the cover of *Photoshop in a Nutshell*, while resembling an owl, does not exist. According to Alison Pirie of the Museum of Comparative Zoology at Harvard University, this bird is entirely a product of the artist's creation.

Owls are easily distinguished from other birds by their forward-facing eyes, lack of a neck, and large heads. Their hearing range approximates that of a human, though their directional hearing is much more sensitive. Some owls have tufts of feathers on their heads that resemble ears, but are actually decorative. Despite popular belief, owls are not actually blind in daylight, and, while they cannot see in complete darkness, their eye structure allows them to see with very little light.

There are two families and approximately 180 species of these birds of prey distributed throughout the world, with the exception of Antarctica. Most species of owl are nocturnal hunters, feeding entirely on live animals, ranging in size from insects to hares.

Edie Freedman designed the cover of this book, using a 19th-century engraving from the Dover Pictorial Archive. The cover layout was produced with Quark XPress 3.32 using the ITC Garamond font. The inside layout was designed by Nancy Priest and implemented in FrameMaker by Mike Sierra. The text and heading fonts are ITC Garamond Light and Garamond Book. The illustrations that appear in the book were created in Adobe Photoshop 4 and Macromedia Freehand 7 by Robert Romano.

Whenever possible, our books use RepKover™, a durable and flexible lay-flat binding. If the page count exceeds RepKover's limit, perfect binding is used.

More Titles from O'Reilly

Web Review Studio Series

GIF Animation Studio

By Richard Koman
1st Edition October 1996
184 pages, Includes CD-ROM
ISBN 1-56592-230-1

GIF animation is bringing the Web to life—without plug-ins, Java programming, or expensive authoring tools. This book details the major GIF animation programs, profiles work by leading designers (including John Hersey, Razorfish, Henrik Drescher, and Erik Josowitz), and documents advanced animation techniques. A CD-ROM includes freeware and shareware authoring programs, demo versions of commercial software, and the actual animation files described in the book. *GIF Animation Studio* is the first release in the new Web Review Studio series.

Shockwave Studio

By Bob Schmitt
1st Edition March 1997
200 pages, Includes CD-ROM
ISBN 1-56592-231-X

This book, the second title in the new Web Review Studio series, shows how to create compelling and functional Shockwave movies for web sites. The author focuses on actual Shockwave movies, showing how the movies were created. The book takes users from creating simple time-based Shockwave animations through writing complex logical operations that take full advantage of Director's power. The CD-ROM includes a demo version of Director and other software sample files.

Designing with JavaScript

By Nick Heinle
1st Edition September 1997
256 pages, Includes CD-ROM
ISBN 1-56592-300-6

Written by the author of the "JavaScript Tip of the Week" web site, this new Web Review Studio book focuses on the most useful and applicable scripts for making truly interactive, engaging web sites. You'll not only have quick access to the scripts you need, you'll finally understand why the scripts work, how to alter the scripts to get the effects you want, and, ultimately, how to write your own groundbreaking scripts from scratch.

Photoshop Web Studio

By Mikkel Aaland
1st Edition October 1997 (est.)
250 pages (est.), ISBN 1-56592-350-2

The special requirements of the Web present many challenges to Photoshop users. This book gives users a wealth of tips and techniques for creating fast, quality images for the Web. The author explains the issues and shares the best tricks from top designers. This book is sure to be *the* desktop reference for anyone creating web images.

O'REILLY™

TO ORDER: **800-998-9938** • *order@oreilly.com* • *http://www.oreilly.com/*
OUR PRODUCTS ARE AVAILABLE AT A BOOKSTORE OR SOFTWARE STORE NEAR YOU.
FOR INFORMATION: **800-998-9938** • **707-829-0515** • *info@oreilly.com*

Graphics

Encyclopedia of Graphics File Formats
By James D. Murray & William vanRyper
2nd Edition April 1996 Includes CD-ROM 1154 pages
ISBN 1-56592-161-5

The *Encyclopedia of Graphics File Formats* is the definitive reference on graphics file formats; the first edition of the book has already become a classic for graphics programmers.

In this second edition, we have retrofitted the entire *Encyclopedia of Graphics File Formats* for display on the Internet's World Wide Web. Using the Enhanced Mosaic browser (included on the CD-ROM), you can navigate the book's contents on the CD-ROM and (if you have an Internet connection) link to the O'Reilly Web Center on the Internet where we maintain an online update service. There you'll find updates, descriptions of new formats, graphics news, and links to additional resources on the World Wide Web. On the CD-ROM, we've also included the updated printed book—still the most portable resource around.

Whether you're a graphics programmer, service bureau, or graphics designer who needs to know the low-level technical details of graphics files, this online resource/book is for you.

For each of more than 100 formats, the product provides quick summary information—How many colors are supported by the format? What type of compression does it use? What's the maxi-

mum image size? What's the platform, the numerical format, and the supporting applications? It also provides extensive text detailing how graphics files are constructed in a particular format. The CD-ROM includes a collection of hard-to-find resources (many that have never before been available outside the organizations that developed them). We've assembled original file format specification documents (covering more than 100 formats) from such vendors as Adobe, Apple, IBM, Microsoft, and Silicon Graphics, along with test images and code examples for many of the formats. The CD-ROM also contains a set of publicly available software and shareware—for Windows, MS-DOS, OS/2, the Macintosh, and UNIX—that will let you convert, view, compress, and manipulate graphics files and images.

Technical requirements for the product: a CD-ROM drive; a PC running Microsoft Windows 3.1, 95, or NT; a Macintosh workstation, or a UNIX workstation supported by Spyglass Enhanced Mosaic. A 256-color monitor is highly recommended.

"At last!!! No more hunting, begging, borrowing, or stealing to find that particular file format information you need—here it is . . . in one place. If you work with graphics files, buy this book. . . . The *EGFF* is useful to file-dissecting neophytes and veterans alike. It is a well-written resource and reference book that you will wonder how you ever did without." —*Microtimes*

O'REILLY™
TO ORDER: **800-998-9938** • order@oreilly.com • http://www.oreilly.com/
OUR PRODUCTS ARE AVAILABLE AT A BOOKSTORE OR SOFTWARE STORE NEAR YOU.
FOR INFORMATION: **800-998-9938** • **707-829-0515** • info@oreilly.com

How to stay in touch with O'Reilly

1. Visit Our Award-Winning Site
http://www.oreilly.com/

★"Top 100 Sites on the Web" —*PC Magazine*
★"Top 5% Web sites" —*Point Communications*
★"3-Star site" —*The McKinley Group*

Our web site contains a library of comprehensive product information (including book excerpts and tables of contents), downloadable software, background articles, interviews with technology leaders, links to relevant sites, book cover art, and more. File us in your Bookmarks or Hotlist!

2. Join Our Email Mailing Lists
New Product Releases
To receive automatic email with brief descriptions of all new O'Reilly products as they are released, send email to:
listproc@online.oreilly.com
Put the following information in the first line of your message (*not* in the Subject field):
subscribe oreilly-news "Your Name" of "Your Organization" (for example: subscribe oreilly-news Kris Webber of Fine Enterprises)

O'Reilly Events
If you'd also like us to send information about trade show events, special promotions, and other O'Reilly events, send email to:
listproc@online.oreilly.com
Put the following information in the first line of your message (*not* in the Subject field):
subscribe oreilly-events "Your Name" of "Your Organization"

3. Get Examples from Our Books via FTP
There are two ways to access an archive of example files from our books:

Regular FTP
• ftp to:
  ftp.oreilly.com
  (login: anonymous
  password: your email address)
• Point your web browser to:
  ftp://ftp.oreilly.com/

FTPMAIL
• Send an email message to:
  ftpmail@online.oreilly.com
  (Write "help" in the message body)

4. Visit Our Gopher Site
• Connect your gopher to:
  gopher.oreilly.com

• Point your web browser to:
  gopher://gopher.oreilly.com/

• Telnet to:
  gopher.oreilly.com
  login: gopher

5. Contact Us via Email
order@oreilly.com
To place a book or software order online. Good for North American and international customers.

subscriptions@oreilly.com
To place an order for any of our newsletters or periodicals.

books@oreilly.com
General questions about any of our books.

software@oreilly.com
For general questions and product information about our software. Check out O'Reilly Software Online at **http://software.oreilly.com/** for software and technical support information. Registered O'Reilly software users send your questions to:
website-support@oreilly.com

cs@oreilly.com
For answers to problems regarding your order or our products.

booktech@oreilly.com
For book content technical questions or corrections.

proposals@oreilly.com
To submit new book or software proposals to our editors and product managers.

international@oreilly.com
For information about our international distributors or translation queries. For a list of our distributors outside of North America check out:
http://www.oreilly.com/www/order/country.html

O'Reilly & Associates, Inc.
101 Morris Street, Sebastopol, CA 95472 USA
TEL   707-829-0515 or 800-998-9938
       (6am to 5pm PST)
FAX   707-829-0104

O'REILLY™
TO ORDER: **800-998-9938** • *order@oreilly.com* • *http://www.oreilly.com/*
OUR PRODUCTS ARE AVAILABLE AT A BOOKSTORE OR SOFTWARE STORE NEAR YOU.
FOR INFORMATION: **800-998-9938** • **707-829-0515** • *info@oreilly.com*

International Distributors

UK, Europe, Middle East and Northern Africa (except France, Germany, Switzerland, & Austria)

INQUIRIES
International Thomson Publishing Europe
Berkshire House
168-173 High Holborn
London WC1V 7AA, UK
Tel: 44-171-497-1422
Fax: 44-171-497-1426
Email: itpint@itps.co.uk

ORDERS
International Thomson Publishing Services, Ltd.
Cheriton House, North Way
Andover, Hampshire SP10 5BE,
United Kingdom
Tel: 44-264-342-832 (UK)
Tel: 44-264-342-806
  (outside UK)
Fax: 44-264-364418 (UK)
Fax: 44-264-342761 (outside UK)
UK & Eire orders:
itpuk@itps.co.uk
International orders:
itpint@itps.co.uk

France
Editions Eyrolles
61 bd Saint-Germain
75240 Paris Cedex 05
France
Fax: 33-01-44-41-11-44

FRENCH LANGUAGE BOOKS
All countries except Canada
Tel: 33-01-44-41-46-16
Email: geodif@eyrolles.com

ENGLISH LANGUAGE BOOKS
Tel: 33-01-44-41-11-87
Email: distribution@eyrolles.com

Australia
WoodsLane Pty. Ltd.
7/5 Vuko Place, Warriewood NSW 2102
P.O. Box 935,
Mona Vale NSW 2103
Australia
Tel: 61-2-9970-5111
Fax: 61-2-9970-5002
Email: info@woodslane.com.au

Germany, Switzerland, and Austria
INQUIRIES
O'Reilly Verlag
Balthasarstr. 81
D-50670 Köln
Germany
Tel: 49-221-97-31-60-0
Fax: 49-221-97-31-60-8
Email: anfragen@oreilly.de

ORDERS
International Thomson Publishing
Königswinterer Straße 418
53227 Bonn, Germany
Tel: 49-228-97024 0
Fax: 49-228-441342
Email: order@oreilly.de

Asia (except Japan & India)
INQUIRIES
International Thomson Publishing Asia
60 Albert Street #15-01
Albert Complex
Singapore 189969
Tel: 65-336-6411
Fax: 65-336-7411

ORDERS
Telephone: 65-336-6411
Fax: 65-334-1617
thomson@signet.com.sg

New Zealand
WoodsLane New Zealand Ltd.
21 Cooks Street (P.O. Box 575)
Wanganui, New Zealand
Tel: 64-6-347-6543
Fax: 64-6-345-4840
Email: info@woodslane.com.au

Japan
O'Reilly Japan, Inc.
Kiyoshige Building 2F
12-Banchi, Sanei-cho
Shinjuku-ku
Tokyo 160 Japan
Tel: 81-3-3356-5227
Fax: 81-3-3356-5261
Email: kenji@oreilly.com

India
Computer Bookshop (India) PVT.
LTD.
190 Dr. D.N. Road, Fort
Bombay 400 001 India
Tel: 91-22-207-0989
Fax: 91-22-262-3551
Email:
cbsbom@giasbm01.vsnl.net.in

The Americas
O'Reilly & Associates, Inc.
101 Morris Street
Sebastopol, CA 95472 U.S.A.
Tel: 707-829-0515
Tel: 800-998-9938 (U.S. & Canada)
Fax: 707-829-0104
Email: order@oreilly.com

Southern Africa
International Thomson Publishing Southern Africa
Building 18, Constantia Park
138 Sixteenth Road
P.O. Box 2459
Halfway House, 1685 South Africa
Tel: 27-11-805-4819
Fax: 27-11-805-3648

O'Reilly & Associates, Inc.
101 Morris Street
Sebastopol, CA 95472-9902
1-800-998-9938

Visit us online at:
http://www.ora.com/

O'REILLY WOULD LIKE TO HEAR FROM YOU

Which book did this card come from?

_____

Where did you buy this book?
- ❏ Bookstore
- ❏ Direct from O'Reilly
- ❏ Bundled with hardware/software
- ❏ Other _____
- ❏ Computer Store
- ❏ Class/seminar

What operating system do you use?
- ❏ UNIX
- ❏ Windows NT
- ❏ Other _____
- ❏ Macintosh
- ❏ PC(Windows/DOS)

What is your job description?
- ❏ System Administrator
- ❏ Network Administrator
- ❏ Web Developer
- ❏ Other _____
- ❏ Programmer
- ❏ Educator/Teacher

❏ Please send me O'Reilly's catalog, containing
a complete listing of O'Reilly books and
software.

Name   Company/Organization

Address

City   State   Zip/Postal Code   Country

Telephone   Internet or other email address (specify network)

neteenth century wood engraving
a bear from the O'Reilly &
ssociates Nutshell Handbook®
*ing & Managing UUCP.

DATE DUE

RECD MAR 2 3 2009

BUS
FIRST CI
Postage will

Demco, Inc. 38-293

O'Reilly & Associates, Inc.
101 Morris Street
Sebastopol, CA 95472-9902